Thinking Through the Past

Thinking Through the Past

A Critical Thinking Approach to U.S. History

Volume I: To 1877

FIFTH EDITION

John Hollitz

College of Southern Nevada

Australia • Brazil • Japan • Korea • Mexico • Singapore • Spain • United Kingdom • United States

CENGAGE
Learning®

**Thinking Through the Past:
A Critical Thinking Approach
to U.S. History, Volume I
Fifth Edition**
John Hollitz

Product Director: Suzanne Jeans

Product Manager: Ann West

Content Developer: Megan
 Chrisman

Product Assistant: Liz Fraser

Marketing Brand Manager: Melissa
 Larmon

Rights Acquisitions Specialist:
 Jennifer Meyer Dare

Manufacturing Planner: Sandee
 Milewski

Art and Design Direction,
 Production Management, and
 Composition: PreMediaGlobal

Cover Image: Town of Pomeioc,
 plate XIX, from 'America,
 Part I', engraved by Theodore
 de Bry (1528–98), 1590
 (engraving), White, John
 (fl.1570–93) (after) / Virginia
 Historical Society, Richmond,
 Virginia, USA / The Bridgeman
 Art Library

For product information and technology assistance,
contact us at **Cengage Learning Customer & Sales
Support, 1-800-354-9706**

For permission to use material from this text or product,
submit all requests online at **www.cengage.com/permissions.**
Further permissions questions can be emailed to
permissionrequest@cengage.com.

Library of Congress Control Number: 2013952535

Student Edition:
ISBN-13: 978-1-285-42743-0
ISBN-10: 1-285-42743-2

Cengage Learning
200 First Stamford Place, 4th Floor
Stamford, CT 06902
USA

Cengage Learning is a leading provider of customized learning
solutions with office locations around the globe, including
Singapore, the United Kingdom, Australia, Mexico, Brazil and Japan.

Locate your local office at **international.cengage.com/region.**

Cengage Learning products are represented in Canada by Nelson
Education, Ltd.

For your course and learning solutions, visit **www.cengage.com.**

Purchase any of our products at your local college store or
at our preferred online store **www.cengagebrain.com.**

Instructors: Please visit **login.cengage.com** and log in to access
instructor-specific resources.

Printed in the United States of America
1 2 3 4 5 6 7 17 16 15 14 13

Contents

3

Evaluating Primary Sources: Was Pennsylvania "The Best Poor Man's Country"?

4

Evaluating One Historian's Argument: The "Hidden Side" of the American Revolution   55

5

Motivation in History: The Founding Fathers and the Constitution   86

6

Ideas in History: Race in Jefferson's Republic   113

7

The Problem of Historical Causation:
The Second Great Awakening   144

8

Grand Theory and History: Democracy and the Frontier   172

9

History as Biography: Historians and Old Hickory   201

10

History "From the Bottom Up": Historians and Slavery   227

11

Ideology and Society: The Bounds of Womanhood in the North and South   249

12

Grand Theory, Great Battles, and Historical Causes: Why Secession Failed

13

The Importance of Historical Interpretation: The Meaning of Reconstruction

Preface

The encouraging response to the fourth edition from students and instructors has prompted me to create a fifth edition of *Thinking Through the Past*. As before, this book is inspired by the idea that interpretation is at the heart of history. That is why learning about the past involves more than mastering facts and dates, and why historians often disagree. As teachers, we know the limitations of the deadly dates-and-facts approach to the past. We also know that encouraging students to think critically about historical sources and historians' arguments is a good way to create excitement about history and to impart understanding of what historians do. The purpose of *Thinking Through the Past,* therefore, is to introduce students to the examination and analysis of historical sources.

FORMAT

To encourage students to think critically about American history, *Thinking Through the Past* brings together primary and secondary sources. It gives students the opportunity to analyze primary sources *and* historians' arguments, and to use one to understand and evaluate the other. By evaluating and drawing conclusions from the sources, students will use the methods and develop some of the skills of critical thinking as they apply to history. Students will also learn about a variety of historical topics that parallel those in U.S. history courses. Unlike most anthologies or collections of primary sources, this book advances not only chronologically, but also pedagogically through different skill levels. It provides students the opportunity to work with primary sources in the early chapters before they evaluate secondary sources in later chapters or compare historians' arguments in the final chapters. Students are also able to build on the skills acquired in previous chapters by considering such questions as motivation, causation, and the role of ideas and economic interests in history.

At the same time, this book introduces a variety of approaches to the past. Topics in *Thinking Through the Past* include social, political, cultural, intellectual, economic, diplomatic, and military history. The chapters look at history "from the top down" and "from the bottom up." Thus students have the opportunity to evaluate history drawn from slave quarters as well as from state houses. In the process, they are exposed to the enormous range of sources that historians use to construct arguments. The primary sources in these volumes include portraits, photographs, maps, letters, fiction, music lyrics, laws, oral histories, speeches, movie posters, magazine and newspaper articles, cartoons, and architectural plans.

The chapters present the primary and secondary sources so students can pursue their own investigations of the material. Each chapter is divided into five parts: a brief introduction, which sets forth the problem in the chapter; the Setting, which provides background information pertaining to the topic; the Investigation, which asks students to answer a short set of questions revolving around the problem discussed in the introduction; the Sources, which in most chapters provide a secondary source and a set of primary sources related to the chapter's main problem; and, finally, a brief Conclusion, which offers a reminder of the chapter's main pedagogical goal and looks forward to the next chapter's problem.

CHANGES TO THE FIFTH EDITION

In the fifth edition, there are significantly revised chapters in both volumes on provocative topics that have been on the cutting edge of recent historical scholarship. These topics are intended to stimulate student interest in American history. In Volume I, chapters on the Constitution, the American West, and Andrew Jackson have been revised with the addition of new source material. As before, changes reflect more recent historical scholarship and have been designed with accessibility in mind. New primary source material in Chapter 8 reflects contemporary historical scholarship on the nineteenth-century American frontier, while Chapter 9 presents a new biographical assessment of young Andrew Jackson that introduces students to a "gambler" and "carouser" who matures into a "formidable leader of men." In Volume II, a significantly revised chapter on racial and ethnic unrest on the home front during World War II is intended to provide students with a broader historical context and to excite a broader mix of contemporary students. Overall, the volumes have been revised with an eye toward making the book a more engaging learning tool. To this end, many other chapters contain new sources that provide additional insights for students as they conduct their historical investigations.

ACKNOWLEDGMENTS

Many people contributed to this book, starting with my own students. Without them, of course, it never would have been created.

I owe many thanks to the people who assisted in various ways with the revisions for this edition. At the College of Southern Nevada, Inter-Library Loan librarian Marion Martin, as always, provided cheerful and invaluable assistance. Numerous colleagues around the country offered useful suggestions regarding revisions and chapter drafts. I am honored by their commitment to *Thinking Through the Past* and thank them for helping to make it a better book.

In particular, I'd like to thank the following individuals who reviewed the fifth edition: Guy Aronoff, Humboldt State University; Terrell Goddard, Northwest Vista College; Li Hongshan, Kent State University at Tuscarawas; Abigail Markwyn, Carroll University; Linda Mollno, Cal Poly Pomona; Craig Perrier, Fairfax County Public Schools; Emily Rader, El Camino College; Alicia Rodriquez, California State University, Bakersfield; Megan Seaholm, University of Texas at Austin; Rebecca Shrum, Indiana University Purdue University Indianapolis; Garth Swanson, Genesee Community College; and Wendy Wall, Binghamton University. The reviewers of the fourth edition were: Andy Ginette, University of Southern Indiana; Terrell Goddard, Northwest Vista College; Charlotte Haller, Worcester State College; Jeffrey Johnson, Augustana College; Jennifer Mata, University of Texas Pan American; Sean O'Neill, Grand Valley State University; Phillip Payne, St. Bonaventure University; and Timothy Thurber, Virginia Commonwealth University. The reviewers of the third edition were Michael D. Wilson, Vanguard University; David A. Canton, Georgia Southern University; Paivi Hoikkala, California State Polytechnic University at Pomona; Kathleen Kennedy, Western Washington University; Monroe H. Little, Jr., Indiana University-Purdue University at Indianapolis; Cathleen Schultz, University of St. Francis; Paul C. Rosier, Villanova University; Marsha L. Weisiger, New Mexico State University; and Katherine A. S. Sibley, St. Joseph's University.

I owe thanks to many others as well for their contribution to the previous editions. Alan Balboni, DeAnna Beachley, Michael Green, Charles Okeke, the late Gary Elliott, colleagues at the Community College of Southern Nevada, offered sources, reviewed portions of the manuscript, shared insights, or simply offered encouragement. Richard Cooper and Brad Nystrom at California State University, Sacramento, listened patiently and offered helpful suggestions at the initial stages of this project. As usual, however, my biggest debt is to Patty. For her enduring support and abiding love, this book is once again dedicated to her.

J. H.

Thinking Through the Past

Introduction

"History," said Henry Ford, "is more or less bunk." That view is still shared by many people. Protests about the subject are familiar. Studying history won't help you land a job. And, besides, what matters is not the past but the present.

Such protests are not necessarily wrong. Learning about ancient Greece, the French Revolution, or the Vietnam War will hardly guarantee employment, even though many employers evaluate job candidates on critical thinking skills that the study of history requires. Likewise, who can deny the importance of the present compared to the past? In many ways, the present and future are more important than the past. Pericles, Robespierre, and Lyndon Johnson are dead; presumably, anyone reading this is not:

Still, the logic behind the history-as-bunk view is flawed because all of us rely upon the past to understand the present, as did even Henry Ford. Besides building the Model T, he also built Greenfield Village outside Detroit because he wanted to re-create a nineteenth-century town. It was the kind of place the automotive genius grew up in and the kind of place he believed represented the ideal American society: small-town, white, native-born, and Protestant. Greenfield Village was Ford's answer to changes in the early twentieth century that were profoundly disturbing to him and to many other Americans of his generation: growing cities, the influx of non-Protestant immigrants, changing sexual morality, new roles and new fashions for women, and greater freedom for young people.

Ford's interest in the past, symbolized by Greenfield Village, reflects a double irony. It was the automobile that helped to make possible many of the changes, like those in sexual morality, that Ford detested. The other irony is that Ford used history—what he himself called "bunk"—to try to better the world. Without realizing it, he became a historian by turning to the past to explain to himself and others what he disliked about the present. Never mind that Ford blamed immigrants, especially Jews, for the changes he decried in crude, hate-filled tirades. The point is that Ford's view of America was rooted in a vision of the past, and his explanation for America's ills was based on historical analysis, however unprofessional and unsophisticated.

All of us use historical analysis all the time, even if, like Ford, we think we don't. In fact, we all share a fundamental assumption about learning from the past: One of the best ways to learn about something, to learn how it came to be, is to study its past. That assumption is so much a part of us that we are rarely conscious of it.

Think about the most recent time you met someone for the first time. As a way to get to know this new acquaintance you began to ask questions about his or her past. When you asked, "Where did you grow up?" or "How long have you lived in Chicago?" you were relying on information about the past to learn about the present. You were, in other words, thinking as a historian. You assumed that a cause-and-effect relationship existed between this person's past and his or her present personality, interests, and beliefs. Like a historian, you began to frame questions and to look for answers that would help to establish causal links.

Because we all use history to make sense of our world, it follows that we should become more skilled in the art of making sense of the past. Ford did it crudely, and ended up promoting the very things he despised. But how exactly do you begin to think more like a historian? For too many students, this challenge summons up images of studying for history exams: cramming names, dates, and facts, and hoping to retain some portion of this information long enough to get a passing grade. History seems like a confusing grab bag of facts and events. The historian's job, in this view, is to memorize as much "stuff" as possible. In this "flash-card" approach, history is reduced to an exercise in the pursuit of trivia, and thinking like a historian is nothing but an exercise in mnemonics—a system of improving the memory.

There is no question that the dates, events, and facts of history are important. Without basic factual knowledge historians could no more practice their craft than biologists, chemists, or astrophysicists could practice theirs. But history is not a static recollection of facts. Events in the past happened only once, but the historians who study those events are always changing their minds about them. Like all humans, historians have prejudices, biases, and beliefs. They are also influenced by events in their own times. In other words, they look at the past through lenses that filter and even distort. Events in the past may have happened only once, but what historians think about them, the meaning they give to those events, is constantly changing. Moreover, because their lenses perceive events differently, historians often disagree about the past. The supposedly "static" discipline of history is actually dynamic and charged with tension.

That brings us to the question of what historians really do. Briefly, historians ask questions about past events or developments and try to explain them just as much as biology, chemistry, or astrophysics, therefore, history is a problem-solving discipline. Historians, like scientists, sift evidence to answer questions. Like scientists, whose explanations for things often conflict, historians can ask the same questions, look at the same facts, and come up with different explanations because they look at the past in different ways. Or they may have entirely different questions in mind and so come away with very different "pasts." Thus history is a process of constant revision. As historians like to put it, every generation writes its own history.

But why bother to study and interpret the past in our own way if someone else will only revise t again in the future? The answer is sobering: If we don't write our own history, someone else will write it for us. Who today would accept as historical truth the notion that the Indians were cruel savages whose extermination was necessary to fulfill an Anglo-Saxon destiny to conquer the continent for democracy and civilization? Who today would accept the "truth" that slaves were racially inferior and happy with their lot on Southern plantations? If we accept these views of Indians and black slaves, we are allowing nineteenth-century historians to determine our view of the past.

Instead, by reconstructing the past as best we can, we can better understand our own times. Like the amnesia victim, without memory we face a bewildering world. As we recapture our collective past, the present becomes more intelligible. Subject to new experiences, a later generation will view the past differently. Realizing that future generations will revise history does not give us a license to play fast and loose with the facts of history. Rather, each generation faces the choice of giving meaning to those facts or experiencing the confusion of historical amnesia.

Finding meaning in the facts of the past, then, is the central challenge of history. It requires us to ask questions and construct explanations—mental activities far different and far more exciting than merely memorizing names, dates, and facts. More important, it enables us to approach history as critical thinkers. The more skilled we become at historical reasoning, the better we will understand our world and ourselves. Helping you to develop skill in historical analysis is the purpose of this volume.

The method of this book reflects its purpose. The first chapter discusses textbooks. History texts have a very practical purpose. By bringing order to the past, they give many students a useful and reassuring "handle" on history. But they are not the Ten Commandments, because, like all works of history, they also contain interpretations. To most readers these interpretations are hard to spot. Chapter 1 examines what a number of college textbooks in American history say and don't say about the Indians at the time of English settlement of the New World. By reading selections from several texts and asking how and why they differ, we can see that texts are not as objective as readers often believe.

If textbooks are not the absolute truth, how can we ever know anything? To answer those questions, we turn next to the raw material of history. Chapter 2, on childhood in Puritan New England, examines the primary sources on which historians rely to reconstruct and interpret the past. What are these sources? What do historians do with them? What can historians determine from them?

With a basic understanding of the nature and usefulness of primary sources, we proceed to Chapter 3 for a closer evaluation. This chapter on the haves and have-nots of colonial Pennsylvania shows how careful historians must be in using primary sources. Does a source speak with one voice or with many? How can historians disagree about the meaning of the same historical facts? By carefully evaluating primary sources in this chapter, you can draw your own conclusions about society in colonial Pennsylvania. You can also better understand how historians often derive different conclusions from the same body of material.

Chapter 3 is good preparation for the evaluation in Chapter 4 of one historian's argument about the unsettling effects of the Revolution on American society. By exploring various attempts to achieve greater equality during the Revolutionary-era, the essay and primary sources in the chapter focus on an often-neglected aspect of the struggle for independence. They also reinforce the lesson that our understanding of the past is influenced by the historical voices that we choose to hear.

One of the most important sources of disagreement among historians is the question of motivation. What drove people to do what they did in the past? The good historian, like the detective in a murder mystery, eventually asks that question. And few topics in American history better illustrate the importance of motivation than that in Chapter 5, the Founding Fathers and their purposes in framing the Constitution. As that topic also shows, questions of motive perhaps cause the most arguments among historians.

Motives in history are related to ideas, the subject of Chapter 6. What power do ideas exert in history? What is their relationship, for example, to the economic motives examined in the previous chapter? In Chapter 6 we try to answer these questions by examining the role of ideology in shaping Jeffersonian policies regarding blacks and Native Americans.

The problem of motivation is also closely linked to the study of historical causation. Different historical interpretations usually involve different views about the causes of things. In considering the questions of motivation and ideology, Chapters 5 and 6 move beyond the question of what happened to the question of why it happened. Chapter 7, on the early-nineteenth-century religious revivals known as the Second Great Awakening, moves even deeper into the realm of why. It considers the extent to which many different factors may interact to produce historical change.

Once we have considered the questions of motivation and causation in history, Chapter 8 examines what historians call a "grand theory" of history, a sweeping or all-encompassing explanation of historical causation. The topic of this chapter is the causal relationship between America's long frontier experience and the development of democratic political institutions. This chapter also considers the problems historians face in trying to fit historical evidence into sweeping hypotheses.

Chapter 9 turns from the influence of grand forces to the influence of "great" individuals. Few individuals were considered greater, by many Americans in the first half of the nineteenth century, than Andrew Jackson. What influence does a "great" individual like Jackson have on history? Are there extraordinary people who shape an entire era? How much can students of history learn about the past by looking at it from the "top down"? How much do they miss by doing so? Such questions are, of course, related to the topics of previous chapters: historical evidence, motivation, causation, and even grand historical theories.

The next chapter examines history from the opposite perspective—from the "bottom up." What can historians learn by looking at the people at the bottom of a society? What challenges face historians who try? In early American history, the best place for using this approach is the issue of slavery. Chapter 10 examines what slavery was like for slaves and why their lives are important to historians.

Many of the chapters just discussed use a single historical essay and an accompanying set of primary sources. Chapter 11 offers an opportunity to pull together the lessons of previous chapters. It compares what two historians have written about a single topic: the position of women in the North and the South before the Civil War. Because the sources in this chapter deal with the impact of ideal images on actual behavior, they enable us to consider, in a single topic, the questions of motivation and causation as well as the influence of ideology in society.

The goal of Chapter 12 is similar to that of Chapter 11: to synthesize, or pull together, the lessons learned in preceding chapters. Here, however, the emphasis is on the problems of historical evidence, causation, and the use of grand theory. Chapter 12 contains two essays on the outcome of the Civil War as well as a small collection of primary sources. It asks you to compare and analyze conflicting arguments by using not only primary sources but also insights drawn from previous chapters.

All of the chapters in this volume encourage you to think more like a historian and to sharpen your critical thinking skills. Chapter 13 returns to a point emphasized throughout this volume: The pursuit of the past cannot occur apart from a consideration of historical interpretation, and differences in historical interpretation matter not just to historians but to everyone. This final chapter examines various interpretations of the political experience of African Americans during Reconstruction. It contains two accounts of black political involvement in Reconstruction and primary documents that illuminate both interpretations. In addition, it underscores the way our view of the past can be used to justify policies and practices in a later time.

By the end of this volume, you will have sharpened your ability to think about the past. You will think more critically about the use of historical evidence and about such historical problems as motivation, causation, and interpretation. Moreover, by exploring several styles of historical writing and various approaches to the past—from those that emphasize politics or economics to those that highlight social developments or military strategy—you will also learn to understand the importance of the past. In short, you will think more like a historian.

Chapter
1

The Truth About Textbooks:
Indians and the Settlement of America

The textbook selections in this chapter illustrate different assumptions textbook writers have had about American Indians and white–Indian relations during the settlement period.

Sources

1. History of the American People (1927), DAVID S. MUZZEY
2. The American Pageant (1966), THOMAS A. BAILEY
3. A People and a Nation (2008), MARY BETH NORTON ET AL.

*O*ne of the best aids to learning history is also one of the biggest hindrances to understanding the past. It is the textbook, the traditional authority on American history. Textbooks impose a welcome order on the past by organizing events chronologically and explaining historical relationships. How, then, do these helpful companions sometimes obscure our understanding of the past?

Readers of textbooks often start with the false assumption that these books simply report facts predetermined by the "dead hand" of the past. That misconception is encouraged by a certain tone: Textbooks seem to speak with authority. "To us as children," historian Frances FitzGerald writes,

> texts were the truth of things: they were American history. It was not just that we read them before we understood that not everything that is printed is the truth, or the whole truth. It was that they, much more than other books, had the demeanor and trappings of authority. They were weighty volumes. They spoke in measured cadences: imperturbable, humorless, and as distant as Chinese emperors.[1]

Many college students make the same mistake, even if their textbooks speak in more familiar tones. They too assume that their history textbooks "contain only the truth of things."

Of course, the case is more complicated. Textbook authors select facts and shape history in ways that reflect their own times. Thus, like all works of history, textbooks contain interpretations. Readers who see only the cold, immovable facts of history have difficulty spotting them, yet the interpretations are there, like graveyard ghosts lurking amid the headstones. Comparing the way textbooks present the same topic is one good way to detect these elusive spirits. In this chapter we examine what several textbooks say about the Indians when Europe discovered America and when England settled Virginia.

SETTING

Ravaged by strange diseases, attacked by land-hungry settlers, and dispossessed from their land, Indians were among the biggest losers in the American past. Because history is mostly written by winners, Native Americans have been big losers in history books too. For a long time, historians treated them as little more than "an exotic, if melancholy, footnote to American history."[2] Worse, their accounts were based on questionable ideas about the Indians' lack of "civilization."

Discussions about population show how historians' assumptions about Indian culture influenced their conclusions. In the early twentieth century, historians believed that 1 million Indians lived north of Mexico in 1492 and that fewer than 10 million lived in the entire Western Hemisphere. In fact, at least 2 million people lived in the United States and Canada, with another 15 million in central Mexico. Some researchers now think the total population of the New World in 1492 was around 60 million. One reason for this difference is that earlier population estimates failed to take into account the devastating effects of Old World germs on Indians. They were also based on an assumption that "uncivilized" Indians were incapable of supporting large numbers of people on their land. Following the lead of anthropologists and ethnographers, historians now understand the sophistication of Native American culture and so have dramatically raised their estimates of the Indian population.

Today's historians also have a much greater understanding of the varied ways that whites and Indians interacted. The Indians' role in American history began with their impact on the environment. English settlers encountered a land already cleared and cultivated, a condition that made English settlement much easier. Cultural exchange began immediately, aided by a rough technological equality between the Europeans and Indians. With the exception of the Europeans' ability to navigate the oceans and make iron into tools and weapons, the technological differences between the English settlers and their indigenous neighbors were not great. While the English learned to cultivate tobacco, corn, squash, and other crops, the Indians quickly learned to use kettles, knives, needles, and guns.

In fact, Native Americans and the European invaders often developed a symbiotic, or mutually dependent, relationship. Initially, Europeans frequently relied on Indian food and skills to survive in a foreign environment. Some New England Puritans, for instance, likely survived their first winter in bark huts that the local Native Americans taught them to construct. Later European settlers depended on Indians to guide them through seemingly trackless forests and to extract a rich harvest of furs from the land. Likewise, Native Americans quickly came to depend on European trade goods.

An understanding of Native American culture makes clear that English settlers were influenced by Indians in ways they did not understand. It also puts some familiar events in Virginia's early history in a new light. When the Jamestown settlers fell ill in 1607, the powerful Indian Chief Powhatan provided food to keep the starving colony alive. Captain John Smith could only explain this gift as an act of God, who had "changed the heart of the savages."[3] Later Smith was captured by Indians and saved from death, so he believed, by Powhatan's daughter Pocahontas. Just before Smith's executioners were supposed to strike their fatal blows, the Indian "princess" threw herself at the Englishman's feet and pleaded for his life. Once again, Smith saw only the hand of God. He did not see that his remarkable "rescue" was a ceremony designed to demonstrate Powhatan's power and desire to have friendly relations with the English. Nor did he understand that Powhatan, who wanted to extend his authority over dozens of unruly tribes around the Chesapeake, viewed the English as a useful ally. Within a year, the suspicious Smith had begun to burn

Indian fields and villages to coerce Powhatan and other chiefs to provide more food to the growing settlement.

Events soon ran their tragic course. After Smith left Virginia in 1609, other settlers continued to use force to extract food from the Indians. In 1613 they also kidnapped Pocahontas and held her ransom. Only when John Rolfe vowed to marry her did Powhatan sign a peace treaty. More settlers poured into Virginia, however, and continued to pressure Indians for land. In 1622 the Indians attacked, wiping out about one-third of Virginia's white population. It was the final blow to the Virginia Company, which soon declared bankruptcy. The attack also led to a new attitude about the Indians. As one settler put it, "Our hands which were before tied with gentleness and fair usage, are now set at liberty by the treacherous violence of the savages. . . . [We] may now . . . invade the Country, and destroy them who sought to destroy us. . . ."[4] Virginians began to exterminate the Indians. Only much later, when they began to examine their own cultural assumptions, would historians question why.

INVESTIGATION

This chapter contains three selections from American history textbooks with varying perspectives about the Indians. The first selection is from a text first published in 1927; the last is from one published in 2008. *Your primary task is to determine how views of the Indians differ in these accounts. A good analysis will address these main questions:*

1. **What does each text say about Indian culture?** What does it reveal about cultural differences among the Indians? How are the Indians and Indian tribes named? Does the language describing the Indians reflect a belief that one's own culture is superior to others (ethnocentrism)?

2. **Is there evidence of cultural exchange between the Indians and Europeans?** Is relevant information about this exchange left out?

3. **Does the text discuss the Indian population at the time of the European discovery of the New World?** Which text has the higher estimate of this population?

4. **What role do the Indians play in the settlement of Jamestown?** Do the Indians aid the settlers? Why do the Indians attack? Why do the English settlers attack the Indians?

5. **Are individual Indians mentioned? If so, how are they portrayed?** What, if anything, does the selection say about Pocahontas? About Powhatan?

You may not be able to find answers to all of these questions in each text. However, you should be able to find enough evidence to come to a well-supported conclusion about the different ways each text treats the Indians.

Before you begin, some cautions may be helpful. First, there is consider-able overlap in these accounts. All of them deal with the Indians on the eve of European discovery and with white–Indian relations in Virginia. Second, none of these selections contain encyclopedic accounts, but rather information that the authors thought was important to an understanding of these topics.

Third, because historians make interpretations by choosing or omitting cer-tain facts, you will need to determine what has been left out of each account. This requires some background, so make sure that you have read your textbook's account of the Native Americans prior to the European conquest. Also read what it has to say about the interaction between the English and Native Americans in Virginia. (Of course, it too contains an interpretation.) Finally, don't dismiss an account simply because it is biased. Your challenge is to make a critical, informed, and fair judgment about the way textbooks have treated the Indians.

SOURCES

History of the American People (1927)
DAVID S. MUZZEY

America is the child of Europe. Until the discoverers and explorers from the maritime nations of western Europe began to come to the shores of these con-tinents, more than four hundred years ago, the vast regions now occupied by the United States, the British Dominion of Canada, and the Latin-American republics of Mexico, Central and South America were a wilderness of tribes of copper-colored barbarians or savages, whose ancestors had crossed by Bering Strait from north-eastern Asia to Alaska, we know not how many centuries before, and had slowly spread southward and eastward to Patagonia and Labrador. These American Indians (or "Amerinds," to use the cable-code name by which scholars distinguish them from the inhabitants of the country of India) showed great diversity of character and attainments, due to differences in climate, soil, food, building material, and the activi-ties necessary to preserve life. The Mayas of Yucatan, the Incas of Peru, the Aztecs of Mexico, the Hopis of New Mexico, the Haidas of Queen Charlotte Island, and the Iroquois of central New York furnish examples of Indian tribes who had learned to construct quite elaborate calendars and temples, to weave beautiful rugs and baskets, to bake pottery, to build houses of clay or of cedar beams, shaped with stone implements and ornamented with huge carved totem poles, to devise rude political institutions, and to raise crops of beans, pumpkins, and Indian corn. Other tribes were sunk in bestial

Source: From David Saville Muzzey, *History of the American People,* 1927, pp. 1, 2, 39, 40, 43

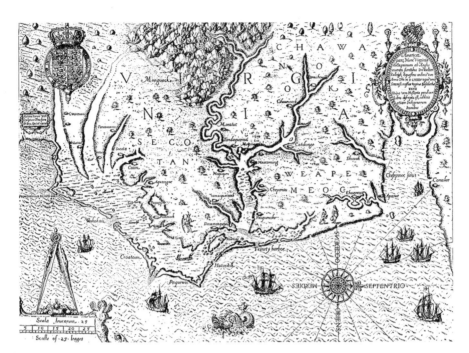

An early map of Virginia [Library of Congress Rare Book and Special Collections Division Washington, D.C. [LC-USZ62-54020]]

savagery, sheltering themselves from wind and snow behind piles of brush-wood, wallowing in the southern mud like hogs, eating roots, grass, snakes, and lizards, and dying by thousands from the ravages of the beasts and the diseases against which they were powerless to protect themselves. Nowhere had they risen above the stage of barbarism. It was for the European settlers to introduce civilization into the New World. They brought hither not only tools for the conquest of the wilderness, such as firearms, iron implements for building and farming, horses, cattle, sheep, and hogs, wheat and barley, vegetables and fruits, but also the forms of government, the religion, the books, and the languages of the Old World. For the ethnologist the American Indians have been a picturesque object of study; for the government, since the days of the earliest settlers, they have been an obstruction to be removed, by methods often unnecessarily cruel, from the path of civilization. They have contributed almost nothing to the making of America. The New World was a virgin continent for the European discoverers and their descendants, to make of it what they would. . . .

. . . On May 6, 1607, three small ships with one hundred and four colonists, of whom a large part were "gentlemen" unused to labor, arrived at the capes guarding the entrance to Chesapeake Bay. Their instructions were to choose a healthful place on a navigable river, by which they might arrive at "some spring which runs the contrary way toward the East India Sea," to avoid giving offense to the Indians, and to conduct themselves "for the good of your country and your own." . . . [T]he colonists' supplies had been almost exhausted during the four and a half months' voyage from England, and they neglected the necessary planting of corn for the search for gold and the passage to the Indies. Indeed, had it not been for the supplies obtained from the Indians, the colony could hardly have lasted through the first winter. As it was, more than half the settlers died of fever from the malarial air and the brackish water of the James. The survivors owed their life, probably, to the energy and resourcefulness of one man, John Smith, a seasoned veteran of many a war in Europe and the hero, in his own tales, of hair-raising adventures among the Turks and the Russians. Smith was a braggart and a martinet, but he made the men work, kept the Indians in awe by a combination of boldness and cleverness, and obtained frequent supplies of corn. . . .

. . . By 1624 there were about a thousand persons in the colony (though more than five times that number had been sent out from England since the first settlement). . . . Yet the results were disappointing. It must be remembered that the colony was not started as an experiment in democracy or a refuge from oppression, but as a business venture. The stockholders were looking for returns on their investment. Hundreds of thousands of dollars had been put into the enterprise and the returns were ridiculously small. . . . An Indian massacre in 1622, which cost the colony three hundred and forty-seven lives, was a good pretext for declaring the government by the company a failure, and two years later James had the charter annulled by the royal judges and took the government into his own hands.

2   The American Pageant (1966)
THOMAS A. BAILEY

The American republic, which is still relatively young, was from the outset singularly favored. It started from scratch on a vast and virgin continent, which was so sparsely peopled by Indians that they could be eliminated or pushed aside. Such a magnificent opportunity for a great democratic experiment may never come again, for no other huge, fertile, and uninhabited areas are left in the temperate zones of this crowded planet. . . .

As the realization gradually dawned that the American continents were a rich prize in their own right, Spain became the dominant exploring and colonizing power in the 1500s. . . .

The bare statistics of Spain's colonial empire are impressive. By 1574, thirty-three years before the first primitive English shelters in Virginia, there were about two hundred Spanish cities and towns in North and South America. A total of 160,000 Spanish inhabitants, mostly men, had brought

Source: Thomas Bailey, *The American Pageant,* 3rd edition, pp. 4, 10, 13–15. Copyright © 1966 by D. C. Heath and Company. Reprinted by permission of Houghton Mifflin Company.

some 5,000,000 Indians under their yoke. Majestic cathedrals dotted the land, printing presses were turning out books, and literary prizes were being awarded. Two distinguished universities were chartered in 1551, one at Mexico City and the other at Lima, Peru. Both of them antedated Harvard, the first college established in the English colonies, by eighty-five years.

It is clear that the Spaniards, who had more than a century's head start over the English, were genuine empire builders. As compared with their Anglo-Saxon rivals, their colonial establishment was larger and richer and as an entity lasted a quarter of a century longer. The English settlers, disagreeable though the thought may be, were more successful than the Spaniards in killing off the Indians. . . .

In 1606, two years after peace with Spain, the finger of destiny pointed to Virginia. A joint-stock company, known as the Virginia Company of London, received a charter from King James I of England for a settlement in the New World. The main attraction was hoped-for gold, although there was some desire to convert the heathen Indians to Christianity and to find a passage through America to the Indies.

The early years at Jamestown proved to be a nightmare for all concerned— except the buzzards. Hundreds of wretched souls perished from disease, from actual starvation ("the starving time," 1609–1610), and later from Indian massacres. Ironically, the woods rustled with game and the rivers flopped with fish. Soft-handed English gentlemen and deported criminals wasted valuable time seeking gold when they should have been hoeing corn. They were spurred to their frantic search by edicts from the directors of the company, who threatened to abandon the colonists if they did not strike it rich.

Virginia was saved from going under at the start largely by the leadership and resourcefulness of an incredible young adventurer, Captain John Smith. Taking over in 1608, he whipped the gold-hungry colonists into line with the rule, "He who will not work shall not eat." The dusky Indian maiden Pocahontas may not have saved the captured Smith's life, as he dramatically relates, by suddenly interposing her head between his and the Indian war clubs. But there can be little doubt that Pocahontas, who married John Rolfe in 1613, helped save the colony by enlisting the aid of the Indians and by helping to preserve the peace during these critical years.

A People and a Nation (2008)
MARY BETH NORTON ET AL.

By approximately 9,000 years ago, the residents of what is now central Mexico began to cultivate food crops, especially maize (corn), squash, beans, avocados, and peppers. In the Andes Mountains of South America,

Source: From Mary Beth Norton. *A People and a Nation,* 8E. © 2008 Wadsworth, a part of Cengage Learning, Inc. Reproduced by permission. www.cengage.com/permissions

people started to grow potatoes. As knowledge of agricultural techniques improved and spread through the Americas, vegetables and maize proved a more reliable source of food than hunting and gathering. Except for those living in the harshest climates, most Americans started to adopt a more sedentary style of life so that they could tend fields regularly. . . .

Wherever agriculture dominated the economy, complex civilizations flourished. Such societies, assured of steady supplies of grains and vegetables, no longer had to devote all their energies to subsistence. Instead, they were able to accumulate wealth, produce ornamental objects, trade with other groups, and create elaborate rituals and ceremonies. In North America, the successful cultivation of nutritious crops, such as maize, beans, and squash, seems to have led to the growth and development of all the major civilizations: first the large city-states of Mesoamerica (modern Mexico and Guatemala) and then the urban clusters known collectively as the Mississippian culture and located in the present-day United States. Each of these societies, many historians and archaeologists now believe, reached its height of population and influence only after achieving success in agriculture. Each later declined and collapsed after reaching the limits of its food supply, with dire political and military consequences.

Archaeologists and historians still know little about the first major Mesoamerican civilization, the Olmecs, who about 4,000 years ago lived near the Gulf of Mexico in cities dominated by temple pyramids. The Mayas and Teotihuacán, which developed approximately 2,000 years later, are better recorded. Teotihuacán, founded in the Valley of Mexico about 300 B.C.E. (Before the Common Era), eventually became one of the largest urban areas in the world, housing perhaps 100,000 people in the fifth century C.E. (Common Era). Teotihuacán's commercial network extended hundreds of miles in all directions; many peoples prized its obsidian (a green glass), used to make fine knives and mirrors. Pilgrims traveled long distances to visit Teotihuacán's impressive pyramids and the great temple of Quetzalcoatl— the feathered serpent, primary god of central Mexico. . . .

Ancient native societies in what is now the United States learned to grow maize, squash, and beans from Mesoamericans, but the exact nature of the relationship of the various cultures is unknown. (No Mesoamerican artifacts have been found north of the Rio Grande, but some items resembling Mississippian objects have been excavated in northern Mexico.) The Hohokam, Mogollon, and ancient Pueblo peoples of the modern states of Arizona and New Mexico subsisted by combining hunting and gathering with agriculture in an arid region of unpredictable rainfall. Hohokam villagers constructed extensive irrigation systems, but even so, they occasionally had to relocate their settlements when water supplies failed. Between 900 and 1150 C.E. in Chaco Canyon, the Pueblos built fourteen "Great Houses," multistory stone structures averaging two hundred rooms. The canyon, at the juncture of perhaps 400 miles of roads, served as a major regional trading and processing center for turquoise, used then as now to create beautiful ornamental objects. Yet the aridity eventually caused the Chacoans to migrate to other sites.

At almost the same time, the unrelated Mississippian culture flourished in what is now the midwestern and southeastern United States. Relying largely on maize, squash, nuts, pumpkins, and venison for food, the Mississippians lived in substantial settlements organized hierarchically. The largest of their urban centers was the City of the Sun (now called Cahokia), near modern St. Louis. Located on rich farmland close to the confluence of the Illinois, Missouri, and Mississippi Rivers, Cahokia, like Teotihuacán and Chaco Canyon, served as a focal point for both religion and trade. At its peak (in the eleventh and twelfth centuries C.E.), the City of the Sun covered more than 5 square miles and had a population of about twenty thousand—small by Mesoamerican standards but larger than any other northern community, and larger than London in the same era. . . .

The Aztecs' histories tell of the long migration of their people (who called themselves Mexica) into the Valley of Mexico during the twelfth century. The uninhabited ruins of Teotihuacán, which by then had been deserted for at least two hundred years, awed and mystified the migrants. Their chronicles record that their primary deity, Huitzilopochtli—a war god represented by an eagle—directed them to establish their capital on an island where they saw an eagle eating a serpent, the symbol of Quetzalcoatl. That island city became Tenochtitlán, the center of a rigidly stratified society composed of hereditary classes of warriors, merchants, priests, common folk, and slaves.

The Aztecs conquered their neighbors, forcing them to pay tribute in textiles, gold, foodstuffs, and human beings who could be sacrificed to Huitzilopochtli. They also engaged in ritual combat, known as flowery wars, to obtain further sacrificial victims. The war god's taste for blood was not easily quenched. In the Aztec year Ten Rabbit (1502), at the coronation of Motecuhzoma II (the Spaniards could not pronounce his name correctly, so they called him Montezuma), thousands of people were sacrificed by having their still-beating hearts torn from their bodies. . . .

The Spaniards came to Tenochtitlán not only with horses and steel weapons but also with smallpox, bringing an epidemic that had begun on Hispaniola. The disease peaked in 1520, fatally weakening Tenochtitlán's defenders. "It spread over the people as great destruction," as elderly Aztec later remembered. "Some it quite covered [with pustules] on all parts—their faces, their heads, their breasts. . . . There was great havoc. Very many died of it." Largely as a consequence, Tenochtitlán surrendered in 1521, and the Spaniards built Mexico City on its site. Cortés and his men seized a fabulous treasure of gold and silver. Thus, not long after Columbus's first voyage, the Spanish monarchs—who treated the American territories as their personal possessions—controlled the richest, most extensive empire Europe had known since ancient Rome. . . .

The initial impulse that led to England's first permanent colony in the Western Hemisphere was, however, economic. A group of merchants and wealthy gentry in 1606 obtained a royal charter for the Virginia Company, organized as a joint-stock company, a forerunner of the modern corporation. . . .

In 1607 the company dispatched 104 men and boys to a region near Chesapeake Bay called Tsenacomoco by its native inhabitants. There in May they established the palisaded settlement called Jamestown on a swampy peninsula in a river they also named for their monarch. They quickly constructed small houses and a Church of England chapel. Ill equipped for survival in the unfamiliar environment, the colonists fell victim to dissension and disease as they attempted to maintain traditional English social and political hierarchies. Familiar with Spanish experience, the gentlemen and soldiers at Jamestown expected to rely on local Indians for food and tribute, yet the residents of Tsenacomoco refused to cooperate. Moreover, through sheer bad luck the settlers arrived in the midst of a severe drought (now known to be the worst in the region for 1,700 years), which persisted until 1612. The lack of rainfall not only made it difficult to cultivate crops but also polluted their drinking water.

The weroance (chief) of Tsenacomoco, Powhatan, had inherited rule over six Algonquian villages and later gained control of some twenty-five others. In late 1607 negotiations with Captain John Smith, one of the colony's leaders, the weroance tentatively agreed to an alliance with the Englishmen. In exchange for foodstuffs, Powhatan hoped to acquire guns, hatchets, and swords, which would give him a technological advantage over the enemies of his people. Each side in the alliance wanted to subordinate the other, but neither succeeded.

The fragile relationship soon foundered on mutual mistrust. The wereoance relocated his primary village in early 1609 to a place the newcomers could not access easily. Without Powhatan's assistance, the settlement experienced a "starving time" (winter 1609–1610), when many died and at least one colonist resorted to cannibalism. In spring 1610 the survivors packed up to leave on a newly arrived ship but en route out of the James River encountered a new governor, more settlers, and added supplies, so they returned to Jamestown. Sporadic skirmishes ensued as the standoff with the Powhatans continued. To gain the upper hand, the settlers in 1613 kidnapped Powhatan's daughter, Pocahontas, and held her hostage. In captivity, she agreed to convert to Christianity and to marry a colonist, John Rolfe. He had fallen in love with her, but she probably married him for diplomatic reasons; their union initiated a period of peace between the English and her people. Funded by the Virginia Company, she and Rolfe sailed to England to promote interest in the colony. She died at Gravesend in 1616, probably of dysentery, leaving an infant son who returned to Virginia as a young adult.

Although their royal charter nominally laid claim to a much wider territory, the Jamestown settlers saw their "Virginia" as essentially corresponding to Tsenacomoco. Powhatan's dominion was bounded on the north by
the Potomac, on the south by the Great Dismal Swamp, and on the west by
the fall line—the beginning of the upland Piedmont. Beyond those boundaries lay the Powhatans' enemies and (especially in the west) lands the
Powhatans feared to enter. English people relied on the Powhatans as
guides and interpreters, traveling along rivers and precontact paths in order to trade with the Powhatans' partners. For more than half a century, settlement in "Virginia" was confined to Tsenacomoco.

In Tsenacomoco and elsewhere on the North American coast, English settlers and local Algonquians focused on their cultural differences, not their
similarities, although both groups held deep religious beliefs, subsisted
primarily through agriculture, accepted social and political hierarchy, and
observed well-defined gender roles. From the outset English men regarded
Indian men as lazy because they did not cultivate crops and spent much of
their time hunting (a sport, not work, in English eyes). Indian men thought
English men effeminate because they did the "woman's work" of cultivation. In the same vein, the English believed that Algonquian women were
oppressed because they did heavy field labor.

The nature of Algonquian and English hierarchies differed. Among
Algonquians like the Powhatans, political power and social status did not
necessarily pass directly through the male line, instead commonly flowing
through sisters' sons. By contrast, English gentlemen inherited their position from their father. English political and military leaders tended to rule
autocratically, whereas Algonquian leaders (even Powhatan) had limited
authority over their people. Accustomed to the European concept of powerful kings, the English overestimated the ability of chiefs to make treaties that
would bind their people.

Furthermore, Algonquians and English had different notions of property
ownership. Most Algonquian villages held their land communally. It could
not be bought or sold absolutely, although certain rights to use the land (for
example, for hunting or fishing) could be transferred. Once, most English
villagers, too, had used land in common, but because of enclosures in the
previous century they had become accustomed to individual farms and to
buying and selling land. The English also refused to accept the validity of
Indians' claims to traditional hunting territories, insisting that only land
intensively cultivated could be regarded as owned or occupied. As one
colonist put it, "salvadge peoples" who "rambled" over a region without
farming it could claim no "title or propertye" in the land. Ownership of such
"unclaimed" property, the English believed, lay with the English monarchy,
in whose name John Cabot had laid claim to North America in 1497.

Above all, the English settlers believed unwaveringly in the superiority
of their civilization. Although in the early years of colonization they often

anticipated living peacefully alongside indigenous peoples, they always assumed that they would dictate the terms of such coexistence. . . . They showed little respect for the Indians when they believed English interests were at stake, as was demonstrated by developments in Virginia once the settlers had finally found the salable commodity they sought.

That commodity was tobacco, the American crop previously introduced to Europe by the Spanish and subsequently cultivated in Turkey. In 1611 John Rolfe planted seeds of a variety from the Spanish Caribbean, which was superior to the strain grown by Virginia Indians. Nine years later, Virginians exported 40,000 pounds of cured leaves, and by the late 1620s shipments had jumped dramatically to 1.5 million pounds. . . .

The spread of tobacco cultivation immeasurably altered life for everyone. Successful tobacco cultivation required abundant land, because the crop quickly drained soil of nutrients. Farmers soon learned that a field could produce only about three satisfactory crops before it had to lie fallow for several years to regain its fertility. Thus the once-small English settlements began to expand rapidly: eager applicants asked the Virginia Company for large land grants on both sides of the James River and its tributary streams. Lulled into a false sense of security by years of peace, Virginians established farms at some distance from one another along the riverbanks—a settlement pattern convenient for tobacco cultivation but dangerous for defense.

Opechancanough, Powhatan's brother and successor, watched the English colonists' expansion and witnessed their attempts to convert natives to Christianity. Recognizing the danger, the war leader launched coordinated attacks all along the James River on March 22, 1622. By the end of the day, 347 colonists (about one-quarter of the total) lay dead, and only a timely warning from two Christian converts saved Jamestown itself from destruction.

CONCLUSION

Now that you have examined these selections, several points should be clear. First, there is no such thing as objective history. Even contemporary textbooks that may seem to be "the whole truth" reflect history's subjectivity. Second, like everyone else, textbook writers are products of their own time. Attitudes about the Indians at different times in the twentieth century surely influenced historians' views about the role of Native Americans in history. Each textbook's publication date is an important clue to why these historians could come to such different conclusions about Indian culture and white–Indian relations. Even historians writing at the same time, however, often do not necessarily share the same values or assumptions. They may also disagree about sources. Today, for instance, some scholars argue that John Smith's account of his Virginia experiences is reliable, while others contend that he was a self-promoter who often embellished the truth. Finally, you may have determined that you need more "firsthand" information to answer the questions in this chapter. That conclusion is a reminder that historians must have more than other historians' accounts to understand the past. They also need primary sources. These valuable sources allow historians to see the past from the perspective of those in it. We turn to them next.

FURTHER READING

William Cronon, *Changes in the Land: Indians, Colonists, and the Ecology of New England* (New York: Hill and Wang, 1983).
Frances FitzGerald, *America Revised: History Schoolbooks in the Twentieth Century* (New York: Vintage, 1979).
James W. Loewen, *Lies My Teacher Told Me: Everything Your American History Textbook Got Wrong* (New York: The New Press, 1995).
Gary B. Nash, *Red, White, and Black: The Peoples of Early America*, 2nd ed. (Englewood Cliffs, N.J.: Prentice Hall, 1982).
David Price, *Love and Hate in Jamestown: John Smith, Pocahontas, and the Heart of a New Nation* (New York: Alfred A. Knopf, 2003).

NOTES

1. Frances FitzGerald, *America Revised: History Schoolbooks in the Twentieth Century* (New York: Vintage, 1979), p. 7.
2. James Axtell, *The European and the Indian: Essays in the Ethnohistory of Colonial North America* (New York: Oxford University Press, 1981), p. 274.
3. John Smith, "Generall Historie of Virginia, New-England, and the Summer Isles" (1624), quoted in Jack P. Greene, *Settlements to Society 1584–1763* (New York: McGraw-Hill, 1966), p. 35.
4. Quoted in Gary B. Nash, *Red, White, and Black: The Peoples of Early America*, 2nd ed. (Englewood Cliffs, N.J.: Prentice Hall, 1982), p. 61.

Chapter

2

The Primary Materials of History: Childhood in Puritan New England

The documents in this chapter are primary sources that relate to Puritan child-rearing practices. Three kinds of sources are given—portraits, written material, and architectural drawings.

Sources

1. Elizabeth Eggington (1664)
2. Henry Gibbs (1670)
3. Letter of Samuel Mather (Age 12) to His Father (ca. 1638)
4. Massachusetts Court Records
5. Lawrence Hammond, Diary Entry for April 23, 1688
6. Cotton Mather on Young Children (1690)
7. *An Arrow Against Profane and Promiscuous Dancing* (1690), INCREASE MATHER
8. Samuel Sewall on the Trials of His Fifteen-Year-Old Daughter (1696)
9. The Well-Ordered Family (1712), BENJAMIN WADSWORTH
10. The Duty of Children Toward Their Parents (1727)
11. A Puritan Primer Warns Against Frivolous Behavior (1671)
12. The Roger Mowry House (ca. 1653)
13. The Eleazer Arnold House (ca. 1684)

*I*n 1671, Puritan minister Eleazar Mather reminded his New England congregation why they had come "unto this land" earlier in the seventeenth century. They left England, he told them, to ensure their children's spiritual welfare— "to leave God in the midst of them."[1] Mather's reminder suggests how seriously the Puritans took their child-rearing duties. The very survival of a godly society in New England depended on the proper molding of their offspring.

To rear children properly, Puritans realized, nothing was more important than education. As the Massachusetts General Court put it in 1647, reading must be taught in the school because it was "one chief project of that old deluder, Satan, to keep men from the knowledge of the Scriptures."[2] So the Puritans taught their children to read and write. And they did write: diaries, journals, tracts, letters, histories, sermons, and notes on sermons. Today, libraries, museums, archives, and historical societies are filled with these historical sources.

To understand what historians do with primary sources, we turn to the Puritans. They left modern historians a narrower range of primary sources than many people who came after them. Today, historians count virtually anything from the recorded past as primary sources, including newspapers, magazines, posters, motion pictures, speeches, and even artifacts such as furniture, coins, or clothing. The highly literate Puritans, nonetheless, created a rich trove of mostly written primary historical material. For that reason, it is fitting that we begin our examination of primary sources by looking at Puritan childhood. Doing so will also tell us about Puritan society's important values and ideals. Then, by comparing Puritan and modern childhood, we can learn a great deal about both Puritan society and our own.

SETTING

The Puritans believed that a godly community was constructed with well-ordered families. Within these families, child rearing was a primary responsibility of parents. They were expected to teach their children basic tenets of religion and the "first principles and grounds of government."[3] However, because a child's salvation was at stake, child rearing was too important to leave to unsupervised parents. Far more than the schools and government do today, Puritan authorities oversaw the upbringing and education of children.

The Puritan family was, above all, a patriarchy. Drawing on traditional English customs and Old Testament injunctions, the Puritans placed authority within the household in the hands of the husband and father. Thus, despite the supervision of family affairs by Puritan authorities, a Puritan father was the divinely ordained ruler of his little commonwealth. In a preindustrial age when most work was done in the home, the father was usually present and his authority was immediate.

Although fathers had final authority in all household matters, mothers of course also played an essential role in the Puritan family. Aside from numerous tasks in and around the home, wives shared the responsibility for rearing children. The education and spiritual salvation of the children, for example, were primarily the mother's concerns. As the minister Cotton Mather declared, "A mother must give the law of God unto them."[4] Mothers thus exercised a great deal of authority over their children. Although fathers had the power to overrule their wives' decisions regarding their children, they were encouraged not to. Cooperation between husbands and wives was the ideal in the Puritan home. As another writer put it, "Children and Servants are . . . as Passengers are in a boat. Husband and Wife are as a pair of oars, to row them to their desired haven."[5]

The little commonwealth had other important characteristics. One was its size. Compared with families in England or even Virginia, families in New England were large, often with six or more children. In addition, the Puritans followed the common colonial practice of apprenticing their children at a young age. At age fourteen, a Puritan child would often be sent for as long as seven years to another family to learn a trade or skill.

Clearly, childhood in Puritan New England was defined by different expectations and values than childhood in most American households in the early twenty-first century. If historians have the ability to travel instantly to other places and times, when they enter Puritan New England they step into a very different world indeed.

INVESTIGATION

This chapter contains several primary sources relating to the Puritan childhood experience. Some are written sources; others are not. As you read and examine them, answer the following central questions:

1. **Based on the evidence in the primary sources, what do you think were the most important characteristics of Puritan childhood?** What expectations and values shaped the Puritan childhood experience?

2. **What does the evidence reveal about the responses of children to the expectations placed on them?** What clues do the sources offer regarding children's behavior or attitudes?

3. **Considering roles, responsibilities, and expectations, how do you think the experience of growing up in Puritan New England differed from your own experience?** What are the main reasons for the differences between Puritan child-rearing practices and those of today? Were Puritan children treated more or less like adults than modern children?

As you study the sources, you can make a short list of what you think were the most important qualities to be instilled in a Puritan child. List as well the most important influences in shaping a Puritan child. Then list the most important qualities you think your parents tried to instill in you. In comparing these lists, you can begin to frame an answer to the third question: How did the experience of growing up in Puritan New England differ from your own?

Once you have determined those differences, you can begin to consider what these primary sources suggest about the reasons for the child-rearing practices in Puritan society. Make a list of the most important influences shaping child-rearing practices in Puritan society and another of the most important influences in your own childhood. This second task will be much easier if you have already read the sections on the Puritans in your textbook. When you are done, some of the important differences between Puritan society and our own should be very clear.

There is no single answer to the central questions of this chapter. Your answers will be determined in part by your biases and experiences. If you compare your answers with those of your classmates, you will quickly discover an axiom of historical inquiry: Even with the same primary sources, historians do not always see the past in the same way.

SOURCES

Portraits

Although artists attempt to capture the likenesses of their subjects, their patrons often want them to do more than that. A portrait may be a view of the subject as he or she wishes to be seen or, in this case, as parents wish their children to be seen. Moreover, as they do today, formal portraits in the seventeenth century captured their subjects' likenesses at special times; historians cannot assume that the subjects looked like this everyday. They also have to be careful about using appearances to draw conclusions about personality or emotions. For instance, these Puritan children are not smiling. Early photographers also did not have their subjects smile. When modern children have their photographs taken, however, photographers usually ask them to smile. Yet modern posed photographs may not reveal their subjects' feelings any more than did the likenesses captured in earlier paintings or photographs. The question to keep in mind, then, is why the Puritans would prefer to have their children portrayed with facial expressions so different from those in modern photographs. Finally, the dress of these Puritan children may seem odd by modern standards. As you examine it, consider whether it suggests anything about children's roles or about parents' expectations regarding proper behavior. Also consider what these portraits may reveal about Puritan attitudes toward material display.

1 Elizabeth Eggington (1664)

Wadsworth Atheneum Museum of Art/Art Resource, NY

The daughter of a ship captain, Elizabeth Eggington wears a pearl necklace and holds a fan in her left hand. Beneath the ribbons that tie her collar is a miniature portrait set in jewels. The letters and numbers in the background are the date of the portrait. This portrait demonstrates that the artist was unable to render the human form accurately. Note, for instance, that Elizabeth Eggington's head, neck, and arms are not proportional to the rest of her body.

2 Henry Gibbs (1670)

Freake-Gibbs Painter, Portrait of Henry Gibbs (1670), oil on canvas, The Clay Center for the Arts & Sciences of West Virginia.

The style of painting seen in this and other Puritan portraits originated in sixteenth-century England in reaction to more sensuous art of the Renaissance. Several elements of this style are evident in this portrait, including the dark background and flatter presentation of forms on the canvas. Like the portrait in the previous source, this one also demonstrates the artist's failure to render human anatomy accurately. Note, too, the clothing worn by Henry, a young boy. Keep in mind that nongender-specific clothing for very young children was typical in the Puritans' time and remained so until the early twentieth century. Finally, note the clothing's rich detail, a mark of the family's prosperous circumstances.

Written Evidence

The answers to some of the questions in the portrait section may not be obvious from an examination of only the paintings. As you read and analyze the written documents, note what values Puritan parents tried to instill in their children and whether independence or creativity was highly prized. Also look for clues to Puritan attitudes about idleness and play. Try to determine whether Puritan parents and children had an egalitarian relationship and whether they recognized the period of prolonged dependence between childhood and adulthood that we call adolescence. Note any evidence of intense psychological pressure on children. Also keep in mind that the punishment of death for the crimes set forth in Source 4 was never actually imposed on a child in Puritan Massachusetts. Think about why Puritan authorities found it necessary to set down such a punishment and what it might indicate about actual behavior. Finally, some observers have argued that children growing up in American society today are often treated like adults by advertisers, Hollywood, parents, schools, and others. As you evaluate this evidence, consider whether Puritan children were treated more or less like adults than modern children are.

Letter of Samuel Mather (Age 12) to His Father (ca. 1638)

Though I am thus well in my body, yet I question whether my soul doth prosper as my body doth; for I perceive, yet to this very day little growth in grace; and this makes me question, whether grace be in my heart or no. I feel also daily great unwillingness to good duties, and the great ruling sin of my heart; and that God is angry with me, and gives me no answers to my prayers, but many times, he even throws them down as dust in my face; and he does not grant my continual requests for the spiritual blessing of the softning of my hard heart. And in all this I could yet take some comfort, but that it makes me to wonder, what God's secret decree concerning me may be; for I doubt whether ever God is wont to deny grace and mercy to his chosen (though uncalled) when they seek unto him, by prayer, for it; and therefore, seeing he doth thus deny it to me, I think that the reason of it is most like to be, because I belong not unto the election of grace. I desire that you would let me have your prayers, as I doubt not but I have them.

Source: Cotton Mather: *Maganlia Christi Americana* (New York: Russell and Russell, 1967), p. 40, reproduced from 1852 ed., originally published in 1702.

4   Massachusetts Court Records

If any child, or children, above sixteen years old, and of sufficient under-standing, shall curse, or smite their natural father, or mother; he or they shall be put to death: unles it can be sufficiently testified that the Parents have been very unchristianly negligent in the education of such children; or so provoked them by extream, and cruel correction: that they have been forced therunto to preserve themselves from death or maiming. . . .

If a man have a stubborn or rebellious son, of sufficient years & uder-standing (viz) sixteen years of age, which will not obey the voice of his Father, or the voice of his Mother, and that when they have chastened him will not harken unto them: then shal his Father & Mother being his natural parents, lay hold on him, & bring him to the Magistrates assembled in Court & testifie unto them, that their Son is stubborn & rebellious & will not obey their voice and chastisement, but lives in sundry notorious crimes, such a son shal be put to death. . . .

For as much as the good education of children is of singular behoof and benefit to any Common-wealth; and wher as many parents & masters are too indulgent and negligent of their duty in that kinde. It is therefore ordered that the Selectmen of every town, in the severall precincts and quarters where they dwell, shall have a vigilant eye over their brethren & neighbours, to see, first that none of them shall suffer so much barbarism in any of their fami-lies as not to indeavour to teach by themselves or others, their children & apprentices so much learning as may inable them perfectly to read the eng-lish tongue, & knowledge of the Capital laws: upon penaltie of twentie shil-lings for each neglect therin. Also that all masters of families doe once a week (at the least) catechize their children and servants in the grounds & principles of Religion, & if any be unable to doe so much: that then at the least they procure such children or apprentices to learn some short orthodox catechism without book, that they may be able to answer unto the questions that shall be propounded to them out of such catechism by their parents or masters or any of the Selectmen when they shall call them to a tryall of what they have learned in this kinde. And further that all parents and masters do breed & bring up their children & apprentices in some honest lawful calling, labour or imploymet, either in husbandry, or some other trade profitable for them-selves, and the Common-wealth if they will not or cannot train them up in learning to fit them for higher imployments. And if any of the Selectmen after admonition by them given such masters of families shal finde them still neg-ligent of their dutie in the particulars aforementioned, wherby children and servants become rude, stubborn & unruly; the said Selectmen with the help of two Magistrates, or the next County court for that Shire, shall take such children or apprentices from them & place them with some masters for years

From The Laws and Liberties of Massachusetts (1648)

(boyes till they come to twenty-one, and girls eighteen years of age compleat) which will more strictly look unto, and force them to submit unto government according to the rules of this order, if by fair means and former instructions they will not be drawn unto it. [1642]

---

5   Lawrence Hammond, Diary Entry for April 23, 1688

This day came into our family Elizabeth Nevenson, daughter of Mr. John Nev[e]nson and Elizabeth his wife, who wilbe 13 yeares of age the 22d day of October next: The verbal Covenant betweene my wife and Mrs. Nevenson is, that she the said Elizabeth shall dwell with my wife as a servant six yeares, to be taught, instructed and provided for as shalbe meet, and that she shall not depart from our family during the said time without my wives, consent.

Source: Massachusetts Historical Society Proceedings, XXVII: p. 146

---

6   Cotton Mather on Young Children (1690)

Multitudes of our *Children* are very much *Un-Catechised,* as to the principles, and sadly *Unnurtured* and *Ungoverned* as to the practices of Christianity. Our Children are miserably both *neglected* and *indulged;* tho' *too much* be made of them, in gratifying of their *unruly wills,* nevertheless *too little* is made of them in providing for their *immortal souls; and some of you have not the Knowledge of God; I speak this to the shame* of your ungodly Tutors. . . .

In like manner, when I understand that any of *you* are ignorant, or naughty and vicious Children, methinks I see the horrid *Lions* of Hell, fetching some of my poor *Lambs* away, and how shall I answer it, if I do not *go out after them!* The following pages are some of my Essays to pluck you out of your Eternal Perdition; and I hope you will read them seriously, frequently, very profitably. . . .

Gracious *little* Children endeavour to *Know* God, as thus an Heavenly *Father* to them. . . .

First, They place on God, the *Affection* which is due unto a *father.* . . .

Secondly, They pay to *God,* the *Reverence* which is due unto a *father.* They dare not therefore be rude, sa[u]cy, impudent, in the special presence of the Lord; nor Talk, nor Sport, nor Sleep, when they should be worshipping of Him. . . .

Thirdly, They yield to God the *submission* which is due unto a *father.* They will by no means dispute the will of God, but render a most full, profound, absolute Obedience thereunto . . . .

Fourthly, They have a *Dependance* on God as *Children* on a *Father.* . . .

Source: Cotton Mather, Addresses to Old Men, and Young Men, and Little Children (Boston, 1690).

Fifthly, They have a *Resemblance* of God, as *Children* of a Father. . . . If any perhaps, of his play-mates or school-mates, go to do any naughty thing, he will zealously rebuke them for it. In a word, These gracious Children, are loth to do any thing that may be displeasing to such a Father as the blessed God. If such a Child be tempted unto *Sabbath-breaking* he thinks, *What shall I dishonour my father so as to take the Devil for my play-fellow!* If he be tempted unto Cursing, Swearing, Lying, or the calling of wicked Names, he thinks, *No, my Heavenly Father does cast Children unto those flames where they shall not have a drop of water to cool their Tongues, for such crimes as these!* He abhors all that is contrary to the thrice-Holy-God.

7 An Arrow Against Profane and Promiscuous Dancing (1690)

INCREASE MATHER

Now they that frequent Promiscuous Dancings, or that send their Children thereunto, walk disorderly, and contrary to the Apostles Doctrine. It has been proved that such a practice is a Scandalous Immorality, and therefore to be removed out of Churches by Discipline, which is the Broom of Christ, whereby he keeps his Churches clean. . . .

The Catechism which Wicked men teach their Children is to Dance and to Sing. Not that Dancing, or Musick, or Singing are in themselves sinful: but if the Dancing Master be wicked they are commonly abused to lasciviousness, and that makes them to become abominable. But will you that are Professors of Religion have your Children to be thus taught? the Lord expects that you should give the Children who'are Baptized into his Name another kind of Education, that you should bring them up in the nurture and admonition of the Lord: And do you not hear the Lord Expostulating the case with you, and saying, you have taken my Children, the Children that were given unto me; the Children that were solemnly engaged to renounce the Pomps of Satan; but is this a light matter that you have taken these my Children, and initiated them in the Pomps and Vanities of the Wicked one, contrary to your Covenant? What will you say-in the day of the Lords pleading with you? we have that charity for you as to believe that you have erred through Ignorance, and not wickedly: and we have therefore accounted it our Duty to inform you in the Truth. If you resolve not on Reformation, you will be left inexcusable. However it shall be, we have now given our Testimony and delivered our own Souls. Consider what we say, and the Lord *give* you understanding in all things.

Source: George M. Waller, ed., *Puritanism in Early America*, 2nd ed. (Lexington: D.C. Health and Company, 1973), pp. 22–23; originally from Increase Mather, *An Arrow Against Profane and Promiscuous Dancing . . .* (Boston, 1698).

Samuel Sewall on the Trials of His Fifteen-Year-Old Daughter (1696)

January 13, 1696

When I came in, past 7. at night, my wife met me in the Entry and told me Betty had surprised them. I was surprised with the abruptness of the Relation. It seems Betty Sewall had given some signs of dejection and sorrow; but a little after dinner she burst out into an amazing cry, which caus'd all the family to cry too: Her Mother ask'd the reason; she gave none; at last said she was afraid she should goe to Hell, her Sins were not pardon'd. She was first wounded by my reading a Sermon of Mr. Norton's, about the 5th of Jan. Text Jn° 7. 34. Ye shall seek me and shall not find me. And those words in the Sermon, Jn° 8. 21. Ye shall seek me and shall die in your sins, ran in her mind, and terrified her greatly. And staying at home Jan. 12. she read out of Mr. Cotton Mather—Why hath Satan filled thy heart, which increas'd her Fear. Her Mother ask'd her whether she pray'd. She answer'd, Yes; but feared her prayers were not heard because her Sins not pardon'd.

Source: M. Halsey Thomas, ed., *The Diary of Samuel Sewall* (New York: Farrar, Straus and Giroux, 1973), I, pp. 345–346.

The Well-Ordered Family (1712)
BENJAMIN WADSWORTH

Parents should govern their children well, restrain, reprove, correct them, as there is occasion. A Christian householder should *rule well his own house.* . . . Children should not be left to themselves, to a loose end, to do as they please; but should be *under tutors and governors,* not being fit to govern themselves. . . . Children being bid to obey their parents in all things. . . plainly implies that parents should give suitable precepts to, and maintain a wise government over their children; so carry it, as their children may both *fear* and *love* them. You should *restrain your children from sin* as much as possible. . . . You should *reprove* them for their faults; yea, if need be, *correct* them too. . . . Divine precepts plainly show that, as there is occasion, you should *chasten* and *correct* your children; you dishonor God and hurt them if you neglect it. Yet, on the other hand, a father should *pity his children. You should not provoke your children to wrathe, lest they be discouraged.* . . . You should by no means carry it ill to them; you should not frown, be harsh, morose, faulting and blaming them when they don't deserve it, but do behave themselves well. If you fault and

Source: Benjamin Wadsworth, *The Well-Ordered Family* (Boston, 1712).

blame your children, show yourself displeased and discontent when they do their best to please you, this is the way to provoke them to wrath and anger, and to discourage them; therefore you should carefully avoid such ill carriage to them. Nor should you ever correct them upon *uncertainties*, without sufficient evidence of their fault. Neither should you correct them in a *rage* or *passion*, but should deliberately endeavor to *convince* them of their fault, their sin; and that 'tis out of love to God's honor and their good (if they're capable of considering such things) that you correct them. Again, you should never be *cruel* nor *barbarous* in your corrections, and if *milder* ones will reform them, more severe ones should never be used. Under this head of *government* I might further say, you should refrain your children *from bad company* as far as possibly you can. . . . If you would not have your sons and daughters destroyed, then keep them from ill company as much as may be. . . . You should not suffer your children needlessly to frequent *taverns*, nor to be abroad *unseasonably on nights*, lest they're drawn into numberless hazards and mischiefs thereby. You can't be too careful in these matters.

---

10   The Duty of Children Toward Their Parents (1727)

God hath commanded saying, Honour thy Father and Mother, and whoso curseth Father or Mother, let him die the Death. Mat. 15, 4.

Children obey your Parents in the Lord, for this is right.

2. Honour thy Father and Mother, (which is the first Commandment with Promise).

3. That it may be well with thee, and that thou mayst live long on the Earth.

Children, obey your Parents in all Things, for that is well pleasing unto the Lord. Col. 3/20.

The Eye that mocketh his Father, and despiseth the Instruction of his Mother, let the Ravens of the Valley pluck it out, and the young Eagles eat it.

Father, I have sinned against Heaven, and before thee. Luke 15, 10.

I am no more worthy to be called thy Son.

No man ever hated his own flesh, but nourisheth and cherisheth it. Ephes. 5/19.

I pray thee let my Father and Mother come and abide with you, till I know what God will do for me. I Sam. 22, 3.

My Son, help thy Father in his Age, and grieve him not as long as he liveth.

Source: Paul Leicester Ford, ed., *The New England Primer* (New York: Dodd, Mead and Co., 1899). Facsimile reprinting of 1727 edition, pp. 20–22.

And if his Understanding fail, have patience with him, and despise him not when thou art in thy full Strength.

Whoso curseth his Father or his Mother, his Lamp shall be put out in obscure Darkness. Prov. 20, 20.

A Puritan Primer Warns Against Frivolous Behavior (1671)

Severall young men playing at foote-ball on the Jce upon the Lords-day are all Drownd

Collection of Picture Research Consultants & Archives.

Architectural Evidence

This section contains sketches and floor plans of two Puritan houses. Like portraits, they must be evaluated carefully. Although floor plans provide only a "bird's eye" view of an interior and by themselves do not answer our primary questions, they can tell us a great deal. First, they reveal the size of the house, a fairly reliable indication of economic circumstances. In addition, they may show the amount of private and common space, thus indicating whether personal privacy was possible. When combined with other sources, they may also indicate whether privacy was even valued. The number and location of fireplaces show how much daytime living space a family had during New England's long winters. Floor plans might even offer clues about the level of household technology, something that would greatly influence the lives of family members. Household sketches give additional information. First, whereas the floor plans here show only the lower floor, the sketches show how much space was provided by the entire house. Second, much like portraits, houses reflect the values of the people who built them. They may be ornate and pretentious or simple and unadorned, qualities that floor plans alone may not reveal.

As you examine the ground-level floor plans and sketches of these two houses, think about the impact that these dwellings might have had on the children growing up in them. Also keep in mind how they compare to the space and design of the home in which you grew up.

 The Roger Mowry House (ca. 1653)

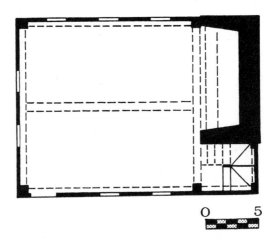

Courtesy of The Fine Arts Library, Harvard College Library, FA 2635.12.

NOTE: Addition on the right was added later.
Courtesy of The Fine Art Library, Harvard CollegeLibrary , FA 2635.12

13 The Eleazer Arnold House (ca. 1684)

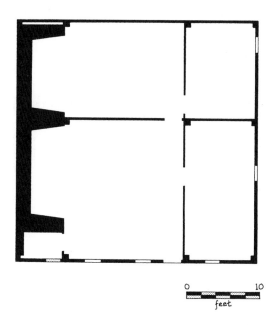

0   10
feet

Courtesy of The Fine Arts Library, Harvard College
Library, FA 2635.12.

Courtesy of The Fine Arts Library, Harvard College Library, FA 2635.12.

CONCLUSION

Our first reaction might be to dismiss Puritan child-rearing practices as strange or even cruel. However, it is important to try to understand the way people in other times viewed such practices. As one historian has said, "History cannot be written unless the historian can achieve some kind of contact with the mind of those about whom he is writing."[6]

It is not easy to make such "contact" with the Puritans. We do not apprentice children. And it is difficult to imagine a child today writing a letter like the one Samuel Mather wrote to his father in 1638. Yet, like us, the Puritans loved their children and, like the Puritans, we recognize the need to "govern" and educate them. Their "raw material" was the same as ours, even if the methods, goals, and results of Puritan child rearing were very different. Just as children are today, young Samuel and other Puritan children were formed by their society's beliefs, values, and material conditions, including religious beliefs that differ greatly from our own. Studying the differences between Puritan and modern child-rearing practices is thus a good way to understand the forces operating in Mather's society and ours.

In Chapter 3, we will discover another reason for historians to make "mental contact" with people in the past. As we will see, primary sources rarely speak with one voice; they express opinions as well as facts. To assess these sources critically, historians must understand the strangers who created them on their terms.

FURTHER READING

Edward Hallett Carr, *What Is History?* (New York: Alfred A. Knopf, 1962).
John Demos, *A Little Commonwealth: Family Life in Plymouth Colony* (New York: Oxford University Press, 1970).
Philip J. Greven, *The Protestant Temperament: Patterns of Child-Rearing/Religious Experience and the Self in Early America* (Chicago: The University of Chicago Press, 1977).
Steven Mintz, *Huck's Raft: A History of American Childhood* (Cambridge: Harvard University Press, 2004).
Gerald F. Moran and Maris A. Vinovskis, *Religion, Family and Life Course: Explorations in the Social History of Early America* (Ann Arbor: University of Michigan Press, 1992).
Edmund Morgan, *The Puritan Family: Religion and Domestic Relations in Seventeenth-Century New England* (New York: Harper and Row, 1966).
Helena M. Wall, *Family and Community in Early America* (Cambridge: Harvard University Press, 1990).

NOTES

1. Steven Mintz, *Huck's Raft: A History of American Childhood* (Cambridge: Harvard University Press, 2004), p. 10.
2. Quoted in Edmund Morgan, *The Puritan Family: Religion and Domestic Relations in Seventeenth-Century New England* (New York: Harper and Row, 1966), p. 88.
3. Quoted in Steven Mintz and Susan Kellogg, *Domestic Revolutions: A Social History of American Family Life* (New York: Free Press, 1988), p. 1.
4. Cotton Mather, *A Family Well-Ordered* (Boston: Bartholomew Green and J. Allen, 1699), p. 37.
5. William Secker, *A Wedding Ring* (Boston: T. G. Green, 1705), p. 52.
6. Edward Hallett Carr, *What Is History?* (New York: Alfred A. Knopf, 1962), p. 27.

Chapter

3

Evaluating Primary Sources: Was Pennsylvania "The Best Poor Man's Country"?

This chapter presents various kinds of primary sources on Pennsylvania before the Revolution. The documents relate to the question of whether Pennsylvania was indeed the land of opportunity that one source claims it was.

Sources

1. An Historical and Geographical Account of Pennsylvania (1698), GABRIEL THOMAS
2. Plantations in Pennsylvania (1743), WILLIAM MORALEY
3. Journey to Pennsylvania (1756), GOTTLIEB MITTELBERGER
4. Advertisement for a Runaway (1759)
5. American Husbandry (1775)
6. William Penn on House Construction in Pennsylvania (1684)
7. Cabin, Berks County
8. Charles Norris's Mansion, Chestnut Street
9. Early Settlements in Pennsylvania (1696)
10. Wealth Distribution in Philadelphia, 1693–1774
11. Acquisition of Land by Former Indentured Servants, 1686–1720

*T*o the Englishman William Moraley, Pennsylvania was a paradise. Moraley was an indentured servant who went to Pennsylvania in 1729 and found "woods and well-manured farms" everywhere. He claimed to have traveled hundreds of miles at no expense because the inhabitants outdid one another in providing him food and "charity." The colony was "the best poor man's country in the world," Moraley asserted in his autobiography. "If this was sufficiently known by the miserable objects we have in our streets," he concluded, "multitudes would be induced to go thither."

As we know, multitudes from many lands did go there. Did they settle in the "best poor man's country"? Or was Moraley's conclusion unwarranted? Historians want to know how much opportunity the countless immigrants to colonial Pennsylvania found. Just as many Americans today worry about their own opportunities, historians are interested in the extent of equality, wealth, and poverty in colonial America. They are curious to know if opportunities for economic advancement were increasing or declining in the colonial period and if some people succeeded at others' expense. Because the people living in that society eventually revolted against Great Britain, historians also want to know whether economic and social conditions in the colonies helped to bring on the American Revolution. In this chapter, we use primary sources to investigate wealth holding and opportunity in this "best poor man's country."

SETTING

By 1759, Pennsylvania was in many ways a prototype of American development. Blessed with a favorable climate, rich soil, and a policy of toleration introduced by Quaker proprietor William Penn, the colony attracted large numbers of English, Irish, German, and Swiss settlers. The Quakers' egalitarianism may not have made them popular in England, but it was appealing to many Europeans looking for a better life.

Many of those drawn to Pennsylvania were indentured servants, bound to their masters for a term of service. Although terms varied over time and differed among colonies, they were often four years and often in exchange for payment of their passage across the Atlantic. As servants, they were considered un-free people rather than "freemen." Their service could also be sold from one master to another, as masters bought or sold their indentures, or contracts. Yet unlike slaves, who had virtually no chance of achieving freedom, indentured servants were not permanently bound. In 1685, about half of the adult males arriving in the colony were indentured. Although that percentage declined by the eighteenth century, the number of servants in Pennsylvania remained high throughout the colonial period. In 1750, for example, nearly 20 percent of Philadelphia's work force was indentured. Within Pennsylvania, servitude itself also changed over time. Until the 1720s, servants arriving in the colony were overwhelmingly English and often served relatives or acquaintances in rural areas. After that decade, the majority were Germans and other non-English immigrants. For them, the impersonal marketplace rather than familial ties shaped their relationships with their masters.

Like its sister colonies, Pennsylvania was overwhelmingly rural, and its farmers produced crops for faraway markets. That trade sped the growth of Philadelphia, which served the same commercial function as other colonial ports. By the middle of the eighteenth century, the City of Brotherly Love challenged Boston as the most important commercial center in the colonies.

The colony was also typical in other ways. Under English common law, which prevailed in Pennsylvania and throughout the colonies, a married woman had almost no legal rights. She was known as a femme coverte, covered by the husband. Under coverture, a term in common law, husbands and wives were considered as one person, and married women were deprived of numerous rights. They had no property or money, including wages, of their own, and had no right to enter into legal contracts. Since their economic opportunities were limited to those of their husbands, the questions of wealth holding and economic advancement did not apply to them. The situation was even worse for the colony's African American population. Slavery was legal in Pennsylvania, as it was in all other American colonies. By 1767, there were nearly 1,400 slaves and maybe 150 free blacks in Philadelphia, a city of some 16,000 residents and home to 20 percent of the colony's bondsmen, its ultimate have-nots. The distribution of wealth and the extent of economic opportunity were irrelevant for them.

If wealth holding and economic advancement in colonial Pennsylvania pertained only to some people, conclusions about the opportunities there must be carefully qualified. The available sources make generalizations even more difficult. Because evidence regarding opportunity in the colonies is limited, historians traditionally have relied on "literary" sources—that is, written descriptions of economic or social conditions. Yet such evidence usually reflects only one person's views. Roughly 2.5 million people lived in the colonies by the middle of the eighteenth century, and their economic circumstances varied greatly. Making valid generalizations from a limited number of individual observations is therefore difficult. So to obtain larger samples, historians frequently turn to such legal documents as tax rolls and wills, which often reflect the experiences of people who seldom left written records and which are often free of the biases seen in literary sources. To make sense of these legal documents, however, researchers usually limit their studies to a particular colony, county, or town. That narrow focus, in turn, makes it difficult to generalize about other places.

The passage of time creates still more difficulties. Nearly a century separated the founding of Pennsylvania in 1681 and the Declaration of Independence in 1776, and opportunities for advancement changed over that time. The expansion of trade, population growth, overcrowding, and urban growth created dynamic patterns of wealth holding and economic advancement. Because colonial society was not static, historians must know how these patterns changed.

To determine if William Moraley was correct about Pennsylvania is thus not easy. It requires careful evaluation of primary sources. We must separate fact from opinion, reconcile conflicting evidence, determine whether sources are representative, and understand the outlook of our subjects.

INVESTIGATION

Imagine that you rent a small plot of land in rural England in the mid-eighteenth century. You wish to settle in a place without extreme wealth or poverty where you can improve your fortunes. An acquaintance in Pennsylvania has just sent you a packet of documents about the colony. It contains an offer for paid passage to Pennsylvania in exchange for a four-year term of service. You must use the information in the documents to determine if you should accept the offer. In other words, you must evaluate the documents in order to determine the extent of social stratification and opportunities for economic advancement in Pennsylvania. Thus, you will need to determine whether the documents contain facts or unsubstantiated opinions, and whether they are representative or atypical. Also keep in mind that some of these sources were written by individuals who did not stay in Pennsylvania. When you are finished, you should be able to answer these main questions about Pennsylvania society:

1. **What was the pattern of wealth distribution?** How much equality and inequality existed in this society? How large was the gap between the haves and the have-nots?

2. **What were the opportunities for indentured servants, once free, to improve their lot in this society?** Do the sources support only one conclusion about that? Are the sources equally reliable? Regarding the chances for individuals to advance themselves, do the sources suggest that this was a fluid or rigid, class-bound society?

3. **Was there greater or less equality as time went on?** Is there evidence that some people were getting rich at the expense of others?

How you answer these questions will determine whether you move to Pennsylvania. Not every document will answer each of these questions, but together they should give you enough evidence to come to some conclusions about the opportunities in colonial Pennsylvania. Because you need to evaluate a large number of sources, creating a chart like the one on the next page will help keep track of the evidence. As you examine each source, write down the selection number in the appropriate boxes.

Evidence of Stratification	Evidence of Social Equality
Evidence of Rigid Class Structure	Evidence of Economic Mobility

When you have finished the chart, your decision should be clearer.

SOURCES

1 Gabriel Thomas was a Welsh yeoman farmer who spent fifteen years in Pennsylvania before departing for England, where this account of the colony was published. In 1706, Thomas returned to Sussex County near Philadelphia, where he owned a thousand-acre plantation. Note the reasons why he thought that conditions were better in Pennsylvania than in England or Wales.

An Historical and Geographical Account of Pennsylvania (1698)
GABRIEL THOMAS

I must needs say, even the present Encouragements are very great and inviting, for Poor People (both Men and Women) of all kinds, can here get three times the Wages for their Labour they can in England or Wales.

I shall instance in a few, which may serve; nay, and will hold in all the rest. The first was a Black-Smith (my next Neighbour), who himself and one Negro Man he had, got Fifty Shillings in one Day, by working up a Hundred

Source: Albert Cook Myers, ed., *Narratives of Early Pennsylvania, West New Jersey, and Delaware 1630–1707* (New York: Barnes and Noble, Inc., 1912), pp. 326–327, 328–329.

Pound Weight of Iron, which at Six Pence per Pound (and that is the common Price in that Countrey) amounts to that Summ.

And for Carpenters, both House and Ship, Brick-layers, Masons, either of these Trades-Men, will get between Five and Six Shillings every Day constantly. As to Journey-Men Shooe-Makers, they have Two Shillings per Pair both for Men and Womens Shooes: And Journey-Men Taylors have Twelve Shillings per Week and their Diet. Sawyers get between Six and Seven Shillings the Hundred for Cutting of Pine-Boards. And for Weavers, they have Ten or Twelve Pence the Yard for Weaving of that which is little more than half a Yard in breadth. . . .

Corn and Flesh, and what else serves Man for Drink, Food and Rayment, is much cheaper here than in England, or elsewhere; but the chief reason why Wages of Servants of all sorts is much higher here than there, arises from the great Fertility and Produce of the Mace; besides, if these large Stipends were refused them, they would quickly set up for themselves, for they can have Provision very cheap, and Land for a very small matter, or next to nothing in comparison of the Purchace of Lands in England; and the Farmers there, can better afford to give that great Wages than the Farmers in England can, for several Reasons very obvious.

As First, their Land costs them (as I said but just now) little or nothing in comparison, of which the Farmers commonly will get twice the encrease of Corn for every Bushel they sow, that the Farmers in England can from richest Land they have.

In the Second place, they have constantly good price for their Corn, by reason of the great and quick vent [passage] into Barbadoes and other Islands; through which means Silver is become more plentiful than here in England, considering the Number of People, and that causes a quick Trade for both Corn and Cattle; and that is the reason that Corn differs now from the Price formerly, else it would be at half the Price it was at then; for a Brother of mine (to my own particular knowledge) sold within the compass of one Week, about One Hundred and Twenty fat Beasts, most of them good handsom large Oxen.

---

2 William Moraley spent nearly five years in the colonies, where he traveled widely. His autobiography describes the relationship between the haves and the have-nots in colonial Pennsylvania. In other passages, Moraley also reveals that he was a drunkard and a thief. Does his character influence his creditability?

Source: The Infortunate: The Voyage and Adventures of William Moraley, an Indentured Servant, University Park: The Pennsylvania State University Press, 1992, pp. 93–95. Copyright © 1992 by The Pennsylvania State University Press. Reproduced by permission of the publisher.

Plantations in Pennsylvania (1743)

WILLIAM MORALEY

At the first Peopling [of] these Colonies, there was a Necessity of employing a great Number of Hands, for the clearing the Land, being over-grown with Wood for some Hundred of Miles; to which Intent, the first Settlers not being sufficient of themselves to improve those Lands, were not only obliged to purchase a great Number of *English* Servants to assist them, to whom they granted great Immunities, and at the Expiration of their Servitude, Land was given to encourage them to continue there; but were likewise obliged to purchase Multitudes of Negro Slaves from *Africa*, by which Means they are become the richest Farmers in the World, paying no Rent, nor giving Wages either to purchased Servants or Negro Slaves; so that instead of finding the Planter Rack-rented, as the *English* Farmer, you will taste of their Liberality, they living in Affluence and Plenty.

The Condition of the Negroes is very bad, by reason of the Severity of the Laws, there being no Laws made in Favour of these unhap[p]y Wretches: For the least Trespass, they undergo the severest Punishment; but their Masters make them some amends, by suffering them to marry, which makes them easier, and often prevents their running away. The Consequence of their marrying is this, all their Posterity are Slaves without Redemption; and it is in vain to attempt an Escape, tho' they often endeavour it; for the Laws against them are so severe, that being caught after running away, they are unmercifully whipped; and if they die under the Discipline, their Masters suffer no Punishment, there being no Law against murdering them. So if one Man kills another's Slave, he is only obliged to pay his Value to the Master, besides Damages that may accrue for the Loss of him in his Business.

The Masters generally allow them a Piece of Ground, with Materials for improving it. The Time of working for themselves, is Sundays, when they raise on their own Account divers Sorts of Corn and Grain, and sell it in the Markets. They buy with the Money Cloaths for themselves and Wives; as for the Children, they belong to the Wives Master, who bring them up; so the Negro need fear no Expense, his Business being to get them for his Master's use, who is as tender of them as his own Children. On Sundays in the evening they converse with their Wives, and drink Rum, or Bumbo, and smoak Tobacco, and the next Morning return to their Master's Labour.

They are seldom made free, for fear of being burthensome to the Provinces, there being a Law, that no Master shall manumise them, unless he gives Security they shall not be thrown upon the Province, by settling Land on them for their Support.

3   Gottlieb Mittelberger was a German immigrant who returned to Germany four years after arriving in America in 1756.

Journey to Pennsylvania (1756)
GOTTLIEB MITTELBERGER

When the ships have landed at Philadelphia after their long voyage, no one is permitted to leave them except those who pay for their passage or can give good security; the others, who cannot pay, must remain on board the ships till they are purchased, and are released from the ships by their purchasers. The sick always fare the worst, for the healthy are naturally preferred and purchased first; and so the sick and wretched must often remain on board in front of the city for 2 or 3 weeks, and frequently die, whereas many a one, if he could pay his debt and were permitted to leave the ship immediately, might recover and remain alive. . . .

The sale of human beings in the market on board the ship is carried on thus: Every day Englishmen, Dutchmen and High-German people come from the city of Philadelphia and other places, in part from a great distance, say 20, 30, or 40 hours away, and go on board the newly arrived ship that has brought and offers for sale passengers from Europe, and select among the healthy persons such as they deem suitable for their business, and bargain with them how long they will serve for their passage money, which most of them are still in debt for. When they have come to an agreement, it happens that adult persons bind themselves in writing to serve 3, 4, 5, or 6 years for the amount due by them, according to their age and strength. But very young people, from 10 to 15 years, must serve till they are 21 years old.

Many parents must sell and trade away their children like so many head of cattle; for if their children take the debt upon themselves, the parents can leave the ship free and unrestrained; but as the parents often do not know where and to what people their children are going, it often happens that such parents and children, after leaving the ship, do not see each other again for many years, perhaps no more in all their lives. . . .

It often happens that whole families, husband, wife, and children, are separated by being sold to different purchasers, especially when they have not paid any part of their passage money.

Source: Frederick M. Binder and David M. Reimers, *The Way We Lived* (Lexington, Mass.: D. C. Heath and Co., 1988), pp. 59–61.

When a husband or wife has died at sea, when the ship has made more than half of her trip, the survivor must pay or serve not only for himself or herself, but also for the deceased.

When both parents have died over half-way at sea, their children, especially when they are young and have nothing to pawn or to pay, must stand for their own and their parents' passage, and serve till they are 21 years old. When one has served his or her term, he or she is entitled to a new suit of clothes at parting; and if it has been so stipulated, a man gets in addition a horse, a woman, a cow. . . .

If some one in this country runs away from his master, who has treated him harshly, he cannot get far. Good provision has been made for such cases, so that a runaway is soon recovered. He who detains or returns a deserter receives a good reward.

If such a runaway has been away from his master one day, he must serve for it as a punishment a week, for a week a month, and for a month half a year. But if the master will not keep the runaway after he has got him back, he may sell him for so many years as he would have to serve him yet. . . .

However hard he may be compelled to work in his fatherland, he will surely find it quite as hard, if not harder, in the new country. Besides, there is not only the long and arduous journey lasting half a year, during which he has to suffer, more than with the hardest work; he has also spent about 200 florins which no one will refund to him. If he has so much money, it will slip out of his hands; if he has it not, he must work his debt off as a slave and poor serf. Therefore let every one stay in his own country and support himself and his family honestly. Besides I say that those who suffer themselves to be persuaded and enticed away by the man-thieves, are very foolish if they believe that roasted pigeons will fly into their mouths in America or Pennsylvania without their working for them.

> **4**   Masters frequently put advertisements in colonial newspapers for runaway indentured servants. As you read this advertisement from the *Pennsylvania Gazette,* you can look for what it reveals about the conditions of indentured servants.

Advertisement for a Runaway (1759)

Germantown, July 18, 1759

Run away on the 13th of this Instant, at Night, from the Subscriber, of said Town, an Apprentice Lad, named Stophel, or Christopher Hergesheimer, about 19 Years of Age, by Trade a Blacksmith, middle sized of his Age, has a sour down-looking Countenance, is of Dutch Extraction, but can talk good English; Had on, and took with him, when he went away, a bluish Cloath Coat, green Nap Jacket, Snuff coloured Breeches, and Linen Jacket and Breeches, all about half wore, two pair of Ozenbrigs Trowsers, two Ditto Shirts, and one pretty fine, a Pair of old Shoes, a Pair of Thread, and a Pair of Cotton Stockings, a good Athlone Felt Hat, and yellowish Silk Handkerchief, wore his own dark brown short Hair, but may cut it off: He had a Hurt on the Inside of his Left-hand, not quite cured, at his going away. Whoever takes him up, and brings or conveys him to his Master, or secures him in the Jail of Philadelphia, shall have Forty Shillings Reward, and reasonable Charges, paid by

Matthew Potter, junior.

Source: Pennsylvania Gazette, August 2, 1759.

5   This guide to life in the English colonies was written anonymously and published in London in 1775 as a promotional tract to encourage potential settlers to move to America. Does this purpose make its information suspect?

American Husbandry (1775)

This country is peopled by as happy and free a set of men as any in America. Out of trade there is not much wealth to be found, but at the same time there is very little poverty, and hardly such a thing as a beggar in the province. This is not only a consequence of the plenty of land, and the rate of labour, but also of the principles of the Quakers, who have a considerable share in the government of the country. It is much to the honour of this sect that they support their own poor in all countries, in a manner much more respectable than known in any other religion.

There are some country gentlemen in Pennsylvania, who live on their estates in a genteel and expensive manner, but the number is but small . . . . [M]oney is scarce in this country, and all the necessaries and conveniences of life cheap, except labour. But in general the province is inhabited by small freeholders, who live upon a par with great farmers in England; and many little ones who have the necessaries of life and nothing more.

Source: Reprinted by permission of the author from Jack P. Greene, *Settlements to Society.* Copyright © 1966. Published by the McGraw-Hill Companies.

In the settled parts of the colony, there are few situations to be found that are without such a neighbourhood as would satisfy country gentlemen of small estates, or country parsons in Britain. There are, besides Philadelphia, many small towns in which are found societies that render the country agreeable; and the country itself is scattered with gentlemen at moderate distances, who have a social intercourse with each other, besides occasional parties to Philadelphia.

The most considerable of the freeholders that do not however rank with gentlemen, are a set of very sensible, intelligent, and hospitable people, whose company, in one that is mixed, improves rather than lessens the agreeableness of it; a circumstance owing to many of them being foreigners, which even gives something of a polish to the manners when we find ourselves in the midst of a country principally inhabited by another people. The little freeholders (there are not many farmers, except near Philadelphia) are in ease and circumstances much superior to the little farmers in England.

The method of living in Pennsylvania in country gentlemen's families, is nearly like that of England: the only business is to ride about the plantation now and then, to see that the overseers are attentive to it; all the rest of the time is filled up with entertaining themselves; country sports, in the parts of the province not fully settled, are in great perfection; they have hunting, but their horses are unequal to those of England; shooting and fishing are much more followed, and are in greater perfection than in England, though every man is allowed both to shoot and fish throughout the province, except the latter in cultivated grounds. . . . It must be at once apparent, that a given income would go much further here than in Britain; this is so strongly a truth, that an income of four or five hundred pounds a year, and a plantation, can hardly be spent without extravagance, or indulging some peculiar expence; whereas that income from an estate in Britain will hardly give a man the appearance of a gentleman. . . .

6   After returning from Pennsylvania, William Penn wrote a tract directed at people interested in moving to the colony. What does it reveal about living conditions? Using evidence in Source 1, try to calculate how much labor would be required to accumulate the amounts shown in Penn's table. (Keep in mind that twenty shillings equals one pound.)

Source: Harold R. Shurtleff, *The Log Cabin Myth: A Study of the Early Dwellings of the English Colonists in North America* (Gloucester, Mass.: Peter Smith, 1967), pp. 124–125; originally from William Penn, *Information and Direction to Such Persons as Are Inclined to America, More Especially Those related to the Province of Pennsylvania* (London, 1684).

William Penn on House Construction in Pennsylvania (1684)

I propose to speak my own Knowledg, and the Observation of others, as particularly as I can; . . . This done, I take my two men, and go to my Lot . . . and then go to felling of Trees, proper for a first House, which will very well serve for the present occasion, and afterwards, be a good out House, till plenty will allow me to build a Better.

To build them, a House of thirty foot long and eighteen broad, with a partition neer the middle, and an other to divide one end of the House into two small Rooms, there must be eight Trees of about sixteen Inches square, and cut off, to Posts of about fifteen foot long, which the House must stand upon; and four pieces, two of thirty foot long, and two of eighteen foot long, for Plates, which must lie upon the top of those Posts, the whole length and bredth of the House, for the Gists [joists] to rest upon. There must be ten Gists of twenty foot long, to bear the Loft, and two false Plates of thirty foot long to lie upon the ends of the Gists for the *Rafters* to be fixed upon, twelve pare of Rafters of about twenty foot, to bear the Roof of the House, with several other smaller pieces; as Wind-Beams, Braces, Studs, etc. which are made of the Waste Timber. For Covering the House, Ends, and Sides, and for the Loft, we use *Clabboard*, which is *Rived feather-edged*, of five foot and a half long, that well Drawn, lyes close and smooth: The Lodging Room may be lined with the same, and filld up between, which is very Warm. These houses usually endure ten years without Repair.

	l.	s.	d.*
For the Carpenters work for such an House, I and my Servants assisting him, together with his diet	07	00	00
For a Barn of the same Building and Dimensions,	05	10	00
For Nailes, and other things to finish Both	03	10	00

The lower flour is the *Ground*, the upper *Clabbord:* This may seem a mean way of Building, but 'tis sufficient and safest for ordinary beginners.

*pounds, shillings, pence

Views of Early Pennsylvania Houses

As you study these pictures of houses in colonial Pennsylvania, note what they reveal about social classes there.

This stone cabin was of an Old World style frequently copied by British immigrants in Pennsylvania until about 1760.

Cabin, Berks County

Courtesy Harvard College Library, Widener Library, 25212.233 vol 1.

8   Charles Norris was the son of a well-to-do Quaker merchant and political leader, Isaac Norris.

Charles Norris's Mansion, Chestnut Street (built 1750)

The Historical Society of Pennsylvania (HSP), Benjamin Evans. Bb862/Ev1Sp87.

9   **Early Settlements in Pennsylvania (1696)**

Map of Early Pennsylvania (1696)

This source is part of a map of the settled portion of Pennsylvania around Philadelphia made in 1696. Like floor plans, maps can be an important primary source for historians and with careful analysis can reveal something about the way people lived. They are especially valuable for determining wealth-holding patterns in colonial society, where most of the wealth was held as land.

In Pennsylvania, proprietor William Penn, the wealthy Quaker land-grant holder, wanted farms to be 450 acres and grouped into townships of about fifty people. In the center of each township was to be a common area of meadows and pasturelands. The scale of miles in these maps will give you a rough idea of the size of the settlers' holdings. (One square mile equals 640 acres.) Locate Philadelphia on the map. The large parcels around Philadelphia are actually townships rather than individual holdings. Keep in mind that such developments as growing population and commerce gave some land on the map of the settled area around Philadelphia greater value than other land. As you examine this map, ask yourself if the settlers followed Penn's wishes regarding land distribution, or if there was inequality in landholding.

Rare Books Section, State Library of Pennsylvania, Harrisburg.

10 This table is a distillation of large numbers of primary documents. It shows the percentage of the wealth held by different segments of the free adult property holders at various times in Philadelphia. The table divides the sample into two general groups: the lower 90 percent of wealth holders and the upper 10 percent. These groups are then further divided. The lower 90 percent are divided into thirds. (For instance, the 0–30 group is the lowest 30 percent of the total sample of Philadelphia property holders in terms of their individual wealth.) The upper 10 percent is divided in half to show the wealth holding of the richest 5 percent of the population. The figures

under each date are the percentage of the wealth owned by each segment of the population. As you examine this table, look for a trend in the distribution of wealth. Then turn back to the map of the settled area around Philadelphia (Source 9). Locate Philadelphia County, Bucks County, and Chester County and consider whether it is likely that the distribution of wealth in Bucks and Chester counties in 1774 was similar to that in Philadelphia County.

Wealth Distribution in Philadelphia, 1693–1774

Segments of Wealth-Holding Population	Percentage of Total Wealth		
	1693	1767	1774
0–30 (poorest)	2.2	1.8	1.1
31–60	15.2	5.5	4.0
61–90	36.6	27.0	22.6
91–100 (richest)	46.0	65.7	72.3
91–95	13.2	16.2	16.8
96–100	32.8	49.5	55.5

Source: Adapted from table in Gary B. Nash, *Race, Class and Politics: Essays on American Colonial and Revolutionary Society* (Urbana: University of Illinois Press, 1986), p. 176.

11 This table illustrates how much land former indentured servants in Pennsylvania acquired over a period of thirty years after completion of their terms of service. The sample tracks a group of servants who were indentured between 1682 and 1686 and became free some time during or after those years. What does this table suggest about poor individuals' opportunities to accumulate property?

Acquisition of Land by Former Indentured Servants, 1686–1720

Number of Acres	Number of Former Servants	%
1–50	27	39.7
51–100	14	20.6
101–150	5	7.4
151–200	10	14.7
200–	12	17.6
Total (Total samples = 196)	68	

Source: Sharon V. Salinner, *"To serve well and faithfully": Labor and Indentured Servants in Pennsylvania, 1682–1800* (Cambridge: Cambridge University Press, 1987), p. 39.

CONCLUSION

Albert Einstein said that a person who dropped a stone from the window of a moving railroad car would see it descend toward the railroad embankment in a straight line. An observer standing on the embankment, however, would see the same stone fall in a parabolic curve, down and forward in the same direction as the train. Our vantage point determines what we see.

The sources in this chapter also reflect that axiom. Historical evidence rarely supports only one conclusion because people in the past saw things differently. Your decision about the wisdom of moving to Pennsylvania also illustrates Einstein's lesson. You and your classmates may not come to the same decision, but that does not necessarily mean you are wrong. The lesson of Einstein's falling stone thus applies to both primary sources and historians' own writings. We can ask the same question of each: Do they reflect the view from the railroad window or from the embankment? Remembering that question will make it easier, starting in the next chapter, to evaluate the writings of historians and the primary sources on which they are based.

FURTHER READING

James A. Henretta and Gregory H. Nobles, *Evolution and Revolution: American Society, 1600–1820* (Lexington, Mass.: D. C. Heath, 1987).

Richard Hofstadter, *America at 1750: A Social Portrait* (New York: Alfred A. Knopf, 1971).

James T. Lemon, *The Best Poor Man's Country: A Geographical Study of Early Southeastern Pennsylvania* (Baltimore: Johns Hopkins University Press, 1972).

Gottlieb Mittelberger, *Journey to Pennsylvania,* ed. Oscar Handlin and John Clive (Cambridge, Mass.: Harvard University Press, 1960).

Sharon V. Salinger, *"To serve well and faithfully": Labor and Indentured Servants in Pennsylvania, 1682–1800* (Cambridge: Cambridge University Press, 1987).

John Van Der Zee, *Bound Over: Indentured Servitude and American Conscience* (New York: Simon and Schuster, 1985).

NOTE

1. Susan E. Klepp and Billy G. Smith, eds., *The Infortunate: The Voyage and Adventures of William Moraley, an Indentured Servant* (University Park: Pennsylvania State University Press, 1992), p. 89.

Chapter
4

Evaluating One Historian's Argument: The "Hidden Side" of the American Revolution

The documents in this chapter are a combination of primary and secondary sources. The chapter presents an essay on social unrest in the revolutionary period and then provides several primary sources that can be used to judge the validity of the essayist's view of the American Revolution.

Secondary Source

Primary Sources

*E*very year, Americans commemorate their nation's birth with fireworks. For some onlookers, exploding Fourth of July rockets are a reminder of the long and bloody war that actually won independence. Today, though, few Americans understand much about the American Revolution. More than two hundred years after the muskets fell silent, this conflict remains enshrouded in myth and misunderstanding.

One reason is the way the tale is often told. Many traditional accounts of the Revolution focus on the leaders in the struggle for independence. Rarely seen are the many other Americans of lesser rank who protested, revolted, fought, suffered, and sacrificed in this long conflict. In addition, even today, many popular accounts present the Revolution only as a struggle to win independence from Great Britain that had little, if any, impact on American society. In fact, all wars are unsettling to societies that fight them and the Revolution was no exception. It would be remarkable if it had been otherwise. After all, the supporters of independence had enlisted an idea with potentially explosive consequences for their own society: equality. As Thomas Jefferson well knew, proclaiming that "all men are created equal" was an effective argument against rule by a monarch. But it could also be a powerful stimulus for change in a society where the majority was not free and equal.

Independence Day celebrations do not cast much light on efforts to fashion a more egalitarian society during the Revolution. Yet these efforts were often accompanied by fireworks of their own. What conflicts within American society were elicited by the fight against British rule? To what extent was the rebellion against British authority in the colonies intertwined with, and even shaped by, protests against inequality within American society? Did these protests make the Revolution, in the words of one historian, a fight over "who should rule at home" as well as for "home rule"?[1] Answers to these questions promise to illuminate the "unknown" American Revolution: the struggles to make American society a more egalitarian and democratic society.

SETTING

If many Americans today are unaware that there might be another side to the American Revolution, historians themselves are partly to blame. Their accounts have not always acknowledged that the fight for independence from Great Britain might have been accompanied by battles over the exercise of power at home. That oversight can be partly explained by the dramatic nature of the conflict between Britain and the revolting colonists. To a large extent, though, it also reflects the historians' own times. Indeed, the American Revolution is an excellent example of the old adage that each generation writes its own history.

For a long time, patriot oratory drowned out rumbles of discontent in the histories of the fight for independence. In fact, through most of the nineteenth century, historians simply reiterated the claims of the Whigs—as those who opposed Britain called themselves—that the Revolution was a struggle to defend liberty against a tyrannical government. Writing in the patriotic afterglow of the War for Independence, the accounts of so-called nationalist historians pictured the enemy in terms that left little room to question the Whigs' cause—or the premise that victory itself ushered in a glorious age of liberty and equality. With America's liberation from a "venal" British government, historian George Bancroft asserted in the 1850s, the "knell of the ages of servitude was rung; those of equality and brotherhood were to come in." Bancroft and other nationalist historians simply found it inconceivable that Americans might also have fought among themselves to achieve "equality and brotherhood."[2]

Later historians would not. At the beginning of the twentieth century, as progressive reformers battled wealthy and powerful corporate interests in the name of the "people," historians such as Carl Becker and Arthur Schlesinger, Sr., sharply attacked the nationalist view of the Revolution. Rather than view the Revolution as a moral struggle between righteousness and treachery, these progressive historians characterized it primarily as a contest over property and power. In Becker's oft-quoted phrase, the Revolution was a battle to gain home rule and determine "who should rule at home." Whether in its causes or its consequences, these historians argued, the Revolution could not be considered apart from economic and social tensions within American society, in particular the struggle by the have-nots of colonial society against a dominant aristocracy.

In time, that view also came in for attack. In the decades after World War II, as Americans engaged in a global cold war against communism, so-called consensus historians denied the existence of deep social divisions in the American past. Progressive historians, they charged, had distorted the nature of the Revolution by viewing it through the lens of their own generation's social and economic battles. Writing in the postwar period, historians such as Daniel Boorstin and Edmund Morgan saw remarkably little social or economic conflict among those who struggled for independence. Instead, they emphasized how colonists from all social ranks rallied together to defend cherished rights.

A generation later, social upheaval had unraveled Americans' sense of Cold War unity. The turmoil of the 1960s and 1970s also helped to refocus historians' attention on the social context of the Revolution. Since the 1960s, though, historians' views of the Revolution have demonstrated little unity. Some historians have concentrated on understanding the context and consequences of the revolutionaries' political ideas. One of the most influential, Gordon Wood, would argue that these ideas were truly radical because they led Americans to question rule by traditional elites and to create more democratic governments. Other historians, however, would point to the limits of change in revolutionary society. In the wake of the civil rights and women's movements, scholars who turned their attention to non-elite groups often emphasized that the Revolution did not bring equality or liberty to all. More recently, some historians have taken a closer look at the actions of common people during the Revolution. Sometimes called neoprogressives, they have highlighted Revolutionary-era class conflict and efforts by ordinary people to create a more egalitarian society. In doing so, these historians have enhanced our understanding of the social and economic influences on Revolutionary leaders. Their work also provides a timely reminder that those who try to understand the fight for independence without also considering struggles over "rule at home" will not fully understand the American Revolution.

INVESTIGATION

Unlike the previous chapters, this one contains a historian's essay—a *secondary source*—as well as a set of primary documents. The secondary source discusses the relationship between the struggle for independence and Americans' "multiple agendas" for radically transforming their society. The primary sources shed light on the essay's argument about the need to broaden our conception of the Revolution beyond the Founding Fathers who led the struggle against Britain. Your challenge is to use these sources to evaluate the essay's conclusions regarding varied efforts of other people to mold their society along more egalitarian and democratic lines. Together, the secondary and primary sources will allow you to determine the various ways that Americans challenged traditional authority and ideas. In the end, you should be able to decide whether and how the American Revolution was a "people's revolution" and what differences that made. Your evaluation should address the following questions:

1. **According to Source 1, how does broadening the story to include non-elite people change our understanding of the American Revolution?** In what ways, according to this source, did these people seek to transform American society? How did their actions shape the crisis with Britain?

2. **What do the primary sources reveal about the desires of common people or outsiders to challenge the status quo—the prevailing ideas or existing state of affairs in American society?** Did their protests share any common themes or ideas?

3. **Do you agree with historian Gary Nash that the protest of non-elite people made the Revolution radical?** In what ways, if at all, did those protests help to define the Revolution?

To complete this assignment, first read Source 1 and determine its argument about the "true radicalism" of the Revolution. Then turn to the primary sources to see what additional evidence they provide about the efforts of outsiders and non-elite Americans to change their society. When you are finished, you should be able to come to some conclusions about the extent to which the Revolution involved a struggle to remake American society along more democratic and egalitarian lines and was thus more than a struggle for independence from Britain.

SECONDARY SOURCE

1

In this source, historian Gary Nash argues that we must see beyond the "mythic" view of the Revolution that usually revolves around the leaders of the American colonies' rebellion against Great Britain. Doing so, Nash maintains, reveals its "radicalism." In this selection, Nash points to the protests of various groups or individuals during the Revolutionary era. Their actions and ideas, he suggests, challenged traditional power arrangements in various ways and illustrate the way many Americans wanted to democratize their society in these years. As you read Nash's account, note the way he links protests against British policies to an increasing willingness to challenge authority in general. In what ways did that attitude manifest itself in the Revolutionary era, according to Nash?

The Unknown American Revolution (2005)
GARY B. NASH

In this [study] the reader will find, I hope, an antidote for historical amnesia. To this day, the public remembers the Revolution mostly in its enshrined, mythic form. This is peculiar in a democratic society because the sacralized story of the founding fathers, the men of marble, mostly concerns the uppermost slice of American revolutionary society. That is what has lodged in our minds, and this is the fable that millions of people in other countries know about the American Revolution.

I ask readers to expand their conception of revolutionary American society and to consider the multiple agendas—the stuff of ideas, dreams, and aspirations—that sprang from its highly diverse and fragmented character. It is not hard today to understand that American people in all their diversity entertain a variety of ideas about what they want their nation to be and what sort of America they want for their children. Much the same was true

Source: Gary B. Nash, The Unknown American Revolution: The Unruly Birth of Democracy and the Struggle to Create America (New York: Viking, 2005), pp. xvi–xvii, 44–45, 46–49, 59, 151, 157–158, 159–160, 171–175, 202–204, 205, 206.

two centuries ago. But from a distance of more than two centuries we don't think about our nation's birth that way. It is more comforting to think about united colonists rising up as a unified body to get the British lion's paw off the backs of their necks. That is a noble and inspiring David and Goliath story, but it is not what actually happened. It is assuredly not the story of radical democracy's work during the Revolution.

This [study] presents a people's revolution, an upheaval among the most heterogeneous people to be found anywhere along the Atlantic littoral in the eighteenth century. The [study's] thrust is to complicate the well-established core narrative by putting before the reader bold figures, ideas, and movements, highlighting the true radicalism of the American Revolution that was indispensable to the origins, conduct, character, and outcome of the world-shaking event.

By "radicalism" I mean advocating wholesale change and sharp transformation rooted in a kind of dream life of a better future imagined by those who felt most dissatisfied with the conditions they experienced as the quarrel with Great Britain unfolded. For a reformed America they looked toward a redistribution of political, social, and religious power; the discarding of old institutions and the creation of new ones; the overthrowing of ingrained patterns of conservative, elitist thought; the leveling of society so that top and bottom were not widely separated; the end of the nightmare of slavery and the genocidal intentions of land-crazed frontiersmen; the hope of women of achieving a public voice. This radicalism directed itself at destabilizing a society where the white male elite prized stability because it upheld their close grip on political, economic, religious, sexual, and social power. This radicalism, therefore, was usually connected to a multifaceted campaign to democratize society. . . .

The pages that follow mostly view the American Revolution through the eyes of those not in positions of power and privilege, though the iconic founding fathers are assuredly part of the story. In reality, those in the nether strata of colonial society and those outside "respectable" society were most of the people of revolutionary America. Without their ideas, dreams, and blood sacrifices, the American Revolution would never have occurred, would never have followed the course that we can now comprehend, and would never have reverberated around the world among oppressed people down to the present day. Disinterring these long-forgotten figures from history's cemetery, along with their aspirations and demands, along with the events and dramatic moments in which they figured so importantly, is offered as an antidote to the art of forgetting. . . .

[I]t is not surprising that imperial decisions made in England as the Seven Years' War drew to a close sparked anger and upheaval in North America. A key element in this destabilization was the remarkable center-stage appearance of lower-class and enslaved people, whom colonial leaders had always hoped to keep in the wings, if not offstage altogether. In some sectors of colonial society, radical insurgency arose quite apart from England's attempts to rule its overseas colonies with a stronger hand. In other cases, external and internal stimuli of radical behavior overlapped and interacted. Whether stimulated externally or ignited internally, ferment during the years from 1761 to 1766 changed the dynamics of social and political relations in the colonies and set in motion currents of reformist sentiment with the force of a mountain wind. Critical to this half decade was the colonial response to England's Stamp Act, more the reaction of common colonists than that of their presumed leaders.

When dawn broke on August 14, 1765, Bostonians tramping to work found an effigy of Andrew Oliver, who was as respectable and well heeled a man as anyone in the city, clad in rags and dangling from a giant elm tree at the crossing of Essex and Orange Streets in the city's South End. This is where a narrow neck of land led from Boston to the farm villages west of the town. Attached to the effigy was the verse. "A goodlier sight who e'er did see? A Stamp-Man hanging on a tree!" Strung up alongside Oliver's effigy was a worn "Jack-Boot with a Head and horns peeping out of the top." The boot was painted green on the bottom—"a Green-ville sole," said the sign. The boot was a clever pun on the unpopular earl of Bute, King George's trusted adviser, and George Grenville, first lord of the Treasury and chancellor of the Exchequer. Colonial Americans regarded these two men as the architects of detested new imperial policies, especially the hated Stamp Act passed by Parliament on March 22, 1765, and scheduled to take effect on November 1. Oliver had been appointed as the distributor of the stamps for Boston and the entire colony of Massachusetts.

Before the day was over, laboring Bostonians, joined by middling townsmen, turned the city upside down. The "Stamp Act crisis," as historians have called it, had begun. In the cascading reactions to the Stamp Act, we can see how discontent over England's tightening of the screws on its American colonies merged with resentment born out of the play of events indigenous to colonial life. A perceptive witness of the mass disorder occurring from one end of the colonies to the other over the Stamp Act would have seen that several revolutions were about to erupt simultaneously. . . .

Bostonians knew vaguely about the tricky constitutional question raised by the Stamp Act: whether Parliament had the right to pass a tax simply to raise revenue—an internal tax—when the colonies had no representation in Parliament. American colonists, with rare exceptions, agreed that Parliament was entitled to pass external taxes meant to control the flow of trade. But ordinary Bostonians knew something beyond a quibble: that Lieutenant Governor Thomas Hutchinson had arranged the appointment of his brother-in-law Andrew Oliver to be the distributor of the hated stamps. Common folk also knew that both men were leaders of the prerogative circle gathered around the royal governor, an imperious group that had recently tried to dismantle Boston's town meeting and showed contempt for ordinary people who dared to think of themselves as entitled to a role in political affairs. All of Boston also knew that their provincial legislature had elected three men to gather with delegates from other colonies to meet in New York in October 1765 to hammer out an intercolonial protest to Parliament about the Stamp Act. The crowd, however, had no intention to wait for the Stamp Act Congress to meet.

At midmorning on August 14, Hutchinson ordered Sheriff Stephen Greenleaf to cut down the effigies, and at that moment the question of rightful authority moved from the chambers of constituted authority to the streets. Quickly, a crowd assembled to stop the sheriff. All day, common Bostonians detained farmers bringing produce into town along Orange Street until they had their goods "stamped" under the great elm standing at the neck of land. At the end of working hours, a mass of laboring men began forming for a mock funeral. Their leader was Ebenezer MacIntosh, a poor shoemaker and veteran of the Seven Years' War. . . . With MacIntosh acting as "the principal leader of the mob," as Governor Francis Bernard described the action, the crowd cut down Oliver's effigy as dark came on and carried it through the streets toward the Town House, the center of government where the legislature met. Then the crowd headed for the South End wharves, where Oliver had built a brick office for distributing the detested stamps. In less than thirty minutes they leveled the building. Saving the timbers, they "stamped" them in derision of the Stamp Act, and hauled them to Oliver's luxurious house at the foot of Fort Hill. At nightfall, they added the timbers to a bonfire atop the hill. By the light of the bonfire, they beheaded Oliver's effigy and then destroyed Oliver's stable house and his horse-drawn coach and chaise—prime emblems of upper-class affluence. Later in the evening, when Lieutenant Governor Hutchinson and Sheriff Greenleaf tried to stop the destruction, the crowd drove them off in a hailstorm of stones after someone cried out: "The Governor and the Sheriff! To your arms, my boys." For another four hours, deep into the night, the crowd tore through Oliver's house, breaking windows and a looking glass said to be the largest in the colonies, demolishing the elegant furniture, emptying the contents of the well-stocked wine cellar, and tearing up the gardens. The next day the shocked Oliver asked to be relieved of his commission as stamp distributor.

Twelve days later it was Lieutenant Governor Thomas Hutchinson's turn. After attacking the handsome houses of the deputy register of the vice admiralty court and the comptroller of Customs, a crowd of men in workaday garb descended on Hutchinson's mansion. Catching the lieutenant governor at dinner with his family, the crowd smashed in the doors with axes and sent the Hutchinsons packing. Working with almost military precision, they reduced the furniture to splinters, stripped the walls bare, chopped through inner partitions until the house was a hollow shell, destroyed the formal gardens, drank the wine cellar dry, stole nine hundred pounds sterling in coin (today this would be about $90,000), scattered books and papers in the street, and carried off every movable object of value. Led again by MacIntosh, the crowd worked into the night, spending almost three hours alone "at the cupola before they could get it down" and then finishing off the building as dawn broke. "Gentlemen of the army, who have seen towns sacked by the enemy," wrote one of the first historians of the Revolution, Boston's William Gordon, "declare they have never before saw an instance of such fury. . . ."

Hutchinson knew why his townsmen hated the tightening of trade regulations and the imposition of a new tax. But only by considering the wrath he had incurred among ordinary people over many years could he have understood their determination to bring his house level with the street. He never admitted such understanding in his correspondence or private conversations that have survived in the documentary record. But it is clear that the crowd was giving vent to years of resentment at the accumulation of wealth and power by the haughty prerogative faction led by Hutchinson. Behind every swing of the ax and every hurled stone, behind every shattered crystal goblet and splintered mahogany chair, lay the fury of a plain Bostonian who had read or heard the repeated references to impoverished people as "rabble" and to Boston's popular caucus, led by Samuel Adams, as a "herd of fools, tools, and sycophants." The mobbish attackers were those who had suffered economic hardship while others fattened their purses just the year before, they had listened to their popular leaders condemn those "who grind the faces of the poor without remorse, eat the bread of oppression without fear, and wax fat upon the spoils of the people." They had heard it said over and over that "luxury and extravagance are. . . destructive of those virtues which are necessary for the preservation of liberty and the happiness of the people." They had burned inwardly at hearing some of the wealthy proclaim from their mansions that poverty was the best inducement for industry and frugality and that "the common people of this town and country live too well." And they had cheered James Otis when he replied that "I am of a quite different opinion, I do not think they live half well enough. . . ."

While crowds took to the streets up and down the Atlantic seaboard shouting "liberty and no stamps," it entered the minds of many colonists that the constant talk about liberty—and its opposite, slavery—might become highly contagious, and applied to an issue far more fundamental than a modest tax imposed by England. In every colony, white leaders began to wonder about how restive slaves might react to the rhetoric fueling the disturbances related to the Stamp Act. While seeking freedom from parliamentary taxes, while deploring English tyranny and supposed attempts to "enslave" colonists, the Americans unexpectedly faced a profound contradiction as they scrambled to suppress enslaved Africans with their own urges to be free. . . .

Nobody in England's North American colonies wanted a more radical change than those who abhorred the practice of enslaving and brutalizing fellow human beings. A crescendo of objections to the continuance of slavery, mounting in the two years before the Declaration of Independence, gave hope that an ancient blotch on humaneness and morality might come to an end in a part of the world where people prided themselves on being part of a redeemer society destined to teach the world at large. The abolitionists' pamphlets that rolled off the presses, mostly in the northern cities, were longer, shriller, and more numerous and trenchant than those of the previous decade. The old argument of the Enlightenment philosophers that slavery was the central impediment to the march of progress continued. So did the insistence that American patriots be consistent about their proclamations of liberty and unalienable rights. But now, with war imminent, the new militancy of slaves and an astounding royal proclamation made the issue of abolition all the more urgent. . . .

Many slaves could not wait for benevolent masters and mistresses to set them free. From northern New England to the Georgia-Florida border, previous strategies to obtain freedom—petitioning legislatures for a general emancipation, bringing individual freedom suits before local courts, and taking flight in the hope of successfully posing as free men and women—now expanded to a fourth highly risky but less complicated option: offering the British their services in exchange for freedom and inducing the British to issue a general proclamation that would provide an opportunity for masses of slaves to burst their shackles.

In Boston, after he had been appointed the military governor of Massachusetts in April 1774, General Thomas Gage was determined to ram the new British policy down the throats of truculent Bostonians. Five months later, he received offers of help in this difficult matter from an unlikely source. Knowing that Governor Gage had dissolved the Massachusetts legislature, thereby foreclosing that avenue of ending slavery, Boston's slaves now offered to take up the sword against their masters. In late September 1774, fourteen months before Virginia's royal governor issued his famous proclamation offering freedom to any slave or indentured servant reaching the British forces, enslaved Bostonians tried to turn rumors of British intentions into concrete policy. "There has been in town a conspiracy of the Negroes," Abigail Adams wrote her husband, now in Philadelphia as a delegate to the First Continental Congress. "At present it is kept pretty private and was discovered by one who endeavored to dissuade them from it; he being threatened with his life, applied . . . for protection." Abigail continued that "They conducted in this way . . . to draw up a petition to the Governor, telling him they would fight for him provided he would arm them and engage to liberate them if he conquered." For white Bostonians, who prided themselves as a different breed from Virginia and Carolina slave masters, this came as a shock. Benjamin Franklin's judgment nearly twenty years before that "every slave may be reckoned a domestic enemy" was being chillingly confirmed. . . .

Slaves in tidewater Virginia did their part to shape English policy on the emancipation issue through a rash of uprisings in early 1775. On April 21, only two days after the minutemen riddled Gage's troops, who were sent to capture the colonial arsenals at Lexington and Concord, determined slaves made their move. John Murray, earl of Dunmore, had already moved from the governor's mansion in Williamsburg, Virginia's capital, to the *Fowey*, a British warship anchored in the lower York River. From here he dispatched a detachment to seize barrels of gunpowder in Williamsburg and bring them to the British warships. Edmund Randolph, Jefferson's son-in-law, later claimed that the governor's intention was to disarm the Virginians and "weaken the means of opposing an insurrection of the slaves . . . for a protection against whom in part the magazine was at first built." Seeing their chance, a number of slaves in Williamsburg offered to join Dunmore and "take up arms." To cow white patriot Virginians, Dunmore now warned that he "would declare freedom to the slaves and reduce the City of Williamsburg to ashes" if the hastily raised militia units threatened him.

Ten days later, on May 1, 1775, Dunmore made an earthshaking decision in favor of what one white Virginian called "the most diabolical" scheme to "offer freedom to our slaves and turn them against their masters." Writing to the secretary of state in London, Dunmore set out his plan "to arm all my own Negroes and receive all others that will come to me whom I shall declare free." It was a policy, remembered South Carolina's William Drayton, that "was already known" by slaves, who "entertain ideas that the present contest was for obliging us to give them their liberty." Near panic engulfed the South. "The newspapers were full of publications calculated to excite the fears of the people—massacres and instigated insurrections were the words in the mouth of every child," remembered Indian superintendent John Stuart. Stuart himself was part of the potential insurrection. Charlestonians drove him from the city after he was suspected of plotting to draw Creek Indians into the conflict on the British side. Stuart fled to Saint Augustine, Florida, to await the British occupation of South Carolina. . . .

The roll call of Virginia revolutionary leaders was also the roll call of Virginia speculators in western land whose rights, they believed, had been obliterated by a series of policy decisions, legal judgments, and Parliamentary acts in 1774, including the Quebec Act. The man who was the principal author of Virginia's Declaration of Rights and Virginia's new state constitution, George Mason, "had watched the Proclamation of 1763 destroy first his beloved Ohio Company and then his hopes of obtaining fifty thousand acres of Kentucky land. . . ." The man who would introduce the Declaration of Independence to the Continental Congress in July 1776, Richard Henry Lee, had been appalled by how the 1763 Proclamation Act and the Quebec Act dashed his Mississippi Land Company's hopes to lay hands on 2.5 million acres. The man who would lead the Continental army, George Washington, had thousands of acres of bounty lands that he purchased cheaply from veterans' claims slip from his hands as a result of the English attempt to stop Virginia land speculation. The man who drafted the Declaration of Independence, Thomas Jefferson, had invested in three land companies that would have given him title to 17,000 acres if the ministry in London had not cracked down. And the man whose fiery speeches helped push the colonies to the brink of revolution, Patrick Henry, saw five of his land ventures disappear like smoke. All these disappointments could be undone through a war that would remove the roadblocks—that is, a double war: against England, and against the ancient inhabitants of the fertile region watered by the Ohio River and its tributaries.

The Quebec Act was obnoxious not only to Virginians but to many colonists speculating in lands north of the Ohio River. The act also fiercely offended Protestant New Englanders because it guaranteed Catholic Canadians the right to worship freely. Hence, they folded the Quebec Act into the other Coercive Acts of 1774 and branded them all as "intolerable." But for the Six Iroquois Nations the Quebec Act promised relief from the frantic speculation and squatting in the lands reserved for the Iroquois and other northern tribes. . . .

As the Iroquois pondered their position, the matter became more urgent when several companies of New Englanders and New Hampshire backwoodsmen, completely unauthorized by the Continental Congress, attacked and captured Fort Ticonderoga and Crown Point on Lake Champlain on May 10–11, 1775. Under the joint command of Benedict Arnold and Ethan Allen (who wrestled dangerously for command of this private expeditionary army), the attack at dawn succeeded without a shot being fired. Surrounding the fort, Allen called out to the British officer, who commanded only about forty men: "Come out of there, you damned old rat." When asked in whose name the Americans were fighting, the ever bull headed Allen replied, "In the name of the Great Jehovah and the Continental Congress." Neither had authorized the attack. But this victory made the Iroquois' problem no less severe. . . .

Another Grand Iroquois council met at the end of July 1775 in Montreal to listen to [Quebec] Governor [Guy] Carleton's plea for Iroquois support. Joseph Brant participated in a mock feast to devour "a Bostonian and drink his blood—an ox having been roasted for the purpose, and a pipe of wine given to drink." Along with some 1,700 Indians, Brant listened intently as Guy Carleton promised the Mohawks that if they took up the hatchet "to defend our country," they would recover all their stolen property after the British put the Americans in their place and forced their obedience to royal authority. . . .

[John] Adams, especially in his public pronouncements, had nervous fits about the leveling spirit breaking out in all the colonies. It was one thing to bring the high and mighty down a rung or two, but quite another to allow those on the bottom rungs to spring upward. Like his cousin Sam, he believed that in a republic the distance between rich and poor should not be too great. But if this leveling of income and wealth shaded into indiscipline or challenges to the authority of the well-born and educated, he saw the beast of anarchy beckoning. Writing from Philadelphia to Abigail, who was tending the farm and raising their four children in Braintree, Massachusetts, three hundred miles to the north, Adams complained that "our struggle has loosened the bands of government everywhere. That children and apprentices were disobedient—that schools and colleges were grown turbulent— that Indians slighted their guardians and Negroes grew insolent to their masters." This casting off of deference disturbed Adams. Released from the bottle, could the genie ever be recaptured?

That the genie was not always masculine also troubled Adams. His wife Abigail tasked him on just this issue. Her husband's long absences from home and the strain of running their farm by herself just outside British-occupied Boston, along with the death of her mother in the fall of 1775, all seemed to bring her to a new state of consciousness about what the looming revolution might hold for the women who were playing such an important role in the nonimportation and homespun movements. "In the Code of Laws which I suppose it will be necessary for you to make," she wrote John on March 31, 1776, "I desire you would remember the ladies, and be more generous and favourable to them than your ancestors." In this much quoted passage, Abigail went from desire to demand. "Do not put such unlimited power into the hand of the husbands. Remember all men would be tyrants if they could. If particular care and attention is not paid to the ladies, we are determined to foment a rebellion, and will not hold ourselves bound by any laws in which we have no voice or representation." A few paragraphs earlier Abigail had wondered about just how real the "passion for liberty" was among those who still kept fellow humans enslaved. Now she pushed the point home about men enslaving women. "That your sex are naturally tyrannical is a truth so thoroughly established as to admit of no dispute, but such of you as wish to be happy willingly give up the harsh title of master for the more tender and endearing one of friend. Why then, not put it out of the power of the vicious and lawless to use us with cruelty and indignity with impunity? Men of sense in all ages abhor those customs which treat us only as the vassals of your sex."

In this letter we see clearly how women of Abigail Adams's intellectual mettle nimbly made the connection between civil and domestic government. The more male leaders railed against England's intentions to "enslave" its colonial "subjects," to rule arbitrarily, to act tyrannically, the more American women began to rethink their own marital situations. The language of protest against England reminded many American women that they too were badly treated "subjects"—the subjects of husbands who often dealt with them cruelly and exercised power over them arbitrarily. Most American women, still bound by the social conventions of the day, were not yet ready to organize in behalf of greater rights. But the protests against England stirred up new thoughts about what seemed arbitrary or despotic in their own society, and many women began to think that what had been endured in the past was no longer acceptable. This paved the way for change. Abigail's reference to the cruelty men used against their wives probably refers to the "rule of thumb" that the law upheld. Deeply imbedded in England's common law, and encoded in Blackstone's *Commentaries on the Laws of England,* the rule of thumb made it permissible for husbands to beat their wives so long as the stick or club did not exceed the thickness of a male thumb. The reference to using women with indignity probably referred to the emotional and psychological domination of wives by husbands. For all his love of Abigail, John's reply to her letter of March 31, 1776, confirmed the point. "As to your extraordinary code of laws," he wrote, "I cannot but laugh." Then referring to the growing insubordination of children, apprentices, Indians, slaves, and college students, he sniffed that "your letter was the first intimation that another tribe more numerous and powerful than all the rest were grown discontented. This is rather too coarse a compliment but you are so saucy, I won't blot it out. . . ."

Abigail was not amused. She knew that it was not the British ministry that stirred up women and others grating against their subordination. Instead of writing John after receiving his dismissive letter, she unburdened herself to her friend Mercy Otis Warren, the sister of John Otis and wife of James Warren, a Massachusetts legislator. "He is very saucy to me in return for a list of female grievances which I transmitted to him," she wrote Mercy. "I think I will get you to join me in a petition to Congress." Why, she wondered, was her husband so insensitive to what seemed an opportunity to enact a more "generous plan," "some laws in our favor upon just and liberal principles" by which the law would curb "the power of the arbitrary and tyrannic to injure us with impunity?" Under revised law, women could gain court protection against abusive husbands and not lose their property and wages to men once they married. For raising just and liberal principles, she bitterly told Mercy, he scoffed at her and called her saucy. "So I have helped the sex abundantly," she closed, "but I will tell him I have only been making trial of the disinterestedness of his virtue, and when weighed in the balance have found it wanting." Mercy Otis Warren, who had already crossed the boundaries of correct female behavior by writing two patriot plays that pilloried Thomas Hutchinson and other Loyalists, sympathized with Abigail and told other women that the criticism of females who interested themselves in politics should be resisted. . . .

Adams tried to end the argument on a high note by complimenting Abigail as a "Stateswoman" as well as "a Farmeress." But for Abigail, the matter was not closed. Years later she insisted that "I will never consent to have our sex considered in an inferior point of light. Let each planet shine in their own orbit. God and nature designed it so—if man is Lord, woman is

Lordess—that is what I contend for." Like a stone cast into a pond, ripples radiated outward from this private family argument auguring currents of change far beyond the Adams family.

PRIMARY SOURCES

The primary sources in this section reflect the concerns and experiences of various people during the struggle for independence. As you evaluate these sources, consider what they reveal about the desire to achieve greater equality and to what extent they support the argument that the American fight for independence from Britain unleashed a struggle to achieve greater equality and rights at home.

2   When the Stamp Act went into effect on November 1, 1765, a crowd of angry men in New York targeted Lieutenant Governor Cadwallader Colden, a defender of British policy in the colonies. The crowd was led by a group of men from the middle rank of New York society that came to be known as the Sons of Liberty. Several days later, Colden recounted the incident in a report to officials in Britain. Note the type of property the mob attacked. Why do you think many of New York's "gentlemen" may have come out to "observe"?

An Account of a Stamp Act Riot (1765)

Sir,

In a day or two after the date of my letter of the 26th of last month. . . the packages of stamped papers were landed from His Majesty's ship *Garland* at noonday without a guard or the least appearance of discontent among the people. . . . But on the evening of the first day of this month the mob began to collect together, and after it became dark they came up to the Fort Gate with a great number of torches, and a scaffold on which two images were placed, one to represent the governor in his grey hairs, & the other the devil by his side. This scaffold with the images was brought up within 8 or 10 feet of the gate with the grossest ribaldry from the mob. As they went from the gate they broke open my coach house, took my chariot out of it & carried it

Source: Cynthia A. Kierner, *Revolutionary America 1750–1815: Sources and Interpretations* (Upper Saddle River, N.J.: Prentice Hall, 2003), pp. 74–75; originally from Cadwallader Colden to Secretary Conway, November 5, 1765, in E. B. O'Callaghan and Berthold Fernow, eds., *Documents Relative to the Colonial History of the State of New York*, 15 vols. (Albany, N.Y., 1853–1887), VII: p. 771.

round the town with the images, & returned to the Fort Gate, from whence they carried them to an open place, where they had erected a gibbet, within 100 yards of the Fort Gate & there hung up the images. After hanging some time they were burnt in a fire prepared for the purpose, together with my chariot, a single horse chair and two sledges, our usual carriages when snow is on the ground, which they took out of my coach house. While this was doing a great number of gentlemen of the town if they can be called so, stood around to observe the outrage on their King's governor. The garrison was at the same time on the ramparts with preparation sufficient to destroy them, but not a single return in words or otherwise was made from any man in the fort, while this egregious insult was performing. . . . It is given out that the mob will storm the fort this night. I am not apprehensive of their carrying out their purpose; probably it might be attended with much bloodshed because a great part of the mob consists of men who had been privateers & disbanded soldiers whose view it is to plunder the town.

This goes by Major James of the Royal Artillery who with much zeal for his Majesty's service put the fort in the best posture of defence he could, for reason which the mob, the same night they insulted their governor, broke open his house, burnt all his furniture, wearing clothes and every thing in it to a great value, at the same time threatening to take away his life in the most shameful manner.

3   In early 1766, the Sons of Liberty took action against two New York merchants who abided by the Stamp Act when they accepted customs documents issued on stamped paper. What does this account of that punishment reveal about the dangers facing the middling men in the Sons of Liberty as they turned to crowd action to protest the Stamp Act?

A Mob Punishes Merchants (1766)

The matter was intended to be done privately, but it got wind, and by ten o'clock I suppose two thousand people attended at the Coffee House, among them most of the principal men in town. The culprits' apologies did not satisfy the people. They were highly blamed and the Sons of Liberty found it necessary to use their influence to moderate the resentments of the people. Two men were dispatched to the collector for the stamped bonds, of which he had thirty in all. He desired liberty to confer with the governor, which was granted. The governor sent word, if the stamps were delivered to him, he would give his word and honor they should not be used; but that if

Source: David Hawke, ed., U.S. Colonial History: Reading and Documents (Indianapolis: The Bobbs-Merrill Company, Inc., 1966), pp. 405–406; originally from John Holt to Mrs. Benjamin Franklin, February 15, 1766, Franklin Papers, XLVIII: p. 92.

the people were not satisfied with this, they might do as they pleased with them. The message being returned to the gathering multitude, they would not agree to the governor's proposal, but insisted upon the stamp being delivered and burnt. One or two men, attended by about a thousand others, were then sent for the stamps, which were brought to the Coffee House; and the merchant who had used them was ordered himself to kindle the fire and consume them, those filled in and all. This was accordingly done amid the huzzas of the people, who were by this time swelled to the number I suppose of about five thousand, and in another hour I suppose would have been ten thousand. The people pretty quietly dispersed soon after, but their resentment was not allayed. Toward the evening,. . . though the Sons of Liberty exerted themselves to the utmost, they could not prevent the gathering of the multitude, who went to Mr. [Charles] Williams' [New York's naval officer] house, broke open the door, and destroyed some of the furniture. But through the influence of the Sons of Liberty and on his most earnest entreaty and promise in the most public manner to ask pardon next day, or do whatever they should require of him, they were prevailed on to leave the house, and then went to the merchants, where after huzzaing for some time, they were prevailed upon to forbear doing any mischief—on consideration that both men were well beloved in town and bore fair character. . . .

. . . [M]any of those of inferior sort, who delight in mischief merely for its own sake or for plunder seem yet to be in such a turbulent disposition that the two mortified gentlemen are still in some danger, but the Sons of Liberty intend to exert themselves in their defense.

---

4 Gouverneur Morris was a New York "aristocrat" opposed to British policies in the colonies. He also kept a close eye on his fellow colonists' responses to British actions. In this source, Morris discusses the people's involvement in anti-British protests after the passage of the Coercive Acts. What are his fears regarding the consequences of such involvement?

A Gentleman Comments on the Mob (1774)

Dear Sir:

You have heard, and you will hear a great deal about politics, and in the heap of chaff you may find some grains of good sense. Believe me, sir, freedom and religion are the only watchwords. We have appointed a committee, or rather we have nominated one. Let me give you a history of it. . . .

Source: Cynthia A. Kierner, *Revolutionary America 1750–1815: Sources and Interpretations* (Upper Saddle River, N.J.: Prentice Hall, 2003), pp. 102–103; originally from Gouverneur Morris to Thomas Penn, May 20, 1774, in Peter Force, ed., *American Archives*, 4th ser., 6 vols. (Washington, D.C., 1837–1853), I: pp. 342–343.

The troubles in America during Grenville's administration. . . stimulated some daring coxcombs to rouse the mob into an attack upon the bounds of order and decency. These fellows became. . . the leaders in all the riots, the bell-weathers of the flock. . . That we have been in hot water with the British Parliament ever since everybody knows. . . The port of Boston has been shut up. These [mobs], simple as they are, cannot be gulled as heretofore. In short, there is no ruling them, and now. . . the heads of the mobility grow dangerous to the gentry, and how to keep them down is the question. While they correspond with the other colonies, call and dismiss popular assemblies, make resolves to bind the consciences of the rest of mankind, bully poor printers, and exert with full force all their other tribunitial powers, it is impossible to curb them. . . .

I stood in the balcony, and on my right hand were ranged all the people of property, with some few poor dependents, and on the other all the tradesmen, etc., who thought it worth their while to leave daily labour for the good of the country. The spirit of the English constitution has yet a little influence left, and but a little. The remains of it, however, will give the wealthy people a superiority this time, but would they secure it they must banish all school-masters and confine all knowledge to themselves. This cannot be. The mob begin to think and to reason. Poor reptiles! It is with them a vernal morning; they are struggling to cast off their winter's slough, they bask in the sunshine, and ere noon they will bite, depend upon it. The gentry begin to fear this. Their committee will be appointed, they will deceive the people and again forfeit a share of their confidence. And if these instances of what with one side is policy, with the other perfidy, shall continue to increase and become more frequent, farewell aristocracy. I see, and I see it with fear and trembling, that if the disputes with Great Britain continue, we shall be under the worst of all possible dominions; we shall be under the domination of a riotous mob.

---

5 Even before 1776, colonies began to create new governments to replace the old ones connected to the imperial government of Great Britain. Three weeks after the Second Continental Congress met in Philadelphia, citizens in one western North Carolina county passed resolutions designed to replace imperial rule there. To what extent do the provisions regarding military affairs and law enforcement reflect democratic or egalitarian sentiments?

Source: Cynthia A. Kierner, *Revolutionary America 1750–1815: Sources and Interpretations* (Upper Saddle River, N.J.: Prentice Hall, 2003), pp. 123–124; originally from W. L. Saunders et al., eds., *The Colonial and State Records of North Carolina*, 30 vols. (Raleigh, Winston, Goldsboro, and Charlotte, 1886–1914), IX: pp. 1282–1284.

Mecklenburg County Resolves (1775)

1. That all commissions civil and military heretofore granted by the Crown to be exercised in these colonies are null and void and the constitution of each particular colony wholly suspended.
2. That the Provincial Congress of each Province under the direction of the great Continental Congress is invested with all legislative and executive powers within their respective Provinces and that no other legislative or executive power does or can exist at this time in any of these colonies.
3. As all former laws are now suspended in this Province and the Congress have not yet provided others we judge it necessary for the better preservation of good order, to form certain rules and regulations for the internal government of this county until laws shall be provided for us by the Congress.
4. That the inhabitants of this county do meet on a certain day appointed by the committee and having formed themselves into nine companies. . . eight in the county and one in the town of Charlotte do choose a Colonel and other military officers who shall hold and exercise their several powers by virtue of this choice and independent of the Crown of Great Britain and former constitution of this Province.
5. That for the better preservation of the peace and administration of justice each of those companies do choose from their own body two discreet freeholders who shall be empowered each by himself and singly to decide and determine all matters of controversy arising within said company under the sum of twenty shillings and jointly and together all controversies under the sum of forty shillings, that so as their decisions may admit of appeal to the convention of the selectmen of the county and also that anyone of these men shall have power to examine and commit to confinement persons accused of petit larceny.
6. That those two selectmen thus chosen do jointly and together choose from the body of their particular body two persons properly qualified to act as constables who may assist them in the execution of their office.
7. That upon the complaint of any persons to either of these selectmen he do issue his warrant directed to the constable commanding him to bring the aggressor before him or them to answer said complaint.

---

6   As in other colonies, by 1775, patriots in Virginia often took it upon themselves to force merchants to sign agreements prohibiting the importation of British goods. This source depicts one such action, probably to enforce resolutions passed by the Williamsburg Convention, which was operating by then as an extralegal government in the colony. The merchants could either comply with non-importation agreements or face the

"alternative": the gallows with a keg of tar and a bag of feathers. Notice, on the left, one merchant being led toward them. To the victim's right, a patriot with scissors in hand is ready to cut off his hair before tarring and feathering him. Finally, notice the mix of people, including women and, at the rear, an African American.

The Alternative of Williamsburg (1775)
PHILIP DAWE

Library of Congress Prints and Photographs Division Washington, D.C. [LC-USZ62-9488].

7

After the decision for independence, the states began to draft constitutions for new state governments. One of the most important issues confronting the framers of these documents was whether to lower, or abolish altogether, the property qualification for voting. Some states, such as Virginia, left the colonial property qualification unchanged. In Pennsylvania, however, voting was opened to all male taxpayers at least twenty-one years of age. As this dialogue between fictional characters published in a Philadelphia newspaper demonstrates, that provision for broad voting rights aroused the concern of some people. What is the argument offered here against such a liberal standard?

"A Dialogue Between Orator Puff and Peter Easy" (1776)

Orator: Now all will be put on a level with respect to this grand right of voting at elections, and that may in time bring them to a level in every other respect, as has happened in other countries.

Peter: This is a great step, neighbour Puff, and may have very extraordinary consequences. Thou must be convinced, I believe, that a large majority of Pennsylvania, at present, consists of freeholders, and honest, industrious, frugal people, who are worth at least fifty pounds each.

Orator: I am convinced of that truth; but what would you argue from that?

Peter: Why, I cannot perceive the propriety or prudence of putting these inhabitants upon a level with the indolent or prodigal, who have not acquired such a small sum as fifty pounds, in a country where the acquiring of such a sum is not difficult, especially for a single man. If the privilege [of voting] extended only to those who had families, here there would not be so much in it; or if there was any other "sufficient evidence" of their attachment to the state required. Besides, it appears clearly to be an injury to all the inhabitants of the state, who are worth *fifty* pounds in real or personal estate. For the right of electing is vested in them, by the laws of Pennsylvania, and in them alone, and therefore the extending the same right to all men without distinction. . . takes away so much of their right, from those who are worth fifty pounds, and proportionately lessens their influence in elections, and therefore in the state. What necessity is there for this general alteration? Can't the liberties and happiness of Pennsylvania be trusted to those men in it, who are worth *fifty* pounds each? And should we go to wreck and ruin, unless we are saved by those who are not worth that sum?. . . Such people, having nothing to lose, and a prospect of gaining by public convulsions, are

Source: Cynthia A. Kierner, *Revolutionary America 1750–1815: Sources and Interpretations* (Upper Saddle River, N.J.: Prentice Hall, 2003), pp. 205–207; originally from *Pennsylvania Evening Post*, October 24, 1776.

always the most ready to engage in seditions, tumultuous and factious proceedings. They are the people to whom artful, delighting, selfish, ambitious, daring, wicked men apply themselves, and make use of to promote their pernicious projects. They are generally the most illiterate and ignorant of the whole of society, and therefore, the most easily imposed on by such men as I have described. . . On the other hand, while the rights of election, that is of sovereignty, as I said, are lodged in those who possess the general property, landed and personal within this state, it will ever be in their interest to keep things quiet, and to have officers go on with regularity; and if the other class grows turbulent, the whole force and dignity of the government can be exerted to keep them in order.

---

8 The large number of petitions for freedom by black slaves during the American Revolution demonstrates that many of them saw the hypocrisy in slaveholders' proclamations of liberty to protest British tyranny. This petition by free blacks to the Massachusetts legislature was one of many calling for the abolition of slavery in the state. Although the legislature never acted on those petitions, the state's supreme court declared slavery unconstitutional in 1783. What are the arguments against slavery in this petition? How do you account for its tone?

Antislavery Petition of Massachusetts Free Blacks (1777)

To the Honorable Counsel & House of [Representa]tives for the State of Massachusetts Bay in General Court assembled, January 13, 1777

The petition of A Great Number of Blackes detained in a State of slavery in the Bowels of a free & Christian Country Humbly sheweth that your Petitioners apprehend that they have in Common with all other men a Natural and Unaliable Right to that freedom which the Grat Parent of the Unavers hath Bestowed equalley on all menkind and which they have Never forfeited by any Compact or agreement whatever—but that wher Unjustly Dragged by the hand of cruel Power from their Derest friends and sum of them Even torn from the Embraces of their tender Parents—from A populous Pleasant and plentiful country and in violation of Laws of Nature and off Nations and in defiance of all the tender feelings of humanity Brough hear Either to Be sold Like Beast of Burthen & Like them Condemnd to Slavery for Life— Among A People Profesing the mild Religion of Jesus A people Not Insensible of the Secrets of Rational Being Nor without spirit to Resent the unjust

Source: Herbert Aptheker, ed., *A Documentary History of the Negro People in the United States from Colonial Times Through the Civil War* (Secaucus, N.J.: The Citadel Press, 1973), pp. 9–10; originally from *Collections, Massachusetts Historical Society*, 5th ser. (Boston, 1877), III: pp. 432–437.

endeavours of others to Reduce them to a state of Bondage and Subjection your honouer Need not to be informed that A Live of Slavery Like that of your petioners Deprived of Every social privilege of Every thing Requisit to Render Life Tolable is far worse then Nonexistence.

[In imitat]ion of the Lawdable Example of the Good People of these States your petitononers have Long and Patiently waited the Evnt of petition after petition By them presented to the Legislative Body of this state and cannot but with Grief Reflect that their Sucess hath ben but too similar they Cannot but express their Astonishment that It have Never Bin Considred that Every Principle from which Amarica has Acted in the Cours of their unhappy Dificultes with Great Briton Pleads Stronger than A thousand arguments in favours of your petioners they therfor humble Beseech your honours to give this petion its due weight & consideration & cause an act of the Legislatur to be past Wherby they may be Restored to the Enjoyments of that which is the Naturel Right of all men—and their Children who wher Born in this Land of Liberty may not be heald as Slaves after they arive at the age of twenty one years so may the Inhabitance of this Stats No longer chargeable with the inconsistancey of acting themselves the part which they condem and oppose in others Be prospered in their present Glorious struggle for Liberty and have those Blessing to them, &c.

 In 1780, seven black residents of Massachusetts petitioned the state legislature to exempt them from taxation. On what grounds do they do so?

Blacks Protest Taxation (1780)

To The Honourable Councel and House of Representives in General Court assembled for the State of the Massachusetts Bay in New England—March 14th A D 1780—

The petition of several poor Negroes & molattoes who are Inhabitant of the Town of Dartmouth Humbly Sheweth—That we being Chiefly of the African Extract and by Reason of Long Bondag and hard Slavery we have been deprived of Injoying the Profits of our Labouer or the advantage of Inheriting Estates from our Parents as our Neighbouers the white peopel do haveing some of us not long Injoyed our own freedom & yet of late, Contrary to the invariable Custom & Practice of the Country we have been & now are Taxed both in our Polls and that small Pittance of Estate which through much hard Labour & Industry we have got together to Sustain our selves &

Source: Herbert Aptheker, ed., *A Documentary History of the Negro People in the United States from Colonial Times Through the Civil War* (Secaucus, N.J.: The Citadel Press, 1973), pp. 15–16; originally from *Archives Division, Massachusetts Historical Society.*

families withal—We apprehand it therefore to be hard usag and [one word is illegible here-ed.] doubtless (if Continued will) Reduce us to a State of Beggary whereby we shall become a Berthan to others if not timely prevented by the Interposition of your Justice & power & yor Petitioners farther sheweth that we apprehand ourselves to be Aggreeved, in that while we are not allowed the Privilage of freemen of the State having no vote or Influence in the Election of those that Tax us yet many of our Colour (as is well known) have cheerfully Entered the field of Battle in the defence of the Common Cause and that (as we conceive) against a similar Exertion of Power (in Regard to taxation) too well Known to need a recital in this place. . . .

. . .We most humbley Request therefore that you would take our unhappy Case into your serious Consideration and in your wisdom and Power grant us Relief from Taxation while under our Present depressed Circumstances and your poor Petioners as in duty bound shall ever pray &c*

*In 1783, the Massachusetts Supreme Court declared that blacks who were subject to taxation were entitled to vote.

10   Joseph Brant, also known as Thayendanegea, was an Iroquois chief who was half white. Brant was in London in 1776 and declared his loyalty to the colonial secretary, Lord George Germain. What did Brant seek to gain from his loyalty to Britain?

Chief Thayendanegea Pledges His Loyalty (1776)

Brother.

When we delivered our speech you answered us in few words, that you would take care and have the grievances of the Six Nations on account of their lands, particularly those of the Mohocks and Oughquagas, removed; and all those matters settled to our satisfaction whenever the troubles in America were ended, and that you hoped the Six Nations would continue to behave with that attachment to the King they had always manifested; in which case they might be sure of his Majesty's favour and protection.

Brother. We return you thanks for this promise, which we hope will be performed, and that we shall not be disappointed, as has often been the case, notwithstanding the warm friendship of the Mohocks to his Majesty and his government, who are so immediately concerned, that the same has been often mentioned by the Six Nations and their getting no redress a matter of surprize to all the Indian Nations.

Source: Documents Relative to the Colonial History of the State of New-York, VIII, 678.

We are not afraid Brother, or have we the least doubt but our brethren the Six Nations will continue firm to their engagements with the King their father. Our Superintendant knows that in order to keep true to their treaties they have at times punished their friends and Allies.

Brother. The troubles that prevail in America and the distance we are from our country, allows us only to say that on our return we shall inform our Chiefs and Warriors what we have seen and heard and join with them in the most prudent measures for assisting to put a stop to those disturbances notwithstanding reports of their generally taking the strongest side. Which was not the case last Summer when we offered to prevent the invasion of Canada and lost several of our people in defending it. The only reason we mentioned the conduct of the Six Nations at that time was, that they might have credit for what they actually did, as we have heard much that affair has been attributed to the Nippissings and other Indians of Canada.

Brother. As we expect soon to depart for our own Country having been long here, we request you, and the great men who take charge of the affairs of government, not to listen to every story that may be told about Indians; but to give ear only to such things as come from our Chiefs and wise men in Council; which will be communicated to you by our Superintendent.

___

11 In response to a shortage of rations in George Washington's Continental Army in 1780, Esther Reed, the wife of Pennsylvania governor Joseph Reed, and other women organized a house-to-house drive to raise funds to support the troops. On July 4, 1780, Reed reported to Washington that the women had raised more than $300,000, though much of it was in deflated paper money. Written to encourage women to contribute funds for the soldiers, "The Sentiments of an American Woman" illustrates how participation in the struggle for independence could justify greater involvement by women in public affairs and politics.

"The Sentiments of an American Woman" (1780)
ESTHER REED

On the commencement of actual war, the Women of America manifested a firm resolution to contribute as much as could depend on them, to the deliverance of their country. Animated by the purest patriotism, they are sensible of sorrow at this day, in not offering more than barren wishes for the success of so glorious a Revolution. They aspire to render themselves more really useful; and this sentiment is universal from the north to the south of the Thirteen United States. Our ambition is kindled by the

Source: "The Sentiments of an American Woman" (Philadelphia, 1780).

same of those heroines of antiquity, who have rendered their sex illustrious, and have proved to the universe, that, if the weakness of our Constitution, if opinion and manners did not forbid us to march to glory by the same paths as the Men, we should at least equal, and sometimes surpass them in our love for the public good. I glory in all that which my sex has done great and commendable. I call to mind with enthusiasm and with admiration, all those acts of courage, of constancy and patriotism, which history has transmitted to us: The people favoured by Heaven, preserved from destruction by the virtues, the zeal and the resolution of Deborah, of Judith, of Esther! The fortitude of the mother of the Massachabees, in giving up her sons to die before her eyes: Rome saved from the fury of a victorious enemy by the efforts of Volumnia, and other Roman Ladies: So many famous sieges where the Women have been seen forgeting the weakness of their sex, building new walls, digging trenches with their feeble hands, furnishing arms to their defenders, they themselves darting the missile weapons on the enemy, resigning the ornaments of their apparel, and their fortune, to fill the public treasury, and to hasten the deliverance of their country; burying themselves under its ruins, throwing themselves into the flames rather than submit to the disgrace of humiliation before a proud enemy.

Born for liberty, disdaining to bear the irons of a tyrannic Government, we associate ourselves to the grandeur of those Sovereigns, cherished and revered, who have held with so much splendour the scepter of the greatest States. The Batildas, the Elizabeths, the Maries, the Catharines, who have extended the empire of liberty, and contented to reign by sweetness and justice, have broken the chains of slavery, forged by tryants in the times of ignorance and barbarity. The Spanish Women, do they not make, at this moment, the most patriotic sacrifices, to encrease the means of victory in the hands of their Sovereign. He is a friend to the French Nation. They are our allies. We call to mind, doubly interested, that it was a French Maid who kindled up amongst her fellow-citizens, the flame of patriotism buried under long misfortunes: It was the Maid of Orleans who drove from the kingdom of France the ancestors of those same British, whose odious yoke we have just shaken off; and whom it is necessary that we drive from this Continent.

But I must limit myself to the recollection of this small number of atchievements. Who knows if persons disposed to censure, and sometimes too severely with regard to us, may not disapprove our appearing acquainted even with the actions of which our sex boasts? We are at least certain, that he cannot be a good citizen who will not applaud our efforts for the relief of the armies which defend our lives, our possessions, our liberty? The situation of our soldiery has been represented to me; the evils inseparable from war, and the firm and generous spirit which has enabled them to support these. But it has been said, that they may apprehend, that, in the course of a long war, the view of their distresses may be lost, and their services be forgottten. Forgotten! never; I can answer in the name of all my sex. Brave Americans, your disinterestedness, your courage, and your constancy will always be dear to America, as long as she shall preserve her virtue.

We know that at a distance from the theatre of war, if we enjoy any tranquility, it is the fruit of your watchings, your labours, your dangers. If I live happy in the midst of my family; if my husband cultivates his field, and reaps his harvest in peace; if, surrounded with my children, I myself nourish the youngest, and press it to my bosom, without being affraid of fee[l]ing myself separated from it, by a ferocious enemy; if the house in which we dwell; if our barns, our orchards are safe at the present time from the hands of those incendiaries, it is to you that we owe it. And shall we hesitate to evidence to you our gratitude? Shall we hesitate to wear a cloathing more simple; hair dressed less elegant, while at the price of this small privation, we shall deserve your benedictions. Who, amongst us, will not renounce with the highest pleasure, those vain ornaments, when-she shall consider that the valiant defenders of America will be able to draw some advantage from the money which she may have laid out in these; that they will be better defended from the rigours of the seasons, that after their painful toils, they will receive some extraordinary and unexpected relief; that these presents will perhaps be valued by them at a greater price, when they will have it in their power to say: *This is the offering of the Ladies.* The time is arrived to display the same sentiments which animated us at the beginning of the Revolution, when we renounced the use of teas, however agreeable to our taste, rather than receive them from our persecutors: when we made it appear to them that we placed former necessaries in the rank of superfluities, when our liberty was interested: when our republican and laborious hands spun the flax, prepared the linen intended for the use of our soldiers; when exiles and fugitives we supported with courage all the evils which are the concomitants of war. Let us not lose a moment; let us be engaged to offer the homage of our gratitude at the altar of military valour, and you, our brave deliverers, while mercenary slaves combat to cause you to share with them, the irons with which they are loaded, receive with a free hand our offering, the purest which can be presented to your virtue,

By an AMERICAN WOMAN

12   Judith Sargent Murray was the daughter of a prominent Massachusetts family and the wife of a merchant. By her own later admission, the American Revolution first led her to question the prevailing attitudes toward women. In 1779, she wrote an essay on "the sexes" and eleven years later, during a period of considerable public discussion regarding women's proper role in the new republic, she submitted a slightly revised version for publication. On what grounds does she argue that women are equal to men?

"On the Equality of the Sexes" (1790)
JUDITH SARGENT MURRAY

Is it upon mature consideration we adopt the idea, that nature is . . . partial in her distributions? Is it indeed a fact, that she hath yielded to one half of the human species so unquestionable a mental superiority? I know that to both sexes elevated understandings, and the reverse, are common. But, suffer me to ask, in what the minds of females are *so* notoriously deficient, or unequal. . . . Will it be said that the judgment of a male of two years old, is more sage than that of a female's of the same age? I believe the reverse is generally observed to be true. But from that period what partiality! how is the one exalted and the other depressed, by the contrary modes of education which are adopted! the one is taught to aspire, and the other is early confined and limited. As their years increase, the sister must be wholly domesticated, while the brother is led by the hand through all the flowery paths of science. Grant that their minds are by nature equal, yet who shall wonder at the *apparent* superiority, if indeed custom becomes *second nature;* nay if it taketh place of nature, and that it doth the experience of each day will evince. At length arrived at womanhood, the uncultivated fair one feels a void, which the employments allotted her are by no means capable of filling. . . . Now, was she permitted the same instructors as her brother,. . . for the employment of a rational mind an ample field would be opened. In astronomy she might catch a glimpse of the immensity of the Deity, and thence she would form amazing conceptions of the august and supreme Intelligence. In geography she would admire Jehova in the midst of his benevolence; thus adapting this globe to the various wants and amusements of its inhabitants. In natural philosophy she would adore the infinite majesty of heaven, clothed in condescension; and as she traversed the reptile world, she would hail the

Source: Sheila L. Skemp, *Judith Sargent Murray: A Brief Biography with Documents* (Boston: Bedford Books, 1998), pp. 177, 178–180; originally from *Massachusetts Magazine*, March 1790, pp. 132–135.

goodness of a creating God. A mind, thus filled, would have little room for the trifles with which our sex are, with too much justice, accused of amusing themselves, and they would thus be rendered fit companions for those, who should one day wear them as their crown. Fashions, in their variety, would then give place to conjectures, which might perhaps conduce to the improvement of the literary world; and there would be no leisure for slander or detraction. Reputation would not then be blasted, but serious speculations would occupy the lively imiginations of the sex. . . .

Will it be urged that those acquirements would supersede our domestick duties, I answer that every requisite in female economy is easily attained; and, with truth I can add, that when once attained, they require no further *mental attention*. Nay, while we are pursuing the needle, or the superintendency of the family, I repeat that our minds are at full liberty for reflection; that imagination may exert itself in full vigor and that if a just foundation early laid, our ideas will then be worthy of rational beings. If we were industrious we might easily find time to arrange them upon paper, or should avocations press too hard for such an indulgence, the hours allotted for conversation would at least become more refined and rational. Should it still be vociferated, "Your domestick employments are sufficient"—I would calmly ask, is it reasonable, that a candidate for immortality, for the joys of heaven, an intelligent being, who is to spend an eternity in contemplating the works of Deity, should at present be so degraded, as to be allowed no other ideas, than those which are suggested by the mechanism of a pudding, or the sewing of the seams of a garment? Pity that all such censurers of female improvement do not go one step further, and deny their future existence; to be consistent they surely ought.

Yes, ye lordly, ye haughty sex, our souls are by nature *equal* to yours; the same breath of God animates, enlivens, and invigorates us; and that we are not fallen lower than yourselves, let those witness who have greatly towered above the various discouragements by which they have been so heavily oppressed; and though I am unacquainted with the list of celebrated characters on either side, yet from the observations I have made in the contracted circle in which I have moved, I dare confidently believe, that from the commencement of time to the present day, there hath been as many females, as males, who, by the *mere force of natural powers*, have merited the crown of applause; who *thus unassisted*, have seized the wreath of fame.

CONCLUSION

Several points should be clear from your analysis of the sources in this chapter. First, primary sources are useful tools to help assess historical arguments. They may reinforce or contradict historians' conclusions, add insights, and raise new questions. Second, as we saw in the first chapter on interpretations in text-books, often what is missing in a discussion about the past is as significant as those things that are part of the story. In this case, it is useful to think about the kinds of protest that were not included in even a small collection of sources intended to illustrate struggles for social equality during the Revolution. Their absence might also be an important clue regarding the limits of the fight over "who should rule at home."

This second point, in turn, is related to a third. These sources remind us that historians must be careful when generalizing about the past. That point is illustrated particularly well in this chapter's secondary source. Some of the old progressive historians at the beginning of the twentieth century argued that the War for Independence was *primarily* the result of social conflicts within American society. The author of Source 1, however, makes a more circum-scribed argument about the relationship between the fight over home rule and the one over who should rule at home. At the same time, the primary sources illustrate that it is not necessarily easy to prove something as sweeping as a social revolution.

These sources also demonstrate two other related points that will be more closely examined in the next chapters. First, historians must understand the ideas that moved people in the past—and the meaning of those ideas to people at the time. In the case of the Revolution, the idea of equality played a central role in the actions of those who supported independence. Yet, as this chapter's sources illustrate, it did not necessarily mean the same thing or hold the same implications in the minds of these Revolutionaries. Finally, historians must understand their subjects' motives. Did Revolutionaries challenge British actions out of principle? Or did more mundane consider-ations related to conflicts within American society move them to a certain course of action? Interpretations of the American Revolution cannot ignore this question. In fact, as we will see next, the question of motives is *central* to historians' interpretations and much of history's detective work is a search for clues to explain them.

FURTHER READING

Sylvia R. Frey, *Water from the Rock: Black Resistance in a Revolutionary Age* (Princeton, N.J.: Princeton University Press, 1991).

Woody Holton, *Forced Founders: Indians, Slaves and the Making of the American Revolution in Virginia* (Chapel Hill: University of North Carolina Press, 1999).

Charles Patrick Neimeyer, *America Goes to War: A Social History of the Continental Army* (New York: New York University Press, 1996).

Mary Beth Norton, *Liberty's Daughters: The Revolutionary Experience of American Women, 1750–1800* (Boston: Little, Brown, 1980).
Gordon S. Wood, *The American Revolution: A History* (New York: Random House, 2002).

NOTES

1. Carl L. Becker, *The History of Political Parties in the Province of New York, 1760–1776* (Madison: University of Wisconsin Press, 1960), p. 22.
2. Cited in Edmund S. Morgan, ed., *The American Revolution: Two Centuries of Interpretation* (Englewood Cliffs, N.J.: Prentice Hall, 1965), p. 73.

Chapter

5

Motivation in History:
The Founding Fathers and the Constitution

This chapter raises the question of motive in historical interpretation. It presents one historian's thesis about the motivation of the Founding Fathers and gives several primary sources by which to judge that thesis.

Secondary Source

1. *Unruly Americans and the Origins of the Constitution* (2007),
   WOODY HOLTON

Primary Sources

2. "Honesty Is the Best Policy" (1786), "CURTIUS"
3. "Honesty Is the Best Policy" (1786), "WILLING TO LEARN"
4. "Half Our Inhabitants . . . Will Become Bankrupt" (1786)
5. George Washington Reacts to Shays's Rebellion (1786)
6. The Founding Fathers Debate the Establishment of Congress (1787)
7. An Antifederalist Mocks the "Aristocratic Party" (1787)
8. A Founder Defends the Constitution's Restraints (1787)
9. "An Antifederalist Defends Paper Money" (1787)
10. *Federalist #10* (1788), JAMES MADISON
11. *Federalist #15* (1788), ALEXANDER HAMILTON

*M*any Americans believe that the Founding Fathers established the Constitution in 1787 to safeguard individual rights. Yet the freedom of speech, the freedom of the press, the right to bear arms, or the right to be secure in one's home are set forth in the Bill of Rights, which did not become part of the Constitution until 1791. And it was not the Federalist proponents of the Constitution who insisted that it be amended to include these rights so cherished today. It was their Antifederalist opponents, who often pointed to similar protections written into state constitutions.

If the Founding Fathers' overriding concern was not to protect Americans' civil liberties from the encroachments of government power, what was it? What was the motivation of the Founding Fathers for replacing the Articles of Confederation with a new and far more powerful central government? As in detective work, the question of motivation is essential to historical inquiry. Unfortunately, the motives of those in the past are sometimes not easy to determine because historical sources rarely reveal clear-cut answers to that question. In fact, motivation is one reason that historians argue about the past.

There are few better examples of historians' disagreement over the question of motivation than their views about the creation of the Constitution. Why was this document drafted, accepted by the Constitutional Convention, and ratified? What, specifically, did the Founders see as the primary defects of the existing government? What dangers did they perceive with the government under the Articles? How would the new government remove them? As we consider these questions in this chapter, we encounter an important aspect of historical detective work.

SETTING

Until the early twentieth century, the Founding Fathers were venerated as demigods who were driven by only the most laudable motives. In this view, the Founders realized that a weak central government under the Articles of Confederation was unable to deal effectively with the numerous threats and dangerous conditions, from hostile foreign nations on the country's periphery to the government's own weak finances. With the Republic in peril, they rose selflessly to their country's aid and formulated a plan for a stronger government that saved the American experiment in self-government. As one American history textbook said in 1892, the Constitutional Convention was an "eminent assemblage of America's noblest patriots and most illustrious historic characters, 'all, all, honorable men.'"[1]

Then, in 1913, historian Charles Beard published *An Economic Interpretation of the Constitution of the United States*. Whereas earlier writers saw a group of patriots, Beard saw men who were personally interested in the fruits of their labor. Writing during the heyday of muckrakers intent on uncovering political corruption and exposing the practices of corporations, Beard focused on the Founding Fathers' backgrounds and property holdings. As merchants and creditors, he concluded, they stood to gain materially from a strong government that would protect private property and pay off the government's Revolutionary War debts, including the debt owed to them. For Beard, the clash over the Constitution reflected a struggle between economic classes. On the one side was a wealthy creditor class; on the other were small farmers and debtors. According to Beard, the printing of paper money by many states, legal under the Articles of Confederation, sharpened the division between these two classes. Such money made it possible for poor debtor farmers to pay back loans with depreciated money, that is, money worth less than that which they had borrowed from creditors. As Beard put it, "No one can pore for weeks over the letters, newspapers and pamphlets of the years 1787–1789 without coming to the conclusion that there was a deep-seated conflict between a popular party based on paper money and agrarian interests and a conservative party . . . resting . . . on financial, mercantile and personal property interests generally."[2] Backed by a minority of Americans because women, blacks, Indians, and those without sufficient property had no voice, the Constitution was an undemocratic document created by a propertied elite who sought protection from popular majorities.

By the middle of the twentieth century, historians began to assault Beard's charge that the Founders were driven by their own financial gain. They were led by Forrest McDonald, who argued that ownership of the government's Revolutionary War debt in the form of bonds had no bearing on whether individuals favored or opposed the Constitution. With McDonald's rebuttal of Beard's argument that the Founders were out to line their own pockets, historians began to explore other concerns that could have led the Founders to push for a new government. Unlike Beard, they relied primarily on the Founders' writings for clues about motivation. Gordon Wood, the most prominent of them, did not ignore the economic context of the Constitution's creation or what he called the Founders' "aristocratic purposes." He argued, though, that the Founders' words must be considered as more than masks for economic interests. In his view, those words reveal unique and creative thinking about the republican government that were "popularly based and [that] embodied what Americans had been groping towards from the beginning of their history." And that is why, he concluded, their handiwork was so "easily adopted."[3]

At the beginnings of a new century, however, historian Howard Zinn and other "neo-Beardians" have reemphasized the Founders' anti-democratic fears. In their view, the Founders' motives did not spring from their pocketbooks, but are to be found in the democratic practices of the states, many of which confronted large state Revolutionary War debts during a deep economic depression. Popular pressure mounted in the states for debt forgiveness and the printing of paper money. Such pressures sometimes culminated in armed uprisings of small debtor farmers, including Shays's Rebellion in Massachusetts in 1786. Such disturbances, these historians argue, helped to focus the Founding Fathers' fears on unchecked democracy and the inability of the Articles of Confederation to counter it. The result was a Constitution that did little to protect individual rights, but much to limit popular influence. As the debate over the Founding Fathers' motives continues, an understanding of history makes one thing clear: Historians in this century are not likely to agree once and for all on the picture that Americans should hold of their nation's founders.

INVESTIGATION

In this chapter, we examine various sources relating to the motives of the Founders for creating the Constitution. The sources are a short excerpt from one historian's recent examination of that question and a small set of primary sources. Before completing the investigation in this chapter, make sure you have read the sections in your textbook on the Confederation period and the Constitution. They will provide useful background. As you consider the sources in this chapter, your job is to determine whether the argument in the secondary source offers a convincing explanation of the Founders' motives. To do this, you must consider to what extent the primary sources support that argument or offer evidence of alternative concerns or motives on the part of the Founders. Formulating answers to the following questions will help you complete this assignment:

1. **What were the Founding Fathers' motives for creating the Constitution, according to the author of Source 1?** How does his explanation conflict with what he calls "high school textbooks and popular histories"?

2. **Is the argument in the secondary source regarding the origins of the Constitution persuasive?** Do its conclusions seem to be justified by the evidence?

3. **Can you use the primary sources to make an alternative case for the creation of the Constitution?** Could a desire to limit popular influence on the government have been driven by other concerns than those suggested by the secondary source? Do the primary sources offer any evidence of that?

4. **How does the explanation of the Founding Fathers' motives in the secondary source in this chapter compare to that suggested by your textbook?** Does the evidence in Chapter 4 regarding changes in American society in the Revolutionary era shed any light on the argument presented in Source 1? Does that chapter's evidence support or undermine this argument?

SECONDARY SOURCE

1

Excerpts from historian Woody Holton locate the motivation behind the Constitution in developments in the states. As you read this selection, consider what role the author assigns to economic and political conditions in the states in his assessment of the Founders' motives. Also consider whether people are usually driven by only one interest. Is it possible that other concerns besides those identified in this source could have driven the Founders?

Unruly Americans and the Origins of the Constitution (2007)

WOODY HOLTON

High school textbooks and popular histories of the Revolutionary War locate the origins of the Constitution in the nasty conflicts that kept threatening to tear the federal convention apart—and in the brilliant compromises that, again and again, brought the delegates back together. Should every state have the same number of representatives in Congress, or should representation be weighted in favor of the more populous ones? Solution: proportional representation in the House of Representatives and state equality in the Senate. Should the national government be allowed to abolish the African slave trade? Solution: yes, but not until 1808. . . .

The textbooks and the popular histories give surprisingly short shrift to the Framers' motivations. What almost all of them do say is that harsh experience had exposed the previous government, under the Articles of Confederation (1781—89), as too weak. What makes this emphasis strange is that the Framers' own statements reveal another, more pressing motive. Early in the Constitutional Convention, James Madison urged his colleagues to tackle "the evils . . . which prevail within the States individually as well as those which affect them collectively." The "mutability" and "injustice" of "the laws of the States" had, Madison declared shortly after leaving Philadelphia, "contributed more to that uneasiness which produced the Convention, and prepared the public mind for a general reform, than those which accrued to our national character and interest from the inadequacy of the Confederation."

Madison's preoccupation with what he later called the "the internal administration of the States" was by no means unique. On the eve of the

convention, expressions of concern about the weakness of Congress, numerous as they were, were vastly outnumbered by complaints against the state
governments. "What led to the appointment of this Convention?" Maryland
delegate John Francis Mercer asked his colleagues. Was it not "the corruption & mutability of the Legislative Councils of the States"?

Once the Constitution had been sent out to the thirteen states for ratification, its supporters affirmed that some of the most lethal diseases it was
designed to cure were to be found within those same states. William Plumer
of New Hampshire embraced the new national government out of a conviction that "our rights & property are now the sport of ignorant unprincipled
State legislators." In the last of the *Federalist Papers*—the series of eighty-five
newspaper essays that are widely seen as America's premier contribution to
political science—Alexander Hamilton praised the Constitution for placing
salutary "restraints" on "the ambition of powerful individuals in single
states."

What was wrong with the state assemblies? Given the modern perception that the Founding Fathers had devoted their lives to the principle of
government by the people, it is jarring to read their specific grievances.
An essay appearing in a Connecticut newspaper in September 1786 complained that the state's representatives paid "too great an attention to popular notions." At least one of those Connecticut assemblymen thoroughly
agreed. In May 1787, just as the federal convention assembled, he observed
that even the southern states, which under British rule had been aristocratic bastions, had "run into the extremes of democracy" since declaring
independence.

What these men were saying was that the American Revolution had gone
too far. Their great hope was that the federal convention would find a way
to put the democratic genie back in the bottle. Alexander Hamilton, the most
ostentatiously conservative of the convention delegates, affirmed that many
Americans—not just himself—were growing "tired of an excess of democracy." Others identified the problem as "a headstrong democracy: a "prevailing rage of excessive democracy," a "republican frenzy," "democratical
tyranny," and "democratic licentiousness."

During the eighteenth century the primary means of land transportation—
other than walking—was the horse. Writers and speakers often expressed
their anxiety about the changes occurring in their fellow Americans by
calling them "unruly steeds." To Silas Deane it seemed that "the reins
of Government" were held with too "feeble a hand."

What had persuaded the Framers and many of the most prominent Americans
of the postwar era that the Revolution had gotten out of hand? Consider the case of James Madison, "the father of the Constitution." Madison
is widely credited with writing the "Virginia Plan," the Constitutional Convention's first draft. Having addressed the convention more often than
all but one other delegate, he went on to become one of the two principal

authors of the *Federalist* Papers, the best-known brief for ratification. When it became clear that roughly half the electorate would refuse to accept the Constitution until it contained a bill of rights, it was Madison who drew up those first ten amendments. . . .

One reason historians have always found Madison such an appealing character is that he himself was something of a bookworm. . . . Yet one subject seemed to fuel Madison with a limitless energy and to draw him from the tranquillity of his study. This was his disgust with the state governments that emerged from the Revolutionary War. Madison's desperate desire to rein in the thirteen state governments was not born in a contemplative philosophical vacuum; it reflected his own day-to-day experience as a political animal. . . .

What really alarmed Madison was the specific legislation the assemblies had adopted. More than anything else, it was the desire to overturn these state laws that set him on the road to Philadelphia. Nor was he alone. Another Constitutional Convention delegate, Pennsylvania's Gouverneur Morris, enumerated various kinds of iniquitous state laws he hoped his colleagues would guard against in the new national charter, concluding that "experience evinces the truth of this remark without having recourse to reading."

What had the thirteen assemblies done wrong? The "evils which had more perhaps than any thing else, produced this convention," Madison told his colleagues in Philadelphia, were the states' countless "Interferences" with "the security of private rights, and the steady dispensation of Justice."

All this talk about "rights" and "Justice" may seem today like glittering generalities. Actually, the transgressions that the Founding Fathers laid at the feet of the thirteen state legislatures were quite specific. Most glaringly representatives had shown excessive indulgence to debtors and taxpayers. They had refused to force farmers to pay what they owed.

Insects, drought—even invading armies—fearsome as they all are, have rarely been what rural Americans dread most. That distinction belongs to the farmers' creditors—not only the men and women who have lent them cash but the merchants who have supplied them with tools and other merchandise on credit and the government officials who press them to pay their back taxes. In the wake of the Revolutionary War the thirteen legislatures had ridden to the farmers' rescue. They had allowed debtors to satisfy their creditors with property—even pine barrens and "old Horses"—instead of hard money (gold and silver). In some cases public officials had temporarily shut down the legal system that was the neglected creditor's only recourse. Worst of all, Congress and every state assembly had funded the war effort partly by printing paper money. They emitted far more currency than the economy could bear, and the result was runaway inflation. In several states a person who owed £1000 could get out of the debt with money that was actually worth only £1. Even after peace was declared in 1783, seven state legislatures printed additional currency.

The state governments also had debtors of their own to worry about. In most states thousands of citizens were behind on their taxes. Just like private debtors, delinquent taxpayers had received too much indulgence from state officials, the Framers believed. What may have seemed like a strictly state-level concern actually had national implications, since Congress relied upon the states for its own funding. The Articles of Confederation delegated the power of raising "Continental" funds to the thirteen state assemblies. To many Americans it seemed the states had botched this task. They knew why, too: representatives were reluctant to load their constituents down with burdensome federal taxes.

Tax relief crippled government operations. Even worse, it prevented public officials from meeting their single largest obligation, namely servicing the enormous debts they had amassed during the war. When Congress and the states failed to redeem the war bonds or even pay interest on them, Madison declared in *Federalist* Number 10, the owners of the securities were not the only ones who suffered. By begetting a "prevailing and increasing distrust of public engagements," this terrible "injustice" had doomed the state and federal governments themselves.

For men like Madison, writing the Constitution was like appealing an unfavorable jury verdict to a higher court. If the thirteen state legislatures could not muster the fortitude to crack down on delinquent debtors and taxpayers, they reasoned, they would create a national government that could.

The Framers believed the only way to prevent state assemblymen from giving the taxpayer a free ride was to get them out of the business of collecting—or not collecting—"Continental" taxes. Article I, Section 8 gave the national government what it had never had before, its own power to tax. Article I, Section 10 imposed a similar crackdown on private debtors. It prohibited the states from rescuing farmers by issuing paper money or by "impairing the obligation of contracts" using any of the other devices they had discovered during the 1780s.

As a result of the protection that Section 10 afforded creditors, more people proclaimed that clause "the best in the Constitution" than any other in the document. Section 10 was even touted as "the soul of the Constitution." Virginia governor Edmund Randolph pronounced Section 10 "a great favourite of mine." Nothing, in the whole Federal Constitution, is more necessary than this very section," a New Jersey Federalist claimed. Two prominent Pennsylvanians, attorney James Wilson and physician Benjamin Rush, independently reached the conclusion that even if the Constitution did nothing more than ban paper money, that alone would still, in Rush's words, be "eno' to recommend it to honest men."

Rush was exaggerating, of course, but suppose for a moment that the Constitution had contained no other provisions besides those found in Sections 8 and 10 of Article I. The danger would have remained that the new national government would itself go easy on debtors and taxpayers—or at least look the other way when the states did so. It was largely in order to eliminate these possibilities that the Framers made the Constitution considerably less responsive to the popular will than any of the states. *Only* one element of the new government, the House of Representatives, would be elected directly by the people, and its initiatives could be derailed by the senators (who would not be chosen directly by the voters until 1913), the president, or the Supreme Court. Whereas most state legislators and even governors had to run for reelection every year, presidents would serve for four years and senators for six. As long as they committed no crimes, judges could remain in office for life.

Even the one element of the national government that would be elected directly by the people, the House of Representatives, would be considerably less responsive to the voters than any of the state assemblies. The reason was that every congressman would represent many more voters than state legislators did. The best way to shield the government from popular pressure, Madison believed, was to "extend the sphere" of both individual election districts and the overall polity. Expanding legislative constituencies would enhance the likelihood that representatives would be wealthy men. Larger districts would also offer congressmen a measure of protection against grassroots pressure. Finally, as Madison famously pointed out in *Federalist* Number 10, the new national government would embrace much greater diversity than any of the states. With a wide variety of interests and proposals jockeying for popular support, none was likely to attract a majority. Thus members of Congress would be free to make their own decisions.

A month before writing *Federalist* Number 10, Madison privately summarized it, employing an expression he did not dare use in that public essay: "Divide et impera, the reprobated axiom of tyranny, is under certain qualifications, the only policy, by which a republic can be administered on just principles." "Divide et impera" is Latin for "divide and conquer."

It appears that by the mid-1780s the vast majority of free Americans shared James Madison's suspicion that the American Revolution had lost its way. And yet many perhaps most, ordinary citizens disagreed with him about what had gone wrong. In fact, both their diagnosis of the nation's political ills and the cures they championed were essentially the reverse of his.

This alternative perspective on the new nation's growing pains was evident even in Madison's home state of Virginia. Indeed, in May 1787, just as the Framers were gathering in Philadelphia, a Virginia tax, designed to reduce the enormous debt that the state government had run up during the Revolutionary War, pushed a group of farmers in Greenbrier County (now part of West Virginia) into rebellion. The leader of the revolt was a local tavern-keeper named Adonijah Mathews.

The war had brought tremendous hardship to men like Mathews, but the peace that followed was, in many ways, even worse. As late as the summer of 1787 the Greenbrier settlements still endured occasional attacks from Native American war parties. Indians were not the settlers' most serious concern, however. The state government sided with the land speculation firms that claimed hundreds of thousands of acres in western counties like Greenbrier, mandating, according to one petition, that the farmers' money be "Extorted" from them by the land jobbers. And yet even land speculation was not the greatest threat. In the 1780s Virginians believed they paid "greater Taxes than any people under the Sun."

In the spring of 1787 Greenbrier farmers tried to redress their grievances. First "some Ilminded person or persons" burned down the county jail. Then at the May meeting of the county court, at least a hundred and fifty Greenbrier citizens signed an "Instrument of Writing" in which they pronounced themselves victims of "Great oppressions." The associators vowed "not to pay the certificate tax"—a special levy aimed at calling in war bonds. The certificate tax required each householder to turn in a certain number of war bonds for every worker under his or her roof. It also taxed property and several specific activities—including tavern-keeping, which may explain why Mathews rose to the forefront of the antitax movement. After "binding themselves to stand by each other, in preventing the Sheriff from taking their property for debt or taxes," the Greenbrier associators "sent copies of the association paper to the other back counties." It was also reported that they had made a still more radical agreement. When the county justices gathered for their August 1787 session, an opponent of the rebellion claimed, the rebels planned to "prevent the Court from Sitting."

Inevitably the Greenbrier uprising put gentry Virginians in mind of the farmers' revolt that had broken out less than a year earlier in Massachusetts. Bay State leaders had made the mistake of blaming the 1786 insurgency on a single charismatic leader—they christened it "Shays's Rebellion," and the name stuck—and officials in Virginia made a similar assumption, ascribing their own backcountry revolt to Mathews, who had recently been successfully sued for debt.

Adonijah Mathews probably never met James Madison. Yet these two Virginians' conflicting views neatly encapsulated the state-level controversies that led to the adoption of the U.S. Constitution. Both what Adonijah Mathews demanded from the House of Delegates (tax relief) and the mechanism by which he sought it (rebellion) indicate that his analysis of the economic and political plight of the United States during the Confederation period was diametrically opposed to the viewpoint that men like James Madison were just then expressing as they themselves rebelled against the state governments of the 1780s by writing the Constitution. Even as the Framers lamented that excessive democracy—an overreliance on the popular will—had turned the United States into a farmers' paradise, many of the farmers themselves complained that they could redress their many grievances only by taking up arms. . . .

From the complex struggles of the 1780s, the Founding Fathers extracted a simple lesson: that the uneducated farmers who seized the ship of state during the American Revolution had damn near driven it aground. From the Founders' perspective, the policies adopted by the state legislatures in the 1780s proved that ordinary Americans were not entirely capable of ruling themselves.

The Framers wove that message right into the fabric of the nation's founding document, and it remains there still. Indeed, the period between Philadelphia's two great signing ceremonies—for the Declaration of Independence in 1776 and for the Constitution in 1787—is often put on display alongside such tragedies as slavery and the persecution of ethnic and religious minorities, to illustrate the dangers of democracy.

But many Americans who lived through the postwar era—probably, in fact, the vast majority of them—saw things differently. They admitted that the state assemblies had badly damaged the American economy. In sharp contrast to the future Framers of the Constitution, however, they attributed the recession of the 1780s to elite, not popular, misrule. . . .

A host of the Framers' contemporaries—men and women whose names have long since been forgotten—were firmly convinced that the recession that followed the Revolutionary War could have been ended without making the United States a less democratic country. Better than we do today, those ordinary farmers understood what was at stake in this great contest. Far from simply griping about particular policies, they were making the case that they possessed the ability to govern themselves.

PRIMARY SOURCES

The primary sources in this section are from debates about economic conditions in the states, debates from the Constitutional Convention, and arguments in favor of and opposed to the Constitution. As you read and analyze these sources, consider what they reveal about the Founding Fathers' motives and whether they support Holton's argument or offer an alternative explanation for the framing of the Constitution.

2, 3

Under the Articles of Confederation, states had the power to issue money. Meanwhile, a severe depression caused by the Revolutionary War had left small debtor farmers with lower crop prices and little money to pay for loans or taxes. In many states, therefore, cash-starved debtors clamored to have their state governments print depreciated paper money and pass laws enabling them to postpone debt payments to creditors. From New York and Rhode Island to South Carolina and Georgia, paper money advocates won out. More than $5,800,000 in such money was emitted by the states in the two years before the Constitutional Convention. This agitation had sparked a fierce debate in the states. "Curtius" and "Willing to Learn," the anonymous authors of these two identically named newspaper essays, take opposing sides in the debate in New Jersey. What are their respective arguments regarding debt forgiveness and the printing of paper money? What does each see as the dangers to the nation of the other's position? Do the arguments in each source apply to the situation facing debtors and creditors today?

"Honesty Is the Best Policy" (1786)
"CURTIUS"

Softly good friend—How came you in debt? "Why we have purchased farms when we had not a shilling in our pockets, these we have secured to the persons from whom we had them, and now the unconscionable mortgagee would take them from us, and we shall be ruined." If you have not paid for those farms you have not bought them, and it is as equitable that you should be ruined. . . . Did the state of New Jersey tell you to involve yourselves? What business had you to buy the land, (or rather steal it, for buy it you did not, since there has been no payment made) when you did not foresee the least probability of clearing yourselves from the incumbrance! . . . You are in debt, and there are ways and means to get out of it, without demolishing public credit for your rescue. . . . The better way would be, by discountenancing every thing that is dishonest, and uniting with those who feel for the real interest of their country, join in every measure that will tend to restore confidence, and confidence once restored their remedy is at hand, the HONEST AND INDUSTRIOUS will never suffer. Deducing, therefore, from the foregoing premises, the inutility of the proposed expedient, a wise and virtuous legislature, cannot conceive themselves authorized, however popular the plan, to enforce the measure.

Source: Jack P. Greene, ed., *Colonies to Nation: 1763–1789* (New York: McGraw-Hill Book Company, 1967), pp. 483–484, 485, 487, 489–490; originally from The *Political Intelligencer, And New-Jersey Advertiser* (New Brunswick and Elizabeth Town), January 4, 1786.

"Honesty Is the Best Policy" (1786)
"WILLING TO LEARN"

I need only appeal to every person's knowledge.

1st. Every one who has observed must know that it has been the custom for many years past, for industrious husbandsmen and mechanics to take

Source: Jack P. Greene, ed., *Colonies to Nation: 1763–1789* (New York: McGraw-Hill Book Company, 1967), pp. 490, 491, 492, 495; originally from The Political Intelligencer, And New-Jersey Advertiser (New Brunswick and Elizabeth Town), January 25, 1787.

money on loan to purchase land and build with, and furnish themselves with materials to work with at their occupation, and thereby they commonly became useful members of the community, and if a creditor called for his money before the debtor could gain it by industry, he could generally procure it on lean of some other person which has given encouragement to those who are now in debt, to become debtors.

2d. It is also known that it has ever been countenanced by our legislature, and by all those men who now hold obligations in their hands, by which they are destroying so many honest industrious members of the community, else how came those obligations in their hands?

3d. It is also well known that the moneyed-men have agreed jointly and severally in a great combination not to let their money on loan, but confine it within their own coffers.

4th. And likewise it is known that the moneyed-men are generally demanding the payment of their debts at this time when they themselves have put it out of the power of the debtor to pay it by the aforesaid hording the money. And the moneyed-men, not yet satisfied, are pressing the matter farther, and wishing for a greater advantage to grind the face of the needy, perhaps thinking that they are honestly providing for their own families; that they may set their nest on high and not be under the necessity of getting their bread by industry, but live by the labour of the honest farmer and mechanic, without being any service to church or state, but that of holding the purse in unrighteous hands—rioting in luxury by means of oppression, and living in idleness by other men's toils.

And seeing this is the true state of the case between the creditor and debtor, it is in vain to tell him "Softly, good friend, how came you in debt; what business had you to buy the land or rather steal it, for buy it you did not?" . . .

Curtius says, "let confidence be restored, it is the best of all funds and then let money be struck."

It is impossible to restore confidence without first striking money, for money is not to be had and many of the honestest men by frequent disappointment, are under the necessity of breaking their engagements, and failing in payment and in fact are become unable to pay money according to their promise; why the man you say is dishonest, he promises and does not perform, you say, no favor ought to be shewn him, you prosecute him and confiscate his estate.

But let money be struck, and he will receive his debts, and manifest an ever ready responsibility to all lawful demands, and the greatest punctuality in the payment of his debts, and by money being circulated, there will be a ready money market, so that the poorest mechanic, if industrious, may be a punctual pay master. . . .

4   By 1786, the pro-creditor policies of the Massachusetts state government
had spurred numerous petitions from poor, debtor farmers in the western
portion of the state. In the following document, farmers from the western
Massachusetts town of Greenwich petitioned the legislature for the issuance of
paper money. According to the petitioners, why is such money necessary?

"Half Our Inhabitants . . . Will Become Bankrupt" (1786)*

To the Honourable Senate and the House of Representatives in General
Court assembled att their next session:

A Petition of the Subscribers humbly sheweth—

That in the time of the late war, being desirous to defend secure and promote
the wrights and liberties of the people, we spared no pains but freely granted all
that aid and assistance of every kind that our civel fathers required of us.

We are sencable also that a great debt is justly brought upon us by the war
and are as willing to pay our shares towards itt as we are to injoy our shars
in independancy and constatutional priviledges in the Commonwealth, if itt
was in our power. And we beleve that if prudant mesuers ware taken and a
moderate quantety of medium to circulate so that our property might sel for
the real value we mite in proper time pay said debt.

But with the greatest submittion we beg leave to informe your Honours that
unles something takes place more favourable to the people, in a little time att
least, one half of our inhabitants in our oppinion will become banckerupt—
how can itt be otherwise—the constables are dayly [selling] our property both
real and personal, our land after itt is [appraised] by the best judges under oath
is sold for about one third of the value of itt, our cattle about one half the
value, the best [E]nglesh hay thirteen shilings per tone. . . . And we beg leave
further to informe your honours that att suits law are very numerous and
the attorneys in our oppinion very extravigent and oppressive in their demands. And when we compute the taxes laid upon us the five preceeding
years: the state and county, town and wartime taxes, the amount is equil
to what our farms will rent for. Sirs, in this situation what have we to live
on—no money to be had; our estates dayly posted and sold, as above described. What can your honours ask of us unles a paper curancy or some
other medium be provided so that we may pay our taxes and debts. Suerly
your honours are not strangers to the distresses of the people but doe know

Source: Samuel Eliot Morison, *Sources and Documents Illustrating the American Revolution
1764–1788 and the Formation of the Federal Constitution* (New York: Oxford University Press,
1965), pp. 208–210.

*Frequent misspellings in this source are part of the original text.

that many of our good inhabitants are now confined in [Jail] for debt and for taxes; maney have fled, others wishing to flee to the State of New York or some other State; and we believe that for two years past four inhabitents have removed from this State to some other State to one that has come from some other State to settle in this State.

Honoured Sirs, are not these imprisonments and fleeing away of our good inhabitents very injurious to the credit or honour of the Commonwealth? will not the people in the neighbouring States say of this State: altho the Massachusets [boast] of their fine constatution, their government is such that itt devours their inhabitents? Notwithstanding all these distresses, we hear of no abatement of sallerys, but his Excellency the Governor must be paid eleven hundred a year out of the moneys collected as before mentoned, and other sallerys and grants to other gentlemen, as your honours very well know. Iff these things are honest, just and rite, we sincearly wish to be convinced of itt but we honestly confess itt is beyond our skill to reconsile these sallerys and grants with the principles of our Constatution. . . .

Jeremiah Powers.

Nehemiah Stebbins,

Zebedee Osborn

January 16th 1786.   *[and 57 other signatures].*

5   When the Massachusetts legislature refused to respond to popular pressures for paper money, debt-ridden small farmers rose in an armed rebellion led by Daniel Shays, a Revolutionary War veteran. Although the rebellion dissipated after rebels engaged state forces in several skirmishes, news of it traveled quickly through the other states. In this letter to Henry Knox of Massachusetts, George Washington recorded his thoughts upon receiving word about the uprising against a state government. What dangers does Washington see in such disturbances? What does he see as a remedy to them?

George Washington Reacts to Shays's Rebellion (1786)

My dear Sir,

* * * I feel, my dear General Knox, infinitely more than I can express you, for the disorders, which have arisen in these States. Good God! Who, besides a Tory, could have foreseen, or a Briton predicted them? Were these people

Source: Jack P. Greene, ed., *Colonies to Nation: 1763–1789* (New York: McGraw Hill, 1967), pp. 507–508; originally from Worthington Chauncey Ford, ed., *The Writings of George Washington* (14 vols., 1889–1893), XI, pp. 103–107.

wiser than others, or did they judge of us from the corruption and depravity of their own hearts? The latter I am persuaded was the case and that notwithstanding the boasted virtue of America we are very little if anything behind them in dispositions to every thing that is bad.

I do assure you, that even at this moment, when I reflect upon the present prospect of our affairs, it seems to me to be like the vision of a dream. My mind can scarcely realize it as a thing in actual existence; so strange . . . does it appear to me. In this, as in most other matters, we are too slow. When this spirit first dawned, probably it might have been easily checked; but it is scarcely within the reach of human ken, at this moment, to say when, where, or how it will terminate. There are combustibles in every State, which a spark might set fire to. . . .

In both your letters you intimate, that the men of reflection, principle, and property in New England, feeling the inefficacy of their present government, are contemplating a change; but you are not explicit with respect to its nature. It has been supposed, that the constitution of the State of Massachusetts was amongst the most energetic in the Union. May not these disorders then be ascribed to an indulgent exercise of the powers of administration? If your laws authorized, and your powers are equal to the suppression of these tumults in the first instance, delay and unnecessary expedients were improper. These are rarely well applied; and the same causes would produce similar effects in any form of government, if the powers of it are not exercised. I ask this question for information. I know nothing of the facts.

That Great Britain will be an unconcerned spectator of the present insurrections, if they continue, is not to be expected. That she is at this moment sowing the seeds of jealousy and discontent among the various tribes of Indians on our frontiers, admits of no doubt in my mind; and that she will improve every opportunity to foment the spirit of turbulence within the bowels of the United States, with a view of distracting our governments and promoting divisions, is with me not less certain. Her first manoeuvres in this will no doubt be covert, and may remain so till the period shall arrive when a decided line of conduct may avail her. . . . We ought not therefore to sleep nor to slumber. Vigilance in watching and vigor in acting is become in my opinion indispensably necessary. If the powers are inadequate, amend or alter them; but do not let us sink into the lowest state of humiliation and contempt, and become a by-word in all the earth. I think with you, that the spring will unfold important and distressing scenes, unless much wisdom and good management is displayed in the interim. . . .

---

6   This selection presents different opinions of delegates at the Constitutional Convention on popular representation in the House of Representatives, referred to here as the "first branch," "larger branch," or "most numerous branch." On what grounds do they argue for or against direct election by the "people" of this body within the government?

The Founding Fathers Debate the Establishment of Congress (1787)

Thursday, May 31

Resol: 4. first clause "that the members of the first branch of the National Legislature ought to be elected by the people of the several States" being taken up,

Mr. Sherman opposed the election by the people, insisting that it ought to be by the State Legislatures. The people he said, immediately should have as little to do as may be about the Government. They want [lack] information and are constantly liable to be misled.

Mr. Gerry The evils we experience flow from the excess of democracy. The people do not want virtue, but are the dupes of pretended patriots. In Massts. it had been fully confirmed by experience that they are daily misled into the most baneful measures and opinions by the false reports circulated by designing men, and which no one on the spot can refute. One principal evil arises from the want of due provision for those employed in the administration of Governmt. It would seem to be a maxim of democracy to starve the public servants. He [Mr. Gerry] mentioned the popular clamour in Massts. for the reduction of salaries and the attack made on that of the Govt. though secured by the spirit of the Constitution itself. He had he said been too republican heretofore: he was still however republican, but had been taught by experience the danger of the levelling spirit.

Mr. Mason argued strongly for an election of the larger branch by the people. It was to be the grand depository of the democratic principle of the Govts. It was, so to speak, to be our House of Commons—It ought to know & sympathise with every part of the community; and ought therefore to be taken not only from different parts of the whole republic, but also from different districts of the larger members of it, which had in several instances particularly in Virga., different interests and views arising from difference of produce, of habits &c &c. He admitted that we had been too democratic but was afraid we . . . incautiously run into the opposite extreme. We ought to attend to the rights of every class of people. He had often wondered at the indifference of the superior classes of society to this dictate of humanity & policy; considering that however affluent their circumstances, or elevated their situations, might be, the course of a few years, not only might but certainly would, distribute their posterity throughout the lowest classes of Society. Every selfish motive therefore, every family attachment,

Source: Gaillard Hunt and James Brown Scott, eds., *The Debates in the Federal Convention of 1787 Which Framed the Constitution of the United States* (New York: Oxford University Press, 1920), pp. 31–33.

ought to recommend such a system of policy as would provide no less carefully for the rights and happiness of the lowest than of the highest orders of Citizens.

Mr. Wilson contended strenuously for drawing the most numerous branch of the Legislature immediately from the people. He was for raising the federal pyramid to a considerable altitude, and for that reason wished to give it as broad a basis as possible. No government could long subsist without the confidence of the people. In a republican Government, this confidence was peculiarly essential. He also thought it wrong to increase the weight of the State Legislatures by making them the electors of the national Legislature. All interference between the general and local Governmts. should be obviated as much as possible. On examination it would be found that the opposition of States to federal measures had proceeded much more from the officers of the States, than from the people at large.

Mr. Madison considered the popular election of one branch of the National Legislature as essential to every plan of free Government. He observed that in some of the States one branch of the Legislature was composed of men already removed from the people by an intervening body of electors. That if the first branch of the general legislature should be elected by the State Legislatures, the second branch elected by the first—the Executive by the second together with the first; and other appointments again made for subordinate purposes by the Executive, the people would be lost sight of altogether; and the necessary sympathy between them and their rulers and officers, too little felt. He was an advocate for the policy of refining the popular appointments by successive filtrations, but thought it might be pushed too far. He wished the expedient to be resorted to only in the appointment of the second branch of the Legislature, and in the Executive & judiciary branches of the Government. He thought too that the great fabric to be raised woul[d] be more stable and durable, if it should rest on the solid foundation of the people themselves, than if it should stand merely on the pillars of the Legislatures.

Mr. Gerry did not like the election by the people. The maxims taken from the British constitution were often fallacious when applied to our situation which was extremely different. Experience he said had shewn that the State legislatures drawn immediately from the people did not always possess their confidence. He had no objection however to an election by the people if it were so qualified that men of honor & character might not be unwilling to be joined in the appointments. He seemed to think the people might nominate a certain number out of which the State legislatures should be bound to choose.

Mr. Butler thought an election by the people an impracticable mode.

On the question for an election of the first branch of the national Legislature by the people.

Massts. ay. Connect. divd. N. York ay. N. Jersey no. Pena. ay. Delawe. divd. Va. ay. N. C. ay. S. C. no. Georg[i]a. ay.

> 7

In this source, "Montezuma," an anonymous author in a Philadelphia newspaper, uses mockery to attack the Federalists' motives for a new government. Note how he associates the structure of the proposed government with anti-democratic views on the part of the Founders.

An Antifederalist Mocks the "Aristocratic Party" (1787)

We the Aristocratic party of the United States, lamenting the many inconveniencies to which the late confederation subjected the *well-born*, the *better kind* of people, bringing them down to the level of the *rabble*, . . . submit to *our friends* in the first class for their inspection, the following defense of our *monarchical, aristocratical democracy*.

1st. As a majority of all societies consist of men who (though totally incapable of thinking or acting in governmental matters) are more readily led than driven, we have thought meet to indulge them in something like a democracy in the new constitution, which part we have designated by the popular name of the House of Representatives. But to guard against every possible danger from this *lower house*, we have subjected every bill they bring forward, to the double negative of our *upper house* and president. Nor have we allowed the *populace* the right to elect their representatives annually . . . lest this body should be too much under the influence and control of their constituents. . . . We have so interwoven continental and state legislatures that they cannot exist separately; whereas we in truth only leave them the power of electing us, for what *can* a provincial legislature do when we possess the exclusive regulation of external and internal commerce, excise, duties, imposts, post-offices and roads; when we and we alone, have the power to wage war, make peace, coin money (if we can get bullion) if not, borrow money, organize the militia and call them forth to execute our decrees, and crush insurrections assisted by a noble body of veterans subject to our nod, which we have the power of raising and keeping even in the time of peace. What have we to fear from state legislatures or even from states, when we are armed with such powers, with a president at our head?. . . I repeat it, what have we to fear armed with such powers, with a president at our head who is captain-general of the army, navy and militia of the United States, who can make and unmake treaties, appoint and commission ambassadors and other ministers, who can grant or refuse reprieves or pardons, who can make judges of the supreme and other continental courts—in short, who will be the source, the fountain of honor, profit and power, whose influence like the rays of the sun, will diffuse itself far and wide, will exhale all *democratical* vapors and break the *clouds of popular insurrection?*. . .

Source: Morton Borden, ed., *The Antifederalist Papers* (East Lansing: Michigan State University Press, 1965), pp. 20–21, 22, 23; originally from *Independent Gazetter,* October, 17, 1787.

We have said nothing about a bill of rights, for we viewed it as an eternal clog upon our designs, as a lock chain to the wheels of government. . . . We have for some time considered the freedom of the press as a great evil—it spreads information, and begets a licentiousness in the people which needs the rein more than the spur; besides, a daring printer may expose the plans of government and lessen the consequence of our president and senate—for these and many other reasons we have said nothing with respect to the "right of the people to speak and publish their sentiments". . . Impressed with a conviction that this constitution is calculated to restrain the influence and power of the LOWER CLASS— to draw that *discrimination* we have so long sought after; to secure to our friends *privileges and offices*, which were not to be . . . [obtained] under the former government, because they were in common; to take the burden of *legislation and attendance on public business* off the commonalty, who will be much better able thereby to prosecute with effect their private business; to destroy that *political thirteen-headed monster*, the state sovereignties; to check the *licentiousness* of the people by making it dangerous to *speak or publish* daring or tumultuary sentiments; to enforce obedience to laws by a *strong executive*, aided by *military pensioners*; and finally to promote the public and private interests of the *better kind* of people—we submit it to your judgment to take such measures for its adoption as you in your wisdom may think fit.

Signed by unanimous order of the lords spiritual and temporal.

MONTEZUMA

---

8 In this source from the debates over the ratification of the Constitution in the Pennsylvania State Ratifying Convention, Federalist James Wilson explains the single most important accomplishment of the Constitution. What does his explanation reveal about the concerns of one Founder?

A Founder Defends the Constitution's Restraints (1787)

I shall conclude at present, and I have endeavored to be as concise as possible, with mentioning, that in my humble opinion, the powers of the general government are necessary, and well defined—that the restraints

Source: Merrill Jensen, ed., *The Documentary History of the Ratification of the Constitution,* (Madison: State Historical Society of Wisconsin, 1976), vol. II, pp. 498–499.

imposed on it, and those imposed on the state governments, are rational and salutary, and that it is entitled to the approbation of those for whom it was intended. . . .

Permit me to make a single observation in this place on the restraints placed on the state governments. If only the following lines were inserted in this Constitution, I think it would be worth our adoption: "No state shall hereafter *emit bills of credit*; make any thing, but gold and silver coin, a *tender* in payment of debts; pass any bills of attainder; ex post facto law; or *law impairing the obligation of contracts*." Fatal experience has taught us, dearly taught us, the value of these restraints. What is the consequence even at this moment? It is true we have no tender law in Pennsylvania; but the moment you are conveyed across the Delaware you find it haunts your journey and follows close upon your heels. The paper passes commonly at twenty-five or thirty percent discount. How insecure is property!

These are a few of those properties in this system, that I think recommend it to our serious attention, and will entitle it to receive the adoption of the United States. Others might be enumerated, and others still will probably be disclosed by experience.

9   Matthew Locke sat in the Continental Congress and was a member of the North Carolina State Ratifying Convention. A farmer who represented the state's small western farmers, he feared that the Constitution concentrated too much power in the central government. How does he defend his state's emission of paper money after the Revolution, a power that the new Constitution would strip from the states?

"An Antifederalist Defends Paper Money" (1787)

I fear greatly for this state, and for other states. I find there has a considerable stress been laid upon the injustice of laws made heretofore. Great [opinions] are thrown on this state for making paper money. I wish those gentlemen who made those observations would consider the necessity which compelled us in a great measure to make such money. I never thought the law which authorized it a good law. If the evil could have been avoided, it would have been a very bad law; but necessity, sir, justified it in some degree. . . . Necessity compelled our [legislature] to pass the law,

From Jonathan Elliot, ed., *The Debates in the Several State Conventions on the Adoption of the Federal Constitution*, Vol. IV (1836).

in order to save vast numbers of people from ruin. I hope to be excused in observing that it would have been hard for our late Continental army to lay down their arms, with which they had valiantly and successfully fought for their country, without receiving or being promised and assured of some compensation for their past services. . . . Congress was unable to pay them, but passed many resolutions and laws in their favor, particularly one that each state should make up the depreciation of the pay of the Continental [regular troops], who were distressed for the want of an adequate compensation for their services. This state could not pay her proportion in specie. To have laid a tax for that purpose would have been oppressive. What was to be done? The only expedient was to pass a law to make paper money, and make it a tender. The Continental [regular troops were] satisfied, and approved of the measure, it being done at their instance in some degree. . . . notwithstanding it was supposed to be highly beneficial to the state, it is found to be injurious to it. Saving expense is a very great object, but this incurred much expense. This subject has for many years embroiled the state; but the situation of the country, and the distress of the people are so great, that the public measures must be accommodated to their circumstances with peculiar delicacy and caution, or another insurrection may be the consequence. . . .

10 The *Federalist* was a collection of documents written by James Madison, John Jay, and Alexander Hamilton to win ratification of the Constitution in New York State. In Federalist #10, Madison explains why liberty is better protected in a large republic than in a smaller, more democratic state. As you read, determine whether Madison's concerns about factions were exclusively economic in nature.

Federalist #10 (1788)

JAMES MADISON

Among the numerous advantages promised by a well-constructed Union, none deserves to be more appreciated than its tendency to break and control the violence of class interest, or faction. The advocate of popular governments never finds himself so much alarmed for their character and fate as when he contemplates their weakness for this dangerous vice.

Source: Excerpted from *The Federalist Papers: A Contemporary Selection,* Abridged and Edited by Lester DeKloster. Copyright © 1976 Wm. B. Eerdmans Publishing Co. Used by permission.

The instability, injustice, and confusion introduced by faction into public councils have, in truth, been the mortal diseases under which popular governments have everywhere perished.

By a faction I understand a number of citizens, whether amounting to a majority or minority of the whole, who are united and actuated by some common impulse of passion, or of interest, adverse to the rights of other citizens, or to the permanent and aggregate interests of the community. . . .

From the protection of differing and unequal abilities for the acquiring of property, there results the possession of different degrees and kinds of property; and from the influence of these differences there follows a division of society into different interests and parties.

The causes of faction are thus sown in the very nature of man. A zeal for different opinions concerning religion, concerning government and on many other points; an attachment to different leaders ambitiously contending for pre-eminence and power: these have divided mankind into parties, inflamed them with mutual animosity, and made them much more disposed to vex and to oppress each other than to co-operate for their common good. Even the most frivolous and fanciful distinctions have been sufficient to kindle the most unfriendly passions and to excite the most violent conflicts.

Withal, the most common and durable source of factions has ever been the unequal distribution of property. Those who hold as opposed to those who are without property have ever formed distinct interests in society. Those who are creditors, and those who are debtors, likewise share different concerns. A landed interest, a manufacturing interest, a mercantile interest, a moneyed interest, with many lesser interests, grow up of necessity in civilized nations, and divide them into different classes, actuated by different sentiments and views. The regulation of these various and interfering interests forms the principal task of modern legislation, and involves the spirit of party and faction in the necessary and ordinary operations of government. . . .

A common passion or interest will, in almost every case, be felt by a majority of the whole; and there is nothing to check the inducements to sacrifice the weaker party or individual. Hence it is that such pure democracies have ever been spectacles of turbulence and contention; have ever been found incompatible with personal security or the rights of property; and have in general been as short in their lives as they have been violent in their deaths. . . .

A republic, on the other hand, by which I mean a government in which a scheme of representation takes place, opens a different prospect and promises the cure for which we are seeking. Let us examine the points in which it varies from pure democracy, and we shall comprehend both the nature of the cure and the efficacy it must derive from the Union.

The two great points of difference between a pure democracy and a republic are: first, the delegation of the government in a republic to a smaller number of citizens elected by the rest; secondly, the greater number of citizens and greater sphere of country over which the republic may be thus extended.

The effect of the first difference is, on the one hand, to refine and enlarge the public views by passing them through the medium of a chosen body of citizens, whose wisdom may best discern the true interest of their country and whose patriotism and love of justice will be least likely to sacrifice it to temporary or partial considerations. Under such conditions it may well happen that the public voice, pronounced by the representatives of the people, will be more consonant to the public good than if pronounced by the people themselves. It is possible, of course, that the effect may unhappily be inverted. Men of factious tempers, of local prejudices or of sinister designs, may, by intrigue, by corruption, or by other means, first obtain the votes and then betray the interests of the people. The question resulting is, then, whether small or extensive republics are most favorable to the election of proper guardians of the public weal; and it is clearly decided in favor of the larger.

For, as each representative will be chosen by a greater number of citizens in the large than in the small republic, it will be more difficult for unworthy candidates to practise with success the vicious arts by which elections are too often carried. Moreover, the suffrages of the people being more free, they will be more likely to center on men who possess the most attractive merit and the most diffusive and established characters.

Hence, it clearly appears that the same advantage which a republic has over a pure democracy in controlling the effects of faction is enjoyed by a large over a small republic—is enjoyed, that is, by the Union over the States composing it. . . .

The influence of factious leaders may kindle a flame within their particular States but will be unable to spread a general conflagration through the other States. A religious sect may degenerate into a political faction in a part of the United States, but the variety of sects dispersed over the entire face of the nation must secure the national councils against any danger from that source. A rage for paper money, for an abolition of debts, for an equal division of property, or for any improper or wicked project, will be less apt to pervade the whole body of the Union than a particular member of it, in the same proportion as such a malady is more likely to taint a particular county or district than an entire State.

In the extent and proper structure of the Union, therefore, we behold a republican remedy for the diseases most incident to republican government.

In this source, Alexander Hamilton deplores the condition of the nation under the Articles of Confederation. What threats to the nation does he perceive? Does this source support the argument in the secondary source that democratic practices of the states were the primary concern of the Founders?

Federalist #15 (1788)
ALEXANDER HAMILTON

We may indeed with propriety be said to have reached almost the last stage of national humiliation. There is scarcely any thing that can wound the pride, or degrade the character of an independent nation, which we do not experience. Are there engagements to the performance of which we are held by every tie respectable among men? These are the subjects of constant and unblushing violation. Do we owe debts to foreigners and to our own citizens contracted in a time of imminent peril, for the preservation of our political existence? These remain without any proper or satisfactory provision for their discharge. Have we valuable territories and important posts in the possession of a foreign power, which by express stipulations ought long since to have been surrendered? These are still retained, to the prejudice of our interests not less than of our rights. . . . Are we entitled by nature and compact to a free participation in the navigation of the Mississippi? Spain excludes us from it. Is public credit an indispensable resource in time of public danger? We seem to have abandoned its cause as desperate and irretrievable. Is commerce of importance to national wealth? Ours is at the lowest point of declension. Is respectability in the eyes of foreign powers a safeguard against foreign encroachments? The imbecility of our Government even forbids them to treat with us: Our ambassadors abroad are the mere pageants of mimic sovereignty. Is a violent and unnatural decrease in the value of land a symptom of national distress? The price of improved land in most parts of the country is much lower than can be accounted for by the quantity of waste land at market, and can only be fully explained by that want of private and public confidence, which are so alarmingly prevalent among all ranks and which have a direct tendency to depreciate property of every kind. Is private credit the friend and patron of industry? That most useful kind which relates to borrowing and lending is reduced within the narrowest limits, and this still more from an opinion of insecurity than from the scarcity of money.

Source: Michael Kammen, ed., *The Origins of the American Constitution: A Documentary History* (New York: Viking Penguin, 1986), pp. 158–159.

CONCLUSION

Historians' efforts to pin down the Founding Fathers' motives remind us of some important points about the study of history. First, because their sources may support more than one conclusion, historians often do not agree on answers to many questions. And because they have not always agreed about the Founders' motives, our views about the founding of the Republic have never been securely fixed. In fact, historians' changing views of the Founders are a reminder that each generation writes its own history. In the early twentieth century, for instance, historian Charles Beard turned to the past with a Progressive-era conviction that discovering hidden economic motives was necessary both to understand the past and to change the present. Later historians, however, did not often share that conviction.

The question of the Founders' motives is also a reminder that historical questions cannot be neatly separated from one another. As Woody Holton demonstrates in Source 1, conclusions about the motives of the Founding Fathers depend in large part on one's assessment of the conditions under the Articles of Confederation: What those conditions were, what was responsible for them, and whether they were as bad as the Federalists claimed. Answers to these questions, in turn, depend on the historical sources we use to understand the past. Holton argues that historians too often rely on sources generated by the Federalists. And those sources, he says, reflect a biased Federalist view regarding conditions in the Confederation period and an unflattering picture of the common people.

Holton's final point holds one last reminder. The Founders, he says, "wove the message right into the fabric" of the Constitution that "ordinary Americans were not entirely capable of ruling themselves." Thus, even today the Confederation period is "often put on display . . . to illustrate the dangers of democracy." That view, he contends, teaches a damaging lesson—that common people should not have more control over their government. The final reminder, then, is this: The past may often *seem* to have little to do with our own lives, but the lessons that historians draw from it may actually have great relevance for our times.

FURTHER READING

Roger H. Brown, *Redeeming the Republic: Federalists, Taxation, and the Origins of the Constitution* (Baltimore: The Johns Hopkins University Press, 1993).

Richard Hofstadter, *The Progressive Historians: Turner, Beard, Parrington* (New York: Alfred A. Knopf, 1968).

Forrest McDonald, *Novus Ordo Seclorum: The Intellectual Origins of the Constitution* (Lawrence: University Press of Kansas, 1985).

Edmund S. Morgan, *Inventing the People: The Rise of Popular Sovereignty in England and America* (New York: W. W. Norton & Company, 1988).

Jack Rokove, *Original Meanings: Politics and Ideas in the Making of the Constitution* (New York: Alfred A. Knopf, 1996).

Garry Wills, *Interpreting America: The Federalist* (Garden City, N.Y.: Doubleday & Company, 1981).

NOTES

1. Richard Miller Devens, *American Progress: Or the Great Events of the Greatest Century* (Springfield, Mass.: C. A. Nichols, 1892), p. 80.
2. Charles A. Beard, *An Economic Interpretation of the Constitution of the United States* (New York: Macmillan Company, 1913), p. 292.
3. Gordon S. Wood, *The Creation of the American Republic* (New York: W. W. Norton and Company, Inc., 1969), p. 615.

Chapter
6

Ideas in History:
Race in Jefferson's Republic

The historian's essay in this chapter discusses Thomas Jefferson's racial views. The primary sources can be used to evaluate the essay's argument.

Secondary Source

1. Within the "Bowels" of the Republic (1979), RONALD T. TAKAKI

Primary Sources

2. Thomas Jefferson on Indians and Blacks (1784)
3. "Address of Little Turtle" (1802)
4. "Jefferson's Reply" (1802)
5. Thomas Jefferson on the Indians' Future (1803)
6. A Jeffersonian Treaty with the Delaware Indians (1804)
7. Indian Land Cessions (1800–1812)
8. A Denunciation of White Tyranny (1811)
9. Thomas Jefferson on Black Colonization (1801)
10. "The Virginia Legislature Debates an Emancipation Prohibition" (1806)
11. A Letter from a Man of Colour (1813)
12. A Black Response to Colonization (1817)

*E*veryone knows that "the pen is mightier than the sword." With that cliché, we often acknowledge the influence of ideas. Historians must do more than that, however, to understand the past. They have to *demonstrate* the power of ideas. Usually, that is not easy. As we saw in chapter 5, people rarely explain what influenced their behavior. Moreover, many people are unaware of the impact of ideas in their lives. As the British economist John Maynard Keynes observed, those who "believe themselves quite exempt from any intellectual influences" are often "slaves" to some moldy idea.[1]

Fortunately, the American past provides numerous opportunities to assess the influence of ideas. In early American history, there may be few better places to look for such evidence than in Thomas Jefferson's study. More than most Americans of his day—and most presidents since—Jefferson was a man of ideas. With interests that ranged from architecture to zoology, his mind was rarely at rest. His views, whether on architecture, government, society, or even zoology, were shaped by thinkers who came before him. Jefferson's own views, in turn, influenced many people in his time and after. In fact, historians have long attempted to trace and understand the enduring influences of those ideas.

Recently, some historians have shifted attention to Jefferson's views about race, specifically, his conclusions about blacks and Native Americans. Few problems engaged his thoughts more frequently than the obvious differences that he saw between whites, blacks, and Indians. Those differences were more than a curiosity, for in Jefferson's view race could not be considered apart from another problem. The author of the Declaration of Independence justified American independence with the ideas of equality and natural rights, but he feared that America's fragile experiment in self-government could survive only in a properly ordered society that promoted a virtuous citizenry. The crucial issues raised by race were whether blacks or Native Americans could ever be such citizens and what appropriate policies should be devised for each. In this chapter, then, we examine influences on Jefferson's thinking. More important, we consider his ideas about race and the status of blacks and Indians that reflected less than the Declaration's lofty sentiments.

SETTING

Modern-day visitors to Monticello—the home Thomas Jefferson designed for himself on a Virginia mountaintop—quickly learn something about the circumstances and mind of its builder. The entrance hall, where Jefferson established a museum to receive guests, provides the first clues about his wide-ranging intellectual pursuits. Walls crowded with mastadon bones and the antlers and skulls of North American mammals attest to his interest in natural history.

Various Indian artifacts, gifts from Lewis and Clark to the president who sponsored their daring expedition across the continent, stand as reminders of Jefferson's curiosity about Native Americans. The sitting room—a classroom for Jefferson's eleven grandchildren—is further proof of his interest in education, as is the library next door, home to some 7,000 volumes on history, law, and politics. Nearby, the greenhouse attests to his abiding passion for horticulture and the study to his fascination with astronomy, meteorology, and archaeology.

If Monticello reveals Jefferson's love of learning, it also demonstrates his attachment to Enlightenment ideals. There, he prominently displayed the busts of such Enlightenment thinkers as John Locke, Isaac Newton, and Voltaire. Like other eighteenth-century intellectuals, Jefferson believed that the universe was orderly and balanced, and that it operated according to certain "natural laws." It followed that these natural laws could be understood through empirical investigation. It also followed that societies and individuals in harmony with nature's laws would be guided by the ideals of order and self-control. Designed in the carefully balanced neoclassical style, Monticello itself is a study in architectural restraint. There, Jefferson spent many hours conducting experiments to understand the natural world. There, too, he carefully ordered his own life. Thus, like the busts of Enlightenment thinkers, the clock that Jefferson placed on the wall of his bed alcove was no accident. The Sage of Monticello had to know the time as soon as he awoke.

If Jefferson's home abounds with evidence of the Enlightenment's impact on its owner, it also reflects an eighteenth-century republican ideal of virtuous independence. Jefferson shared with other eighteenth-century republican thinkers a belief that property ownership and political liberties were inseparable. He also assumed that a virtuous citizenry was necessary to maintain republican government. Such citizens were property holders who supported themselves through their own labor. Possessed of independent means, they were beholden to no one. Self-controlled and guided by reason, they were the surest safeguard against irrational mobs and the tyrants who manipulated them. Because only an agricultural society provided opportunity for widespread property ownership in Jefferson's day, small or middling yeoman farmers—sturdy, industrious, and aware of their rights—represented the firmest foundation upon which to build a republic. As Jefferson declared in his *Notes on the State of Virginia*, "Corruption of morals in the mass of cultivators is a phenomenon of which no age nor nation has furnished an example."[2]

For the same reason, Alexander Hamilton's policies posed a dangerous threat to the republic because they fostered the development of cities and factories. Filled with propertyless mobs, cities were dens of vice that corrupted morals. In Europe's cities, Jefferson had witnessed hoards of such propertyless, subservient, and idle people. An economy based on manufacturing and commerce naturally led to large numbers of such citizens. Lacking the yeoman's virtues and independent means, they were easily manipulated by demagogues and tyrants. No wonder Jefferson concluded that as long as "we have land to labor . . . let us never see our citizens occupied at a workbench."[3]

Set against this ideological backdrop, Monticello was not only Jefferson's home, but also a place where he could live beholden to no man. On his mountaintop, where he produced his own food and other necessities, Jefferson had achieved on a grand scale the independence that republican society required to maintain a virtuous citizenry. Of course, he did this by making dependents of many others. On his four farms, up to 135 slaves worked in fields and shops and at household chores. Many of them lived in small rooms beneath terraces that flanked the north and south ends of Monticello, while others lived in huts along "Mulberry Row," the plantation road where the stables and workshops were located. Jefferson may have been deeply disturbed by the "abominable crime" of slavery but he never freed any of his own slaves while he lived because he was, ironically, absolutely dependent on them. Slaves provided the means to live according to Enlightenment and republican ideals. From their labor came the leisure to pursue scientific inquiry and to reason about such questions as the best way to ensure the continuation of self-government.

When Jefferson took to his study to ponder the preservation of republican society, the black slaves all around him figured prominently in his mind, as did Native Americans who inhabited the land to the west—land that would eventually have to be brought under cultivation if America were to remain an agrarian republic. Although most Indians were as far removed from Jefferson's Virginia piedmont as blacks were close at hand, Jefferson saw both groups through the same lenses of Enlightenment thought and republican ideology. Thus, he subjected both to empirical analysis as he pondered whether either was capable of fitting into an orderly republican society of rational, self-restrained, and independent citizens. Given Jefferson's eighteenth-century outlook, the prospects for either group would seem bleak, for in his mind black slaves were utter dependents and Indians utterly unrestrained.

INVESTIGATION

The colonists justified their revolt against British rule with a republican ideology based on the idea of equality and natural rights. Historians have long been curious about the impact of that ideology on Americans and their society in the early years of the new nation. In particular, they want to know how ideas unleashed by the American Revolution affected Americans' views about race and whether the Revolution brought about changes in race relations in the postrevolutionary generation. As the author of the Declaration of Independence, the third president of the United States, and a large slaveholder, Thomas Jefferson has frequently been at the center of historians' investigations of these questions. First, they want to know Jefferson's views about Native Americans and blacks and to what extent they were influenced by a republican ideology rooted in the principle of human equality. They are curious about how Jefferson dealt intellectually with his own paradoxical situation as an eloquent spokesman for liberty and a plantation owner who never personally disowned slavery. In other words, they seek to understand to what extent Jefferson's own actions were influenced by his ideas, especially given the long-standing allegations (and recent genetic evidence) regarding Jefferson's sexual relationship with his slave Sally Hemings. Second, they are curious as to what extent Jefferson's policies regarding blacks and Native Americans, as well as those of his Jeffersonian Republican successors, reflected his views. Finally, they want to know the ways in which the lives of blacks and Native Americans changed because of ideas advanced during the Revolution—ideas with whom few people are more closely associated than Jefferson himself.

Source 1 is an exploration of Jefferson's views about blacks and Native Americans. The author argues that the policies advocated by Jefferson toward both groups were influenced by a republican vision of American society. Your job, therefore, is to come to a conclusion about the connection between Jeffersonian ideas and early nineteenth-century policies regarding blacks and Native Americans. To do that, you must come to an understanding of the essay's argument about Jefferson's political and social vision and his racial views. You must then evaluate the views expressed in the primary sources regarding the place of blacks and Indians in American society. Answering the following questions will help you complete this assignment:

1. **How did Jefferson's views regarding blacks and Native Americans differ?** What accounts for the difference, according to historian Ronald Takaki, in Source 1?

2. **How were Jefferson's views about each group related to his fears about the preservation of republican society?** What policies did Jefferson advocate toward each?

3. **Do the primary sources provide evidence of Jefferson's fears about the threat posed by blacks and Indians to the republic?** What evidence do the sources provide that Jefferson's concerns were widespread or that they actually influenced policies regarding these groups?

4. **What evidence do the primary sources provide that African Americans or Native Americans themselves were influenced by ideas about race or equality in the early republic?** Do the primary sources indicate that racial prejudice became more or less rigid in this period?

Before you begin, review your textbook's analysis of the political and social impact of the American Revolution and the ideology that supported it. Also read your textbook's discussion of the Jeffersonian Republican vision of American society and the domestic policies of Jefferson and his successors, James Madison and James Monroe. Pay particular attention to what it says about the situation confronting blacks and Native Americans in the early republic and about Jeffersonian Republican policies toward these groups.

SECONDARY SOURCE

1
In this selection, historian Ronald Takaki argues that Jefferson's views of blacks and Native Americans were influenced by a vision of American society that emphasized the need for the homogeneity, moral purity, and self-control of its citizens. This vision, according to the author, led Jefferson to argue for the exclusion of one group from a "homogeneous" American society and the inclusion of the other in it. As you read this selection, note how Takaki tries to establish a link between Jefferson's vision for the republic and the specific policies that he advocated regarding each group. How do the decisions of many of Jefferson's fellow Virginia slaveholders to voluntarily free slaves in the post-Revolutionary period fit into Takaki's argument regarding Jefferson's racial fears? Also consider what significance he sees in the allegations of a sexual liaison between Jefferson and Sally Hemings. To what extent do Jefferson's actions conform to his ideas?

Within the "Bowels" of the Republic (1979)
RONALD T. TAKAKI

While an enemy is within our bowels, the first object is to expel him.
—*Thomas Jefferson,*
Notes on the State of Virginia

As he called for the expulsion of the British "enemy" from the "bowels" of the emerging nation, Jefferson used rhetoric strikingly similar . . . to express his concern for moral purity in the new republican society. . . . Many years after the British had been forced out, President Jefferson told James Monroe that he looked forward to distant times when the American continent would be covered with "a people speaking the same language, governed in similar forms, and by similar laws." Beneath this vision of America's future, which would shortly lead him to expand the republican nation through the purchase of the Louisiana, lay a rage for order, tidiness, and uniformity which

Source: Ronald T. Takaki, *Iron Cages: Race and Culture in Nineteenth-Century America* (New York: Alfred A. Knopf, 1979), pp. 36–37, 39, 42, 43–45, 46, 47, 48, 49, 50, 55–56, 58–59, 60, 61, 62, 63, 64. Copyright © 1979 by Ronald T. Takaki. Used by permission of Alfred A. Knopf, a division of Random House, Inc.

made him recoil with horror from the possibility of "either blot or mixture on that surface." The purging of the British only created greater pressures to expel other "enemies" from within the "bowels" of American society, as we shall see in an analysis of Jefferson's republican ideology, his insistence on black colonization, and his views on the assimilation of the Indian. . . .

Republicanism, in Jefferson's view, required a homogeneous population. Unless everyone could be converted into . . . what Dr. [Benjamin] Rush called "republican machines," the republic would surely disintegrate into anarchy. Like Dr. Rush, Jefferson believed peace with England did not mean the end of the Revolution. The people themselves still had to be made uniform and a consensus of values and interests established. This homogeneity might be achieved by discouraging the rapid increase of immigrants into the country. . . .

But what should be done to render the people already here into a more "homogeneous" body? Like Rush, Jefferson placed much of his faith in education. . . . [E]ducation would render the people—"the ultimate guardian of their own liberty"—independent and self-controlled.

Such education was indispensable in a society where the people ruled. Unless they were properly educated and unless they were trained to restrain vigilantly their passions, they would constitute the greatest threat to order. Indeed, like the immigrants whom Jefferson feared, they could even explode into "unbounded licentiousness" and bring down the curtains of the new republic. . . .

Unless men in America obeyed their moral sense and exercised self-control, Jefferson feared, they would "live at random" and destroy republican order. This was an especially frightening prospect in a slaveholding society where white men like Jefferson had to guard themselves not only against "the strongest of all human passions" but also against "the most boisterous passions." The possessor of inordinate power over black men and women, Jefferson recognized the need for slavemasters, free from the king and external authority, to exercise great vigilance against their own despotism. Both passions, he anxiously believed, would continue to undermine republican self-control as long as the new nation lacked complete purity and as long as blacks remained within the "bowels" of republican society. . . .

Not only did slavery, in Jefferson's view, violate the black's right to liberty, it also undermined the self-control white men had to have in a republican society. In *Notes on the State of Virginia*, he described what he believed was the pernicious influence of slavery upon republican men:

> There must doubtless be an unhappy influence on the manners of our people produced by the existence of slavery among us. The whole commerce between master and slave is a perpetual exercise of the most boisterous passions, the most unremitting despotism on the one part, and degrading submissions on the other. . . .

During the 1780s, after the enactment of the Virginia manumission law, some ten thousand slaves were given their freedom; Jefferson, however, did not manumit his own bondsmen. To have done so would have been financially disastrous for this debt-ridden planter. "The torment of mind," he cried out, "I will endure till the moment shall arrive when I shall not owe a shilling on earth is such really as to render life of little value." Dependent on the labor of his slaves to pay off his debts, Jefferson hoped he would be able to free them and "put them ultimately on an easier footing," which he stated he would do the moment "they" had paid the debts due from the estate, two-thirds of which had been "contracted by purchasing them." Unfortunately, he remained in debt until his death.

As a slavemaster, Jefferson personally experienced what he described as the "perpetual exercise of the most boisterous passions." He was capable of punishing his slaves with great cruelty. He had James Hubbard, a runaway slave who had been apprehended and returned in irons to the plantation, whipped and used as an example to the other slaves. "I had him severely flogged in the presence of his old companions," Jefferson reported. . . .

Like his fellow slaveholders, Jefferson was involved in the buying and selling of slaves and viewed them in economic terms. "The value of our lands and slaves, taken conjunctly, doubles in about twenty years," he observed casually. "This arises from the multiplication of our slaves, from the extension of culture, and increased demands for lands." His was not a merely theoretical observation: Jefferson's ownership of land and slaves made him one of the wealthiest men in his state. Yet he continued to expand his slave holdings. In 1805, he informed John Jordan that he was "endeavoring to purchase young and able negro men." His interest in increasing his slave property was again revealed in a letter to his manager regarding "a breeding woman." Referring to the "loss of 5 little ones in 4 years," he complained that the overseers did not permit the slave women to devote as much time as was necessary to the care of their children. "They view their labor as the 1st object and the raising of their children but as secondary," Jefferson continued, "I consider the labor of a breeding woman as no object, and that a child raised every 2 years is of more profit than the crop of the best laboring man." Little wonder that, by 1822, Jefferson owned 267 slaves.

Yet, despite his view of slave women as "breeders" and slave children as "profits," Jefferson insisted he would be willing to make a sacrifice and free all of his slaves, if they could be removed from the United States. "I can say," he asserted, "with conscious truth, that there is not a man on earth who would sacrifice more than I would to relieve us from this heavy reproach, in any practicable way. . . ."

Why not, Jefferson asked in *Notes on the State of Virginia*, emancipate the blacks but keep them in the state? "Deep-rooted prejudices entertained by the whites," he fearfully explained, "ten thousand recollections, by the blacks, of the injuries they have sustained; new provocations; the real distinctions which nature has made and many other circumstances, will divide us into parties, and produce convulsions, which will probably never end but in the extermination of the one or the other race." Unless colonization accompanied emancipation, whites would experience the horror of race war. Yet, unless slavery were abolished, whites would continue to face the danger of servile insurrection and the violent rage springing from "ten thousand recollections" of injuries. "As it is," Jefferson declared, "we have the wolf by the ears, and we can neither hold him, nor safely let him go. Justice is in one scale, and self-preservation in the other." The slave revolt in Santo Domingo intensified his anxieties. "It is high time we should foresee," he wrote to James Monroe in 1793, "the bloody scenes which our children certainly, and possibly ourselves (south of Potomac) have to wade through, and try to avert them." . . . The dread of slave rebellion, which Jefferson and other whites felt, was evident in the violent suppression of the Gabriel Prosser conspiracy of 1800. During the hysteria, twenty-five blacks were hanged. Five years later, Jefferson observed that the insurrectionary spirit among the slaves had been easily quelled, but he saw it becoming general and more formidable after every defeat, until whites would be forced, "after dreadful scenes and sufferings to release them in their own way. . . ." He predicted that slavery would be abolished—"whether brought on by the generous energy of our own minds" or "by the bloody process of St. Domingo" in which slaves would seize their freedom with daggers in their hands. . . .

Even if emancipation could be achieved peacefully, colonization would still be required as one of the conditions for the liberation of slaves. Though Jefferson regarded blacks as members of humankind, endowed with moral sense, he believed that blacks and whites could never coexist in America because of "the real distinctions" which "nature" had made between the two races. "The first difference which strikes us is that of color," Jefferson explained. Regardless of the origins of the Negro's skin color, this difference was "fixed in nature." "And is this difference of no importance? Is it not the foundation of a greater or less share of beauty in the two races? Are not the fine mixtures of red and white, the expressions of every passion by greater or less suffusions of color in the one, preferable to that eternal monotony, which reigns in the countenances, that immovable veil of black which covers the emotions of the other race?" To Jefferson, white was beautiful. . . .

White "superiority," for Jefferson, was also a matter of intelligence. He acknowledged that the "opinion" that blacks were "inferior" in faculties of reason and imagination had to be "hazarded with great diffidence." Evaluation of intelligence was problematical: It was a faculty which eluded the research of all the senses, the conditions of its existence were various and variously combined, and its effects were impossible to calculate. "Great tenderness," he added, was required "where our conclusion would degrade a whole race of man from the rank in the scale of beings which their Creator may perhaps have given them." Thus, Jefferson advanced it as a "suspicion" only that blacks "whether originally a distinct race, or made distinct by time and circumstances," were "inferior" to whites in the endowments of both body and mind. Jefferson stated he was willing to have his "suspicion" challenged, even refuted. . . .

In his investigation of the black's "inferior" intelligence, however, Jefferson was more interested in "proofs" which supported rather than refuted his "suspicion." . . . Unlike Rush, Jefferson did not view black "inferiority" as a consequence of slavery or as a social rather than a biological condition. Instead he seized evidence which set blacks apart as "a distinct race," and which emphasized the importance of biology over conditions or circumstances in the determination of intelligence. . . .

Jefferson's descriptions of the Negro involved more than the assertion of black intellectual inferiority: They depicted blacks as dominated by their bodies rather than their minds, by their sensations rather than their reflections. They appeared to be a libidinal race. "They [black men] are more ardent after their female; but love seems with them to be more an eager desire, than a tender delicate mixture of sentiment and sensation." Blacks, in Jefferson's mind, represented the body and the ascendancy of the instinctual life—those volcanic forces of passions he believed whites had to control in republican society.

Here, for Jefferson, in the midst of the society which had destroyed the authority of the king, expelled the enemy from its "bowels," and established a republic of self-governing men, was the presence of a race still under the rule of the passions, created with moral sense but without sufficient intelligence to serve the conscience. . . .

Still, regardless of whether blacks were to be included or excluded, Jefferson was articulating a general fear. If the republican experiment were to succeed and if the new nation were to realize the vision of a "homogeneous" republic, it had to preserve what Franklin described as the "lovely White." It must not allow its people to be "stained" and become a nation of mulattoes. "Their amalgamation with the other colour," Jefferson warned, "produces a degradation to which no lover of his country, no lover of excellence in the human character can innocently consent." If this mixture were to occur, it would surely mean that whites had lost control of themselves and their lustful passions, and had in their "unbounded licentiousness" shattered the very experiment in self-government which they had undertaken during the American Revolution.

This was precisely why the Thomas Jefferson/Sally Hemings relationship, whether imagined or actual, was so significant. If the philosopher of republicanism could not restrain what he called "the strongest of all the human passions" and if the author of jeremiads against miscegenation were guilty of "staining" the blood of white America, how could white men in the republic ever hope to be self-governing? . . .

The question of the relationship between race and republican society could not ignore the presence of the native American. Jefferson knew this, and his racial concerns did not revolve exclusively around blacks. . . . As a white expansionist and an agrarian philosopher in search of "vacant lands," Jefferson was fully conscious of the Indian's existence.

During the struggle to expel the British, Jefferson had two views of the Indian's future in the new nation: He could be civilized and assimilated, or he could be removed and possibly exterminated. Thus, Jefferson declared to the chief of the Kaskaskias that he hoped "we shall long continue to smoke in friendship together," and that "we, like you, are Americans, born in the same land, and having the same interests." Yet, at the same time, Jefferson did not hesitate to advocate removal of hostile Indians beyond the Mississippi and even total war upon them. "Nothing will reduce those wretches so soon as pushing the war into the heart of their country," he wrote angrily in 1776. "But I would not stop there. I would never cease pursuing them while one of them remained on this side [of] the Mississippi." And he went further. Quoting from the instructions the Congress had given the commissioners to the Six Nations, he continued: "We would never cease pursuing them with war while one remained on the face of the earth." His two views—civilization and extermination—were not contradictory: They were both consistent with his vision of a "homogeneous" American society.

To civilize the Indian meant, for Jefferson, to take him from his hunting way of life and convert him into a farmer. As President of the United States, he told the Potawatomies:

> We shall . . . see your people become disposed to cultivate the earth, to raise herds of the useful animals, and to spin and weave, for their food and clothing. These resources are certain: they will never disappoint you: while those of hunting may fail, and expose your women and children to the miseries of hunger and cold. We will with pleasure furnish you with implements for the most necessary arts, and with persons who may instruct you how to make and use them. . . .

Jefferson believed that Indians, like blacks and all humankind, were endowed with an innate "moral sense of right and wrong," which, like the "sense of tasting and feeling" in every man, constituted "a part of his nature." But while Jefferson assigned conscience to both the Indian and the black, he made a crucial distinction between them in the area of intelligence. "I am safe in affirming," he wrote to the Marquis de Chastellux in 1785, "that the proofs of genius given by the Indians of N. America, place them on a level with whites in the same uncultivated state. . . . I believe the Indian then to be in body and mind equal to the white man. I have supposed the black man, in his present state, might not be so." Thus, what made the Indian "equal" or potentially so was his intelligence. . . . If the Indians' circumstances could be changed, white Americans would "probably" find that the native Americans were "formed in mind as well as body, on the same module with the 'Homo sapiens Europaeus.'" Thus, in Jefferson's mind, Indians had a potential blacks did not have: They had the intelligence capable of development which could enable them to carry out the commands of their moral sense.

This meant that Indians did not have to be a "problem" in America's future: They could be assimilated and their oneness with white America would reaffirm the republican civilization and the "progress" Jefferson hoped to realize. Time and again President Jefferson called upon the Indians to intermarry and live among whites as "one people." To the Delawares, Mohicans, and Munries, he declared:

> When once you have property, you will want laws and magistrates to protect your property and persons, and to punish those among you who commit crimes. You will find that our laws are good for this purpose; you will wish to live under them, you will unite yourselves with us, join in our Great Councils and form one people with us, and we shall all be Americans; you will mix with us by marriage, your blood will run in our veins, and will spread with us over this great island.

In 1803 President Jefferson urged Colonel Benjamin Hawkins to encourage the Indians to give up hunting and turn to agriculture and household manufacture as a new way of life. Indians must learn how a little land, well cultivated, was superior in value to a great deal, unimproved. . . .

What the Indian would be required to amputate was not only his identity and culture but also his land. The civilizing of the Indian was a crucial part of Jefferson's strategy to acquire Indian land for white settlement and the expansion of white agrarian society. . . . In a "Confidential Message" to Congress in 1803, he outlined how this could be done.

> First: to encourage them to abandon hunting, to apply to the raising stock, to agriculture and domestic manufactures, and thereby prove to themselves that less land and labor will maintain them in this, better than in their former mode of living. The extensive forests necessary in the hunting life will then become useless, and they will see advantage in exchanging them for the means of improving their farms. . . . Secondly: to multiply trading-houses among them, and place within their reach those things which will contribute more to their domestic comfort than the possession of extensive but uncultivated wilds. Experience and reflection will develop to them the wisdom of exchanging what they can spare and we want, for what we can spare and they want.

So, for whites to obtain western lands the Indians must be led to agriculture, manufactures, and thus to civilization. . . .

The purchase of the Louisiana Territory in 1803 offered Jefferson the opportunity to pursue at once the two possibilities he saw for the Indian—removal and incorporation. The vast new territory, he calculated, could be "the means of tempting all our Indians on the East side of the Mississippi to remove to the West. . . ." In his draft of an amendment to the Constitution, Jefferson included a specific provision for such a removal: "The legislature of the Union shall have authority to exchange the right of occupancy in portion where the U.S. have full rights for lands possessed by Indians within the U.S. on the East side of the Mississippi: to exchange lands on the East side of the river for those . . . on the West side. . . ." Though the amendment remained in draft form, the Louisiana Territorial Act of 1804 did contain a clause which empowered the President to effect Indian emigration. Not all Indians would be "transplanted," however. If Indians chose civilization, Jefferson explained to the Cherokees, they would be allowed to remain where they were; if they chose to continue the hunter's life, they would be permitted to leave and settle on lands beyond the Mississippi. Calling the Cherokees "my children," he promised them that the United States would be the friends of both parties, and would be willing, as far as could be reasonably asked, to satisfy the wishes of both.

Still, all Indians, whether they were farmers or hunters, were subject to removal, and even extermination, if they did not behave. Should any tribe be foolhardy enough to take up the hatchet against the United States, the President wrote Governor Harrison, the federal government should seize the whole country of that tribe and drive them across the Mississippi as the only condition of peace. As Anglo-American tensions mounted in 1808, President Jefferson told the Ottawas, Chippewas, Potawatomies, and Senecas that white Americans considered them "a part of ourselves" and looked to their welfare as "our own." If they sided with the British, however, they would have to abandon forever the land of their fathers. "No nation rejecting our friendship, and commencing wanton and unprovoked war against us, shall ever after remain within our reach. . . ."

Ultimately, for Jefferson, it made no difference whether Indians were removed to the Rocky Mountains, "extirpated from the earth," or allowed to remain in the United States. Indians as Indians could not be tolerated in the republican civilization the American Revolution had created. The new nation must have a "homogeneous" population—a people with the same language and laws, good cabins and enclosed fields, owners of private property. Diversity itself was dangerous in the republican society, especially diversity which included groups and cultures close to nature and the instinctual life. . . .

Regardless of whether they were viewed in terms of their labor or their land, both blacks and Indians, for Jefferson, were under the domination of the body or the instinctual life. While both of them, like whites, were endowed with moral sense, they were both deficient in reason: Black intelligence was inferior and Indian intelligence was undeveloped. Thus both lacked the self-control and rational command Jefferson believed were essential qualities republicans and civilized men must have. In a republican society, men could not live "at random," and all behavior had to be "a matter of calculation" or else the strongest passions would overwhelm the moral sense and rationality. The hope Jefferson held for white America was the creation of a perfect society through the rule of reason and the expulsion of "enemies" from the "bowels" of the new republic.

PRIMARY SOURCES

The primary sources in this section reflect Jefferson's attitudes toward African Americans and Native Americans as well as their own views about their circumstances. As you read these sources, look for connections between Jeffersonian ideas about race and policies toward these two groups. Also consider what ideas influenced the responses of blacks and Indians to their situations.

2   In these passages from *Notes on the State of Virginia,* Jefferson reveals his view about the differences between blacks and Indians. What bearing would his conclusions about each group have on their "fitness" for life in a republican society?

Thomas Jefferson on Indians and Blacks (1784)

Before we condemn the Indians of this continent as wanting genius, we must consider that letters have not yet been introduced among them. Were we to compare them in their present state with the Europeans, north of the Alps, when the Roman arms and arts first crossed those mountains, the comparison would be unequal, because, at that time, those parts of Europe were swarming with numbers; because numbers produce emulation, and multiply the chances of improvement, and one improvement begets another. Yet I may safely ask, how many good poets, how many able mathematicians, how many great inventors in arts or sciences, had Europe, north of the Alps, then produced? And it was sixteen centuries after this before a Newton could be formed. I do not mean to deny that there are varieties in the race of man, distinguished by their powers both of body and mind. I believe there are, as I see to be the case in the races of other animals. . . .

The first difference [between blacks and Indians] which strikes us is that of color. Whether the black of the negro resides in the reticular membrane between the skin and scarf-skin, or in the scarf-skin itself; whether it proceeds from the color of the blood, the color of the bile, or from that of some other secretion, the difference is fixed in nature, and is as real as if its seat and cause were better known to us. And is this difference of no importance? Is it not the foundation of a greater or less share of beauty in the two races? Are not the fine mixtures of red and white, the expressions of every passion by greater or less suffusions of color in the one, preferable to that eternal monotony, which reigns in the countenances, that immovable veil of black

Source: Adrienne Koch and William Peden, eds., *The Life and Selected Writings of Thomas Jefferson* (New York: Random House, 1944), pp. 212–213, 256, 257, 258–259.

which covers the emotions of the other race? Add to these, flowing hair, a more elegant symmetry of form, their own judgment in favor of the whites, declared by their preference of them, as uniformly as is the preference of the Oran-utan for the black woman over those of his own species. The circumstance of superior beauty, is thought worthy [of] attention in the propagation of our horses, dogs, and other domestic animals; why not in that of man? . . .

A black after hard labor through the day, will be induced by the slightest amusements to sit up till midnight, or later, though knowing he must be out with first dawn of the morning. They are at least as brave, and more adventuresome. But this may perhaps proceed from a want of forethought, which prevents their seeing a danger till it be present. When present, they do not go through it with more coolness or steadiness than the whites. They are more ardent after their female; but love seems with them to be more an eager desire, than a tender delicate mixture of sentiment and sensation. Their griefs are transient. Those numberless afflictions, which render it doubtful whether heaven has given life to us in mercy or in wrath, are less felt, and sooner forgotten with them. In general, their existence appears to participate more of sensation than reflection. To this must be ascribed their disposition to sleep when abstracted from their diversions, and unemployed in labor. An animal whose body is at rest, and who does not reflect must be disposed to sleep of course. Comparing them by their faculties of memory, reason, and imagination, it appears to me that in memory they are equal to the whites; in reason much inferior, as I think one could scarcely be found capable of tracing and comprehending the investigations of Euclid; and that in imagination they are dull, tasteless, and anomalous. . . . Most of them, indeed, have been confined to tillage, to their own homes, and their own society; yet many have been so situated, that they might have availed themselves of the conversation of their masters; many have been brought up to the handicraft arts, and from that circumstance have always been associated with the whites. Some have been liberally educated, and all have lived in countries where the arts and sciences are cultivated to a considerable degree, and all have had before their eyes samples of the best works from abroad. The Indians, with no advantages of this kind, will often carve figures on their pages not destitute of design and merit. They will crayon out an animal, a plant, or a country, so as to prove the existence of a germ in their minds which only wants cultivation. They astonish you with strokes of the most sublime oratory; such as prove their reason and sentiment strong, their imagination glowing and elevated. But never yet could I find that a black had uttered a thought above the level of plain narration; never saw even an elementary trait of painting or sculpture. In music they are more generally gifted than the whites with accurate ears for tune and time, and they have been found capable of imagining a small catch.* Whether they will be equal to the

*A short rhythmical composition.

composition of a more extensive run of melody, or of complicated harmony, is yet to be proved. Misery is often the parent of the most affecting touches in poetry. Among the blacks is misery enough, God knows, but no poetry. Love is the peculiar work of the poet. Their love is ardent, but it kindles the senses only, not the imagination.

3, 4   Little Turtle [Mischecanocquah] was a Miami chief who had fought against General Anthony Wayne at the Battle of Fallen Timbers in 1794 near Toledo, Ohio. In early 1802, he met with President Thomas Jefferson in Washington, D.C. What problems does Little Turtle see in the application of the Treaty of Greenville, which he and other chiefs had signed after the battle? How would you characterize Jefferson's response?

"Address of Little Turtle" (1802)

Father, A Treaty was made six years since at Greenville between the President of the United States and your children the Red People.

Father, I with some of my Brethren made certain objections to that Treaty, but finally thought it best it should be signed, and we wish to adhere to it, and hope our white brethren will do so.

My Father, at that Treaty it was understood that the white people would be the fathers friends and protectors of the red People, that they would use their best endeavours to maintain friendship and good understanding between us and the United States, and we believe it has been generally attended to both by the White and Red People.

My Father, and Brothers, by the Treaty it was mentioned that certain reservations should be made for the white people in our Country that the white people should not settle over the line described by the Treaty, that no individual of the white people should be allowed to purchase any land of the Indians, nor any Indians to sell to individuals of the White people, but that when your children were willing to sell any of their lands it should be sold to the United States, which we think a very happy circumstance, because the United States will not allow their Red Brothers to be cheated.

Father some parts of the Treaty has not been so well understood as could be wished[.] [O]ne part which was not understood was mentioned to the President of the United States four years since at Philadelphia concerning the lands at Fort St. Vincenes. By the Treaty the United States were to have all the land which had before been ceded by the Indians to the English or French.

Source: Barbara B. Oberg, ed., *The Papers of Thomas Jefferson* (Princeton: Princeton University Press, 2009) Vol. 36, pp. 280–281, 282–283.

Father, we think some of the white people are settling over the line and we are fearful some of our young men may interrupt the harmony which prevails between the Red and White people, as the white people are considered out of the protection of the United States, when they settle over the line, and as the Chiefs cannot be at all places to watch over their young men. . . .

Father, by the Treaty of Greenville your children were promised a certain quantity of goods and money should be paid them annually, and this they expected would have been done.

Father, when the goods arrive your Children meet with pleasure to receive them; but father we are sorry to mention that the goods do not come in good order, that more or less of our annuities have always been unfit for use and particularly the powder, we believe it is your wish that they should be delivered in good order. . . .

Father, We wish to reap advantages from cultivating the Earth as you do, and request ploughs and other necessary tools may be put into the hands of the Interpreter at Fort Wayne to be dealt out to any who will receive and make use of them for the purpose intended.

Father, Should this request be granted nothing shall be wanting on the part of your children the Chiefs, to introduce husbandry among their children, if the United States will furnish them with the proper utensils. But Father nothing can be done to advantage unless the great Council of the Sixteen fires now assembled, will prohibit any person from selling any Spiritous Liquors among their Red Brothers.

Father, the introduction of this poison has been prohibited in our camps, but not in our Towns, where many of our Hunters, for this poison, dispose of not only their furs &ca. but frequently of their guns & Blankets and return to their families destitute.

Father, Your children are not wanting in Industry, but it is the introduction of this fatal poison, which keeps them poor. Your children have not that command over themselves you have, therefore before any thing can be done to advantage this evil must be remedied.

Father, When our White Brothers come to this land our forefathers were numerous and happy: but since their intercourse with the white people, and owing to the introduction of this fatal poison we have become less numerous and happy.

"Jefferson's Reply" (1802)

BROTHERS & FRIENDS OF THE MIAMIS, POUTEWATAMIES & WEEAUHS

I recieve with great satisfaction the visit you have been so kind as to make us at this place, and I thank the great spirit who has conducted you to us in health and safety, it is well that friends should sometimes meet, open their minds mutually, and renew the chain of affection, made by the same great spirit, and living in the same land with our brothers the red men, we consider ourselves as of the same family; we wish to live with them as one people, and to cherish their interests as our own, the evils which of necessity encompass the life of man are sufficiently numerous, why should we add to them by voluntarily distressing & destroying one another? peace, brothers, is better than war, in a long & bloody war, we lose many friends, and gain nothing, let us then live in peace and friendship together, doing to each other all the good we can, the wise and good on both sides desire this, and we must take care that the foolish and wicked among us shall not prevent it, on our part, we shall endeavor in all things to be just & generous towards you, and to aid you in meeting those difficulties which a change of circumstances is bringing on, we shall with great pleasure see your people become disposed to cultivate the earth to raise herds of the useful animals, and to spin and weave, for their food & clothing, these resources are certain: they will never disappoint you, while those of hunting may fail, and expose your women & children to the miseries of hunger & cold, we will with pleasure furnish you with implements for the most necessary arts, and with persons who may instruct you how to make and use them.

I consider it as fortunate that you have made your visit at this time when our wise men from the sixteen states are collected together in council, who being equally disposed to befriend you can strengthen our hands in the good we all wish to render you.

The several matters you opened to us in your speech the other day, and those on which you have since conversed with the Secretary at war, have been duly considered by us, he will now deliver answers, and you are to consider what he says, as if said by myself, and that what we promise we shall faithfully perform.

Th: Jefferson
Jan. 7, 1802.

Source: Barbara B. Oberg, ed., *The Papers of Thomas Jefferson* (Princeton: Princeton University Press, 2009), Vol. 36, pp. 286–287.

5   Jefferson wrote this letter to William Henry Harrison, governor of the Indiana territory. As you read it, note how Jefferson proposes to change the Indians' way of life and the advantage he sees in doing so. Also note whether he sees the Indians as brothers, or in some other relationship. How would you compare the message here to that in Source 3? Does Jefferson appear to want what is best for the Indians?

Thomas Jefferson on the Indians' Future (1803)

[T]his letter being unofficial and private, I may with safety give you a more extensive view of our policy respecting the Indians, that you may the better comprehend the parts dealt out to you in detail through the official channel, and observing the system of which they make a part, conduct yourself in unison with it in cases where you are obliged to act without instruction. *Our* system is to live in perpetual peace with the Indians, to cultivate an affectionate attachment from them, by everything just and liberal which we can do for them within the bounds of reason, and by giving them effectual protection against wrongs from our own people. The decrease of game rendering their subsistence by hunting insufficient, we wish to draw them to agriculture, to spinning and weaving. The latter branches they take up with great readiness, because they fall to the women, who gain by quitting the labors of the field for those which are exercised within doors. When they withdraw themselves to the culture of a small piece of land, they will perceive how useless to them are their extensive forests, and will be willing to pare them off from time to time in exchange for necessaries for their farms and families. To promote this disposition to exchange lands, which they have to spare and we want, for necessaries, which we have to spare and they want, we shall push our trading uses, and be glad to see the good and influential individuals among them run in debt, because we observe that when these debts get beyond what the individuals can pay, they become willing to lop them off by a cession of lands. At our trading houses, too, we mean to sell so low as merely to repay us cost and charges, so as neither to lessen or enlarge our capital. This is what private traders cannot do, for they must gain; they will consequently retire from the competition, and we shall thus get clear of this pest without giving offence or umbrage to the Indians. In this way our settlements will gradually circumscribe and approach the Indians, and they will in time either incorporate with us as citizens of the United States, or remove beyond the Mississippi. The former is certainly the termination of their history most happy for themselves; but, in the whole course of this, it is essential to cultivate their love. As to their fear, we presume that our strength and their weakness is now so visible that they must see we have only to shut our hand to crush them, and that all our liberalities to them proceed from motives of pure humanity only. Should any tribe be fool-hardy enough to take up the hatchet at any time, the seizing the whole country of that tribe, and driving them across the Mississippi, as the only condition of peace, would be an example to others, and a furtherance of our final consolidation.

Source: Merrill D. Peterson, *Thomas Jefferson: Writings* (New York: Literary Classics of the United States, Inc., 1984), pp. 1117–1119.

6   In 1804, William Henry Harrison signed a treaty with the Delaware tribe, one of eleven Indian treaties negotiated by Harrison between 1803 and 1809. Were its terms consistent with the Jeffersonian ends described in the previous source?

A Jeffersonian Treaty with the Delaware Indians (1804)

The Delaware tribe of Indians finding that the annuity which they receive from the United States, is not sufficient to supply them with the articles which are necessary for their comfort and convenience, and afford the means of introducing amongst them the arts of civilized life, and being convinced that the extensiveness of the country they possess, by giving an opportunity to their hunting parties to ramble to a great distance from their towns, is the principal means of retarding this desirable event; and the United States being desirous to connect their settlements on the Wabash with the state of Kentucky: therefore the said United States, by William Henry Harrison, governor of the Indiana territory, superintendent of Indian affairs, and their commissioner plenipotentiary for treating with the Indian tribes northwest of the Ohio river; and the said tribe of Indians, by their sachems, chiefs, and head warriors, have agreed to the following articles, which when ratified by the President of the United States, by and with the advice and consent of the Senate, shall be binding on the said parties.

ARTICLE 1. The said Delaware tribe, for the considerations hereinafter mentioned, relinquishes to the United States forever, all their right and title to the tract of country which lies between the Ohio and Wabash rivers, and below the tract ceded by the treaty of Fort Wayne, and the road leading from Vincennes to the falls of Ohio.

ARTICLE 2. The said tribe shall receive from the United States for ten years, an additional annuity of three hundred dollars, which is to be exclusively appropriated to the purpose of ameliorating their condition and promoting their civilization. Suitable persons shall be employed at the expense of the United States to teach them to make fences, cultivate the earth, and such of the domestic arts as are adapted to their situation; and a further sum of three hundred dollars shall be appropriated annually for five years to this object. The United States will cause to be delivered to them in the course of the next spring, horses fit for draft, cattle, hogs and implements of husbandry to the amount of four hundred dollars. The preceding stipulations together with goods to the amount of eight hundred dollars which is now delivered to the said tribe, (a part of which is to be appropriated to the satisfying certain individuals of the said tribe, whose horses have been taken by white people) is to be considered as full compensation for the relinquishment made in the first article. . . .

Source: Commissioner of Indian Affairs, *Treaties Between the United States of America, and the Several Indian Tribes, from 1778 to 1837* (1837; reprint, Millwood, N.Y.: Kraus Reprint Co., 1975), pp. 104–105.

7   As you examine these maps of Indian land cessions in the early nineteenth century, locate the general area of the Delaware cession outlined in the previous source. What does this map reveal about the
effectiveness of Jeffersonian means for dealing with the Indians?

Indian Land Cessions (1800–1812)

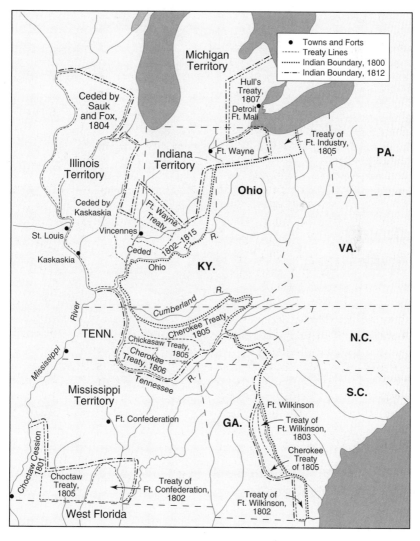

© 2015 Cengage Learning

Indian Land Cessions, Indiana (1783–1840)

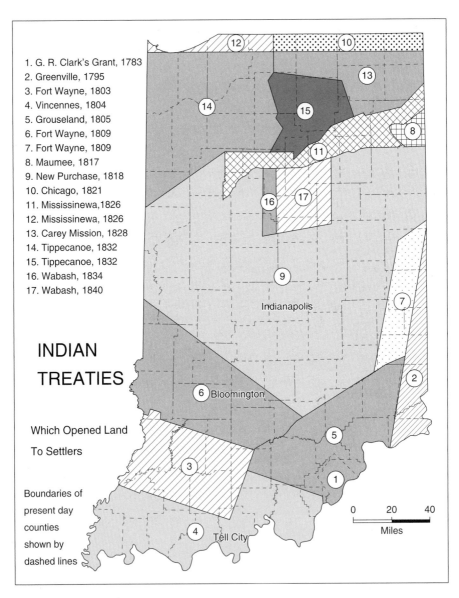

1. G. R. Clark's Grant, 1783
2. Greenville, 1795
3. Fort Wayne, 1803
4. Vincennes, 1804
5. Grouseland, 1805
6. Fort Wayne, 1809
7. Fort Wayne, 1809
8. Maumee, 1817
9. New Purchase, 1818
10. Chicago, 1821
11. Mississinewa, 1826
12. Mississinewa, 1826
13. Carey Mission, 1828
14. Tippecanoe, 1832
15. Tippecanoe, 1832
16. Wabash, 1834
17. Wabash, 1840

INDIAN
TREATIES

Which Opened Land
To Settlers

Boundaries of
present day
counties
shown by
dashed lines

Indianapolis

Bloomington

Tell City

0   20   40
Miles

© 2015 Cengage Learning

8
As settlers advanced into the trans-Appalachian West in the first years of the nineteenth century, the Shawnee chief Tecumseh attempted to unify Indian tribes into a confederation to resist further white encroachment. Note the rhetoric with which he tries to rally the Choctaws and Chickasaws. How would you compare it to the patriots' during the American Revolution? What does this speech reveal about the outcome of Jeffersonian treaty-making?

A Denunciation of White Tyranny (1811)

[H]ave we not courage enough remaining to defend our country and maintain our ancient independence? Will we calmly suffer the white intruders and tyrants to enslave us? Shall it be said of our race that we knew not how to extricate ourselves from the three most dreadful calamities—folly, inactivity and cowardice? . . . Soon your mighty forest trees, under the shade of whose wide spreading branches you have played in infancy, sported in boyhood, and now rest your wearied limbs after the fatigue of the chase, will be cut down to fence in the land which the white intruders dare to call their own. Soon their broad roads will pass over the grave of your fathers, and the place of their rest will be blotted out forever. The annihilation of our race is at hand unless we unite in one common cause against the common foe. . . .

Sleep not longer, O Choctaws and Chickasaws, in false security and delusive hopes. Our broad domains are fast escaping from our grasp. Every year our white intruders become more greedy, exacting, oppressive and overbearing. Every year contentions spring up between them and our people and when blood is shed we have to make atonement whether right or wrong, at the cost of the lives of our greatest chiefs, and the yielding up of large tracts of our lands. Before the palefaces came among us, we enjoyed the happiness of unbounded freedom, and were acquainted with neither riches, wants nor oppression. How is it now? Wants and oppression are our lot; for are we not controlled in everything, and dare we move without asking, by your leave? Are we not being stripped day by day of the little that remains of our ancient liberty? Do they not even kick and strike us as they do their black-faces? How long will it be before they will tie us to a post and whip us, and make us work for them in their corn fields as they do them? Shall we wait for that moment or shall we die fighting before submitting to such ignominy? . . .

. . . Choctaws and Chickasaws, you have too long borne with grievous usurpation inflicted by the arrogant Americans. Be no longer their dupes. If there be one here tonight who believes that his rights will not sooner or later be taken from him by the avaricious American pale faces, his ignorance ought to excite pity, for he knows little of the character of our common foe.

Source: W. C. Vanderwerth, *Indian Oratory: Famous Speeches by Noted Indian Chieftains* (Norman: University of Oklahoma Press, 1971), pp. 62–65.

9

Jefferson wrote this letter to James Monroe, the governor of Virginia, during his first year as president and shortly after a slave rebellion near Richmond, Virginia, organized by a slave named Gabriel Prosser. Although this slave conspiracy was quickly smashed, it renewed whites' fears about the blacks in their midst and led the Virginia legislature to take up the question of colonization. What practical problems does Jefferson see in removing "troublesome" blacks?

Thomas Jefferson on Black Colonization (1801)
WASHINGTON, NOV. 24, 1801

Dear Sir—I had not been unmindful of your letter of June 15, covering a resolution of the House of Representatives of Virginia, and referred to in yours of the 17th inst. The importance of the subject, and the belief that it gave us time for consideration till the next meeting of the Legislature, have induced me to defer the answer to this date. . . .

The idea seems to be to provide for these [blacks] by a purchase of lands; and it is asked whether such a purchase can be made of the U S in their western territory? A very great extent of country, north of the Ohio, has been laid off into townships, and is now at market, according to the provisions of the acts of Congress, with which you are acquainted. There is nothing which would restrain the State of Virginia either in the purchase or the application of these lands; but a purchase, by the acre, might perhaps be a more expensive provision than the H of Representatives contemplated. Questions would also arise whether the establishment of such a colony within our limits, and to become a part of our union, would be desirable to the State of Virginia itself, or to the other States—especially those who would be in its vicinity?

Could we procure lands beyond the limits of the U S to form a receptacle for these people? On our northern boundary, the country not occupied by British subjects, is the property of Indian nations, whose title would [have] to be extinguished, with the consent of Great Britain; & the new settlers would be British subjects. It is hardly to be believed that either Great Britain or the Indian proprietors have so disinterested a regard for us, as to be willing to relieve us, by receiving such a colony themselves; and as much to be doubted whether that race of men could long exist in so rigorous a climate.

Source: Merrill D. Peterson, *Thomas Jefferson: Writings* (New York: Literary Classics of the United States, Inc., 1984), pp. 1096, 1097–1098.

On our western & southern frontiers, Spain holds an immense country, the occupancy of which, however, is in the Indian natives, except a few insulated spots possessed by Spanish subjects. It is very questionable, indeed, whether the Indians would sell? whether Spain would be willing to receive these people? and nearly certain that she would not alienate the sovereignty. The same question to ourselves would recur here also, as did in the first case: should we be willing to have such a colony in contact with us? However our present interests may restrain us within our own limits, it is impossible not to look forward to distant times, when our rapid multiplication will expand itself beyond those limits, & cover the whole northern, if not the southern continent, with a people speaking the same language, governed in similar forms, & by similar laws; nor can we contemplate with satisfaction either blot or mixture on that surface. Spain, France, and Portugal hold possessions on the southern continent, as to which I am not well enough informed to say how far they might meet our views. But either there or in the northern continent, should the constituted authorities of Virginia fix their attention, of preference, I will have the dispositions of those powers sounded in the first instance.

The West Indies offer a more probable & practicable retreat for them. Inhabited already by a people of their own race & color; climates congenial with their natural constitution; insulated from the other descriptions of men; nature seems to have formed these islands to become the receptacle of the blacks transplanted into this hemisphere. Whether we could obtain from the European sovereigns of those islands leave to send thither the persons under consideration, I cannot say; but I think it more probable than the former propositions, because of their being already inhabited more or less by the same race. The most promising portion of them is the island of St. Domingo, where the blacks are established into a sovereignty *de facto*, & have organized themselves under regular laws & government. I should conjecture that their present ruler might be willing, on many considerations, to receive even that description which would be exiled for acts deemed criminal by us, but meritorious, perhaps, by him. The possibility that these exiles might stimulate & conduct vindicative or predatory descents on our coasts, & facilitate concert with their brethren remaining here, looks to a state of things between that island & us not probable on a contemplation of our relative strength, and of the disproportion daily growing; and it is overweighed by the humanity of the measures proposed, & the advantages of disembarrassing ourselves of such dangerous characters. Africa would offer a last & undoubted resort, if all others more desirable should fail us. Whenever the Legislature of Virginia shall have brought it's [sic] mind to a point, so that I may know exactly what to propose to foreign authorities, I will execute their wishes with fidelity & zeal.

10   In the aftermath of Gabriel's Rebellion, a failed Virginia slave uprising in 1800, the state legislature considered several proposals to limit or ban altogether the manumission (freeing) of slaves. After several unsuccessful attempts to restrict manumission, in early 1806 the House of Delegates debated a bill to prevent slave holders from emancipating their slaves "by any means." At the same time, the delegates debated a substitute bill preventing slave holders from emancipating slaves in their wills but allowing emancipation by deed, that is, while slave holders were still alive. As you read these excerpts from the debate, notice the grounds upon which delegates argued, particularly their appeals to individual rights and republican principles and concerns for public safety. Are the arguments and fears expressed here similar to those voiced by Jefferson?

"The Virginia Legislature Debates an Emancipation Prohibition" (1806)

HOUSE OF DELEGATES, JANUARY 15, ****

The bill to prevent the emancipation of Slaves under consideration, in committee of the whole.

Mr. Love offered a substitute for the bill, which substitute went to prevent emancipation *by Will*, and to prevent emancipations to take effect at a distant day. He said he conceived the right to emancipate ought not to be taken away; But that the emancipators ought themselves, to feel the consequences, and be responsible for them, and not leave them to their posterity.

Mr. Robertson observed, that the gentleman (Mr. Love) had contended that the citizens should not be deprived of the right of emancipation, and yet his substitute went to deprive them of that right. If they ought not to be deprived of the power of emancipating by *Deed*, neither ought they to be deprived of the power of emancipating by *Will*. The question (said Mr. R.) is, shall emancipation be tolerated or not? He conceived the question ought to be decided without argument, as investigation might have a tendency to produce those very evils we would avoid. He would, however, state some facts for the consideration of the committee. The preponderance of the blacks in numbers, other the whites, in the eastern parts of the state, is, perhaps, greater than gentlemen have apprehended. The number of the blacks is above 340,000; of the whites, above 336,000; thus there may be of each, about 176,000 above 16 years of age. In order to ascertain the force of each, deduct from the number of the whites the females, who would be a weight on them destructive to their energy in a contest; but the females of the blacks would be as ferocious and formidable as the males. Thus the force

Source: Virginia *Argus* (January 17, 1806), pp. 2–3.

of the blacks is to the whites as 2 to 1. This proves the peculiar necessity of measures of precaution in Virginia.

Laws to prohibit emancipation are not found in other states; but their situation is dissimilar. The number of their whites preponderates greatly. In Virginia it is not so; and a law to prevent emancipation was necessary. For if the blacks see all of their color slaves, it will seem to them a disposition of Providence, and they will be content. But if they see others like themselves free, and enjoying rights, they are deprived of, they will repine.

Those blacks who are free, obtain some education; they obtain a knowledge of facts, by passing from place to place in society; they can thus organize insurrection. They will, no doubt, unite with the slaves. Tell us not of principles. Those principles have been annihilated by the existence of slavery among us. Mr. R. hoped the substitute would not prevail.

Mr. Love said the part of the community from which he came was not much interested. That slaves there did not bear the proportion of one to ten of the number in some other parts . . . . It is proper (said Mr. L.) to retain the right of emancipation. Meritorious services may be rendered by a slave. He may preserve the life or property of his master, and the master should have the power of emancipation, that such services might be rewarded . . . .

Mr. Minor said that if the bill in any form passed, he would prefer the substitute. He was surprised that now, when moral rights are so well understood, a proposition should come from such a quarter as this does, destructive to liberty. In past days these walls have rung with eulogies on liberty. A comparison between those times and the present is degrading to us. We may be equal in intelligence and virtue, but not in the love of liberty. Can we contravene the bill of rights which declares that "all men are by nature free," and shut against this race, the door of hope? The legislature have no right to do a moral wrong. What will be the situation of the blacks if you shut this only door through which they can enter the sacred ground of liberty? They will be fixed in the deepest state of damnation, despair without hope. In such a situation they will prefer death to existence. They now wait patiently in hopes of relief. "Divide and conquer" is as true in policy as it is as a military maxim. The free blacks are sureties for the slaves. It will be their interest to give information of insurrection . . . .

Mr. Robertson was really astonished at the speech that had just been delivered. The gentleman (Mr. Minor) would suffer a mountain of vice to exist, but he stumbles at a mole-hill. Mr. R. said he was actuated by a desire for the public happiness. He was conscious emancipation was destructive to the happiness of the state. The law formerly in existence had forbidden emancipation. We only propose to restore it. Every gentleman who is a slave holder, is an offender against *principle*, and need not feel so squeamish at the present proposal. To cut off all hope of emancipation, will produce content on the part of the slaves. And we have seen that the free blacks are wretched, as much so as the slaves. The proposed measure is necessary. I advocate it from policy; and not because I am less friendly to the rights of men than those who oppose the bill . . . .

Mr. Semple . . . The are now 20,000 free blacks among us. When they shall become more numerous, they will furnish the officers and soldiers around whom the slaves will rally. We cannot now avoid the evil of slavery. Partial emancipation was not the proper remedy. If it proceeds, and they continue to mix with the whites as they have already done, as we daily see, I know not what kind of people the Virginians will be in one hundred years.

Mr. Johnston (the speaker) said the question was, is emancipation an evil or not? He conceived it was an evil, as it related to morality and public security. The free blacks are idle and vicious, and they corrupt the slaves. This mischief was most alarming. The bill would remedy it; but the substitute does nothing . . . .

The substitute was rejected by the committee. The bill was lost on the question to read it a third time. Ayes 73—Noes 75 . . . .

---

11   When the Pennsylvania legislature considered a bill designed to halt the movement of free blacks to the state in 1813, James Forten, a free black Philadelphia sailmaker, wrote a pamphlet against the measure. Due to the efforts of Forten and others, the legislature failed to pass the measure. What principles does he use to support his case? Are they consistent with Thomas Jefferson's republican ideology?

A Letter from a Man of Colour (1813)

We hold this truth to be self-evident, that God created all men equal, and is one of the most prominent features in the Declaration of Independence, and in that glorious fabrick of collected wisdom, our noble Constitution. This idea embraces the Indian and the European, the Savage and the Saint, the Peruvian and the Laplander, the white Man and the African, and whatever measures are adopted subversive of this inestimable privilege, are in direct violation of the letter and spirit of our Constitution, and become subject to the animadversion of all, particularly those who are deeply interested in the measure.

These thoughts were suggested by the promulgation of a late bill, before the Senate of Pennsylvania, to prevent the emigration of people of colour into this state. It was not passed into a law at this session and must in consequence lay over until the next, before when we sincerely hope, the white men, whom we should look upon as our protectors, will have become convinced of the inhumanity and impolicy of such a measure, and forbear to deprive us of those inestimable treasures, Liberty and Independence. . . . We grant there are a number of worthless men belonging to our colour, but there are laws

Source: Gary B. Nash, *Race and Revolution* (Madison, Wis.: Madison House, 1990), pp. 190–192.

of sufficient rigour for their punishment, if properly and duly enforced. We wish not to screen the guilty from punishment, but with the guilty do not permit the innocent to suffer. If there are worthless men, there are also men of merit among the African race, who are useful members of Society. The truth of this let their benevolent institutions and the numbers clothed and fed by them witness. Punish the guilty man of colour to the utmost limit of the laws, but sell him not to slavery! If he is in danger of becoming a publick charge prevent him! If he is too indolent to labour for his own subsistence, compel him to do so; but sell him not to slavery. By selling him you do not make him better, but commit a wrong, without benefitting the object of it or society at large. Many of our ancestors were brought here more than one hundred years ago; many of our fathers, many of ourselves, have fought and bled for the Independence of our country. Do not then expose us to sale. Let not the spirit of the father behold the son robbed of that Liberty which he died to establish, but let the motto of our Legislators be: "The Law knows no distinction." . . .

12　In late 1816, the American Colonization Society was formed with the object of transporting free blacks to Africa. Early the next year, a meeting of free blacks in Philadelphia wrote a protest against the aim of the society. On what grounds do they argue against it? How do their ideas compare to Jefferson's?

A Black Response to Colonization (1817)

Whereas our ancestors (not of choice) were the first successful cultivators of the wilds of America, we their descendants feel ourselves entitled to participate in the blessings of her luxuriant soil, which their blood and sweat manured; and that any measure or system of measures, having a tendency to banish us from her bosom, would not only be cruel, but in direct violation of those principles, which have been the boast of this republic.

Resolved, That we view with deep abhorrence the unmerited stigma attempted to be cast upon the reputation of the free people of color, by the promoters of this measure, "that they are a dangerous and useless part of the community," when in the state of disfranchisement in which they live, in the hour of danger they ceased to remember their wrongs, and rallied around the standard of their country.

Resolved, That we never will separate ourselves voluntarily from the slave population in this country; they are our brethren by the ties of consanguinity, of suffering, and of wrong; and we feel that there is more virtue in suffering privations with them, than fancied advantages for a season.

Source: Herbert Aptheker, ed., *A Documentary History of the Negro People in the United States: From Colonial Times Through the Civil War* (Secaucus, N.J.: The Citadel Press, 1973), pp. 71–72.

Resolved, That without arts, without science, without a proper knowledge of government, to cast into the savage wilds of Africa the free people of color, seems to us the circuitous route through which they must return to perpetual bondage.

Resolved, That having the strongest confidence in the justice of God, and philanthropy of the free states, we cheerfully submit our destinies to the guidance of Him who suffers not a sparrow to fall, without his special providence.

Resolved, That a committee of eleven persons be appointed to open a correspondence with the honorable Joseph Hopkinson, member of Congress from this city, and likewise to inform him of the sentiments of this meeting, when they in their judgment may deem it proper.

CONCLUSION

Thomas Jefferson and his ideas continue to inspire Americans. The homage paid to him by modern political candidates across the ideological spectrum alone is testament to the enduring power of his ideas and his continuing hold on our imaginations. In the words of one historian, Jefferson remains for Americans of all political persuasions "an American icon" and his "'self-evident . . . truths' constitute an American creed."[4] It is no wonder that, as another historian has remarked, Jefferson is the only president whose name "forms an adjective of general meaning."[5] Thus, Jacksonian, for instance, refers to a particular era, whereas we routinely refer to Jeffersonian traditions, principles, or legacies with the understanding that they transcend his own era.

As the sources in this chapter demonstrate, however, closer inspection reveals that the Jeffersonian legacy is complex and contradictory. On the one hand, Jefferson distilled and eloquently expressed ideas about nature, society, and rights inherited from other thinkers and in the process linked the American nation to universal principles and rights. On the other hand, this chapter's sources reveal a profoundly troubling side to Jefferson and his legacy. The same eighteenth-century "laws of nature" that Jefferson advanced in the name of individual rights and "the pursuit of happiness" held conclusions for him that excluded groups of people from those same blessings. Just as he so memorably advanced Enlightenment ideas of nature to condemn tyranny and proclaim universal rights, his application of "reason" to understand the laws of nature led him to other, darker conclusions about how equal people really were. With his "empirical evidence," moreover, Jefferson did more, in his Monticello study, than transmit to posterity the racial prejudices of his age. Rather, he helped to develop a justification for the debasement of non-whites and their exclusion from the full pursuit of opportunities in the republic that he helped to create.

Thus, we continue to struggle with Jefferson. Whether we define him as an icon or hypocrite, that struggle is in its own way an acknowledgment that ideas matter. Wrestling with Jefferson also reminds us that the influence of ideas may run in many, even contradictory, directions. Realizing that, in turn, helps us understand why historians do not always find it easy to trace their influence. The sometimes elusive impact of ideas, in fact, is one reason why historians often disagree about the causes of things. Where one historian, for instance, might relate an individual's stance to a firmly held philosophy, another might ascribe it to economic or financial self-interest. In the end, though, it is often with the enduring historical thread we call ideas that historians connect seemingly unrelated developments in the past. As we shall see in Chapter 7, these threads may even link Thomas Jefferson to a development that on the surface seems far removed from the Sage of Monticello—the transformation of nineteenth-century American religion.

FURTHER READING

Annette Gordon-Reed, *Thomas Jefferson and Sally Hemings: An American Controversy* (Charlottesville: University Press of Virginia, 1997).
John C. Miller, *The Wolf by the Ears: Thomas Jefferson and Slavery* (New York: The Free Press, 1977).
Gary B. Nash, *Race and Revolution* (Madison, Wis.: Madison House, 1990).
Francis Paul Prucha, *American Indian Policy in the Formative Years: The Indian Trade and Intercourse Acts, 1780–1834* (Cambridge, Mass.: Harvard University Press, 1970).
Bernard W. Sheehan, *Seeds of Extinction: Jeffersonian Philanthropy and the American Indian* (Chapel Hill: The University of North Carolina Press, 1973).
Anthony F. C. Wallace, *Jefferson and the Indians: The Tragic Fate of the First Americans* (Cambridge: Harvard University Press, 1999).

NOTES

1. Quoted in Robert L. Heilbroner, *The Worldly Philosophers* (New York: Simon and Schuster, 1967), p. 12.
2. Thomas Jefferson, *Notes on the State of Virginia*, in Adrienne Koch and William Peden, *The Life and Selected Writings of Thomas Jefferson* (New York: Random House, 1944), p. 280.
3. Ibid., p. 280.
4. Peter S. Onuf, *The Mind of Thomas Jefferson* (Charlottesville: University of Virginia Press, 2007), p. 1.
5. Joyce Appleby, "Jefferson and His Complex Legacy" in Peter S. Onuf, *Jeffersonian Legacies* (Charlottesville: University Press of Virginia, 1993), p. 1.

Chapter

7

The Problem of Historical Causation: The Second Great Awakening

The sources in this chapter relate to the question of what accounts for the extended period of religious ferment in the early nineteenth century known as the Second Great Awakening.

Secondary Source

1. The Second Great Awakening and the Transformation of American Christianity (1989), NATHAN O. HATCH

Primary Sources

2. "The Methodist Discipline" (1798)
3. "On Predestination" (1809)
4. A Defense of Camp Meetings (1814)
5. *Book of Mormon* (1830)
6. "Plea for the West" (1835) LYMAN BEECHER
7. A Methodist "Circuit-Rider" Discusses Education and the Ministry (1856)
8. *Negro Methodists Holding a Meeting in Philadelphia* (ca. 1812)
9. A Former Slave Discusses the Appeal of Methodism (1856)
10. Frances Trollope's Account of a Camp Meeting (1829)
11. Harriet Martineau on the Condition of American Women (1837)
12. Rebeccah Lee on the Appeal of Christianity (1831)
13. Philadelphia Journeymen Protest Their Conditions (1828)
14. Occupations of Methodist Converts in Philadelphia (1830s)
15. Alexis de Tocqueville on the Condition of Americans (1835)

*N*obody knows for sure how many people showed up at the Cane Ridge revival in 1801. Some observers put the crowd at 10,000, while others said it was two-and-a-half times that size. Likewise, no one is certain exactly what happened at this massive Kentucky camp meeting. Enemies of the revival, pointing to the six men lying with a woman under a preacher's stand on Saturday night, claimed that "more souls were begot than saved" at Cane Ridge.[1] If the accounts of most contemporaries are any guide, though, more people experienced ecstasy beside the preacher's stand than below it. Even hard-bitten Kentuckians were astounded. One of them saw a "vast sea of human beings . . . agitated as if by a storm." While seven ministers preached simultaneously, he reported, "some of the people were singing, others praying, some crying for mercy in the most piteous accents, while others were shouting most vociferously." The resulting noise was "like the roar of Niagara."[2] Meanwhile, grown men crawled on all fours barking like dogs. Other men and not a few women rolled on the ground shouting and shrieking. Still other worshippers were overcome with the "jerks," their entire bodies twitching and shaking uncontrollably "as if," according to another witness, "they must . . . fly asunder."[3]

Cane Ridge was the biggest camp meeting during the religious revivals known as the Second Great Awakening. Today, it also remains perhaps the most famous event in this decades-long period of religious intensity. Yet there is more to the Second Great Awakening than backwoods camp meetings like Cane Ridge. Beginning about 1800 and extending into the 1830s, this period of intense religious ferment would leave thousands converted—and not just around frontier campfires. By the 1820s and 1830s, revivalism had spread from the backwoods of Kentucky to New York and beyond. In fact, long after the fires were extinguished at Cane Ridge, the Second Great Awakening's preachers were reaping their most abundant harvests in the bustling commercial and manufacturing centers of the Northeast. Moreover, the Awakening was marked by much more than revival tents and fiery preachers. Denominations like the Baptists and Methodists that emphasized a more emotional approach to religion grew dramatically. Older groups such as the Congregationalists, the descendant of the old Puritan Church, and the Episcopalians, the descendant of the Church of England, were thrown on the defensive. At the same time, many new religious groups were born, including the Disciples of Christ and the Mormons. Together, these changes would help to transform American Christianity in the first decades of the nineteenth century.

The new and dramatically expanding religious groups of the Second Great Awakening offer a fertile field for historians searching for the origins of this remarkable religious phenomenon. Despite the obvious enthusiasm exhibited at Cane Ridge and elsewhere, modern historians do not trace the Second Great Awakening to supernatural causes—or explain it as merely the work of skilled preachers. Rather, they seek explanations in the lives of the converted. Exploring the roots of the Second Great Awakening challenges historians to identify important patterns of historical experience and to establish causal links between seemingly unrelated developments. Often, neither task is easy. Yet if the most important job of historians is to explain the causes of events, then their most useful explanations do not merely state the obvious. In this chapter, then, we take up the problem of historical causation by exploring the links between the worldly and otherworldly concerns of Americans drawn to the revival tent in the early nineteenth century.

SETTING

The search for explanations for the Second Great Awakening began even while its fires raged. Echoing defenses heard during the First Great Awakening in the 1740s and 1750s, some clergymen suggested that religious enthusiasm was a response to waning religious zeal, declining church membership, and increasing moral waywardness. Like their counterparts during the colonial revival, ministers often laid much of the blame for this deplorable state of affairs on a decline in respect for religious authorities and the spread of deism and other forms of rational religion, which emphasized the orderly nature of the universe and God's reasonableness. Two circumstances in particular drew their attention: disestablishment of churches after the American Revolution and the triumph of the Jeffersonian Republicans in 1800. The separation of church and state, they argued, removed ministers from their exalted position in American society, while the election of 1800 swept into power rationalists, deists, and supporters of an anticlerical French Revolution. The Awakening's defenders saw an even more disturbing problem when they looked westward. As thousands of pioneers trekked across the Appalachian mountains, alarmed Easterners feared that their western cousins had slipped into a sink of violence, vice, and immorality. Often without churches and surrounded, in the words of one Connecticut Methodist, by "the offscouring of the earth," Westerners were in urgent need of redemption at the hands of Protestant missionary societies.[4] The Second Great Awakening, according to this view, reimposed sobriety and order on society.

Although historians are less interested in justifying the Second Great Awakening than in explaining it, they often echo some of these conclusions. Many educated Americans, they argue, *had* found Enlightenment rationalism emotionally unsatisfying. Likewise, growing numbers of unlettered and unchurched pioneers in the trans-Appalachian West were ripe for conversion at the hands of evangelical preachers whose simple, emotional preaching aimed at the heart rather than the head. Yet many Americans far removed from the frontier also succumbed to religious enthusiasm, and this has led to more comprehensive explanations for the revivals.

Many historians, for instance, trace the appeal of revival religion to broad and disruptive economic or social changes. Some point to the growing number of immigrants, many of them Catholics from Germany or Ireland. Entering an over-whelmingly Protestant nation, these "outsiders" were often met with hostility. At the same time, they may have helped invigorate Protestantism as both religion and religious doctrines assumed heightened importance for many native-born Americans. Other historians, however, contend that revivalism was a response to changes associated with a rising market economy in the early nineteenth century. In this view, many Americans pulled up stakes from settled communities in search of economic opportunities in booming towns and cities and then flocked to revivals to reestablish a lost sense of order in their lives. For many native-born Americans and immigrants alike, movement was in a westward direction. In newly opened western areas, people found themselves in a disordered and frequently violent frontier society. Moreover, there as elsewhere in American society, alcohol consumption was very high even by modern standards, approaching four gallons of pure alcohol per capita by the late 1820s. In such a society, the bonds of family were frequently tested. Given these conditions, some students have tied the Second Great Awakening to stresses on family life. Pointing to the Great Awakening's disproportionate number of female converts, other students conclude that revivals helped women develop a separate sphere free from the male dominance in traditional, patriarchal households. Finally, some scholars maintain that the revivals were fueled by class tensions created by the changing relations between employers and workers in workshops and new factories. In this view, the revivals were a way for an emerging capitalist elite to keep the working class in line by promoting within it the values of sobriety and industry and a belief in individual responsibility.

Still other historians dispute the causal connection between the Awakening and the expansion of capitalism while acknowledging that class tensions had something to do with this religious phenomenon. They conclude that religious enthusiasm was a response to the increasingly democratic nature of American society. In this view, common people in increasing numbers challenged the control of American Christianity by educated elites. One result, they point out, was worship services based on emotional preaching rather than logical, finely spun arguments. Another was a theology emphasizing individual free will and the promise of salvation for all, rather than salvation for a few, at the hands of God. At a time when all adult white males could vote and increasing numbers were free to make decisions affecting their own well-being, it seemed only natural that they should be able to control their own salvation. In short, enthusiastic religion fit the experience of most Americans far better than Calvinism's doctrine of predestination, that is, salvation by God's election.

Clearly, historians disagree about the relationship between religious developments and economic or social changes. As a consequence, even today they remain divided on whether revivalism was, as its early defenders suggested, a powerful means for social control. Pointing to the evangelical roots of the temperance and other moral reform movements of the 1820s and 1830s, many historians argue that evangelism reflected a desire to establish order in an unruly society. Whether it arose out of a desire to civilize dissolute westerners or make industrious workers for a growing capitalist economy, they contend, the Second Great Awakening represented a conservative antidote to social disorder. Other historians deny that revivalism was merely a means for social control— or that religious developments are mere responses to economic or social concerns. They argue instead that religious ideas can also be prime movers in history and that those who seek an explanation for the revivals must therefore understand what one scholar called the "ideological universe in which the historical actors lived."[5] Modern historians, in short, continue to disagree about religion's role in society. At the same time, few episodes in American history present a better opportunity to assess the causal relationship between economic, social, and religious developments than the Second Great Awakening. And for that reason, more than for the strange behavior it sometimes elicited, it merits our attention today.

INVESTIGATION

The sources in this chapter illuminate various aspects of the Second Great Awakening. The essay by historian Nathan Hatch deals with the changes in American Christianity during the Awakening and their connection to a democratic culture that developed out of the American Revolution. Those changes, he argues, are best seen in such denominations as the Baptists and Methodists, which emphasized an emotional approach to religion, and in new religious groups, as represented by the Disciples of Christ and the Church of Jesus Christ of Latter-day Saints (Mormons). Arising first in England, the Baptist and Methodist religions emphasized plain preaching and the individual's ability to save oneself, although their appeal was limited until the end of the eighteenth century. The Disciples of Christ and the Mormon religions began in this country and represented brand new groups in the early nineteenth century. Founded in 1830 by former Presbyterian Alexander Campbell, the Disciples merged two years later with another evangelical group known simply as the Christians, led by another former Presbyterian named Barton Stone. By the eve of the Civil War, the Disciples had become the fifth largest Protestant denomination in the country. Organized in 1830, the Mormon Church arose in the heavily evangelized area of upstate New York known as the "Burned-Over District" for the intensity of the revival activity there. Founder Joseph Smith, a twenty-four-year-old son of a struggling upstate New York farmer, claimed to have translated golden tablets containing the record of ancient people who had inhabited the Americas. Published as the *Book of Mormon* in 1830, this "American Scripture" would quickly attract a growing band of adherents.

Obviously, these "insurgent" religious groups differed in important ways. According to the essay (Source 1), however, they also shared significant traits.

Those common features, Nathan Hatch argues, are the key to understanding the rise of the Second Great Awakening and the way it transformed American Protestantism. Your initial job, then, is to understand those traits and what they reveal about the roots of this religious phenomenon. Second, with the help of a small set of primary sources, you can assess the validity of the essay's argument about the forces that led to the Awakening. Finally, using both the secondary and primary sources in this chapter, you can offer a causal explanation of your own that considers the importance of various social, economic, or cultural factors. Your analysis should address the following questions:

1. **What is the connection between the "democratic spirit" of American culture in the early nineteenth century and the appeal of insurgent religious groups of the Second Great Awakening, according to Nathan Hatch's essay (Source 1)?** What role did the American Revolution play in the growing appeal of these groups during the Awakening, according to the essay?

2. **What evidence do the primary sources and the essay provide to support Nathan Hatch's explanation regarding the growth of insurgent religious groups during the Second Great Awakening?** Do there appear to have been social bases for it?

3. **Do the primary sources offer alternative explanations for the appearance of the Second Great Awakening?** What do they indicate were the major sources of support for it?

4. **What clues does the evidence provide about why different social groups were drawn to insurgent religious denominations or a more emotional style of religious worship?** What special appeals did the Awakening have for women? For African Americans? For white workingmen?

Before you begin, read your textbook's account of changes in early nineteenth-century Protestantism and its discussion of the political, social, and economic changes in the first decades of the nineteenth century. Be careful to notice any connections it makes between these changes and developments in American Protestantism in this period.

SECONDARY SOURCE

1

In this selection, historian Nathan O. Hatch discusses the reasons for the appeal of what he calls the "insurgent" religious groups of the Second Great Awakening, primarily the Baptists, Methodists, Mormons, and the Disciples of Christ. These movements had wide appeal in the early nineteenth century. As you read this source, note the doctrines and styles of worship they shared. According to Hatch, what do these common features have to do with the rapid growth of these groups during the Awakening? Does he pinpoint a specific or more general causal factors in explaining the Awakening? What do you think Gary Nash, the author of the essay on the social consequences of the American Revolution in Chapter 4, would have to say about Hatch's explanation regarding the roots of the Second Great Awakening and its impact on American Christianity?

The Second Great Awakening and the Transformation of American Christianity (1989)
NATHAN O. HATCH

This [study] is about the cultural and religious history of the early American republic and the enduring structures of American Christianity. It argues both that the theme of democratization is central to understanding the development of American Christianity, and that the years of the early republic are the most crucial in revealing that process. The wave of popular religious movements that broke upon the United States in the half century after independence did more to Christianize American society than anything before or since. Nothing makes that point more clearly than the growth of Methodist and Baptist movements among white and black Americans. Starting from scratch just prior to the Revolution, Methodism in America grew at a rate that terrified other more established denominations. By 1820 Methodist membership numbered a quarter million; by 1830 it was twice that number. Baptist membership multiplied tenfold in the three decades after the Revolution; the number of churches increased from five hundred to over twenty-five hundred. The black church in America was born amidst the crusading vigor of these movements and quickly assumed its own distinct character and broad appeal. By the middle of the nineteenth century, Methodist and Baptist churches had splintered into a score of separate denominations, white and black. In total these movements eventually constituted two-thirds of the Protestant ministers and church members in the United States. . . .

This [study] examines five distinct traditions, or mass movements, that developed early in the nineteenth century: the [Disciples of Christ], the Methodists, the Baptists, the black churches, and the Mormons. Each was led by young men of relentless energy who went about movement-building as self-conscious outsiders. They shared an ethic of unrelenting toil, a passion for expansion, a hostility to orthodox belief and style, a zeal for religious reconstruction, and a systematic plan to realize their ideals. However diverse their theologies and church organizations, they all offered common

Source: From Nathan O. Hatch, *The Democratization of American Christianity*, pp. 3, 4–6, 9–11, 13–14, 170, 171–173. Copyright © 1989. Reprinted by permission of the publisher, Yale University Press.

people, especially the poor, compelling visions of individual self-respect and collective self-confidence. Like the Populist movement at the end of the nineteenth century, these movements took shape around magnetic leaders who were highly skilled in communication and group mobilization.

Abstractions and generalities about the Second Great Awakening as a conservative force have obscured the egalitarianism powerfully at work in the new nation. As common people became significant actors on the religious scene, there was increasing confusion and angry debate over the purpose and function of the church. A style of religious leadership that the public deemed "untutored" and "irregular" as late as the First Great Awakening became overwhelmingly successful, even normative, in the first decades of the republic. Ministers from different classes vied with each other to serve as divine spokesmen. Democratic or populist leaders associated virtue with ordinary people and exalted the vernacular in word, print, and song. . . .

The American Revolution is the most crucial event in American history. The generation overshadowed by it . . . stands at the fault line that separates an older world, premised on standards of deference, patronage, and ordered succession, from a newer one that continues to shape our values. The American Revolution and the beliefs flowing from it created a cultural ferment over the meaning of freedom. Turmoil swirled around the crucial issues of authority, organization, and leadership.

Above all, the Revolution dramatically expanded the circle of people who considered themselves capable of thinking for themselves about issues of freedom, equality, sovereignty, and representation. Respect for authority, tradition, station, and education eroded. Ordinary people moved toward these new horizons aided by a powerful new vocabulary, a rhetoric of liberty that would not have occurred to them were it not for the Revolution. In time, the issue of the well-being of ordinary people became central to the definition of being American, public opinion came to assume normative significance, and leaders could not survive who would not, to use Patrick Henry's phrase, "bow with utmost deference to the majesty of the people." . . .

America's nonrestrictive environment permitted an unexpected and often explosive conjunction of evangelical fervor and popular sovereignty. It was this engine that accelerated the process of Christianization within American popular culture, allowing indigenous expressions of faith to take hold among ordinary people, white and black. This expansion of evangelical Christianity did not proceed primarily from the nimble response of religious elites meeting the challenge before them. Rather, Christianity was effectively reshaped by common people who molded it in their own image and who threw themselves into expanding its influence. Increasingly assertive common people wanted their leaders unpretentious, their doctrines self-evident and down-to-earth, their music lively and singable, and their churches in local hands. It was this upsurge of democratic hope that characterized so many religious cultures in the early republic and brought Baptists, Methodists, Disciples of Christ, and a host of other insurgent groups to the fore. The rise of evangelical Christianity in the early republic is, in some measure, a story of the success of common people in shaping the culture after their own priorities rather than the priorities outlined by gentlemen such as the framers of the Constitution.

It is easy to miss the democratic character of the early republic's insurgent religious movements. The Methodists, after all, retained power in a structured hierarchy under the control of bishops. The Mormons reverted to rule by a single religious prophet and revelator. And groups such as the Disciples of Christ, despite professed democratic structures, were eventually controlled by such powerful individuals as Alexander Campbell, who had little patience with dissent. . . .

The democratization of Christianity, then, has less to do with the specifics of polity and governance and more with the incarnation of the church into popular culture. In at least three respects the popular religious movements of the early republic articulated a profoundly democratic spirit. First, they denied the age-old distinction that set the clergy apart as a separate order of men, and they refused to defer to learned theologians and traditional orthodoxies. All were democratic or populist in the way they instinctively associated virtue with ordinary people rather than with elites, exalted the vernacular in word and song as the hallowed channel for communicating with and about God, and freely turned over the reins of power. These groups also shared with the Jeffersonian Republicans an overt rejection of the past as a repository of wisdom. By redefining leadership itself, these movements reconstructed the foundations of religion in keeping with the values and priorities of ordinary people.

Second, these movements empowered ordinary people by taking their deepest spiritual impulses at face value rather than subjecting them to the scrutiny of orthodox doctrine and the frowns of respectable clergymen. . . . What had been defined as "enthusiasm" was increasingly advocated from the pulpit as an essential part of Christianity. Such a shift in emphasis, accompanied by rousing gospel singing rather than formal church music, reflected the common people's success in defining the nature of faith for themselves. . . .

The early republic was also a democratic movement in a third sense. Religious outsiders, flushed with confidence about their prospects, had little sense of their limitations. They dreamed that a new age of religious and social harmony would naturally spring up out of their efforts to overthrow coercive and authoritarian structures. This upsurge of democratic hope, this passion for equality, led to a welter of diverse and competing forms, many of them structured in highly undemocratic ways. The Methodists under Francis Asbury, for instance, used authoritarian means to build a church that would not be a respecter of persons. This church faced the curious paradox of gaining phenomenal influence among laypersons with whom it would not share ecclesiastical authority. Similarly, the Mormons used a virtual religious dictatorship as the means to return power to illiterate men. Yet despite these authoritarian structures, the fundamental impetus of these movements was to make Christianity a liberating force; people were given the right to think and act for themselves rather than depending upon the mediations of an educated elite. The most fascinating religious story of the early republic is the signal achievements of these and other populist religious leaders—outsiders who used democratic persuasions to reconstruct the foundations of religious authority. . . .

Leaders without formal training (Barton Stone, the [Disciple of Christ]; William Miller, the Adventist; Francis Asbury, the Methodist; John Leland, the Baptist; Richard Allen, the African Methodist Episcopal; and Joseph Smith, the Latter-day Saint) went outside normal denominational frameworks to develop large followings by the democratic art of persuasion. These are inherently interesting personalities, unbranded individualists, who chose to storm heaven by the back door. Widely diverse in religious convictions, they were alike in their ability to portray, in compelling terms, the deepest hopes and aspirations of popular constituencies. It was said that Joseph Smith had "his own original eloquence, peculiar to himself, not polished, not studied, not smoothed and softened by education and refined by art." A New England clergyman, who resented uneducated and unrefined greenhorns presuming to speak in the Lord's name, put it this way: "They measure the progress of religion by the numbers who flock to their standards, not by the prevalence of faith and piety, justice and charity and the public virtues in society in general." This new style of gospel minister, remarkably attuned to popular sentiment, amazed Tocqueville. "Where I expect to find a priest," he said, "I find a politician."

These individuals were reacting to deep cultural shifts transforming the relationship between leaders and people; focusing on the issue of leadership allows a clear view of this process. Most important, it shows that the fundamental religious debates in the early republic were not merely a clash of intellectual and theological differences but also a passionate social struggle with power and authority. Deep-seated class antagonism separated clergy from clergy. The learned and orthodox disdained early Methodism's new revival measures, notions of free will, and perfectionism. But they despaired that the wrong sort of people had joined Methodism—people who rejected social authority's claim to religious power. While the eighteenth century had seen a steady growth of authority based on popular appeal, particularly in various forms of religious dissent, the Revolution quickened the pace. Those who defended clerical authority as the right of a gentry minority were pitted against rough-hewn leaders who denied the right of any one class of people to speak for another. The early republic witnessed a popular displacement of power from the uncommon man, the man of ideas in American politics and religion. It is the intent of this study to tell at least part of this complicated story: how ordinary folk came to distrust leaders of genius and talent and to defend the right of common people to shape their own faith and submit to leaders of their own choosing. . . .

To the rebellious leaders of populist religious movements, inspired by the rhetoric of the Revolution, nothing represented ecclesiastical tyranny more than the Calvinist clergy with their zeal for theological systems, doctrinal correctness, organizational control, and cultural influence. The Congregationalist[s] had long enjoyed a privileged position in New England towns, a position [they] maintained well into the nineteenth century. In 1801 Congregationalists and Presbyterians joined forces in the Plan of Union to expand [their] influence into the western missionary field. In addition, this coalition of moderate Calvinist leaders forged a chain of voluntary associations to further extend its influence, among which were the American Board of Commissioners for Foreign Missions (1810), the American Home Missionary Society (1826), the American Tract Society (1825), and the American Sunday School Union (1824).

Whatever the real power and influence of Calvinism, its enemies feared a menacing hydra, much as Jacksonians were obsessed with the power of a "monster" bank. No theme united the interests of insurgent groups between 1780 and 1830 more than an exaggerated opposition to official Christianity. In the face of the efforts of Calvinist coalitions to buttress Christian civilization, populist religious leaders worked with equal determination to withstand the control that [Presbyterian minister] Lyman Beecher and others worked to exert over the religious affairs of the nation. Many [involved in populist religious movements] perceived tyrannical intent in the coordinated Calvinist schemes and launched a ferocious crusade against every facet of Calvinist orthodoxy. They fought its ordered and predictable form of religious experience, its rigid theological systems, its high-toned clericalism (what [Baptist leader] John Leland called "pharisaic pomp"), its penchant for cultural domination (what [Methodist preacher] Freeborn Garrettson called a "thirst for preeminence"), and its attempt to legislate morality. . . .

People nursed at least four related complaints against [Calvinist] orthodoxy: its implicit endorsement of the status quo, its tyranny over personal religious experience, its preoccupation with complicated and arcane dogma, and its clerical pretension and quest for control. People at the bottom end of the social scale have rarely warmed to the doctrines of predestination. The anguish of injustice and poverty makes unacceptable the implication that God is ordaining, and taking pleasure in, whatever happens. African-Americans, for instance, found little place for predestination in their understanding of Christianity. In Wilkinson County, Mississippi, a slave gravedigger, with a younger helper, asked a white stranger a question:

> "Massa, may I ask you something?"
> "Ask what you please."

"Can you 'splain how it happened in the fust place, that the white folks got the start of the black folks, so as to make dem slaves and do all de work?"

The younger helper, fearing the white man's wrath, broke in: "Uncle Pete, it's no use talking. It's fo'ordained. The Bible tells you that. The Lord fo'ordained the Nigger to work, and the white man to boss."

"Dat's so. Dat's so. But if dat's so, then God's no fair man!"

The forms of Christianity that prospered among African-Americans were not accepting of the status quo. They supported a moral revulsion of slavery and promised eventual deliverance, putting God on the side of change and freedom.

For many white people, on the other hand, Calvinist assumptions seemed as pervasive as the air they breathed. Numerous accounts of Methodist, Universalist, and [Disciples of Christ] conversions indicate that common folk had internalized guilt and unworthiness, prompted by predestinarian preaching. But Calvinist sermons seemed to offer few means of spiritual release. Caleb Rich, an early proponent of Universalism, described the fear that plagued him as he grew up in rural New England. His Congregational minister in Sutton, Massachusetts, taught that Christ would have but few "trophies of his Mission into the world, while his antagonist would have his countless millions." "My situation appeared more precarious than a ticket in a lottery, where there was an hundred blanks to one prize." . . .

While Methodists, Disciples, and Mormons disagreed radically on what constituted belief in the gospel, they all shared an intense hostility to the passive quality of Calvinist religious experience, and they all made salvation imminently accessible and immediately available. Methodists, Universalists, Freewill Baptists, and [Disciples of Christ] all described conversion as finding gospel liberty. The renegade Presbyterian Barton W. Stone recounted that he and other pioneers of the [Disciples of Christ] church preached emphatically that the individual could exercise faith at any time: "We urged upon the sinner to believe *now,* and receive salvation—that in vain they looked for the Spirit to be given them, while they remained in unbelief . . . that no previous qualification was required, or necessary in order to believe in Jesus, and come to him. . . . When we began first to preach these things, the people appeared as just awakened from the sleep of ages—they seemed to see for the first time that they were responsible beings." . . .

PRIMARY SOURCES

The following primary sources reveal the messages preached during the Second Great Awakening and their appeal to various groups. These sources may support the argument in the essay regarding the roots of the Awakening or suggest alternative explanations.

2   Making use of camp meetings, Peter Cartwright [see Source 7] and other Methodist preachers evangelized heavily in rural and western frontier areas in the early nineteenth century. While traveling in the West, Cartwright always carried with him a copy of the "Methodist Discipline," a code of behavior for members of the church. As you read its rules for personal conduct, consider the moral order that the "Methodist Discipline" promoted. Why might such a code of behavior appeal to Americans in the early nineteenth century, especially those in rural and frontier areas?

"The Methodist Discipline" (1798)

There is one only condition previously required of those who desire admission into these societies, *a desire to flee from the wrath to come, and to be saved from their sins.* But wherever this is really fixed in the soul, it will be shewn by its fruits. It is therefore expected of all who continue therein, that they should continue to evidence their desire of salvation,

First, By doing no harm, by avoiding evil of every kind: especially that which is most generally practised: Such as,

The taking the name of God in vain:

The profaning the day of the Lord, either by doing ordinary work thereon, or by buying or selling.

Drunkenness: or drinking spirituous liquors, unless in cases of necessity:

The buying or selling of men, women, or children, with an intention to enslave them:

Fighting, quarrelling, brawling, brother *going to law* with brother; returning evil for evil; or railing for railing: the *using many words* in buying or selling:

The *buying or selling goods that have not paid the duty:*

The *giving or taking things on usury,* i.e. unlawful interest:

Uncharitable or *unprofitable* conversation: particularly speaking evil of magistrates or of ministers:

Doing to others as we would not they should do unto us:

Doing what we know is not for the glory of God: As,

The *putting on of gold and costly apparel:*

The *taking such diversions* as cannot be used in the name of the Lord Jesus;

The *singing* those *songs,* or *reading* those *books,* which do not tend to the knowledge or love of God:

Softness and needless self-indulgence:

Laying up treasure upon earth:

Borrowing without a probability of paying; or taking up goods without a probability of paying for them. . . .

Source: Thomas Coke and Francis Asbury, *The Doctrines and Discipline of the Methodist Episcopal Church in America 1798* (Wesleyan Heritage Publications, 2000), pp. 126–127, 142–143, 151, 162.

You are supposed to have the *Faith that overcometh the world*. To you therefore it is not grievous,

I. Carefully to abstain from doing evil: in particular,

1. Neither to *buy* nor *sell* any thing at all on the Lord's-day.

2. To taste no spirituous liquor, *no dram* of any kind, unless prescribed by a physician.

3. To be *at a word* both in buying and selling.

4. Not to *mention the fault* of any *behind his back*, and to stop those short that do.

5. To wear no *needless ornaments*, such as rings, earrings, necklaces, lace, ruffles.

6. To use no *needless self-indulgence*.

II. Zealously to maintain good works; in particular,

1. To *give aims* of such things as you possess, and that according to your ability.

2. To *reprove* those who sin in your sight, and that in love and meekness of wisdom.

3. To be patterns of *diligence* and *frugality*, of *self-denial*, and taking up the cross daily.

III. Constantly to attend on all the ordinances of GOD; in particular,

1. To be at church, and at the LORD'S table, and at every public meeting of the bands, at every opportunity.

2. To use private prayer every day; and family prayer, if you are the head of a family.

3. Frequently to read the scriptures, and meditate thereon. And,

4. To observe, as days of fasting or abstinence, all *Fridays* in the year. . . .

Of Dress

Quest. SHOULD we insist on the rules concerning dress?

Answ. By all means. This is no time to give any encouragement to superfluity of apparel. Therefore give no tickets to any, till they have left off superfluous ornaments. In order to this, 1. Let every one who has the charge of a circuit, read the thoughts upon dress, at least once a year in every large society. 2. In visiting the classes, be very mild, but very strict. 3. Allow of no exempt case: Better one suffer than many. 4. Give no tickets to any that wear high heads, enormous bonnets, ruffles, or rings. . . .

Of the Sale and Use of Spirituous Liquors

Quest. WHAT directions shall be given concerning the sale and use of spirituous liquors?

Answ. If any member of our society retail or give spirituous liquors, and any thing disorderly be transacted under his roof on this account, the preacher who has the oversight of the circuit shall proceed against him as in the case of other immoralities; and the person accused shall be cleared, censured, suspended or excluded according to his conduct, as on other charges of immorality.

 Verse was a popular form of expression for defenders of revival religion during the Second Great Awakening. What does this doggerel suggest about the sources of revivalism's appeal?

"On Predestination" (1809)

If all things succeed
  Because they're decreed
And immutable impulses rule us;
  Then praying and preaching,
  And all such like teaching,
Is nought but a plan to befool us.
  If destiny and fate,
  Guide us this way and that,
As the coachman with bits guides his horses;
  There's no man can stray,
  But all go the right way,
As the stars in their different courses.
. . . .
  If this be the way,
  As some preachers say,
That all things were order'd by fate;
  I'll not spend my pence,
  To pay for nonsense,
If nothing will alter my state.
. . . .
  Then with all he must pass
  For a dull, senseless ass,
Who depends upon predestination.

Source: Elias Smith, *Herald of Gospel Liberty,* September 15, 1809.

Revivalist preacher Lorenzo Dow offered this defense of camp meetings in response to the attacks of orthodox preachers. On what grounds does he defend them?

A Defense of Camp Meetings (1814)

You may support your distinction and feed your pride, but in a religious point of view all men are on a level, and the good man feels it so. The very fact, your aversion to worship your Creator with the poor and despised, proves to me that you have neither part nor lot in the matter; that you know not God nor his worship, and that to follow your advice would be the sure road to perdition. The Lord hath declared his intention and purpose to exalt the humble whilst he will pull down high looks.

Source: Lorenzo Dow, *History of Cosmopolite; or the Four Volumes of Lorenzo Dow's Journal* (Wheeling, Va., 1848), p. 593.

5 The area along the Erie Canal in upstate New York was the scene of intense revival activity. It was also the birthplace of the Church of Jesus Christ of Latter-day Saints (Mormons), founded in 1830 by Joseph Smith. Smith claimed to be a prophet and to have translated ancient scripture that told the story of Israelites and other inhabitants in pre-Columbian America. Although Mormon preaching lacked the emotionalism of the revivalists, it initially attracted many people from this area of intense revival activity. In these passages from the *Book of Mormon*, the prophet Nephi explains the path to salvation and indicts churches that will appear in modern times. Are the themes expressed here similar to those emphasized in other sources?

Book of Mormon (1830)

25 Adam fell that men might be; and men are, that they might have joy.

26 And the Messiah cometh in the fulness of time, that he may redeem the children of men from the fall. And because that they are redeemed from the fall they have become free forever, knowing good from evil; to act for themselves and not to be acted upon, save it be by the punishment of the law at the great and last day, according to the commandments which God hath given.

27 Wherefore, men are free according to the flesh; and all things are given them which are expedient unto man. And they are free to choose liberty and eternal life, through the great Mediator of all men, or to choose captivity and death, according to the captivity and power of the devil; for he seeketh that all men might be miserable like unto himself.

Source: Book of Mormon, 2 Nephi 2:25–29; 28:12–15 (Salt Lake City, Utah: The Church of Jesus Christ of Latter-day Saints, 1986).

28 And now, my sons, I would that ye should look to the great Mediator, and hearken unto his great commandments; and be faithful unto his words, and choose eternal life, according to the will of his Holy Spirit;

29 And not choose eternal death, according to the will of the flesh and the evil which is therein, which giveth the spirit of the devil power to captivate, to bring you down to hell, that he may reign over you in his own kingdom. . . .

12 Because of pride, and because of false teachers, and false doctrine, their churches have become corrupted, and their churches are lifted up; because of pride they are puffed up.

13 They rob the poor because of their fine sanctuaries; they rob the poor because of their fine clothing; and they persecute the meek and the poor in heart, because in their pride they are puffed up.

14 They wear stiff necks and high heads; yea, and because of pride, and wickedness, and abominations, and whoredoms, they have all gone astray save it be a few, who are the humble followers of Christ; nevertheless, they are led, that in many instances they do err because they are taught by the precepts of men.

15 O the wise, and the learned, and the rich, that are puffed up in the pride of their hearts, and all those who preach false doctrines, and all those who commit whoredoms, and pervert the right way of the Lord, wo, wo, wo be unto them, saith the Lord God Almighty, for they shall be thrust down to hell!

---

6 Father of *Uncle Tom's Cabin* author, Harriet Beecher Stowe, Lyman Beecher was one of the most influential Second Great Awakening preacher. He was also a vocal critic of alcohol consumption and, like many Protestant temperance advocates, of growing immigration, especially Catholic immigration. In this source, Beecher reveals another potential source for the invigoration of Protestantism in the early nineteenth century.

"Plea for the West" (1835)
LYMAN BEECHER

. . . [I]If this nation is, in the providence of God, destined to lead the way in the moral and political emancipation of the world, it is time she understood her high calling, and were harnessed for the work. For mighty causes, like

Source: Lyman Beecher, *Plea for the West* (New York: Arno Press, 1977; originally published 1835), pp. 10–12, 49–50, 115–117.

floods from distant mountains, are rushing with accumulating power, to their consummation of good or evil, and soon our character and destiny will be stereotyped forever.

It is equally plain that the religious and political destiny of our nation is to be decided in the West. There is the territory, and there soon will be the population, the wealth, and the political power. The Atlantic commerce and manufactures may confer always some peculiar advantage on the East. But the West is destined to be the great central power of the nation, and under heaven, must affect powerfully the cause of free institutions and the liberty of the world.

The West is a young empire of mind, and power, and wealth, and free institutions, rushing up to a giant manhood with a rapidity and a power never before witnessed below the sun. And if she carries with her the elements of her preservation, the experiment will be glorious—the joy of the nation—the joy of the whole earth, as she rises in the majesty of her intelligence and benevolence, and enterprise, for the emancipation of the world.

It is equally clear, that the conflict which is to decide the destiny of the West, will be a conflict of institutions for the education of her sons, for purposes of superstition, or evangelical light; of despotism, or liberty. . . .

This danger from uneducated mind is augmenting daily by the rapid influx of foreign emigrants, unacquainted with our institutions, unaccustomed to self-government, inaccessible to education, and easily accessible to prepossession, and inveterate credulity, and intrigue, and easily embodied and wielded by sinister design. In the beginning this eruption of revolutionary Europe was not anticipated, and we opened our doors wide to the influx and naturalization of foreigners. But it is becoming a terrific inundation; it has increased upon our native population from five to thirty-seven percent, and is every year advancing. It seeks, of course, to settle down upon the unoccupied territory of the West, and may at no distant day equal, and even outnumber the native population. What is to be done to educate the millions which in twenty years Europe will pour out upon us?. . .

Four years ago the Catholic population was estimated at half a million, and in the single year of 1832 one hundred and fifty thousand were added, and the numbers every year since have greatly increased, and the Catholics predict still greater numbers the current and coming years. A great proportion of them are poor; and though in various forms an oppressive taxation swallows up all the earnings they do not consume or squander, the revenue fails, it is said, to support their clergy. Their multiplied and multiplying institutions, cathedrals of royal splendor, and colleges, and nunneries, and cheap schools, and free schools rise therefore to attest the sincerity and energy of political European patronage.

But the numerical power, without augmentation, would be too small to accomplish the end; and, therefore, Catholic Europe is throwing swarm on swarm upon our shores. They come, also, not undirected. There is evidently a supervision abroad—and one here—by which they come, and set down together, in city or country, as a Catholic body, and are led or followed quickly by a Catholic priesthood, who maintain over them in the land of strangers and unknown tongues an ascendency as absolute as they are able to exert in Germany itself.

Their embodied and insulated condition, as strangers of another tongue, and their unacquaintance with protestants, and prejudices against them, and their fear and implicit obedience of their priestbood, and aversion to instruction from book, or tract, or Bible, but with their consent, tends powerfully to prevent assimilation. . . .

7   Peter Cartwright was a convert of the Cane Ridge camp meeting in Kentucky in 1801. He went on to become a leading Methodist "circuit-rider" in Kentucky and Indiana before settling in Illinois, where he served as a presiding elder in the Methodist Episcopal Church and went into politics. In this passage from his autobiography, the unschooled Cartwright discusses whether ministers needed to be educated in theology. Do you think his conclusions would have been shared by his frontier parishioners?

A Methodist "Circuit-Rider" Discusses Education and the Ministry (1856)

Suppose, now, [Methodism's founder] Mr. [John] Wesley had been obliged to wait for a literary and theologically-trained band of preachers before he moved in the glorious work of his day, what would Methodism have been in the Wesleyan connection to-day? Suppose the Methodist Episcopal Church in these United States had been under the necessity of waiting for men thus qualified, what would her condition have been at this time? In despite of all John Wesley's prejudices, he providentially saw that to accomplish the glorious work for which God had raised him up, he must yield to the superior wisdom of Jehovah, and send out his "lay preachers" to wake up a slumbering world. . . .

The Presbyterians, and other Calvinistic branches of the Protestant Church, used to contend for an educated ministry, for pews, for instrumental music, for a congregational or stated salaried minister. The Methodists

Source: W. P. Strickland, ed., Autobiography of Peter Cartwright (Cincinnati, Ohio: Cranston and Curts, 1856), pp. 78–80.

universally opposed these ideas; and the illiterate Methodist preachers actually set the world on fire—the American world, as least—while they were lighting their matches!

Methodist preachers were called, by literary gentlemen, illiterate, ignorant babblers. I recollect once to have come across one of these Latin and Greek scholars, a regular graduate in theology. In order to bring me into contempt in a public company he addressed me in Greek. In my younger days I had learned considerable [amounts] of German. I listened to him as if I understood it all, and then replied in Dutch. This he knew nothing about, neither did he understand Hebrew. He concluded that I had answered him in Hebrew, and immediately caved in, and stated to the company that I was the first educated Methodist preacher he ever saw.

I do not wish to undervalue education, but really I have seen so many of these educated preachers who forcibly remind me of lettuce growing under the shade of a peach-tree, or like a gosling that had got the straddles by wading in the dew, that I turn away sick and faint. Now, this educated ministry and theological training are no longer an experiment. Other denominations have tried them, and they have proved a perfect failure; and is it not strange that Methodist preachers will try to gather up these antiquated systems, when enlightened Presbyterians and Congregationalists have acknowledged that the Methodist plan is the best in the world, and try to improve, as they say, our system, alleging that our educational institutions have created a necessity for theological institutes? Verily, we have fallen on evil times. Is it possible that now, when we abound in education, that we need Biblical instruction more than when we had no education, or very little? Surely if we ever needed Bible instruction, it was when we could derive no benefit from literary institutions. This is my common-sense view of the subject.

Blacks and the Revivalist Religion

The appeal of revivalism and "insurgent" Christianity was not confined to whites during the Second Great Awakening. In fact, by the first decades of the nineteenth century, large numbers of both slave and free blacks were drawn into the Methodist and Baptist camps. Although they would retreat from these positions in coming decades, at the turn of the nineteenth century Methodists and Baptists condemned slavery and welcomed blacks as equals in their churches. What do this painting and the following account by a free black man of his earlier life in bondage reveal about the appeal of Methodism in the slave quarters?

8 *Negro Methodists Holding a Meeting in Philadelphia (ca. 1812)*

The Metropolitan Museum of Art / Art Resource, NY

9 A Former Slave Discusses the Appeal of Methodism (1856)

My mistress and her family were all Episcopalians. The nearest church was five miles from our plantation, and there was no Methodist church nearer than ten miles. So we went to the Episcopal church, but always came home as we went, for the preaching was above our comprehension, so that we could understand but little that was said. But soon the Methodist religion was brought among us, and preached in a manner so plain that the way faring man, though a fool, could not err therein. The new doctrine produced great consternation among the slaveholders. It was something which they could not understand. It brought glad tidings to the poor bondman; it bound up the brokenhearted; it opened the prison doors to them that were bound, and let the captive go free. As soon as it got among the slaves, it spread from plantation to plantation, until it reached ours, where there were but few who did not experience religion.

Source: John Thompson, *The Life of John Thompson, A Fugitive Slave* (Worcester, Mass., 1856), pp. 18–19.

Women and the Revivals

Women played a large role in the Second Great Awakening, an aspect of the revivals noted by many observers. Frances Trollope and Harriet Martineau were Europeans who traveled widely in America in the early nineteenth century. Rebeccah Lee, on the other hand, was the wife of a Connecticut minister. What do these sources reveal about the possible origins of revivalism's appeal to women?

Frances Trollope's Account of a Camp Meeting (1829)

But how am I to describe the sounds that proceeded from this strange mass of human beings? I know no words which can convey an idea of it. Hysterical sobbings, convulsive groans, shrieks and screams the most appalling, burst forth on all sides. I felt sick with horror. As if their hoarse and overstrained voices failed to make noise enough, they soon began to clap their hands violently. . . .

Many of these wretched creatures were beautiful young females. The preachers moved about among them, at once exciting and soothing their agonies. I heard the muttered "Sister! dear sister!" I saw the insidious lips approach the cheeks of the unhappy girls; I heard the murmured confessions of the poor victims, and I watched their tormentors, breathing into their ears consolations that tinged the pale cheek with red. Had I been a man, I am sure I should have been guilty of some rash act of interference; nor do I believe that such a scene could have been acted in the presence of Englishmen without instant punishment being inflicted; not to mention the salutary discipline of the treadmill, which, beyond all question, would, in England, have been applied to check so turbulent and so vicious a scene.

Source: Frances Trollope, *Domestic Manners of the Americans* (1832; repr., New York: Vintage Books, 1949), pp. 172–173.

Harriet Martineau on the Condition of American Women (1837)

[H]er husband's hair stands on end at the idea of her working, and he toils to indulge her with money: she has liberty to get her brain turned by religious excitements, that her attention may be diverted from morals, politics, and philosophy; and, especially, her morals are guarded by the strictest observance of propriety in her presence. In short, indulgence is given her as a substitute for justice. . . .

. . . [M]arriage is the only object left open to woman. Philosophy she may pursue only fancifully, and under pain of ridicule: science only as a pastime, and under a similar penalty. Art is declared to be left open: but the necessary learning, and, yet more, the indispensable experience of reality, are denied to her. Literature is also said to be permitted: but under what penalties and restrictions? Nothing is thus left for women but marriage.—Yes; Religion, is the reply. . . .

As for the occupations with which American ladies fill up their leisure; what has been already said will show that there is no great weight or diversity of occupation. Many are largely engaged in charities, doing good or harm according to the enlightenment of mind which is carried to the work. In New England, a vast deal of time is spent in attending preachings, and other religious meetings: and in paying visits, for religious purposes, to the poor and sorrowful. The same results follow from this practice that may be witnessed wherever it is much pursued. In as far as sympathy is kept up, and acquaintanceship between different classes in society is occasioned, the practice is good. In as far as it unsettles the minds of the visitors, encourages a false craving for religious excitement . . . the practice is bad.

Source: Harriet Martineau, *Society in America* (Gloucester, Mass.: Peter Smith, 1968), pp. 292–293, 305.

12   Rebeccah Lee on the Appeal of Christianity (1831)

To the Christian religion we owe the rank we hold in society, and we should feel our obligations. It is that, which prevents our being treated like beasts of burden—which secures us the honourable privilege of human companionship in social life, and raises us in the domestic relations to the elevated stations of wives and mothers. Only seriously reflect upon the state of our sex, in those regions of the globe unvisited and unblessed with the light of Christianity; we see them degraded to a level with the brutes, and shut out from the society of lordly *man*; as if they were made by their Creator, not as the companions, but as the slaves and drudges of domineering masters. . . . Let each one then ask herself, how much do I owe?

Source: Nancy F. Cott, *The Bonds of Womanhood: "Woman's Sphere" in New England, 1780–1835* (New Haven, Conn.: Yale University Press, 1977), pp. 131–132; originally from Mrs. Rebeccah Lee, *An Address, Delivered in Marlborough, Connecticut, September 7, 1831.*

Workers and Revivalism in Philadelphia

By the 1820s, such eastern cities as Philadelphia were hotbeds of revival activity. As you examine these sources, keep in mind that journeymen (unlike master craftsmen) were hired workers. Do these sources reveal a possible connection between workers' economic concerns and revivalism's appeal?

Philadelphia Journeymen Protest Their Conditions (1828)

We, the Journeymen Mechanics of the City and County of Philadelphia, conscious that our condition in society is lower than justice demands it should be, and feeling our inability, individually, to ward off from ourselves and families those numerous evils which result from an unequal and very excessive accumulation of wealth and power into the hands of a few, are desirous of forming an Association, which shall avert as much as possible those evils with which poverty and incessant toil have already inflicted, and which threaten ultimately to overwhelm and destroy us. And in order that our views may be properly understood, and the justness of our intention duly appreciated, we offer to the public the following summary of our reasons, principles and objects.

If unceasing toils were actually requisite to supply us with a bare, and in many instances wretched, subsistence; if the products of our industry or an equitable proportion of them, were appropriated to our actual wants and comfort, then would we yield without a murmur to the stem and irrevocable decree of necessity. But this is infinitely wide of the fact. We appeal to the most intelligent of every community, and ask—Do not you, and all society, depend solely for subsistence on the products of human industry? Do not those who labour, while acquiring to themselves thereby only a scanty and penurious support, likewise maintain in affluence and luxury the rich who never labour?

Do not all the streams of wealth which flow in every direction and are emptied into and absorbed by the coffers of the unproductive, exclusively take their rise in the bones, marrow, and muscles of the industrious classes? In return for which, exclusive of a bare subsistence, (which likewise is the product of their own industry,) they receive—not any thing! . . .

The real object, therefore, of this association, is to avert, if possible, the desolating evils which must inevitably arise from a depreciation of the intrinsic value of human labour; to raise the mechanical and productive classes to that condition of true independence and inequality [sic] which their practical skill and ingenuity, their immense utility to the nation and their growing intelligence are beginning imperiously to demand: to promote, equally, the happiness, prosperity and welfare of the whole community—to aid in conferring a due and full proportion of that invaluable promoter of happiness, leisure, upon all its useful members; and to assist, in conjunction with such other institutions of this nature as shall hereafter be formed throughout the union, in establishing a just balance of power, both mental, moral, political and scientific, between all the various classes and individuals which constitute society at large.

Source: John R. Commons et al., eds., *A Documentary History of American Industrial Society* (Cleveland, 1910), V: pp. 84–85, 89–90.

Occupations of Methodist Converts in Philadelphia (1830s)

Occupation	No.	%
Gentlemen	0	0
Professional	3	2.9
Merchant and Retailer	16	15.5
Manufacturer	1	0.9
Lower white-collar	4	3.9
Master Craftsman	10	9.7
Journeyman	64	62.1
Unskilled labor and street trade	5	4.9
Total	103	99.9

Source: Bruce Laurie, *Working People of Philadelphia, 1800–1850* (Philadelphia: Temple University Press, 1980), p. 47; originally from First Presbyterian Church in Southwark, Minutes, 1830–1840, Presbyterian Historical Society, Philadephia; First Presbyterian Church of Southwark, Trustees Minutes, 1818–1832, Presbyterian Historical Society, Philadelphia; and Centennial Publishing Committee, *History of Ebenezer Methodist Church, Southwark* (Philadelphia: J. B. Lippincott, 1892); and city directories, 1830–1835.

Alexis de Tocqueville, a French aristocrat who traveled extensively in the United States in the early 1830s, published his observations about American manners, society, and politics in *Democracy in America*. In what ways did a "general equality of condition" influence Americans' attitudes, according to Tocqueville? How might conditions or attitudes that he perceived encourage revivalism? Are these conditions and attitudes the same as those identified in Nathan Hatch's essay?

Alexis de Tocqueville on the Condition of Americans (1835)

Amongst the novel objects that attracted my attention during my stay in the United States, nothing struck me more forcibly than the general equality of conditions. I readily discovered the prodigious influence which this primary fact exercises on the whole course of society, by giving a certain direction to public opinion, and a certain tenor to the laws; by imparting new maxims to the governing powers, and peculiar habits to the governed. I speedily perceived that the influence of this fact extends far beyond the political character and the laws of the country, and that it has no less empire over civil society than over the Government; it creates opinions, engenders

Source: Alexis de Tocqueville, Democracy in America, 1835.

sentiments, suggests the ordinary practices of life, and modifies whatever it does not produce. The more I advanced in the study of American society, the more I perceived that the equality of conditions is the fundamental fact from which all others seem to be derived, and the central point at which all my observations constantly terminated. . . .

When the ranks of society are unequal, and men unlike each other in condition, there are some individuals invested with all the power of superior intelligence, learning, and enlightenment, whilst the multitude is sunk in ignorance and prejudice. Men living at these aristocratic periods are therefore naturally induced to shape their opinions by the superior standard of a person or a class of persons, whilst they are averse to recognize the infallibility of the mass of the people.

The contrary takes place in ages of equality. The nearer the citizens are drawn to the common level of an equal and similar condition, the less prone does each man become to place implicit faith in a certain man or a certain class of men. But his readiness to believe the multitude increases, and opinion is more than ever mistress of the world. . . .

We shall have occasion to see that, of all the passions which originate in, or are fostered by, equality, there is one which it renders peculiarly intense, and which it infuses at the same time into the heart of every man: I mean the love of well-being. The taste for well-being is the prominent and indelible feature of democratic ages. It may be believed that a religion which should undertake to destroy so deep seated a passion, would meet its own destruction thence in the end; and if it attempted to wean men entirely from the contemplation of the good things of this world, in order to devote their faculties exclusively to the thought of another, it may be foreseen that the soul would at length escape from its grasp, to plunge into the exclusive enjoyment of present and material pleasures. The chief concern of religions is to purify, to regulate, and to restrain the excessive and exclusive taste for well-being which men feel at periods of equality; but they would err in attempting to control it completely or to eradicate it. They will not succeed in curing men of the love of riches: but they may still persuade men to enrich themselves by none but honest means.

This brings me to a final consideration, which comprises, as it were, all the others. The more the conditions of men are equalized and assimilated to each other, the more important is it for religions, whilst they carefully abstain from the daily turmoil of secular affairs, not needlessly to run counter to the ideas which generally prevail, and the permanent interests which exist in the mass of the people. For as public opinion grows to be more and more evidently the first and most irresistible of existing powers, the religious principle has no external support strong enough to enable it long to resist its attacks. . . .

. . . As social conditions become more equal, the number of persons increases who, although they are neither rich enough nor powerful enough to exercise any great influence over their fellow-creatures, have nevertheless acquired or retained sufficient education and fortune to satisfy their own wants. They owe nothing to any man, they expect nothing from any man; they acquire the habit of always considering themselves as standing alone, and they are apt to imagine that their whole destiny is in their own hands. . . .

Although the desire of acquiring the good things of this world is the prevailing passion of the American people, certain momentary outbreaks occur, when their souls seem suddenly to burst the bonds of matter by which they are restrained, and to soar impetuously towards heaven. In all the States of the Union, but especially in the half-peopled country of the Far West, wandering preachers may be met with who hawk about the word of God from place to place. Whole families—old men, women, and children—cross rough passes and untrodden wilds, coming from a great distance, to join a camp-meeting, where they totally forget for several days and nights, in listening to these discourses, the cares of business and even the most urgent wants of the body. Here and there, in the midst of American society, you meet with men, full of a fanatical and almost wild enthusiasm, which hardly exists in Europe. From time to time strange sects arise, which endeavor to strike out extraordinary paths to eternal happiness. Religious insanity is very common in the United States.

CONCLUSION

By now you have probably decided whether you agree with the conclusions in Nathan Hatch's essay. You may have also discovered that the question of historical causation is inseparable from other questions. One was the subject of Chapter 5: motivation. To study the appeal of revivalism and the "insurgent" religious groups during the Second Great Awakening necessarily forces us to understand the motives of those who embraced it. And to do that requires us to consider various influences affecting the converted. Often, that forces us to consider the subject of the last chapter: the role of ideas in history. Nathan Hatch suggests that a democratic ideology stemming from the American Revolution permeated American culture by the early nineteenth century and reshaped religion. Hatch's study of the Second Great Awakening also demonstrates that questions of causation and the role of individuals in history are closely related. Were religious leaders like Peter Cartwright, Barton Stone, and Joseph Smith prime movers in history or did they merely serve some large, underlying forces? As we shall see in later chapters, historians have different answers. Finally, perhaps you found one underlying cause to explain the changes in American Protestantism in the early nineteenth century. Alexis de Tocqueville traced much of what he saw during his travels in the United States back to a perceived equality of condition among Americans. The search for historical causes sometimes leads historians, as it did Tocqueville, to an all-encompassing explanation. In other words, they advance a "grand" theory. In Chapter 8, we turn to one such interpretation of history.

FURTHER READING

Whitney R. Cross, *The Burned-over District: The Social and Intellectual History of Enthusiastic Religion in Western New York, 1800–1850* (New York: Harper & Row, Publishers, 1965).

Paul E. Johnson, *A Shopkeeper's Millennium: Society and Revivals in Rochester, New York, 1815–1837* (New York: Hill and Wang, 1987).

George M. Marsden, *Religion and American Culture* (New York: Harcourt Brace Jovanovich, 1990).

Albert J. Raboteau, *Slave Religion: The "Invisible Institution" in the Antebellum South* (New York: Oxford University Press, 1978).

Bernard A. Weisberger, *They Gathered at the River: The Story of the Great Revivalists and Their Impact upon Religion in America* (Chicago: Quadrangle Books, 1966).

NOTES

1. Quoted in Bernard Weisberger, *They Gathered at the River: The Story of the Great Revivalists and Their Impact upon Religion in America* (Chicago: Quadrangle Books, 1966), p. 36.
2. Quoted in Charles A. Johnson, *The Frontier Camp Meeting: Religion's Harvest Time* (Dallas, Tex.: Southern Methodist University Press, 1955), p. 64.
3. Quoted in Weisberger, *They Gathered at the River*, p. 34.
4. Ibid., p. 11.
5. Curtis D. Johnson, *Islands of Holiness: Rural Religion in Upstate New York, 1790–1860* (Ithaca, N.Y.: Cornell University Press, 1989), p. 7.

Chapter
8

Grand Theory and History:
Democracy and the Frontier

The documents in this chapter deal with the frontier experience and Frederick Jackson Turner's theory about its importance in American history.

Secondary Source

Primary Sources

*I*n 1822, a young Ohio clerk named Jedediah Smith joined a fur-trading party heading up the Missouri River for the Yellowstone country. The fearless, Bible-toting Methodist spent three years in the Rockies, braving fierce storms, forbidding terrain, and suspicious Indians. Still, it was a fruitful outing. While traveling through Wyoming's Wind River Range, he located South Pass, a future gateway through the Rockies for thousands of westward-bound migrants. And when he returned to St. Louis in 1825, he carried 9,000 pounds of beaver pelts. The West had cast its spell on him. Less than a month later, Smith led a party of seventy men back up the Missouri. By the time the trapper returned five years later, he had trekked beyond the Rockies into the wastes of the Great Basin and across the Mojave desert to California—the first American to enter the Mexican province by land.

Smith and other trappers represented the leading edge of American penetration into the West. Yet when he sold his fur business in 1830 to get into the growing Santa Fe trade, the trappers' days were just about over. In fact, when Smith returned to St. Louis that year, he saw many settlers hard on his heels. Drifting back down the Missouri, he passed a host of new towns where none had been before. And more newcomers were on the way. In 1830, more people lived west of the Appalachian Mountains than had lived in the original states in 1790. Indeed, so quickly did settlers displace fur trappers that when Smith died in an Indian attack near the Cimarron River in 1831, he and other mountain men had already become legends—outsized characters from a bygone era.

The West has long evoked powerful and romantic images for many Americans. There, larger-than-life figures, whether explorers, trappers, or the settlers who followed, triumphed over nature and, usually, the native inhabitants. In the process, they pushed the frontier ever westward, bringing "civilization" to an "untamed" land. For many historians, however, this version of national expansion and the images that inevitably accompany it mislead more than they inform. In their view, western history presented as a story of pioneers marching westward, bringing civilization and "progress" with them, ignores many other participants in the western past and overlooks important costs and consequences of the region's development. In this chapter, we turn to the West with this tension in mind. We consider first a grand theory about the long frontier experience as a decisive influence in the nation's past. Like all grand theories, it attributes numerous and far-reaching consequences to a single force. We then consider a set of primary sources that offer numerous other angles from which to consider the nature and significance of the western experience.

SETTING

It did not take long for Americans to create their first frontier heroes out of fur traders like Jedediah Smith. It took historians far longer to acknowledge the influence of the frontier on American society. First the frontier had to become history. In 1890, the U.S. Census Bureau announced the closing of the frontier. Three years later, a young University of Wisconsin historian named Frederick Jackson Turner read his paper called "The Significance of the Frontier in American History" at the World Columbian Exposition in Chicago. Although Turner's "frontier thesis" was ignored at the time, after the turn of the century historians gradually began to acknowledge it.

Even then, many of them were not impressed. In the nineteenth century, most historians ignored the West. They often defined history as "past politics" and emphasized the European roots of American political institutions. Turner, who grew up in rural Wisconsin a generation removed from the frontier, resented the Eastern and European slant to American history. His essay challenged that anti-Western bias and the orthodox definition of history as political narrative. Instead, Turner offered nothing less than a sweeping reassessment of the formation of American society. His "frontier thesis" was a grand explanation of American uniqueness from a Western perspective.

Despite its chilly reception, Turner's thesis gradually became historical orthodoxy. His argument may have challenged a conventional definition of history, but it also confirmed popular thinking. As Theodore Roosevelt noted, Turner "put into definite shape a good deal of thought that has been floating around rather loosely."[1] One idea blowing in the late nineteenth-century breezes was a belief in America's "manifest destiny" to spread American culture and institutions abroad. Turner's thesis was published just after the frontier officially closed and when nostalgia over its passing was growing. Just when many Americans saw new "frontiers" overseas, Turner's thesis confirmed a nationalist assumption that American expansion and democracy were inseparable. It also reflected the pervasive influence of Charles Darwin's theory of evolution on American thought. Like many post-Darwinian thinkers, Turner assumed that societies evolved from a primitive to a "civilized" stage. This Darwinian model of social evolution reinforced both expansionist desires and assumptions about Anglo-Saxon superiority. Indeed, many Americans argued that it was their duty as "Anglo-Saxons" to bring civilization to the "backward" peoples of the world.

Given a receptive audience, Turner's thesis became part of popular thought. It was embraced and popularized by many prominent Americans, from Theodore Roosevelt and Woodrow Wilson to Herbert Hoover. Future president Hoover, for instance, would declare in a widely read article in 1922 that "American individualism has received much of its character from our contacts with the forces of nature on a new continent."[2] In addition to crystallizing popular thinking, Turner's argument was comprehensive, comprehensible, and romantic. Reading Turner, Americans for more than a century have seen his thesis as a key to understanding a cherished part of the nation's past. In one bold stroke, Turner had broadened Americans' history and captured their imaginations.

This grand theory about the nation's frontier experience has drawn much fire, however, from modern historians. In our time, many historians turn to the past with fewer nationalistic assumptions than Turner demonstrated, and they have uncovered a darker and less unified history of the West. Such contemporary Western historians as Patricia Limerick, Gerald Nash, and Donald Worster argue that the conquest of the West was often accompanied by oppression, exploitation, and environmental destruction. These "new Western historians" include in the story of Western settlement people who never appeared on Turner's frontier: women, blacks, Hispanics, Asians, and Indians. Doing so, they argue, reveals some of the flaws in Turner's conception of the frontier. It was not empty space into which Americans moved. Nor did settlers always enter it, as Turner's had, from somewhere back East. And they did not necessarily cast off their cultural baggage and develop new institutions and customs. Thanks to the work of these historians, the Western experience looks much different today than it did to Turner— and students today have a far wider range of sources and perspectives with which to evaluate it.

INVESTIGATION

Because the frontier thesis gave legend and romance a central role in the nation's past, readers even today are inclined to judge it with their hearts rather than their heads. Your main challenge, therefore, is to evaluate Turner's thesis critically. Using Turner's own evidence (Source 1) and that in the primary sources, determine whether his thesis is a useful tool to explain Americans' institutions and character. Your evaluation should address the following questions:

1. **What important effects did the frontier have on American society and character, according to Turner?** What is his evidence that the frontier promoted individualism and a "composite nationality"?

2. **What was the relationship between the frontier and American political institutions?** How does Turner attempt to demonstrate a relationship between democracy and the frontier?

3. **What is Turner's evidence for social breakdown and evolution on the frontier?** What role do the government, corporations, cities, or religious organizations play in Turner's frontier?

4. **How do the experiences of specific groups of people, as reflected in the primary sources, support or modify Turner's view of Western settlement?** Does Turner's thesis reflect a mythic view of the West or real experiences?

SECONDARY SOURCE

1   Like the vast stretches of the West in which even Jedediah Smith occasionally got lost, Turner's frontier thesis is both alluring and deceptive. It is just as easy to be drawn into his argument as it is to lose one's way once there. Readers must be careful not to be ambushed by Turner's prose or by the simplicity of his thesis. They must be alert, inquisitive, and as interested in the small details of the trees as in the grand vision of the forest. As you read, therefore, notice the way Turner defines the frontier. Consider whether he sees it as a line of settlement, a type of society, a specific area or region, or a social process. Also be careful to note his evidence for the transforming power of the frontier.

The Significance of the Frontier in American History (1893)
FREDERICK JACKSON TURNER

In a recent bulletin of the superintendent of the census for 1890 appear these significant words: "Up to and including 1880 the country had a frontier of settlement; but at present the unsettled area has been so broken into by isolated bodies of settlement that there can hardly be said to be a frontier line. In the discussion of its extent, its westward movement, etc., it cannot, therefore, any longer have a place in the census reports." This brief official statement marks the closing of a great historic movement. Up to our own day American history has been in a large degree the history of the colonization of the Great West. The existence of an area of free land, its continuous recession, and the advance of American settlement westward, explain American development. Behind institutions, behind constitutional forms and modifications, lie the vital forces that call these organs into life, and shape them to meet changing conditions. Now, the peculiarity of American institutions is the fact that they have been compelled to adapt themselves to the changes of an expanding people—to the changes involved in crossing a continent, in winning a wilderness, and in developing at each area of this progress out of the primitive economic and political conditions of the frontier into the complexity of city life. . . . Thus American development has exhibited not merely advance along a single line, but a return to primitive conditions on a continually advancing frontier line, and a new development for that area. American social development has been continually beginning over again on the frontier. This perennial rebirth, this fluidity of American life, this expansion westward with its new opportunities, its continuous touch with the simplicity of primitive society, furnish the forces dominating American character. The true point of view in the history of this nation is not the Atlantic coast, it is the Great West. . . .

Source: Proceedings of the Forty-First Annual Meeting of the State Historical Society of Wisconsin (Madison, Wis., 1894), pp. 79–112.

In this advance, the frontier is the outer edge of the wave—the meeting point between savagery and civilization. Much has been written about the frontier from the point of view of border warfare and the chase, but as a field for the serious study of the economist and the historian it has been neglected.

What is the frontier? It is not the European frontier—a fortified boundary line running through dense populations. The most significant thing about it is, that it lies at the hither edge of free land. In the census reports it is treated as the margin of that settlement which has a density of two or more to the square mile. The term is a classic one, and for our purpose does not need sharp definition. . . .

. . . Now, the frontier is the line of most rapid and effective Americanization. The wilderness masters the colonist. It finds him a European in dress, industries, tools, modes of travel, and thought. It takes him from the railroad car and puts him in the birch canoe. It strips off the garments of civilization, and arrays him in the hunting shirt and the moccasin. It puts him in the log cabin of the Cherokee and the Iroquois, and runs an Indian palisade around him. Before long he has gone to planting Indian corn and plowing with a sharp stick; he shouts the war cry and takes the scalp in orthodox Indian fashion. In short, at the frontier the environment is at first too strong for the man. He must accept the conditions which it furnishes, or perish, and so he fits himself into the Indian clearings and follows the Indian trails. Little by little he transforms the wilderness, but the outcome is not the old Europe. . . . The fact is, that here is a new product that is American. At first, the frontier was the Atlantic coast. It was the frontier of Europe in a very real sense. Moving westward, the frontier became more and more American. *As successive terminal moraines result from successive glaciations, so each frontier leaves its traces behind it, and when it becomes a settled area the region still partakes of the frontier characteristics.* Thus the advance of the frontier has meant a steady movement away from the influence of Europe, a steady growth of independence on American lines. And to study this advance, the men who grew up under these conditions, and the political, economic and social results of it, is to study the really American part of our history. . . .

The Frontier Furnishes a Field for Comparative Study of Social Development

. . . The United States lies like a huge page in the history of society. Line by line as we read from west to east we find the record of social evolution. It begins with the Indian and the hunter; it goes on to tell of the disintegration of savagery by the entrance of the trader, the path-finder of civilization; we read the annals of the pastoral stage in ranch life; the exploitation of the soil by the raising of unrotated crops of corn and wheat in sparsely settled farming communities; the intensive culture of the denser farm settlement; and finally the manufacturing organization with city and factory system. This page is familiar to the student of census statistics, but how little of it has been used by our historians. Each of these areas has had an influence in our economic and political history; the evolution of each into a higher stage has worked political transformations.

Composite Nationality

First, we note that the frontier promoted the formation of a composite nationality for the American people. The coast was preponderantly English, but the later tides of continental immigration flowed across to the free lands. This was the case from the early colonial days. The Scotch-Irish and the Palatine Germans, or "Pennsylvania Dutch," furnished the stock of the colonial frontier. With these people were also the free indentured servants, or redemptioners, who at the expiration of their time of service passed to the frontier. Governor Spottswood of Virginia writes in 1717, "The inhabitants of our frontiers are composed generally of such as have been transported hither as servants, and, being out of their time, settle themselves where land is to be taken up and that will produce the necessarys of life with little labour." Very generally these redemptioners were of non-English stock. In the crucible of the frontier the immigrants were Americanized, liberated and fused into a mixed race, English in neither nationality or characteristics. The process has gone on from the early days to our own. . . .

National Tendencies of the Frontier

It is safe to say that the legislation with regard to land, tariff, and internal improvements—the American system of the nationalizing Whig party—was conditioned on frontier ideas and needs. But it was not merely in legislative action that the frontier worked against the sectionalism of the coast. The economic and social characteristics of the frontier worked against sectionalism. The men of the frontier had closer resemblances to the Middle region than to either of the other sections. Pennsylvania had been the seed-plot of frontier emigration, and, although she passed on her settlers along the Great Valley into the west of Virginia and the Carolinas, yet the industrial society of these Southern frontiersmen was always more like that of the Middle region than like that of the tide-water portion of the South, which later came to spread its industrial type throughout the South.

The Middle region, entered by New York harbor, was an open door to all Europe. The tide-water part of the South represented typical Englishmen, modified by a warm climate and servile labor, and living in baronial fashion on great plantations; New England stood for a special English movement—Puritanism. The Middle region was less English than the other sections. It had a wide mixture of nationalities, a varied society, the mixed town and county system of local government, a varied economic life, many religious sects. In short it was a region mediating between New England and the South, and the East and the West. It represented that composite nationality which the contemporary United States exhibits, that juxtaposition of nonEnglish groups, occupying a valley or a little settlement, and presenting reflections of the map of Europe in their variety. It was democratic and non-sectional, if not national; "easy, tolerant and contented;" rooted strongly in material prosperity. It was typical of the modern United States. It was least sectional, not only because it lay between

North and South, but also because with no barriers to shut out its frontiers from its settled region, and with a system of connecting waterways, the Middle region mediated between East and West as well as between North and South. Thus it became the typically American region. Even the New Englander, who was shut out from the frontier by the Middle region, tarrying in New York or Pennsylvania on his westward march, lost the acuteness of his sectionalism on the way. . . .

It was this nationalizing tendency of the West that transformed the democracy of Jefferson into the national republicanism of Monroe and the democracy of Andrew Jackson. The West of the War of 1812, the West of Clay, and Benton, and Harrison, and Andrew Jackson, shut off by the Middle states and the mountains from the coast sections, had a solidarity of its own with national tendencies. On the tide of the Father of Waters, North and South met and mingled into a nation. Interstate migration went steadily on—a process of cross-fertilization of ideas and institutions. . . .

Growth of Democracy

But the most important effect of the frontier has been in the promotion of democracy here and in Europe. As has been pointed out, the frontier is productive of individualism. Complex society is precipitated by the wilderness into a kind of primitive organization based on the family. The tendency is anti-social. It produces antipathy to control, and particularly to any direct control. The tax-gatherer is viewed as a representative of oppression. Professor [Herbert L.] Osgood, in an able article, has pointed out that the frontier conditions prevalent in the colonies are important factors in the explanation of the American revolution, where individual liberty was sometimes confused with absence of all effective government. The same conditions aid in explaining the difficulty of instituting a strong government in the period of the confederacy. The frontier individualism has from the beginning promoted democracy.

The frontier states that came into the Union in the first quarter of a century of its existence came in with democratic suffrage provisions, and had reactive effects of the highest importance upon the older states whose people were being attracted there. It was *western* New York that forced an extension of suffrage in the constitutional convention of that state in 1820, and it was *western* Virginia that compelled the tide-water region to put a more liberal suffrage provision in the constitution framed in 1830, and to give to the frontier region a more nearly proportionate representation with the tide-water aristocracy. The rise of democracy as an effective force in the nation came in with western preponderance under Jackson and William Henry Harrison, and it meant the triumph of the frontier—with all of its good and with all of its evil elements. An interesting illustration of the tone of frontier democracy in 1830 comes from the . . . debates in the Virginia convention.* . . . A representative from western Virginia declared: "But, sir, it is not the increase of population in the West

*To revise the state constitution in 1829–1830.

which this gentleman ought to fear. It is the energy which the mountain breeze and western habits impart to those emigrants. They are regenerated, politically I mean, sir. They soon become *working politicians*; and the difference, sir, between a *talking* and a *working* politician is immense. The Old Dominion has long been celebrated for producing great orators; the ablest metaphysicians in policy; men that can split hairs in all abstruse questions of political economy. But at home, or when they return from congress, they have negroes to fan them asleep. But a Pennsylvania, a New York, an Ohio, or a western Virginia statesman, though far inferior in logic, metaphysics and rhetoric to an old Virginia statesman, has this advantage, that when he returns home he takes off his coat and takes hold of the plough. This gives him bone and muscle, sir, and preserves his republican principles pure and uncontaminated."

So long as free land exists, the opportunity for a conpetency [*sic*] exists, and economic power secures political power. But the democracy born of free land, strong in selfishness and individualism, intolerant of administrative experience and education, and pressing individual liberty beyond its proper bounds, has its dangers as well as its benefits. Individualism in America has allowed a laxity in regard to governmental affairs which has rendered possible the spoils system, and all the manifest evils that follow from the lack of a highly developed civic spirit. In this connection may be noted also the influence of frontier conditions in permitting lax business honor, inflated paper currency and wild-cat banking. The colonial and revolutionary frontier was the region whence emanated many of the worst forms of an evil currency. The West in the War of 1812 repeated the phenomenon on the frontier of that day, while the speculation and wild-cat banking of the period of the crisis of 1837 occurred on the new frontier belt of the next tier of states. Thus each one of the periods of lax financial integrity coincides with periods when a new set of frontier communities had arisen, and coincides in area with these successive frontiers for the most part. The recent Populist agitation is a case in point. Many a state that now declines any connection with the tenets of the Populists, itself adhered to such ideas in an earlier stage of the development of the state. A primitive society can hardly be expected to show the intelligent appreciation of the complexity of business interests in a developed society. The continual recurrence of these areas of paper-money agitation is another evidence that the frontier can be isolated and studied as a factor in American history of the highest importance. . . .

Intellectual Traits

From the conditions of frontier life came intellectual traits of profound importance. The works of travellers along each frontier from colonial days onward describe for each certain traits, and these traits have, while softening down, still persisted as survivals in the place of their origin, even when a higher social organization succeeded. The result is that to the frontier the American intellect owes its striking characteristics. That coarseness and strength combined with acuteness and inquisitiveness, that practical, inventive turn of mind, quick to find expedients, that masterful grasp of material things, lacking in the artistic but powerful to effect great ends, that restless, nervous energy, that dominant individualism, working for good and for evil, and withal that buoyancy and exuberance which comes with freedom,—these are traits of the frontier, or traits called out elsewhere because of the existence of the frontier. Since the days when the fleet of Columbus sailed into the waters of the New World, America has been another name for opportunity, and the people of the United States have taken their tone from the incessant expansion which has not only been open but has even been forced upon them. He would be a rash prophet who should assert that the expansive character of American life has now entirely ceased. Movement has been its dominant fact, and, unless this training has no effect upon a people, the American intellect will continually demand a wider field for its exercise. But never again will such gifts of free land offer themselves. For a moment at the frontier the bonds of custom are broken, and unrestraint is triumphant. There is not *tabula rasa*. The stubborn American environment is there with its imperious summons to accept its conditions; the inherited ways of doing things are also there; and yet, in spite of environment, and in spite of custom, each frontier did indeed furnish a new field of opportunity, a gate of escape from the bondage of the past; and freshness, and confidence, and scorn of older society, impatience of its restraints and its ideas, and indifference to its lessons, have accompanied the frontier. What the Mediterranean Sea was to the Greeks, breaking the bond of custom, offering new experiences, calling out new institutions and activities, that, and more, the ever retreating frontier has been to the United States directly, and to the nations of Europe more remotely. And now, four centuries from the discovery of America, at the end of a hundred years of life under the Constitution, the frontier has gone, and with its going has closed the first period of American history.

PRIMARY SOURCES

The primary sources in this chapter relate to Americans' frontier experience in the first half of the nineteenth century. Settlers had moved from the Ohio of Jedediah Smith's youth early in the century to the Pacific coast by mid-century. These sources reflect the experiences of different groups in the West and therefore may reveal a variety of perspectives.

Fur Trappers in the Far West

In "The Significance of the Frontier in American History," Turner wrote that "the wilderness masters the colonist. It finds him a European in dress, industries, tools, modes of travel, and thought. . . . It strips off the garments of civilization, and arrays him in the hunting shirt and the moccasin." When Turner wrote those words, he may have had in mind scenes captured by Alfred Jacob Miller, an American artist who ventured into the Rocky Mountains and the Far West in 1837. From hundreds of sketches of trappers who, said Miller, "lead the van in the march of civilization," he later painted numerous watercolors.[3] But the West was also a fertile ground for business enterprise. By the first decades of the nineteenth century, fur-trading companies had already established a pattern that would be followed by later railroad, mining, and timber companies. Control and direction of these enterprises lay with capitalists and managers outside the region. Is it more important that fur trappers dressed in "hunting shirt and . . . moccasin," as seen in Source 2, or that they usually took orders from company officials in the East, as revealed in Source 3?

Sketch of Trappers (1837)
ALFRED JACOB MILLER

The Walters Art Museum, Baltimore. acc. #37.1940.29.

N. J. Wyeth's Instructions for Robert Evans at the Fort Hall Trading Post (1834)

Fort Hall July 31st, 1834 as a gent. and Partner of the Columbia River Fishing and Trading Co I leave you the following instructions for your government during the time you may remain in charge of Fort Hall:

1st   You will remain untill you are relieved by another superintendent, or untill the expiration of your time of service with the Co unless you are obliged to evacuate by starvation or hostility of the Indians in either of which cases you will endeavor to cash what goods you are obliged to leave securely.

2nd   In trading you will adhere to the Tariff which is annexed and on no account deviate therefrom and you will give no credit to any one.

3rd   You will give no supplies to any of your men unless the Co are $20 in their debt by the acts which have been handed you, you will be able to ascertain when this is the case.

4th   You will have the animals left here guarded by one man in the day time and put into the Fort at night.

5th   You will keep one centry at night on duty untill your Fort is entirely finished and afterward and if any guard is found asleep you will note it in your Journal and for this and similar purposes you will keep a book in which you will enter all remarkable occurrences. . . .

Source: Clyde A. Milner II, *Major Problems in the History of the American West* (Lexington, Mass.: D. C. Heath and Co., 1989), p. 177.

The Indians' West

The pre–Civil War West was not an uninhabited land when settlers arrived. The following sources reveal information about white-Indian interaction. Keep in mind how a recognition of the Indian experience modifies Turner's thesis.

Frederick W. Beechy was an Englishman who commanded a voyage in 1825 to the Bering Strait between Russia and Alaska. Stopping along the coast of Mexican California, Beechy observed life in several of the missions established by Franciscan missionaries. This excerpt from his narrative of his voyage to the Pacific captures the close but ambivalent relationship between the missionaries and Native American converts.

Mission Life in California (1831)

FREDERICK W. BEECHY

The object of the missions is to convert as many of the wild Indians as possible, and to train them up within the walls of the establishment in the exercise of a good life, and of some trade, so that they may in time be able to provide for themselves and become useful members of civilized society. As to the various methods employed for the purpose of bringing proselytes to the mission, there are several reports, of which some were not very creditable to the institution; nevertheless, on the whole I am of opinion that the priests are innocent, from a conviction that they are ignorant of the means employed by those who are under them. Whatever may be the system, and whether the Indians be really dragged from their homes and families by armed parties, as some assert, or not, and forced to exchange their life of freedom and wandering for one of confinement and restraint in the missions, the change according to our ideas of happiness would seem advantageous to them, as they lead a far better life in the missions than in their forests, where they are in a state of nudity, and are frequently obliged to depend solely upon wild acorns for their subsistence. . . .

Having become Christians they are put to trades, or if they have good voices they are taught music, and form part of the choir of the church. Thus there are in almost every mission weavers, tanners, shoemakers, bricklayers, carpenters, blacksmiths, and other artificers. Others again are taught husbandry, to rear cattle and horses; and some to cook for the mission: while the females card, clean, and spin wool, weave, and sew; and those who are married attend to their domestic concerns.

In requital of these benefits, the services of the Indian, for life, belong to the mission, and if any neophyte should repent of his apostacy from the religion of his ancestors and desert, an armed force is sent in pursuit of him, and drags him back to punishment apportioned to the degree of aggravation attached to his crime. It does not often happen that a voluntary convert succeeds in his attempt to escape, as the wild Indians have a great contempt and dislike for those who have entered the missions, and they will frequently not only refuse to re-admit them to their tribe, but will sometimes even discover their retreat to their pursuers. This animosity between the wild and converted Indians is of great importance to the missions, as it checks desertion. . . .

The children and adults of both sexes, in all the missions, are carefully locked up every night in separate apartments, and the keys are delivered into the possession of the padre; and as, in the daytime, their occupations

Source: Frederick W. Beechy. *Narrative of a Voyage to the Pacific and Bering Strait,* Vol 2, (New York: Da Capo Press, 1968; originally published 1831), pp. 17, 18–19, 21–23.

lead to distinct places, unless they form a matrimonial alliance, they enjoy very little of each other's society. It, however, sometimes happens that they endeavour to evade the vigilance of their keepers, and are locked up with the opposite sex; but severe corporeal punishment, inflicted in the same manner as is practised in our schools, but with a whip instead of a rod, is sure to ensue if they are discovered. Though there may be occasional acts of tyranny, yet the general character of the padres is kind and benevolent, and in some of the missions, the converts are so much attached to them that I have heard them declare they would go with them, if they were obliged to quit the country. It is greatly to be regretted that, with the influence these men have over their pupils, and with the regard those pupils seem to have for their masters, the priests do not interest themselves a little more in the education of their converts, the first step to which would be in making themselves acquainted with the Indian language. Many of the Indians surpass their pastors in this respect, and can speak the Spanish language, while scarcely one of the padres can make themselves understood by the Indians. . . .

Having served ten years in the mission, an Indian may claim his liberty, provided any respectable settler will become surety for his future good conduct. A piece of ground is then allotted for his support, but be is never wholly free from the establishment, as part of his earnings must still be given to them. We heard of very few to whom this reward for servitude and good conduct had been granted; and it is not improbable that the padres are averse to it, as it deprives them of their best scholars. When these establishments were first founded, the Indians flocked to them in great numbers for the clothing with which the neophytes were supplied; but after they became acquainted with the nature of the institution, and felt themselves under restraint, many absconded. Even now, notwithstanding the difficulty of escaping, desertions are of frequent occurrence, owing probably, in some cases, to the fear of punishment—in others to the deserters having been originally inveigled into the mission by the converted Indians or the neophytes, as they are called by way of distinction to Los Gentíles, or the wild Indians—in other cases again to the fickleness of their own disposition.

5 Black Hawk was a Sauk Indian who in 1832 led an uprising of Sauk and Fox Indians in Illinois and Wisconsin. Facing famine, the Indians sought to reoccupy land they had previously abandoned. The Illinois militia, which included a young captain named Abraham Lincoln, was mobilized to remove the Indians. The result was the Black Hawk War. Later, the Sauk and Fox would be removed to Indian lands west of the Mississippi. Here Black Hawk discusses events leading to the war.

Autobiography (1833)

BLACK HAWK

During this summer, I happened at Rock Island, when a great chief arrived, (whom I had known as the great chief of Illinois, [governor Cole,] in company with another chief, who, I have been told, is a great writer, [judge Jas. Hall.] I called upon them and begged to explain to them the grievances under which me and my people were laboring, hoping that they could do something for us. The great chief, however, did not seem disposed to council with me. He said he was no longer the great chief of Illinois—that his children had selected another father in his stead, and that he now only ranked as they did. I was surprised at this talk, as I had always heard that he was a good, brave, and great chief. But the white people never appear to be satisfied. When they get a good father, they hold councils, (at the suggestion of some bad, ambitious man, who wants the place himself,) and conclude, among themselves, that this man, or some other equally ambitious, would make a better father than they have, and nine times out of ten they don't get as good a one again.

I insisted on explaining to these two chiefs the true situation of my people. They gave their assent: I rose and made a speech, in which I explained to them the treaty made by Quàsh-quà-me, and three of our braves, according to the manner the trader and others had explained it to me. I then told them that Quàsh-quà-me and his party *denied*, positively, having ever sold my village; and that, as I had never known them to *lie*, I was determined to keep it in possession.

I told them that the white people had already entered our village, *burnt our lodges, destroyed our fences, ploughed up our corn, and beat our people:* that they had brought *whisky* into our country, *made our people drunk*, and taken from them their *horses, guns*, and *traps*; and that I had borne all this injury, without suffering any of my braves to raise a hand against the whites.

My object in holding this council, was to get the opinion of these two chiefs, as to the best course for me to pursue. I had appealed in vain, time after time, to our agent, who regularly represented our situation to the great chief at St. Louis, whose duty it was to call upon our Great Father to have justice done to us; but instead of this, we are told *that the white people want our country, and we must leave it to them!*

I did not think it possible that our Great Father wished us to leave our village, where we had lived so long, and where the bones of so many of our people had been laid. The great chief said that, as he was no longer a chief, he could do nothing for us; and felt sorry that it was not in his power to aid us—nor did he know how to advise us. Neither of

Source: Donald Jackson, ed., *Black Hawk: An Autobiography* (Urbana: University of Illinois Press, 1964), pp. 102–104.

them could do any thing for us; but both evidently appeared very sorry. It would give me great pleasure, at all times, to take these two chiefs by the hand.

That fall I paid a visit to the agent, before we started to our hunting grounds, to hear if he had any good news for me. He had news! He said that the land on which our village stood was now ordered to be sold to individuals; and that, when sold, *our right* to remain, by treaty, would be at an end, and that if we returned next spring, we would be *forced* to remove!

We learned during the winter, that *part* of the lands where our village stood had been sold to individuals, and that the *trader* at Rock Island had bought the greater part that had been sold. The reason was now plain to me, why *he* urged us to remove. His object, we thought, was to get our lands. We held several councils that winter to determine what we should do, and resolved, in one of them, to return to our village in the spring, as usual; and concluded, that if we were removed by force, that the *trader*, agent, and others, must be the cause; and that, if found guilty of having us driven from our village, they should be *killed!* The trader stood foremost on this list. He had purchased the land on which my lodge stood, and that of our *grave yard* also! Ne-a-pope promised to kill him, the agent, interpreter, the great chief at St. Louis, the war chief at fort Armstrong, Rock Island, and Ke-o-kuck—these being the principal persons to blame for endeavoring to remove us.

Images and Reports from the West

Immigrants, travelers, and artists in the West often left revealing evidence about conditions there. As you read and examine these sources, note how the observations they make and the experiences they relate support or modify Turner's thesis.

 This description was from Baird's guidebook for immigrants and travelers to the West.

View of the Valley of the Mississippi (1832)
ROBERT BAIRD

The peculiarities . . . of character, which may be said to distinguish the population of the West, are all created by the peculiar circumstances in which the people have been placed in that new world. They are,

Source: Robert Baird, *View of the Valley of the Mississippi: Or the Emigrant's and Traveller's Guide to the West* (1832).

1. *A spirit of adventurous enterprise:* a willingness to go through any hardship or danger to accomplish an object. It was the spirit of enterprise which led to the settlement of that country. The western people think nothing of making a long journey, of encountering fatigue, and of enduring every species of hardship. The great highways of the west—its long rivers—are familiar to very many of them, who have been led by trade to visit remote parts of the valley.

2. *Independence of thought and action.*—They have felt the influence of this principle from their childhood. Men who can endure any thing: that have lived almost without restraint, free as the mountain air, or as the deer and the buffalo of their forests—and who know that they are Americans all—will act out this principle during the whole of life. I do not mean that they have such an amount of it as to render them *really* regardless alike of the opinions and the feelings of everyone else. But I have seen many who have the virtue of independence greatly per-verted or degenerated. . . .

3. *An apparent roughness,* which some would deem *rudeness of manners.*

---

7   George Caleb Bingham was a Missouri artist whose work often reflected political themes. A Whig representative in the Missouri General Assembly in the late 1840s, Bingham was no stranger to the political scenes he created in such paintings as *The Stump Orator.* As one St. Louis reporter enthused:

> It is not an attempt to caricature, but an effort to draw an unexaggerated represen-tation of an assemblage which is familiar to every one in the west. The postures—the dress, as clean and neat as the humble means of western life will justify—the little knot of busy politicians around the finely dressed Demagogue, in the back-ground—the idiotic expression of an unfortunate inebriate behind the speaker . . . give to the whole a merit, a richness and a beauty to which ordinary language cannot do justice.[4]

As you examine this painting, determine whether it reflects themes in Turner's frontier thesis.

Stump Speaking (1854)

GEORGE CALEB BINGHAM

Stump Speaking (oil on canvas), Bingham, George Caleb (1811–79)/Private Collection/The Bridgeman Art Library International.

8 It is impossible to discuss the settlement of the West without acknowledging the role played by the Latter-day Saints, or Mormons. When they entered the Salt Lake Valley in 1847, the Mormons immediately began laying plans for a city that reflected collective community action and a desire to live in an orderly society. It was a pattern of settlement that they would duplicate over a large portion of the West. As you read this source, ask yourself if the Mormons' approach to settlement conforms to Turner's thesis.

Brigham Young on Land Distribution (1848)

It is our intention to have the five acre lots next to the city accommodate the mechanics and artisans, the ten acres next, then the twenty acres, followed by the forty and eighty acre lots, where farmers can build and reside. All these lots will be enclosed in one common fence, which will be seventeen miles and fifty-three rods long, eight feet high; and to the end that every man may be satisfied with his lot and prevent any hardness that might occur by any method of dividing the land, we have proposed that it shall all be done by ballot, or casting lots, as Israel did in days of old.

Source: Leonard J. Arrington, *Great Basin Kingdom: An Economic History of the Latter-day Saints* (Lincoln: University of Nebraska Press, 1966), p.52.

9 Antonio Franco Coronel came to California in 1834 and settled in Los Angeles. When gold was discovered in the Sierra foothills, *Californios* (Californians of Spanish descent) headed to the gold fields from as far away as San Diego. Coronel was among them. By 1849, when many other people had arrived in the mining camps, racial and ethnic conflict had flared up. Note Coronel's explanation for the hostility toward the Spanish.

Life in the Gold Fields (1849)

ANTONIO FRANCO CORONEL

I arrived at the Placer Seco [about March, 1849] and began to work at a regular digging.

In this place there was already a numerous population of Chileans, Peruvians, Californians, Mexicans, and many Americans, Germans, etc. The camps were almost separated according to nationalities. All, some more, some less, were profiting from the fruit of their work. Presently news was circulated that it had been resolved to evict all of those who were not American citizens from the placers because it was believed that the foreigners did not have the right to exploit the placers.

One Sunday, [notices] appeared in writing in Los Pinos and in several places, that anyone who was not an American citizen must abandon the place within twenty-four hours and that he who did not comply would be obliged to by force. This was supported by a gathering of armed men, ready to make that warning effective.

There was a considerable number of people of various nationalities who understood the order to leave—they decided to gather on a hill in order to be on the defensive in case of any attack. On the day in which the departure of the foreigners should take place, and for three or four more days, both forces remained prepared, but the thing did not go beyond cries, shots, and drunken men. Finally all fell calm and we returned to continue our work. Daily, though, the weakest were dislodged from their diggings by the strongest.

Source: Antonio Franco Coronel, "Casas de California," Ms., 1877 (BANC MSS C-D 61), the Bancroft Library, University of California, Berkeley. Reprinted by permission of the Bancroft Library.

After this agitation had calmed down, a Frenchman named Don Augusto and a Spaniard named Luis were seized—persons with whom I had dealt and who appeared to me to be honorable and of fairly good upbringing. All who had known them had formed the same opinion as I, and this seizure caused great surprise. Some of the most prominent people met together and commissioned me to investigate the reason for these arrests. I went to an American I had known in Los Angeles, one Richard, who had been a cavalry sergeant—I asked him to look into it for me. He answered immediately that they had been accused by an Irish fellow (an old man) of having stolen from him four pounds of gold from the place where he had buried it. I gave an account of my constituents and then, without loss of time, five pounds of gold was gathered from among all of us to see if payment would set these prisoners free. I approached the leader, whose appearance was disagreeable and ferocious. Wanting to vindicate the two men, I presented my plan to him through an interpreter. I told him we knew them as good men who had sufficient resources of their own and no need to appropriate those of another. Nevertheless, I had here five pounds of gold, one more than the old Irishman said they had stolen from him. He took the five pounds of gold and told me that he would go to report to his group—that I should return in the afternoon, some two or three hours later. Before the hour he had indicated to me, we saw the movement of armed men, the major part under the influence of liquor. Afterward we saw a cart leave with our two unfortunates, their arms tied behind their backs. Two men guarded them from on top of the cart, which was followed by a large crowd, some on foot and others on horseback. On the cart there was an inscription, poorly written in charcoal or something similar, which said that whoever might intercede for them would suffer the same punishment. They reached an oak tree where the execution was to take place. When the ropes had been hung around their necks, they asked to write something to their families and to arrange their affairs. For having made this request, one of the men received a slap in the face. Then, suddenly, they moved the cart and the unlucky men were hanged.

This act horrified me and it had the same effect upon many others—in two days I raised camp and headed toward the northern placers.

The reason for most of the antipathy against the Spanish race was that the greater portion was composed of Sonorans who were men accustomed to prospecting and who consequently achieved quicker, richer results— such as the *Californios* had already attained by having arrived first and acquiring understanding of this same art. Those who came later [mainly Anglo Americans], were possessed by the terrible fever to obtain gold, but they did not get it because their diggings yielded but little or nothing, or because their work did not correspond to what they took out. Well, these men aspired to become rich in a minute and they could not resign themselves to view with patience the better fortune of others. Add to this fever that which the excessive use of liquor gives them. Add that generally among so many people of all nationalities there are a great number of lost people, capable of all conceivable crimes. The circumstance that there were no laws nor authorities who could protect the rights and lives of men gave to these men advantages over peaceful and honorable men. Properly speaking, there was no more law in those times than that of force, and finally, the good person, in his own defense, had to establish the law of retaliation.

 This drawing of a San Francisco saloon captures the diversity of people in California by the mid-nineteenth century. Think about whether such a scene fits Turner's depiction of frontier society.

A San Francisco Saloon (1855)
FRANK MARRYAT

Bar of a Gambling Saloon, by Frank (Francis) Marryat, litho by J. Brandard, 1855, from Mountains and Molehills . . . or a Burnt Journal. From the Collection of the New York Historical Society [cat #48381].

11   Juan Cortina, the son of prominent Mexican family, fought against the
United States in the Mexican-American War. After watching Mexicans
cheated of their land and reduced to second-class citizens following the
war, he led a resistance to American rule in the Rio Grande Valley. After a raid on
Brownsville, Texas, during which Cortina and his followers proclaimed a Republic
of the Rio Grande, the United States Army and Texas Rangers forced Cortina and
his band across the Rio Grande River to Mexico, where he remained.

A Call for Mexicans to Resist (1859)
JUAN CORTINA

Mexicans! When the State of Texas began to receive the new organization
which its sovereignty required as an integrant part of the Union, flocks of
vampires, in the guise of men, came and scattered themselves in the settlements, without any capital, except the corrupt heart and the most perverse
intentions. Some, brimful of laws, pledged to us their protection against the
attacks of the rest; others assembled in shadowy councils, attempted and
excited the robbery and burning of the houses of our relatives on the other
side of the river Bravo; while others, to the abusing of our unlimited confidence, when we intrusted them with our titles, which secured the future of
our families, refused to return them under false and frivolous pretexts; all,
in short, with a smile on their faces, giving the lie to that which their black
entrails were meditating. Many of you have been robbed of your property,
incarcerated, chased, murdered, and hunted like wild beasts, because your
labor was fruitful, and because your industry excited the vile avarice which
led them. A voice infernal said, from the bottom of their soul, "kill them; the
greater will be our gain!" Ah! this does not finish the sketch of your situation. It would appear that justice had fled from this world, leaving you to
the caprice of your oppressors, who become each day more furious towards
you; that, through witnesses and false charges, although the grounds may
be insufficient, you may be interred in the penitentiaries, if you are not previously deprived of life by some keeper who covers himself from responsibility, by the pretence of your flight. There are to be found criminals covered
with frightful crimes, but they appear to have impunity until opportunity
furnish them a victim; to these monsters indulgence is shown, because they
are not of our race, which is unworthy, as they say, to belong to the human
species. But this race, which the Anglo-American, so ostentatious of its own
qualities, tries so much to blacken, depreciate, and load with insults, in a
spirit of blindness, which goes to the full extent of such things so common on

Source: House Executive Documents, 36th Cong., 1st sess., H. Exec. Doc., no 52, ser. 1050
(Washington, D.C.: Thomas H. Ford, Printer, 1860), pp. 79–82.

this frontier, does not fear, placed even in the midst of its very faults, those subtle inquisitions which are so frequently made as to its manners, habits, and sentiments; nor that its deeds should be put to the test of examination in the land of reason, of justice, and of honor. This race has never humbled itself before the conqueror, though the reverse has happened, and can be established; for he is not humbled who uses among his fellow-men those courtesies which humanity prescribes; charity being the root whence springs the rule of his actions. But this race, which you see filled with gentleness and inward sweetness, gives now the cry of alarm throughout the entire extent of the land which it occupies, against all the artifice interposed by those who have become chargeable with their division and discord. This race, adorned with the most lovely disposition towards all that is good and useful in the line of progress, omits no act of diligence which might correct its many imperfections, and lift its grand edifice among the ruins of the past, respecting the ancient traditions and the maxims bequeathed by their ancestors, without being dazzled by brilliant and false appearances. . . .

Mexicans! Is there no remedy for you? Inviolable laws, yet useless, serve, it is true, certain judges and hypocritical authorities, cemented in evil and injustice, to do whatever suits them, and to satisfy their vile avarice at the cost of your patience and suffering; rising in their frenzy, even to the taking of life, through the treacherous hands of their bailiffs. The wicked way in which many of you have been oftentimes involved in persecution, accompanied by circumstances making it the more bitter, is now well known; these crimes being hid from society under the shadow of a horrid night, those implacable people, with the haughty spirit which suggests impunity for a life of criminality, have pronounced, doubt ye not, your sentence, which is, with accustomed insensibility, as you have seen, on the point of execution.

Mexicans! My part is taken; the voice of revelation whispers to me that to me is entrusted the work of breaking the chains of your slavery, and that the Lord will enable me, with powerful arm, to fight against our enemies, in compliance with the requirements of that Sovereign Majesty, who, from this day forward, will hold us under His protection. On my part, I am ready to offer myself as a sacrifice for your happiness; and counting upon the means necessary for the discharge of my ministry, you may count upon my coöperation, should no cowardly attempt put an end to my days. . . .

Women and the Frontier

Of course, women were very much a part of the frontier. As you examine the following sources, consider whether the frontier experience of women differed from that of male settlers and whether it offered new opportunities for women or simply strengthened familiar roles.

12 In 1837, Caroline Kirkland moved with her husband to a frontier village in Michigan, where they settled on 800 acres of land. Two years later, Kirkland published her first book, based on that experience. In it, she offered readers a realistic portrayal of the frontier, especially the life facing women.

A New Home—Who 'll Follow? (1839)
CAROLINE KIRKLAND

Woman's little world is overclouded for lack of the old familiar means and appliances. The husband goes to his work with the same axe or hoe which fitted his hand in his old woods and fields, he tills the same soil, or perhaps a far richer and more hopeful one—he gazes on the same book of nature which he has read from his infancy, and sees only a fresher and more glowing page; and he returns to his home with the sun, strong in heart and full of self-gratulation on the favorable change in his lot. But he finds the home-bird drooping and disconsolate. *She* has been looking in vain for the reflection of any of the cherished features of her own dear fire-side. She has found a thousand deficiencies which her rougher mate can scarce be taught to feel as evils. What cares he if the time honored cupboard is meagerly represented by a few oak-boards lying on pegs and called shelves? His tea-equipage shines as it was wont—the biscuits can hardly stay on the brightly glistening plates. Will he find fault with the clay-built oven, or even the tin "reflector"? His bread never was better baked. What does he want with the great old cushioned rocking-chair? When he is tired he goes to bed, for he is never tired till bed-time. Women are the grumblers in Michigan, and they have some apology. Many of them have made sacrifices for which they were not at all prepared, and which detract largely from their every day stores of comfort. The conviction of good accruing on a large scale does not prevent the wearing sense of minor deprivations.

Another large class of emigrants is composed of people of broken fortunes, or who have been unsuccessful in past undertakings. These like or dislike the country on various grounds, as their peculiar condition may vary. Those who are fortunate or industrious look at their new home with a kindly eye. Those who learn by experience that idlers are no better off in Michigan than elsewhere, can find no term too virulent in which to express their angry disappointment. The profligate and unprincipled lead stormy and uncomfortable lives any where; and Michigan, *now* at least, begins to regard such characters among her adopted children, with a stern and unfriendly eye, so that the few who may have come among us, hoping for the unwatched and unbridled license which we read of in regions nearer to the setting sun, find themselves marked and shunned as in the older world.

Source: Caroline M. Kirkland, *A New Home—Who 'll Follow?* (New Haven: College & University Press, 1965; originally published 1839), pp. 186–188.

As women feel sensibly the deficiencies of the "salvage" state, so they are the first to attempt the refining process, the introduction of those important nothings on which so much depends. Small additions to the more delicate or showy part of the household gear are accomplished by the aid of some little extra personal exertion. "Spinning money" buys a looking-glass perhaps, or "butter money" a nice cherry table. [Sweet briers] and wood-vine; or wild-cucumber, are sought and transplanted to shade the windows. Narrow beds round the house are bright with balsams and Sweet Williams, four o'clocks, poppies and marigolds; and if "th' old man" is good natured, a little gate takes the place of the great awkward *bars* before the door. By and bye a few apple-trees are set out; sweet briars grace the door yard, and lilacs and currant-bushes; all by female effort—at least I have never yet happened to see it otherwise where these improvements have been made at all. They are not all accomplished by her own hand indeed, but hers is the moving spirit. . . .

---

13   Friedrich Richard Petri, a German immigrant, settled on a farm near Fredericksburg, Texas, in the 1840s. The women milking the cows in this scene are Petri's sisters. This and other paintings by Petri detail the rigors of frontier life.

The Pioneer Cowpen (1849)
FRIEDRICH RICHARD PETRI

Pioneer Cowpen, 1849, Petri, Friedrich Richard/UT Texas Memorial Museum Collection/Center for American History, UT-Austin.

The Western Environment

The extraction of the West's resources, in particular its mineral wealth, drew many settlers into the region in the years before the Civil War. In fact, numerous mineral strikes helped to reinforce the popular image of the frontier as a fertile field for individual advancement. The sources in this section reveal other themes associated with resource extraction, however, that Frederick Jackson Turner may have missed.

14   Edward Gould Buffum was part of a regiment sent to California in 1847 during the Mexican War. After the war, Buffum set out for the gold fields of the Sierra Nevada and two years later published his vivid account of life there. In it, he observed the destruction that came with the mining boom in the Sierras and hinted who the biggest winners were likely to be.

Six Months in the Gold Mines (1850)
EDWARD GOULD BUFFUM

I do not believe, as was first supposed, that the gold-washings of northern California are "inexhaustible." Experience has proved, in the workings of other placers, that the rich deposits of pure gold found near the surface of the earth, have been, speedily displaced, and that with an immense influx of labouring population, they have totally disappeared. Thus, in Sonora, where many years ago fifteen and twenty, and even fifty dollars per day, were the rewards of labour, it is found difficult at present with the common implements to dig and wash from the soil more than from fifty cents to two dollars per day to a man. So has it been partially in the richer and more extensive placers of California. When first discovered, are the soil was molested by the pick and the shovel, every little rook crevice, and every river bank was blooming with golden fruits, and those who first struck them, without any severe labour, extracted the deposits. As the tide of emigration began to flow into the mining region, the lucky hits upon rich deposits, of course, began to grow scarcer, until, when an immense population was scattered throughout the whole golden country, the success of the mining operations began to depend more upon the amount of labour performed than upon the good fortune to strike into an unfurrowed soil, rich in gold. When I first saw the mines, only six months after they were worked, and when not more than three thousand people were scattered over the immense territory, many ravines extending for miles along the mountains were turned completely upside down, and portions of the river's banks resembled huge canals that had been excavated. And now, when two years have elapsed, and

Source: Edward Gould Buffum, *Six Months in the Gold Mines* (Philadelphia: Lea and Blanchard, 1850), pp. 104–106, 107–108.

a population of one hundred thousand, daily increasing, have expended so great an amount of manual labour, the old ravines and river banks, which were abandoned when there were new and unwrought placers to go to, have been wrought and re-wrought, and some of them with good success. Two years have entirely changed the character of the whole mining region at present discovered. Over this immense territory, where the smiling earth covered and concealed her vast treasures, the pick and the shovel have created canals, gorges, and pits, that resemble the labours of giants. . . .

Never in the history of the world was there such a favourable opportunity as now presents itself in the gold region of California for a profitable investment of capital; and the following are some of the modes in which it may be applied. I have before shown, and experience and observation have demonstrated it to me, that the beds of the tributaries to the two great rivers that flow from the Sierra Nevada are richer in gold than their banks have yet proved to be. There are many points, at each one of which the river can easily be turned from its channel by a proper application of machinery. Dams are then to be created and pumps employed in keeping the beds dry. Powerful steam machines are to be set in operation for the purpose of tearing up the rocks, and separating the gold from them. The hills and plains are also to be wrought. Shafts are to be sunk in the mountain sides, and huge excavators are to bring to the surface the golden earth, and immense machines, worked by steam power, made to wash it. The earth, which had been previously washed in the common rockers, is to be re-washed in a more scientifically constructed apparatus, and the minute particles of gold, which escape in the common mode of washing, and which are invisible to the naked eye, are to be separated by a chemical process.

15   Hydraulic mining, which directed powerful streams of water onto rocks and soil, became a common method of mineral extraction during the Gold Rush. It also left hillsides scarred and streams and rivers clogged with debris. In addition, such mining required expensive equipment and a large amount of labor, which could be paid for only by corporations.

Hydraulic Mining in California's Gold Fields (1862)

Oakland Museum of California.

CONCLUSION

In looking west to explain American development, Frederick Jackson Turner forced Americans to take Western history seriously. As a result, generations of historians have continued to evaluate and reinterpret the Western experience. Turner's thesis was, if anything, grand. According to it, the frontier fostered such traits as inde-pendence, individuality, and self-reliance. At the same time, it also shaped the democratic character of the nation's political institutions. Indeed, Turner's essay was nothing less than an exploration of the unity of the American experience.

As we have seen, any historical argument that attributes so many effects to one grand cause is bound to attract critics. With the support of evidence in the primary sources, you may have become one of them. You probably glimpsed as well some of the many other perspectives, besides Turner's westward-moving frontier line, by which to understand Western history. Some students, for instance, might conclude, based on evidence here, that the frontier was less a westward-moving line of white settlement than a meeting ground of diverse peoples and cultures. In considering the points of view of women and non-whites, or the activities or corporations and even the impact of expansion on the West's land resources, the Western past begins to look far more complex than Turner's thesis suggested. In fact, his unifying thread of the frontier running through the nation's past, reshaping both institutions and the American character, may look badly frayed, if not broken.

Nonetheless, students of history make a mistake if they dismiss Turner's thesis out of hand. In looking to the West to explain American development, Turner inspired generations of historians to reinterpret the frontier experience. He thus forced Americans to reconsider their past, just as Charles Beard did when writing about the Founding Fathers two decades later. After Beard, historians could not look at the Founders without thinking about economic interests. After Turner, they could not dismiss the West and pretend to understand American history. Nor could they define history merely as the actions of political elites, because Turner had found significance in the lives of millions of ordinary people. Beard himself declared that Turner's essay "was destined to have a more profound influence on thought about American history than any other essay or volume ever written on the subject."[5] Students of American history are thus indebted to Turner. Although his was not the last word on the West, what he had to say remains the starting point for understanding the significance of the frontier in American history.

FURTHER READING

Patricia Nelson Limerick, *The Legacy of Conquest: The Unbroken Legacy of the American West* (New York: W. W. Norton, 1987).

Cathy Luchetti and Carol Olwell, *Women of the West* (St. George, Utah: Antelope Island Press, 1982).

Gerald D. Nash, *Creating the West: Historical Interpretations 1890–1990* (Albuquerque: University of New Mexico Press, 1991).

Malcolm Rohrbough, *The Trans-Appalachian Frontier: Peoples, Societies, Institutions, 1775–1850* (New York: Oxford University Press, 1978).

Donald Worster, *Under Western Skies: Nature and History in the American West* (New York: Oxford University Press, 1992).

NOTES

1. Quoted in Richard Hofstadter, *The Progressive Historians* (New York: Alfred A. Knopf, 1968), p. 230.
2. Herbert Hoover, "American Individualism," *World's Work* 43 (April 1922), p. 585.
3. Quoted in Alfred Jacob Miller, *The West of Alfred Jacob Miller* (Norman: University of Oklahoma Press, 1968), opposite plate 29.
4. Quoted in Nancy Rash, *The Painting and Politics of George Caleb Bingham* (New Haven, Conn.: Yale University Press, 1991), p. 97.
5. Quoted in Hofstadter, *The Progressive Historians*, pp. 47–48.

Chapter

9

History as Biography:
Historians and Old Hickory

This chapter's documents give a portrait of Andrew Jackson. The secondary source discusses his early, formative years, and the primary sources offer more perspectives on the man and the times.

Secondary Source

1. *American Lion* (2008), JON MEACHAM

Primary Sources

2. Jackson on His Experiences During the Revolution (n.d.)
3. Andrew Jackson to Charles Henry Dickinson (1806)
4. Andrew Jackson to Rachel Jackson (1813)
5. Andrew Jackson to William Blount (1812)
6. Andrew Jackson (1817)
7. Old Hickory (1819), JOHN VANDERLYN
8. Andrew Jackson on the Second Bank of the United States (1830)
9. Andrew Jackson's Second Annual Message to Congress (1830)
10. Andrew Jackson to John Coffee (1832)
11. Andrew Jackson to Joel Poinsett (1832)
12. Andrew Jackson's Nullification Proclamation (1832)

*W*hen Andrew Jackson was inaugurated, a huge crowd filled the streets and avenues leading to the Capitol. Restrained only by a ship's cable, it surged two-thirds of the way up the steps leading to the portico. Senator Daniel Webster declared that even he had never seen such a crowd. When General Jackson appeared between the portico's columns, the throng roared. "Never can I forget the spectacle," noted another observer, "nor the electrifying moment when the eager, expectant eyes of that vast and motley multitude caught sight . . . of their adored leader."[1] When Jackson stood and looked out over the crowd, the roar grew louder still.

The din continued during the ten-minute inaugural speech. When he finished, President Jackson pushed through the mob to a carriage waiting to take him to the White House. There another crowd nearly crushed him as he tried to shake well-wishers' hands. By the time Old Hickory fled to a nearby hotel, the guests were into the refreshments. They grabbed food and drink from the waiters, stomped in mud-covered boots on satin-covered chairs, broke china and glassware, and spilled pails of liquor on the carpet. "The mob . . . poured in in one uninterrupted stream of mud and filth," said one congressman. "What a scene did we witness!" said another guest, who was horrified by "a rabble, a mob, of boys, negros [*sic*], women, children, scrambling, fighting, romping."[2]

Andrew Jackson's raucous inauguration in 1829 marked the beginning of the "age of Jackson," an era dominated by the policies and presence of Old Hickory. It is evidence of a powerful bond between Jackson and many of his countrymen. In this chapter, we meet the man who stood above the inaugural crowd just as he towered above his peers in power and influence. We consider what his life reveals about the nameless people in the crowd below. And well we should. The man we encounter here decisively defeated the British at New Orleans in a battle that transformed a disastrous war into a magnificent triumph in most Americans' minds. He helped destroy the Creek and Seminole nations and later, as president, forced the Cherokees onto their tragic "Trail of Tears." Singlehandedly, he destroyed the Second Bank of the United States and faced down the South Carolina nullifiers. He also helped turn party politics into a game of spoils for the winners. Indeed, there are few better subjects for considering the individual's role in history than this man who gave his name to his age.

SETTING

Frontier dueler, hero of the Battle of New Orleans, Indian fighter, veteran of several vitriolic political campaigns, and enemy of "special privilege," Andrew Jackson was no stranger to conflict or controversy. The scholars who have attempted to explain what his rise reveals about American society are equally combative. In the early twentieth century, historians argued that Jackson's triumph grew naturally from the democratization of American society. Frederick Jackson Turner was one of the first historians to associate Jackson with democratic trends in the early nineteenth century. To Turner, Jackson's election to the presidency represented the triumph of the West over a more conservative and less democratic East. A generation later, some historians countered that Jackson's career reflected instead a deep clash between economic groups. Arthur Schlesinger, Jr., for instance, said Jackson led a movement "to control the power of the capitalistic groups, mainly Eastern, for the benefit of non-capitalist groups, farmers and laboring men, East, West, and South."[3] In the 1950s, historian Richard Hofstadter argued that Jackson's victory actually represented the triumph of capitalism. Jackson's antimonopoly rhetoric, he said, was "closely linked to the ambitions of the small capitalist" in the expanding commercial market economy of the early nineteenth century.[4]

About the same time, historian Marvin Meyers challenged Hofstadter's view, maintaining that Jackson's age was characterized by a desire to escape an increasingly competitive and individualistic society. Jackson and his supporters, he said, longed for "a chaste republican order," where "the seductions of risk and novelty, greed and extravagance, rapid motion and complex dealings" could be resisted.[5] Still later, other researchers challenged the view that Old Hickory and his Democratic Party were the champions of democratic reforms. They questioned, for instance, how much support Jackson had among the working class. More recently, Michael Rogin and other historians who have examined Jackson's treatment of the Indians also dispute the democratic character of his policies.

Often lost in discussions about the age of Jackson are Old Hickory himself and the role he played in shaping his age. Partly, that is because modern historians reject the "great man" view of the past. In the nineteenth century, many historians looked to the past for heroic deeds and inspiration. They assumed that a few extraordinary individuals molded their times. Writer Thomas Carlyle said that "the History of the world is but the Biography of great men."[6] Although historians today continue to write biographies, it is not often with this "great man" view. Today, they study individual lives in search of understanding, not heroes. They do not believe that people stand outside their societies and impose their greatness on history. Historians now acknowledge the extent to which individuals are influenced by their times and circumstances. Still, when we consider Andrew Jackson, we must also wonder about one person's exceptional ability to influence events.

INVESTIGATION

Today, sober students of history who have the benefit of hindsight can see Andrew Jackson more clearly than did the drunken Inaugural Day revelers. You are thus in a better position to assess his influence and to answer the central question of this chapter: How did Andrew Jackson's background and personality influence the course of the nation? To answer this main question, however, you must also address several others:

1. **What does the selection by historian Jon Meacham (Source 1) reveal as Jackson's most important personality traits?** What does it reveal about the most important early influences on him?

2. **What do the primary sources reveal about Jackson and his personality?** In what ways do the actions and attitudes revealed in these sources reflect the young man and the influences on him discussed in Source 1? What do the sources reveal about the way Jackson interacted with others, specifically, the way he dealt with those who disagreed with him?

3. **How would you characterize Jackson's views and actions regarding the Second Bank of the United States, the Indians, and South Carolina's nullification of the Tariff of 1832?** To what extent did those views and actions reflect Jackson's personality or his early life influences?

4. **Based on the sources in this chapter and information provided by your textbook, what do you think Jackson's background and personality had to do with his widespread appeal?** What important developments in American society made that background and personality so appealing to many Americans by the 1820s?

The primary sources in this chapter deal in part with two important issues that Jackson confronted as president: Indian removal and South Carolina's nullification of the Tariff in 1832. The secondary source, on the other hand, deals with Jackson's life before he was elected president in 1828. Reading the section in your textbook on Andrew Jackson and his administration, therefore, will provide you with useful background before you begin. Note whether your textbook emphasizes a relationship between Jackson's personality or background and his actions as president regarding important issues.

SECONDARY SOURCE

1   In this excerpt from his study of Andrew Jackson, biographer Jon Meacham focuses on Old Hickory's early years up to early 1815. Meacham discusses how Jackson's youth was characterized by war and the death of loved ones. A "gambler, and a carouser" as a young man, Meacham notes that Jackson matured into "a formidable leader of men." Based on the information in this source, what would you conclude were the most important influences in shaping Jackson's personality or character?

American Lion (2008)
JON MEACHAM

Jackson Grew Up an outsider, living on the margins and at the mercy of others. Traveling to America from Ireland in 1765, his father, the senior Andrew Jackson, and his mother, Elizabeth Hutchinson Jackson, moved into a tiny community a few hundred miles northwest of Charleston, in a spot straddling the border between North and South Carolina. . . .

Jackson's father, meanwhile, was trying to establish himself and his family in the New World. Though a man, his son recalled, of "independent" means, he was, it seems, poorer than his in-laws, who might have made him feel the disparity. While the other members of the extended family began prospering, Jackson moved his wife and two sons, Hugh and Robert, to Twelve Mile Creek, seven miles from the heart of Waxhaw. His wife was pregnant when the first Andrew Jackson died unexpectedly. It was a confusing, unsettling time. The baby was almost due, a snowstorm—rare in the South—had struck, and Jackson's pallbearers drank so much as they carried his corpse from Twelve Mile Creek to the church for the funeral that they briefly lost the body along the way.

Soon thereafter, on Sunday, March 15, 1767, Mrs. Jackson gave birth to her third son, naming him Andrew after her late husband. He was a dependent from delivery forward. Whether the birth took place in North or South Carolina has occupied historians for generations (Jackson himself thought it was South Carolina), but the more important fact is that Andrew Jackson came into the world under the roof of relatives, not of his own parents. Growing up, he would be a guest of the houses in which he lived, not a son, except of a loving mother who was never the mistress of her own household. . . . Even in his mother's lifetime, Jackson felt a certain inferiority to and distance from others. "His childish recollections were of humiliating dependence and galling discomfort, his poor mother performing household drudgery in return for the niggardly maintenance of herself and her children," said [Jackson's niece] Mary Donelson Wilcox. . . . He was not quite part of the core of the world around him. He did not fully belong, and he knew it.

God and war dominated his childhood. His mother took him and his brothers to the Waxhaw Presbyterian meetinghouse for services every week, and the signal intellectual feat of his early years was the memorization of the Westminster Shorter Catechism. Most stories about the young Jackson also paint a portrait of a child and young man full of energy, fun, and not a little fury. Like many other children of the frontier, he was engaged in a kind of constant brawl from birth—and in Jackson's case, it was a brawl in which he could not stand to lose ground or points, even for a moment. . . .

Source: Jon Meacham: *American Lion: Andrew Jackson in the White House* (New York: Random House, 2008), pp. 9, 10–13, 14, 15, 20–21, 22, 25–26, 28–29, 30–31, 32–33.

Perhaps partly because he was fatherless, he may have felt he had to do more than usual to prove his strength and thus secure, or try to secure, his place in the community. "Mother, Andy will fight his way in the world," a neighborhood boy recalled saying in their childhood. Clearly Jackson seethed beneath the surface, for when flummoxed or crossed or frustrated, he would work himself into fits of rage so paralyzing that contemporaries recalled he would begin "slobbering." His prospects were not auspicious: here was an apparently unbalanced, excitable, insecure, and defensive boy coming of age in a culture of confrontation and violence. It was not, to say the least, the best of combinations. . . .

The birth of the Republic was, for Jackson, a time of unrelenting death. . . . By 1778, the South was the focus of the Revolutionary War, and the British fought brutally in Georgia and the Carolinas. In 1779, Andrew's brother Hugh, just sixteen, was fighting at the front and died, it was said, "of heat and fatigue" after a clash between American and British troops at the Battle of Stono Ferry, southwest of Charleston. It was the first in a series of calamities that would strike Jackson, who was twelve.

The British took Charleston on Friday, May 12, 1780, then moved west. The few things Jackson knew and cherished were soon under siege. On Monday, May 29, at about three o'clock in the afternoon, roughly three hundred British troops under the command of Lieutenant Colonel Banastre Tarleton killed 113 men near Waxhaw and wounded another 150. It was a vicious massacre: though the rebels tried to surrender, Tarleton ordered his men forward, and they charged the Americans, a rebel surgeon recalled, "with the horrid yells of intimated demons." Even after the survivors fell to the ground, asking for quarter, the British "went over the ground, plunging their bayonets into everyone that exhibited any signs of life."

The following Sunday was no ordinary Sabbath at Waxhaw. The meetinghouse was filled with casualties from the skirmish, and the Jacksons were there to help the wounded. "None of the men had less than three or four, and some as many as thirteen gashes on them," Jackson recalled.

He was so young, and so much was unfolding around him: the loss of a brother, the coming of the British, the threat of death, the sight of the bleeding and the dying in the most sacred place he knew, the meetinghouse. The enemy was everywhere, and the people of Waxhaw, like people throughout the colonies, were divided by the war, with Loyalists supporting George III and Britain, and others, usually called Whigs, throwing in their lot with the Congress. As Jackson recalled it, his mother had long inculcated him and his brothers with anti-British rhetoric, a stand she took because of her own father, back in Ireland. . . .

In the split between the revolutionaries and the Loyalists Jackson saw firsthand the brutality and bloodshed that could result when Americans turned on Americans. "Men hunted each other like beasts of prey," wrote Amos Kendall, the Jackson intimate who spent hours listening to Jackson reminisce, "and the savages were outdone in cruelties to the living and indignities on the dead." . . .

In April 1781, after a night spent on the run from a British party, he and his brother Robert were trapped in one of their Crawford relatives' houses.* A neighboring Tory alerted the redcoats, and soon Andrew and Robert were surrounded. The soldiers ransacked the house, and an imperious officer ordered Jackson to polish his boots.

Jackson refused. "Sir," he said, with a striking formality and coolness under the circumstances for a fourteen-year-old, "I am a prisoner of war, and claim to be treated as such." The officer then swung his sword at the young man. Jackson blocked the blade with his left hand, but he could not fend it off completely. "The sword point reached my head and has left a mark there . . . on the skull, as well as on the fingers," Jackson recalled. His brother was next, and when he too refused the order to clean the boots, the officer smashed the sword over Robert's head, knocking him to the floor.

In some ways, Andrew was strengthened by the blows, for he would spend the rest of his life standing up to enemies, enduring pain, and holding fast until, after much trial, victory came. Robert was not so fortunate. The two boys were taken from the house to a British prison camp in Camden, about forty miles away. The journey was difficult in the April heat: "The prisoners were all dismounted and marched on foot to Camden, pushed through the swollen streams and prevented from drinking," Jackson recalled. The mistreatment continued at the camp. "No attention whatever was paid to the wounds or to the comfort of the prisoners, and the small pox having broken out among them, many fell victims to it," Jackson said. Robert was sick, very sick. Their mother managed to win her sons' release, and, with a desperately ill Robert on one horse and Mrs. Jackson on another a barefoot Andrew—the British had taken his shoes and his coat—had to, as he recalled, "trudge" forty-five miles back to Waxhaw.

They made a ragged, lonely little group. En route, even the weather turned against them. "The fury of a violent storm of rain to which we were exposed for several hours before we reached the end of our journey caused the small pox to strike in and consequently the next day I was dangerously ill," Jackson recalled. Two days later Robert died. "During his confinement in prison," Jackson's earliest biography said, Robert "had suffered greatly; the wound on his head, all this time, having never been dressed, was followed by an inflammation of the brain, which in a few days after his liberation, brought him to his grave."

Two Jackson boys were now dead at the hands of the British, Elizabeth nursed Andrew, now her only living child, back from the precipice—and then left, to care for two of her Crawford* nephews who were sick in Charleston.

Jackson never saw her again. In the fall of 1781 she died in the coastal city tending to other boys, and was buried in obscurity. Her clothes were all that came back to him. Even by the rough standards of the frontier in late-eighteenth-century America, where disease and death were common, this was an extraordinary run of terrible luck. . . .

*The Crawfords were in-laws of Jackson's mother.

Jackson spiraled downward and lashed out in the aftermath of his mother's death. Before now, living in other people's houses, Jackson had learned to manage complicated situations, maneuvering to maintain a passably cheerful (and grateful) face among people who gave him shelter hut apparently little else. "He once said he never remembered receiving a gift as a child, and that, after his mother's death, no kind, encouraging words ever greeted his ear," recalled Mary Donelson Wilcox.

The Revolutionary War drew to a close with the American victory at Yorktown, Virginia, on the afternoon of Friday, October 19, 1781. Two years later, on Wednesday, September 3, 1783, came the Treaty of Paris, and the United States was now an independent nation. For Jackson, though, the end of war brought little peace. Living for a time with some Crawford relatives, Jackson got into a fight with one of their guests, a Captain Galbraith. Jackson thought him "of a very proud and haughty disposition," and the two found themselves in an argument, and "for some reason," Jackson recalled, "I forget now what, he threatened to chastise me." Jackson replied with a flash of fire. "I immediately answered, 'that I had arrived at the age to know my rights, and although weak and feeble from disease, I had the courage to defend them, and if he attempted anything of that kind I would most assuredly send him to the other world.'" That was enough for Jackson's current Crawford host to shuffle him off to another relative. Having the unstable orphan around presented too many problems, not least the possibility of his attacking other guests.

Then came a crucial interlude in Jackson's life: a sojourn in the cultivated precincts of Charleston. He had come into some money—either from his grandfather or perhaps from the sale of his mother's property—and used it to finance a trip to the coast where he fell in with a fast, sophisticated circle. Some Charlestonians had retreated to the Waxhaw region during the worst of the fighting on the coast, so Jackson had something of an entrée when he arrived. Here he found the pleasures of the turf, of good tailors, and of the gaming tables. "There can be little doubt that at this period he imbibed that high sense of honour, and unstudied elegance of air for which he has since been distinguished," wrote the early Jackson biographer Henry Lee—as well as little doubt that his love of racehorses and fine clothes had its beginnings in Charleston, too.

After Jackson returned to Waxhaw, he grew restless. From 1781 to 1784, he tried his hand at saddle making and school teaching—neither seems to have gone very well—and then left South Carolina for good. For the rest of his life, for a man who adored talk of family, friends, and old times, Jackson mentioned Waxhaw very little, the only exceptions being conversation about his mother and about Revolutionary War action in the region—both things that he could claim as his own. . . .

In 1787, after a brief period of study in Salisbury, North Carolina, Jackson received his license to practice law in that state. A wild man, he worked hard and played even harder for the next four years. He challenged the first lawyer he ever tried a case against to a duel (the challenge fizzled) and arranged for the town's prostitutes to arrive in the midst of a society Christmas ball. "He was the most roaring, rollicking, game-cocking, card-playing, mischievous fellow that ever lived in Salisbury," a contemporary recalled. . . .

He was not born in a station that granted him automatic access to the upper reaches of the nascent American gentry. He had to work his way into those circles with whatever he had at hand—and what he had was a charm that made other men like him and want to join him in exploits that crossed the line of respectability, but never so dramatically that they could not stumble back into the good graces of their wives and neighbors by morning. One day Jackson would draw on his capacity to make others love and follow him in the service of larger causes. But his raw ability to lead—and his sense of adventure and his infectious fearlessness—was already evident in North Carolina.

Tennessee was not yet a state when Jackson, then twenty-one, moved to Nashville in October 1788 and took up residence as a boarder in the house of Mrs. John Donelson, the widow of a founder of the settlement. The Donelsons were among the territory's great families. The patriarch, Colonel John Donelson, was a surveyor who had been a member of the Virginia House of Burgesses before striking out to the west. His 1779–80 voyage on the Cumberland River aboard the flatboat *Adventure* was one of the prevailing stories of the age, and his mysterious death—he was shot to death in the wilderness, perhaps by Indians, perhaps by robbers—only added to his legend.

The colonel, though, survives in history mostly as the father of the wife of Andrew Jackson. Born about 1767—the year Jackson was born—Rachel Donelson came from a clan as distinguished in early American life as Jackson's was anonymous. Rachel was a beautiful young woman with a strong sense of fun—and when Rachel met Jackson in the autumn of 1788 on the Cumberland, she was another man's wife. Rachel Donelson and Lewis Robards of Mercer County, Kentucky, had been married since 1785; they had met and courted during a Donelson family sojourn in Kentucky. At twenty-seven, Robards was a decade older than the seventeen-year-old Rachel, and the marriage was difficult from the start. . . .

With Rachel in Natchez, and Jackson in Tennessee, in the winter of 1790–91. . . . Jackson learned Robards had obtained a divorce. Jackson rushed back to Natchez and married Rachel there. Only two years later, in December 1793, did it become clear that Robards had only *petitioned* for a divorce in December 1790. It was not granted until September 1793, which meant that Jackson had been "married" to another man's wife for several years. By January 1794, all was put right, and Jackson and Rachel were legally married in a ceremony in Tennessee.

Or so Jackson, as a presidential candidate, would later have the world—and history—believe. The weight of the evidence, however, suggests the two lived together as husband and wife and even referred to themselves as married—there are two surviving references to Rachel as "Mrs. Jackson" from late 1790 and early 1791—*before* Robards took the initial step of filing for a divorce. Their passion for each other was apparently deep enough to lead them, despite their later claims to the contrary, to choose to live in adultery in order to provoke a divorce from Robards. By the looser standards of the frontier in the last years of the eighteenth century, such a course would not have damaged their reputations, particularly if—as was the case here—the woman's family approved. . . .

. . . Jackson's pride led him into peril more than once. In Knoxville in the autumn of 1803, in the midst of a quarrel with Tennessee governor John Sevier over which man would become major general of the state militia, Jackson alluded to his own past "services" to the state. "Services?" Sevier replied. "I know of no great service you have rendered the country, except taking a trip to Natchez with another man's wife."

"Great God!" Jackson roared. "Do you mention *her* sacred name?"

Then, according to a contemporary's recollection, "several shots were fired in a crowded street. One man was grazed by a bullet; many were scared; but, luckily, no one was hurt." The story is chiefly interesting for the light it sheds on Jackson's sensitivities about Rachel's honor. "Sevier had touched on a subject that was, with Jackson, like sinning against the Holy Ghost: unpardonable," recalled the source.

No one died in the Sevier shootout, but Jackson could, and did, kill in cold blood. In 1806, an argument over a horse race—the dispute also apparently included a slur against Rachel—degenerated into a duel between Jackson and a man in Nashville named Charles Dickinson. Jackson was determined to have satisfaction, waving off reports that Dickinson might leave the city before the showdown. "It will be in vain, for I'll follow him over land and sea," Jackson said.

At seven o'clock on the morning of Friday, May 30, 1806, on the Red River in Logan County, Kentucky, Jackson and Dickinson faced each other at twenty-four feet. Jackson let Dickinson shoot first, and he hit Jackson in the chest with a bullet. Though wounded, Jackson coolly leveled his own pistol at his opponent, and fired. The trigger caught halfway; Jackson cocked the gun again and fired, killing Dickinson. Only later, as his boot filled with blood after he had left the dueling ground, did the extent of Jackson's wound become clear. He carried Dickinson's bullet in his body until he died. Even in pain—the wound complicated his health for decades— Jackson never let his mask drop. "If he had shot me through the brain, sir," Jackson told a friend, "I should still have killed him.". . .

Jackson was forty-five years old when America and Britain went to war in 1812, and he was viewed as a formidable leader of men. By this time he had served as attorney general for Tennessee in its territorial days, in 1791; been elected to the U.S. House of Representatives in 1796; moved to the U.S. Senate in 1797; served as a judge from 1798 to 1804; and, in 1802, had also become major general of the state militia. All the while he struggled to build his planting and commercial interests, from buying huge tracts of land to running a frontier store. "He loves his country and his countrymen have full confidence in him," Tennessee governor Willie Blount wrote to the secretary of war at the outbreak of hostilities in 1812. "He delights in peace; but does not fear war. He has a peculiar pleasure in treating his enemies as such; with them his first pleasure is to meet them on the field. At the present crisis he feels a holy zeal for the welfare of the United States, and at no period of his life has he been known to feel otherwise." Since his mother and his brothers had died for the Union, he would defend the nation to the death.

It was not only courage and conviction that turned Jackson into a great general and a transformative president. He cared about his followers, thought of them as his family, and communicated this warmth in word and deed. Speaking of his men at a low moment in the War of 1812, Jackson promised to "act the part of a father to them." Many leaders say such things and do not mean them, and many followers dismiss such sentiments as words without substance. Jackson was different. He proved his love in times of crisis, earning capital with his troops that both gave him a nickname and formed a bond of affection and respect between himself and his followers that lasted for the rest of his life.

In the cold winter of 1812–13, just months after the United States declared war on Great Britain, Jackson assembled his volunteers—2,071 in all—to march south, toward New Orleans. Jackson's army set off in January 1813, and, five hundred miles later, at Natchez, federal military authorities told Jackson to hold up, and soon the secretary of war ordered him to disband and return to Nashville. By now 150 of Jackson's men were sick, 56 could not sit up, and Jackson had a total of eleven wagons for the trip. "They abandon us in a strange country," he angrily wrote to Governor Blount, adding: *"And I will make every sacrifice to add to their comfort."* . . . As they prepared to move out, the doctor, Samuel Hogg, asked Jackson what he was to do.

Jackson did not hesitate. "To do, sir? You are to leave not a man on the ground."

"But the wagons are full," Hogg said, "and they will convey not more than half."

"Then let some of the troops dismount, and the officers must give up their horses to the sick," Jackson replied. "Not a man, sir, must be left behind."

Hogg took Jackson at his word, and asked for the general's own horses, which Jackson handed over. In wonder and with admiration his men watched this tall, determined figure press on. . . . On foot, he saw them home, and by the time they arrived in Nashville they were calling him "Old Hickory." Jackson had done what his own parents never had. He had stayed the course with those in his charge, and delivered them from danger. He had done a father's work. . . .

. . . While Rachel was still nursing Jackson back to health, news arrived that Creek Indians under the leadership of Red Eagle had massacred white settlers at Fort Mims, a fortification about forty miles north of Mobile. Red Eagle (his father was Scottish, his mother Creek) had been influenced by Tecumseh, the Shawnee chief who hoped to unite the Indians into a force that, armed and supplied by the British and the Spanish, would crush the white Americans who were usurping their land. "Let the white race perish!" Tecumseh said. "War now! War always! War on the living! War on the dead!"

Men like Jackson had long been troubled by visions of Indians colluding with London and Madrid to check American expansion, threaten the Union, and possibly undo the Revolution. To Jackson it was a given that the Indians—in this case the Creeks—were in league with America's European rivals.

The Creek attack on Fort Minis had taken place on Monday, August 30, 1813. It was brutal; as a historian of Alabama described it. 250 whites, including women and children, "were butchered in the quickest manner, and blood and brains bespattered the whole earth. The children were seized by the legs, and killed by batting their heads against the stockading. The women were scalped, and those who were pregnant were opened, while they were alive, and the embryo infants let out of the womb." Until then, the Creeks had been fighting a factional war; by assaulting Fort Mims, the tribe irrevocably widened the conflict. That the fort had provided protection for settlers who had themselves attacked Red Sticks—named for their red war clubs—made no difference to the whites in the region who panicked at reports of the massacre.

They sent for Jackson. "Those distressed citizens of that frontier [have] . . . implored the brave Tennesseans for aid," he said. "They must not ask in vain." Forcing himself into battle—he was in terrible shape from [a recent] brawl—Jackson won a bloody victory at Tallushatchee, a village filled with Red Sticks. "We shot them like dogs," said David Crockett. Richard Keith Call, then a lieutenant under Jackson, was troubled by the toll Jackson's men had exacted. "We found as many as eight or ten dead bodies in a single cabin," Call said. "Some of the cabins had taken fire, and half consumed human bodies were seen amidst the smoking ruins." The bloodshed was repulsive. "In other instances dogs had torn and feasted on the mangled bodies of their masters," Call said. "Heart-sick I turned from the revolting scene."

Jackson, however, believed justice had been done. "We have retaliated for the destruction of Fort Mims," he told the governor of Tennessee. Difficult months followed. Supplies were few, and the troops' discontent tested Jackson's hold over his men. (Matters turned so grim that Jackson ordered the executions of six militiamen.) Still, he triumphed, winning victories from Talladega to Horseshoe Bend. The Creek War ended in August 1814—nearly a year after Fort Mims—with Jackson's winning the cession of twenty-three million acres of land to the United States (three fifths of modern-day Alabama and one fifth of Georgia).

Jackson never rested. Though he had crushed the Creeks, he still believed the Indians a live threat, a willing tool in the hands of the British and the

Spanish. To the south, he defended Mobile against a British attack and then struck to the east, at Spanish Florida, where he was convinced that Madrid (and London) was "aiming the hostile Indians to butcher our women and children." He threatened Pensacola, which prompted the Spanish authorities there to seek British protection; soon Jackson took the city's major fort, and then turned back to the west, toward New Orleans. It was late November 1814. . . .

Jackson engaged the enemy in a climactic battle on Sunday, January 8, 1815, winning a victory reminiscent of Shakespeare's Henry V at Agin-court. Though the battle came after the war had ended—news of the treaty signed in Ghent on Christmas Eve would not reach New Orleans for several weeks—the victory was stunning. The British lost nearly three hundred men, with another twelve hundred wounded and hundreds more taken prisoner or missing. Only thirteen Americans died, with thirty nine more suffering wounds. "It appears that the unerring hand of providence shielded my men from the powers of balls, bombs and rockets, when every ball and bomb from our guns carried with them the mission of death," Jackson said. Gazing across the battlefield as the cannon smoke lifted, John Coffee thought "the slaughter was shocking," and soon living British soldiers who had hidden beneath their fallen comrades' red coats rose from the heaps of corpses. "I never had so grand and awful an idea of the resurrection as on that day," Jackson recalled.

He was now a national, in fact international, figure of renown. In the city on Monday, January 23, 1815, the city's ranking Roman Catholic priest thanked God for Jackson: "It is Him we intend to praise, when considering you, general, as the *man of His right hand*. . . . Immortal thanks be to His Supreme Majesty, for sending us such an instrument of His bountiful designs!". . .

PRIMARY SOURCES

The primary sources in this chapter reflect Jackson's personality and his stands on important issues during his presidency: the Second Bank of the United States, Indian removal, and nullification. The sources are divided into three sections: writings and personal correspondence that reveal his personality, portraits of Jackson, and sources relating to President Jackson's views on the bank, Indian removal, and nullification. As you consider these sources, determine whether they support the view of Jackson presented Meacham's essay (Source 1).

Jackson's Personality

Some of Jackson's personality traits show through clearly in his writings. The following description of his early life, as well as letters to associates and to his wife Rachel, reveals something about his personality. What labels would you apply to Jackson?

This description was probably written late in life.

Jackson on His Experiences During the Revolution (n.d.)

When we were taken prisoners we were thrown into jail in Camden with about 250 others. My brother, couisin and myself, as Soon as our relationship was known, were separated from each other. No attention whatever was paid to the wounds or to the comfort of the prisoners, and the small pox having broken out among them, for the want of proper care, many fell victims to it. I frequently heard them groaning in the agonies of death and no regard was paid to them. Before our exchange took place I also had become infected with the contagion. Having only two horses in our company when we left Camden, and my brother, on account of weakness caused by a severe bowel complaint and the wound he had received on his head, being obliged to be held on the horse, and my mother riding the other, I was compelled to walk the whole way. The distance to the nearest house to Camden where we stopped that night was forty five miles and the enemy having taken my shoes and jacket I had to trudge along barefooted. The fury of a violent storm of rain to which we were exposed for several hours before we reached the end of our journey caused the small pox to strike in and consequently the next day I was dangerously ill. No attention having been given to my brothers wound or to his illness until after his release, two days subsequent to it he expired. As soon as my recruiting health would permit, my mother hastened to Charleston to administer to the comfort of two of her nephews, Wm. & Jas Crawford then prisoners at this place. On her return She died about three miles from Charleston. When my mother left home I staid with my Uncle Major Crawford. Captain Galbraith in charge of Comissary Stores, ammunition &c. for the American Army, was then staying with my Uncle, and being of a very proud and haughty disposition, for some reason, I forget now what, he threatened to chastise me. I immediately, answered, "that I had arrived at the age to know my rights, and although weak and feeble from disease, I had courage to defend them, and if he attempted anying of that kind I would most assuredly Send him to the other world."

Source: Excerpted from Sam B. Smith and Harriet Chappell Owsley, *The Papers of Andrew Jackson,* University of Tennessee Press, 1980. Reprinted by permission.

Charles Henry Dickinson was reputed to be the best shot in Tennessee. Unfortunately, while drunk he made some irreverent remarks about Rachel Jackson, and Old Hickory killed him in a duel.

Andrew Jackson to Charles Henry Dickinson (1806)

May 23rd. 1806.

Sir.

Your conduct and expressions relative to me of late have been of such a nature and so insulting that requires, and shall have, my notice—Insults may be given by men, of such a kind, that they must be noticed, and the author treated with the respects due a gentleman, altho (as in the present instance) he does not merit it—You have, to disturb my quiet, industriously excited Thomas Swann to quarrel with me, which involved the peace and harmony of society for a while—You on the tenth of January wrote me a very insulting letter, left this country and caused this letter to be delivered after you had been gone some days; and securing yourself in safety from the contempt I held you in, have a piece now in the press, more replete with blackguard abuse, than any of your other productions; and are pleased to state that you would have noticed me in a different way than through the press, but my cowardice would have found a pretext to evade that satisfaction, if it had been called for &c &c. I hope sir your courage will be an ample security to me, that I will obtain speedily that satisfaction due me for the insults offered—and in the way my friend, who hands you this, will point out—He waits upon you, for that purpose, and with your friend, will enter into immediate arrangements for this purpose—I am &c.

Andrew Jackson

Source: Excerpted from Sam B. Smith and Harriet Chappell Owsley, *The Papers of Andrew Jackson,* University of Tennessee Press, 1980. Reprinted by permission.

In December 1813, Jackson was engaged in the Creek Campaign. He was waiting for reinforcements at Fort Strother in the Mississippi Territory, the heart of the Creek nation.

Andrew Jackson to Rachel Jackson (1813)

Head quarters Fort Strother
Decbr 29th. 1813. $\frac{1}{2}$ past 11 oclock at night

My love

    . . . I am fearfull when I get supplies up, which I am making every exer-
tion to do I shall have no men to fight with The shamefull desertion from
their posts of the Volunteer Infantry—The Violated Pledge of the cavalry &
mounted infantry under their own proper signatures, and the apathy displayed in the interior of the state by the fireside Patriotts will sink the reputation of our State—and I weep for its fall—and with it the reputation of the
once brave and patriotic Volunteers—who a few privations, sunk from the
highest elevation of patriots—to mere, wining, complaining, sedioners and
mutineers—to keep whom from open acts of mutiny I have been compelled
to point my cannon against, with a lighted match to destroy them—This was
a grating moment of my life—I felt the pangs of an affectionate parent, compelled from duty, to chastise his child—to prevent him from destruction &
disgrace and it being his duty he shrunk not from it—even when he knew
death might ensue—This was a painfull moment, but it is still more painfull,
to hear of their disorderly, and disgracefull conduct on their return—had
I have been with them this should not have happened . . . There abandon-
ment of the service may destroy the campaign and leave our frontier again
exposed to the Tomhawk of the ruthless savage . . .

Andrew Jackson

Source: Excerpted from Sam B. Smith and Harriet Chappell Owsley, *The Papers of Andrew Jackson,* University of Tennessee Press, 1980. Reprinted by permission.

5   Andrew Jackson to William Blount* (1812)

Hermitage June 5th. 1812

Dear sir,

    I have this moment returned from the State of Georgia. My heart bleeds
within me at hearing of the wanton massacre of our women and children by
a party of Creeks since I left home.

*Blount was a Tennessee politician and land speculator.

Source: Excerpted from Sam B. Smith and Harriet Chappell Owsley, *The Papers of Andrew Jackson,* University of Tennessee Press, 1980. Reprinted by permission.

With infinite regret I learned that Genl. Johnson at the head of 500 men was in the neighborhood of this massacre, at the time of its perpetration, and yet omitted to send a detachment against these marauders or to follow them himself, with his whole force. Thus far they have escaped with impunity carrying off an unfortunate woman along with them. But this cruel outrage must not go unrevengd. The assassins of Women and Children must be punishd.

Now Sir the object of *Tecumpsies* visit to the creek nation is unfolding to us. That incendiary, the emissary of the *Prophet*, who is himself the tool of England, has caused our frontier to be stained with blood, and our peacefull citizens to fly in terror from their once happy abodes.

The sooner we strike, the less resistance we shall have to overcome; and a terrible vengeance inflicted at once upon one tribe may have its effect upon all others.

Even the wretches upon the wabash might take some warning from such a lesson. We must therefore march to the heart of the Creek Nation: a competent force can be raised at the shortest notice; for the spirit of the whole people is on fire. They burn to carry fire and sword to the heart of the Creek Nation, and to learn these wretches in their own Towns and villages what it is to massacre Women and Children at a moment of profound peace. I wait therefore for your Orders! Give me permission to procure provisions and munitions of war, and I pledge myself for the ballance. Twenty five hundred brave men from the 2nd Division will be ready on the first signal to visit the Creek towns, and bring them to terms without the aid of presents. . . . I have the honour to be with great consideration yours Respectfully

Andrew Jackson

Andrew Jackson's Portraits

Andrew Jackson's actions and his image were very familiar to Americans by 1828. In fact, he may have been the most painted of all presidents, and his likeness could be seen on tavern signs and in parlors throughout the land. Most portraits of Jackson emphasized his military experience, as Jackson often sat for them in military dress. Do these portraits capture traits that are also revealed in Jackson's writings?

6   Andrew Jackson (1817)

As did many paintings of Jackson, this one emphasizes his military exploits. Why do you think he might have appreciated such portraits?

National Portrait Gallery, Smithsonian Institution/Art Resource, NY.

Old Hickory (1819)
JOHN VANDERLYN

This portrait was painted in New York City during Jackson's visit there after his military campaign in Florida against the Seminoles. The artist and naturalist John James Audubon declared this portrait the only good likeness of Jackson he had seen.

The Museum of the City of New York/Art Resource, NY

President Andrew Jackson on the Second Bank of the United States, Indian Removal, and Nullification

Jackson made many important decisions as president that helped shape the nation's future. Few of these decisions were more important than his actions regarding the bank, the removal of tribes in the Southeast to land west of the Mississippi River, or South Carolina's nullification of the federal tariff passed in 1832. Do these sources reveal personality traits reflected in the other sources? Did Jackson's stance with regard to these issues reflect the influence of his early years?

8

In 1832, Jackson vetoed the recharter of the Second Bank of the United States. Two years earlier, he had explained his objections to the bank. Note Jackson's reasons for opposing the bank and the fears they reflect.

Andrew Jackson on the Second Bank of the United States (1830)

The present Bank is dangerous to Liberty:

1. Because in the number, wealth, and standing of its officers and stock-holders, in its power to make loans or withold them, to call oppressively upon its debtors or indulge them, build houses, rent lands & houses, and make donations for political or other purposes, it embodies a forceful influence which may be wielded for the agrandisement of a favorite individual a particular interest, or a separate party.

2. Because it concentrates in the hands of a few men, a power over the money of the country, which may be perverted to the oppresion of the people, and in times of public calamity, to the embarrasment of the government.

3. Because much of its stock is owned by foreigners, through the management of which an avenue is opened to a foreign influence in the most vital concern of the Republic.

4. Because it always is governed by interest and will even support *him* who supports *it*. An ambitious or dishonest president may thus always unite all of its power and influence in his support, while an honest one who thwarts its views, will never fail to encounter the weight of its opposition. . . .

But if we yield to the Federal Government this power, it is one which ought not to be exercised—Because if it puts the community, at large and their property at the mercy of a corporation which will in the end pursue its own interest—It will have millions of capital—The deposits of the Government, averaging probably about Six millions more, as well as the deposits of individuals to a much larger amount. With these means and backed by the name and influence of the United States, it is to have the power to establish as many Branches in its respective States as it choose, and these States are to have no power to impose a collect of any tax—When it is the interest of the Bank to give an artificial value to property they will accommodate freely. . . .

They will likewise have the power of setting the rates of exchange both foreign arid domestic at such rates as may best promote their own interests— making them low when they wish to purchase Bills, and high whenever it may best suit them to sell—. . . .

These are powers so vast, and the temptations to use them so great, that no man who loves his country and wishes society protected against avarice and injustice, ought willingly to see confered upon any set man whatsoever— . . . .

When such Bank shall have been a short time in operation and its Branches planted in the respective States, it can and probably will control

Source: Andrew Jackson's *Memorandum Book* 1829–32, Jackson Papers, Library of Congress.

the election, and through them the politics of the country.—It will always be governed by a view of its own interest, and opposing those who may have independence enough to resist, or object to its unjust pretentions.

Andrew Jackson's Second Annual Message to Congress (1830)

It gives me pleasure to announce to Congress that the benevolent policy of the government, steadily pursued for nearly thirty years, in relation to the removal of the Indians beyond the white settlements is approaching to a happy consummation. Two important tribes have accepted the provision made for their removal at the last session of Congress, and it is believed that their example will induce the remaining tribes also to seek the same obvious advantages.

The consequences of a speedy removal will be important to the United States, to individual States, and to the Indians themselves. The pecuniary advantages which it promises to the government are the least of its recommendations. It puts an end to all possible danger of collision between the authorities of the General and State governments on account of the Indians. It will place a dense and civilized population in large tracts of country now occupied by a few savage hunters. By opening the whole territory between Tennessee on the north and Louisiana on the south to the settlement of the whites it will incalculably strengthen the southwestern frontier and render the adjacent States strong enough to repel future invasions without remote aid. It will relieve the whole State of Mississippi and the western part of Alabama of Indian occupancy, and enable those States to advance rapidly in population, wealth, and power. It will separate the Indians from immediate contact with settlements of whites; free them from the power of the States; enable them to pursue happiness in their own way and under their own rude institutions; will retard the progress of decay, which is lessening their numbers, and perhaps cause them gradually, under the protection of the Government and through the influence of good counsels, to cast off their savage habits and become an interesting, civilized, and Christian community. These consequences, some of them so certain and the rest so probable, make the complete execution of the plan sanctioned by Congress at their last session an object of much solicitude.

Toward the aborigines of the country no one can indulge a more friendly feeling than myself, or would go further in attempting to reclaim them from their wandering habits and make them a happy, prosperous people. I have endeavored to impress upon them my own solemn convictions of the duties and powers of the General Government in relation to the State authorities. For the justice of the laws passed by the States within the scope of their reserved powers they are not responsible to this Government. As individuals we may

Source: Andrew Jackson, Second Annual Message, December 6, 1830, in James D. Richardson, A Compilation of the Messages and Papers of the Presidents (New York: Bureau of National Literature, n.d.), III: pp. 1082–1085.

entertain and express our opinions of their acts, but as a Government we have as little right to control them as we have to prescribe laws for other nations. . . .

Humanity has often wept over the fate of the aborigines of this country, and Philanthropy has been long busily employed in devising means to avert it, but its progress has never for a moment been arrested, and one by one have many powerful tribes disappeared from the earth. . . . What good man would prefer a country covered with forests and ranged by a few thousand savages to our extensive Republic, studded with cities, towns, and prosperous farms, embellished with all the improvements which art can devise or industry execute, occupied by more than 12,000,000 happy people, and filled with all the blessings of liberty, civilization, and religion?

The present policy of the Government is but a continuation of the same progressive change by a milder process. The tribes which occupied the countries now constituting the Eastern States were annihilated or have melted away to make room for the whites. The waves of population and civilization are rolling to the westward, and we now propose to acquire the countries occupied by the red men of the South and West by a fair exchange, and, at the expense of the United States, to send them to a land where their existence may be prolonged and perhaps made perpetual. Doubtless it will be painful to leave the graves of their fathers; but what do they more than our ancestors did or than our children are now doing? To better their condition in an unknown land our forefathers left all that was dear in earthly objects. Our children by thousands yearly leave the land of their birth to seek new homes in distant regions. . . .

And is it supposed that the wandering savage has a stronger attachment to his home than the settled, civilized Christian? Is it more afflicting to him to leave the graves of his fathers than it is to our brothers and children? Rightly considered, the policy of the General government toward the red man is not only liberal, but generous. He is unwilling to submit to the laws of the States and mingle with their population. To save him from this alternative, or perhaps utter annihilation, the General Government kindly offers him a new home, and proposes to pay the whole expense of his removal and settlement.

10   Andrew Jackson to John Coffee* (1832)

WASHINGTON, April 7, 1832.

D'r Genl, In my last I informed you that we had just concluded a treaty with the creek Indians, who had ceded all their lands east of the Mississippi river to the United States with certain reservations to chiefs and heads of families. This treaty has been ratified by the senate by a unanimous vote.

*General John Coffee was an adviser to Jackson.

*John Ridge was the leader of the Cherokees who resisted removal from their land.

Source: "To Brigadier-General John Coffee," John Spencer Bassett, ed., in Correspondence of Andrew Jackson (Washington, D.C.: Carnegie Institution of Washington, 1929), IV: pp. 429–430.

Clay and Calhoun in the first instance trying to raise opposition to it, but finding their whole strength nine, they abandoned their opposition. This I name to you to show you the malignity of these men, and to what they stoop in their opposition. They would if they could, overturn heaven and earth, to prostrate me, but providence athwarts all their wicked designs, and will turn it to the benefit of our happy country.

The object of the government now is, to have all their reservations surveyed and laid off as early as we can. They will sell and move to the west, so soon as this is done, and the commissioner of the General Land office is preparing his instructions to forward to you with the necessary funds, so soon as the appropriation is made for this purpose and the object of this letter is to advise you thereof that you may be prepared with the necessary surveyors to compleat the surveys of the reservations as early as possible. When the reserves are surveyed it will require but a short time to compleat the ballance and have it into markett, for the reserves are to be bounded by sectional lines, and the improvements as nearly in the center, as possible.

I hope you will be able to do something with the chickasaws before you are called away on this business. The cherokee delegation are still here, and it is now believed before they leave here will propose to treat with us for their intire removal. The decision of the supreme court has felt still born, and they find that it cannot coerce Georgia to yield to its mandate, and I believe Ridge* has expressed despair, and that it is better for them to treat and move. In this he is right, for if orders were issued tomorrow one regiment of militia could not be got to march to save them from destruction and this the opposition know, and if a colision was to take place between them and the Georgians, the arm of the government is not sufficiently strong to preserve them from destruction. . . .

 ## Andrew Jackson to Joel Poinsett* (1832)

WASHINGTON, December 2, 1832.

My D'r Sir, Your two letters of Novr. 24 and 25th last have been received, and I hasten to answer them.

I fully concur with you in your views of Nullification. It leads directly to civil war and bloodshed and deserves the execration of every friend of, the country. Should the civil power with your aid as a *posse comitatus*[1] prove not

---

*Joel Poinsett was a South Carolina Unionist.

1. *Posse comitatus:* a body of men armed with legal authority, in this case to resist South Carolina's secession.

Source: "To Joel R. Poinsett," John Spencer Bassett, ed., in *Correspondence of Andrew Jackson* (Washington, D.C.: Carnegie Institution of Washington, 1929), IV: pp. 493–494.

strong enough to carry into effect the laws of the Union, you have a right to call upon the Government for aid and the Executive will yield it as far as he has been vested with the power by the constitution and the laws made in pursuance thereof.

The precautionary measures spoken of in your last letter have been in some degree anticipated. Five thousand stand of muskets with corresponding equipments have been ordered to Castle Pinckney; and a Sloop of war with a smaller armed vessel (the experiment) will reach Charleston harbor in due time. The commanding officer of Castle Pinckney will be instructed by the Secretary of War to deliver arms and their equipment to your order. Taking a receipt for them, and should the emergency arise he will furnish to your requisition such ordnance and ordnance stores as can be spared from the arsenals.

The Union must be preserved; and its laws duly executed, but by proper means. With calmness and firmness such as becomes those who are conscious of being right and are assured of the support of public opinion, we must perform our duties without suspecting that there are those around us desiring to tempt us into the wrong. We must act as the instruments of the law and if force is offered to us in that capacity then we shall repel it with the certainty, even should we fall as individuals, that the friends of liberty and union will still be strong enough to prostrate their enemies.

Your union men should act in concert: Their designation as unionists should teach them to be prepared for every emergency: and inspire them with the energy to overcome every impediment that may be thrown in the way of the laws of their constitution, whose cause is now not only their cause but that of free institutions throughout the world. They should recollect that perpetuity is stamped upon the constitution by the blood of our Fathers—by those who atcheived as well as those who improved our system of free Government. For this purpose was the principle of amendment inserted in the constitution which all have sworn to support and in violation of which no state or states have the right to secede, much less to dissolve the union. Nullification therefore means insurrection and war; and the other states have a right to put it down: and you also and all other peaceable citizens have a right to aid in the same patriotic object when summoned by the violated laws of the land. Should an emergency occur for the arms before the order of the Secretary of war to the commanding officer to deliver them to your order, shew this to him and he will yield a compliance. . . . I am great haste yr. mo obdt. Servt.

---

12 After South Carolina passed an Ordinance of Nullification in 1832, Jackson moved decisively to put down the state's defiance of the federal tariff. As you read this excerpt from his proclamation, note whether it reflects any of Jackson's personality traits.

Andrew Jackson's Nullification Proclamation (1832)

This, then, is the position in which we stand: A small majority of the citizens of one State in the Union have elected delegates to a State convention; that convention has ordained that all the revenue laws of the United States must be repealed, or that they are no longer a member of the Union. The governor of that State has recommended to the legislature the raising of an army to carry the secession into effect, and that he may be empowered to give clearances to vessels in the name of the State. No act of violent opposition to the laws has yet been committed, but such a state of things is hourly apprehended. And it is the intent of this instrument to *proclaim*, not only that the duty imposed on me by the Constitution "to take care that the laws be faithfully executed" shall be performed to the extent of the powers already vested in me by law, or of such others as the wisdom of Congress shall devise and intrust to me for that purpose, but to warn the citizens of South Carolina who have been deluded into an opposition to the laws of the danger they will incur by obedience to the illegal and disorganizing ordinance of the convention; to exhort those who have refused to support it to persevere in their determination to uphold the Constitution and laws of their country; and to point out to all the perilous situation into which the good people of that State have been led, and that the course they are urged to pursue is one of ruin and disgrace to the very State whose rights they affect to support.

Fellow-citizens of my native State, let me not only admonish you, as the First Magistrate of our common country, not to incur the penalty of its laws, but use the influence that a father would over his children whom he saw rushing to certain ruin. In that paternal language, with that paternal feeling, let me tell you, my countrymen, that you are deluded by men who are either deceived themselves or wish to deceive you. Mark under what pretenses you have been led on to the brink of insurrection and treason on which you stand. . . .

The laws of the United States must be executed. I have no discretionary power on the subject; my duty is emphatically pronounced in the Constitution. Those who told you that you might peaceably prevent their execution deceived you; they could not have been deceived themselves. They know that a forcible opposition could alone prevent the execution of the laws, and they know that such opposition must be repelled. Their object is disunion. But be not deceived by names. Disunion by armed force is *treason*. Are you really ready to incur its guilt? If you are, on the heads of the instigators of the act be the dreadful consequences; on their heads be the dishonor, but on yours may fall the punishment. On your unhappy State will inevitably fall all the evils of the conflict you force upon the Government of your country. . . .

Source: State Papers on Nullification (Boston, 1834), pp. 29–31.

CONCLUSION

As we saw in Chapter 8, historians for a long time defined history as "past poli-tics." They focused on mostly white, male political and military leaders like Andrew Jackson. Biography was perfectly suited to this approach to the past. Here personality and character, rather than vast impersonal forces, could determine the outcome of history. Indeed, if Jackson's life reveals anything, it is that one individual can influence history. Although it is often difficult to do, understanding one personality can thus be a good way to learn about the past. Old Hickory's life is a reminder that historians who attempt to understand even an era "of the common man" can do so through the life of one extraordinary person.

Still, even the most influential people are constrained by powerful political, economic, social, and cultural forces beyond their control. Thus, historians, even biographers, cannot ignore ordinary people who, in many if not always obvious ways, limit the actions of the prominent and powerful. That is one reason why many historians today focus on the lives of obscure, poor, or seemingly powerless people. As we will see in Chapter 10, such a "bottom-up" approach to history yields a very different perspective on the past.

FURTHER READING

James Barber, *Old Hickory: A Life Sketch of Andrew Jackson* (Washington, D.C.: National Portrait Gallery, Smithsonian Institution, 1990).
Andrew Burstein, *The Passions of Andrew Jackson* (New York: Alfred A. Knopf, 2003).
John A. Garraty, *The Nature of Biography* (New York: Alfred A. Knopf, 1957).
Michael Paul Rogin, *Fathers and Children: Andrew Jackson and the Subjugation of the American Indian* (New Brunswick: Transaction Publishers, 1991).
Harry Watson, *Liberty and Power: The Politics of Jacksonian America* (New York: Hill and Wang, 1990).
Sean Wilentz, *Andrew Jackson* (New York: Henry Holtand Company, 2005).

NOTES

1. Quoted in Robert V. Remini, *The Election of Andrew Jackson* (Philadelphia: J. B. Lippincott, 1963), p. 200.
2. Quoted in Robert V. Remini, *Andrew Jackson and the Course of American Freedom, 1822–1832* (New York: Harper & Row, 1981), p. 178.
3. Quoted in Charles Sellers, "Andrew Jackson Versus the Historians," in *American Themes: Essays in Historiography*, ed. Frank Otto Gatel and Allen Weinstein (New York: Oxford University Press, 1968), p. 143.
4. Quoted in ibid., p. 144.
5. Quoted in ibid., p. 147.
6. Quoted in Edward Hallett Carr, *What Is History?* (New York: Alfred A. Knopf, 1962), p. 68.

Chapter
10

History "From the Bottom Up": Historians and Slavery

The sources in this chapter—an essay drawing from a slaveholder's records and various primary sources—present evidence on slave life in the antebellum South.

Secondary Source

Primary Sources

*L*ike many planters, the lord of the magnificent Cumberland Valley estate saw himself as a kind slave master. The owner of nearly one hundred slaves instructed his overseer "to treat them with great humanity, feed and cloath them well, and work them in moderation." "My negroes," he declared, "shall be treated humanely."[1] Yet this plantation master sometimes whipped and chained his slaves. When he believed his wife's maid was "guilty of a great deal of impudence," he ordered her whipped with perhaps as many as fifty lashes. He had even less patience with runaways. When four of his slaves escaped and were later captured, he put two of them in shackles until he could sell or exchange them. On another occasion, he offered fifty dollars for the capture of a fugitive and "ten dollars for every hundred lashes any person will give him to the amount of three hundred."[2]

This "humane" planter who whipped and chained his slaves was Andrew Jackson. Old Hickory illustrates the contradictions of slavery and the self-deception the institution induced. "Kind" masters often meted out frightening punishment. They condemned their chattel as "lazy," never realizing that it was irrational for slaves to work diligently. They did not see in the faces of slave children the clear evidence of their own sexual liaisons in the slave quarters. Nor did they really know their slaves, certainly not as well as their slaves had to know them. As one former slave put it, "The only weapon of self defence [*sic*] I would use successfully, was that of deception."[3]

If slavery blinded slaveholders to its harsh realities, historians have also suffered from nearsightedness when examining the peculiar institution. Through much of the twentieth century, most historians were not interested in the bottom of society. Andrew Jackson's life mattered; those of his slaves did not. Yet we cannot comprehend America's past without understanding slavery. And that is impossible without knowing slavery's impact on slaves. So in this chapter we look at history "from the bottom up." We examine the lives slaves led within an institution filled with contradictions, deception, and self-deception.

SETTING

Like slave masters, historians often saw what they wanted to when they looked at slave life. Early twentieth-century historian Ulrich B. Phillips, for instance, studied the lives of slaves as a Southerner sympathetic to the slaveholder. His observations about slaves and their interaction with masters were tainted by racist assumptions. Indeed, Phillips concluded that slavery was a paternalistic institution that trained Africans in the ways of a superior white civilization. When views about the status of blacks in American society began to change, so did assessments about slavery and its impact on African Americans.

In 1956, historian Kenneth Stampp published *The Peculiar Institution,* a direct assault on Phillips's view of slavery. Where Phillips saw slavery as benevolent, Stampp characterized it as harsh and oppressive. In his study *Slavery* (1959), Stanley Elkins went further, arguing that the trauma of enslavement had obliterated slaves' African cultural roots. Moreover, Elkins attempted to show that slaves retained little power to shape their own personalities, so emotionally devastating was bondage. Applying modern theories of social psychology, Elkins asserted that many slaves came to assume their masters' view of them as inferior and dependent "Sambos."

Phillips, Elkins, and Stampp shared an assumption that blacks were molded by white masters. Phillips saw slaves as beneficiaries of slavery; Stampp and Elkins saw them as helpless victims. As African Americans fought for civil rights and even black separation in the 1960s, other historians began to question whether slaves had been passive victims of white domination. Elkins's thesis came in for particular attack, even though it had challenged Phillips's paternalistic view. Many critics found incorrect and offensive Elkins's characterization of black slaves as helpless, childlike "Sambos." In such books as John Blassingame's *The Slave Community* (1972), Eugene Genovese's *Roll, Jordan, Roll* (1974), and Herbert Gutman's *The Black Family in Slavery and Freedom* (1976), historians began to examine slavery from the slaves' point of view. They discovered a resilient culture in the slave quarters and portrayed blacks not as passive objects but as people who maintained a separate culture and shaped their own lives.

More recently, other historians have criticized Blassingame, Genovese, Gutman, and other modern scholars for ignoring or distorting the role of women in slave society. They argue that these historians were so intent on negating the Sambo image of the black male that they usually reduced the slave woman's role to insignificance or, in the words of one, sometimes "impos[ed] the Victorian model of domesticity and maternity on the pattern of black female slave life."[4] Meanwhile, such students of slavery as Deborah Gray White, Jacqueline Jones, and Elizabeth Fox-Genovese explored the world of the female slave. They discovered that slave women had different roles than men and that the male supremacy of the plantation house was not necessarily to be found in the slave quarters. As Deborah Gray White concluded, "They were not submissive, subordinate, or prudish and . . . they were not expected to be so."[5]

Such revelations, whether about male or female slaves, have not come easily. Because literacy was withheld from slaves by law, they rarely left written records. So historians have relied on such nontraditional sources as songs, folklore, slave narratives, and even material objects to reconstruct life in the slave quarters. Although these sources are sometimes difficult to interpret, they offer big rewards. Thanks to fresh assumptions about their sources and subjects, historians now understand more fully the impact of the peculiar institution on slaves and the slaves' impact on their society.

INVESTIGATION

By its very nature, of course, slavery was oppressive. Yet historians have not stopped at that obvious conclusion. Although they acknowledge great variety in slaves' circumstances, historians have come to conclusions about all aspects of the peculiar institution, from the profitability of plantations to the culture of slaves. Your main goal in this chapter is to answer another question that historians have asked about slavery: What was life like for plantation slaves in the decades before the Civil War? That is a very broad question. In formulating an answer to it, therefore, you will need to address several related questions:

1. **In what ways were slaves able to shape their own world on James Hammond's Silver Bluff plantation, according to Source 1?** What evidence does the essay offer for a separate culture among slaves? What role did religion play?

2. **To what extent were Hammond's slaves able to resist the oppression of slavery?** Was the plantation an all-powerful institution that made slaves helpless and passive, or did slaves have opportunities to exercise power?

3. **Do the primary sources support or contradict the essay's conclusions about the nature of plantation slavery?** What do they reveal about the pleasures and suffering that slaves experienced? How did female slaves' experiences differ from those of their male counterparts?

4. **What were the most important factors affecting the slave experience?** Was the relationship between Hammond and his slaves typical?

Read the sections in your textbook on antebellum slavery for additional background before you begin, paying particular attention to its conclusions about the nature of plantation slavery.

SECONDARY SOURCE

1 Historian Drew Gilpin Faust's essay on the relationship between master and slaves on James Henry Hammond's South Carolina plantation is based on Hammond's extensive plantation records. Although Faust bases her discussion about planter–slave relations on documents produced by a white master, they reveal a great deal about slave autonomy and power and the existence of a separate slave community on the plantation. With the primary sources, you will be able to evaluate Faust's findings with evidence from other slaves and plantations. As you read this selection, note how Hammond attempted to assert mastery over his slaves and whether psychological manipulation or physical punishment was more important in his efforts to achieve control. Also pay attention to the ways Hammond's slaves tried to undermine his efforts

to dominate them. Finally, note what Hammond's slaves did at the end of the Civil War, and Faust's explanation for their behavior.

Community, Culture, and Conflict on an Antebellum Plantation (1980)
DREW GILPIN FAUST

A dozen miles south of Augusta, Georgia, the Savannah River curves gently, creating two bends that were known to ante-bellum steamboat captains as Stingy Venus and Hog Crawl Round. Nearby, on the South Carolina shore, a cliff abruptly rises almost thirty feet above the water. Mineral deposits in the soil give the promontory a metallic tinge, and the bank and the plantation of which it was part came as early as colonial times to be called Silver Bluff.

In 1831, an opportune marriage placed this property in the hands of twenty-four-year-old James Henry Hammond. An upwardly mobile lawyer, erstwile schoolmaster and newspaper editor, the young Carolinian had achieved through matrimony the status the Old South accorded to planters alone; when he arrived to take possession of his estate, he found and carefully listed in his diary 10,800 acres of land, a dwelling, assorted household effects, and 147 bondsmen. But along with these valued acquisitions, he was to receive a challenge he had not anticipated. As he sought to exert his mastery over the labor force on which the prosperity of his undertaking depended, he was to discover that his task entailed more than simply directing 147 individual lives. Hammond had to dominate a complex social order already in existence on the plantation and to struggle for the next three decades to control what he called a "system of roguery" amongst his slaves.

Hammond astutely recognized that black life on his plantation was structured and organized as a "system," the very existence of which seemed necessarily a challenge to his absolute control—and therefore, as he perceived it, a kind of "roguery." Because Hammond's mastery over his bondsmen depended upon his success at undermining slave society and culture, he established a carefully designed plan of physical and psychological domination in hopes of destroying the foundations of black solidarity. Until he relinquished management of the estate to his sons in the late 1850s, Hammond kept extraordinarily detailed records. Including daily entries concerning the treatment, work patterns, and vital statistics of his slaves, they reveal a striking portrait of slave culture and resistance and of the highly structured efforts Hammond took to overpower it. . . . While Hammond sought to assert both dominance and legitimacy, the slaves at Silver Bluff strove to maintain

Source: Excerpted from Drew Gilpin Faust, "Culture, Conflict, and Community: The Meaning of Power on an Antebellum Plantation," *Journal of Social History*, Vol. 14, No. 1 (Fall 1980). Reprinted by permission.

networks of communication and community as the bases of their personal and cultural autonomy. This struggle, which constantly tested the ingenuity and strength of both the owner and his slaves, touched everything from religion to work routines to health, and even determined the complex pattern of unauthorized absences from the plantation. . . .

The desire to control black religious life led Hammond to endeavor to replace independent black worship with devotions entirely under white direction. At first he tried to compel slaves into white churches simply by making black ones unavailable, and even sought to prevent his neighbors from permitting black churches on their own lands. But soon he took positive steps to provide the kind of religious environment he deemed appropriate for his slaves. For a number of years he hired itinerant ministers for Sunday afternoon slave services. By 1845, however, Hammond had constructed a Methodist Church for his plantation and named it St. Catherine's after his wife.

The piety of the Hammond slaves became a source of admiration even to visitors. A house guest on the plantation in the 1860s found the services at St. Catherine's "solemn and impressive," a tribute, she felt, to Hammond's beneficent control over his slaves. "There was a little company of white people," she recalled, "the flower of centuries of civilization, among hundreds of blacks but yesterday . . . in savagery, now peaceful, contented, respectful and comprehending the worship of God. . . . By reason of Senator Hammond's wise discipline," the visitor assured her readers, there was no evidence of "religious excesses," the usual "mixture of hysteria and conversion" that she believed characterized most black religion. These slaves, it appeared to an outsider, had abandoned religious ecstasy for the reverential passivity prescribed for them by white cultural norms.

Hammond had taken great pains to establish just such white standards amongst his slaves, and the visitor's description of the behavior he succeeded in eliciting from his bondsmen would undoubtedly have pleased him. But even Hammond recognized that the decorous behavior of his slaves within the walls of St. Catherine's was but an outward compliance with his directives. He seemed unable to eradicate black religious expression, evidences of which appeared to him like tips of an iceberg indicating an underlying pattern of independent belief and worship that persisted among his slaves. Twenty years after his original decision to eliminate the slave church, Hammond recorded in his plantation diary, "Have ordered all church meetings to be broken up except at the Church with a white preacher." Hammond's slaves had over the preceding decades tested their master's initial resolve, quietly asserting their right to their own religious life in face of his attempt to deny it to them. . . .

The struggle for power manifested in the conflict over religious autonomy was paralleled in other areas of slave life on the Hammond domain. Just as Hammond sought from the time of his arrival in 1831 to control religious behavior, so too he desired to supervise work patterns more closely. "When

I first began to plant," he later reminisced, "I found my people in very bad subjection from the long want of a master and it required of me a year of severity which cost me infinite pain." The slaves, accustomed to a far less rigorous system of management, resented his attempts and tried to undermine his drive for efficiency. "The negroes are trying me," Hammond remarked in his diary on more than one occasion during the early months of his tenure. In response, he was firm, recording frequent floggings of slaves who refused to comply with his will. When several bondsmen sought to extend the Christmas holiday by declining to return to work as scheduled, Hammond was unyielding, forcing them back to the fields and whipping them as well.

As the weeks passed, the instances of beatings and overt insubordination noted in plantation records diminished; a more subtle form of conflict emerged. Over the next decade, this struggle over work patterns at Silver Bluff fixed on the issue of task versus gang labor. The slaves clearly preferred the independent management of their time offered by the task system, while Hammond feared the autonomy it provided the bondsmen. . . .

Although at this time Hammond succeeded in establishing the gang as the predominant form of labor at Silver Bluff, the victory was apparently neither final nor total. Indeed, it may simply have served to regularize the pattern of poorly performed work Hammond had viewed as a form of resistance to the gang system. He continued to record hoeing that ignored weeds, picking that passed over bulging cotton bolls, and cultivating that destroyed both mule and plough. But eventually the slaves here too won a compromise. By 1850, Hammond was referring once again in his correspondence and in his plantation diary to task work, although he complained bitterly about continuing poor performance and the frequent departure of many bondsmen from the fields as early as midafternoon.

Hammond seemed not so much to master as to manipulate his slaves, offering a system not just of punishments, but of positive inducements, ranging from picking contests to single out the most diligent hands, to occasional rituals of rewards for all, such as Christmas holidays; rations of sugar, tobacco and coffee; midsummer barbecues; or even the pipes sent all adult slaves from Europe when Hammond departed on the Grand Tour. The slaves were more than just passive recipients of these sporadic benefits; they in turn manipulated their master for those payments and privileges they had come to see as their due. Hammond complained that his bondsmen's demands led him against his will to countenance a slave force "too well fed & otherwise well treated," but he nevertheless could not entirely resist their claims. When after a particularly poor record of work by slaves in the fall of 1847 Hammond sought to shorten the usual Christmas holiday, he ruefully recorded on December 26 that he had been "persuaded out of my decision by the Negroes."

Hammond and his slaves arrived at a sort of accommodation on the issue of work. But in this process, Hammond had to adjust his desires and expectations as significantly as did his bondsmen. His abstract notions of order and absolute control were never to be fully realized. He and his slaves reached a truce that permitted a level of production acceptable to Hammond and a level of endeavor tolerable to his slaves. . . .

For some Silver Bluff residents, however, there could be no such compromise. Instead of seeking indirectly to avoid the domination inherent to slavery, these individuals confronted it, turning to arson and escape as overt expressions of their rebelliousness. Throughout the period of his management, Hammond referred to mysterious fires that would break out in the gin house on one occasion, the mill house or the plantation hospital the next. While these depredations could not be linked to specific individuals and only minimally affected the operation of the plantation, running away offered the angry slave a potentially more effective means of immediate resistance to the master's control. Between 1831 and 1855, Hammond recorded fifty-three attempts at escape by his bondsmen. Because he was sometimes absent from the plantation for months at a time during these decades, serving in political office or travelling in Europe, it seems unlikely that this list is complete. Nevertheless, Hammond's slave records provide sufficient information about the personal attributes of the runaways, the circumstances of their departure, the length of their absence and the nature of their family ties to demonstrate the meaning and significance of the action within the wider context of plantation life.

The most striking—and depressing—fact about Silver Bluff's runaways is that Hammond records no instance of a successful escape. A total of thirty-seven different slaves were listed as endeavoring to leave the plantation. Thirty-five percent of these were repeaters, although no slave was recorded as making more than three attempts. Newly purchased slaves who made several efforts to escape were often sold; those with long-term ties to the Silver Bluff community eventually abandoned the endeavor. . . .

While the decision to run away might appear to be a rejection of the ties of black community as well as the chains of bondage, the way in which escape functioned at Silver Bluff shows it usually to have operated somewhat differently. Because there were no runaways who achieved permanent freedom and because most escapees did not get far, they remained in a very real sense a part of the slave community they had seemingly fled. Forty-three percent of the runaways at the Bluff left with others. The small proportion—sixteen percent of the total—of females were almost without exception running with husbands or joining spouses who had already departed. Once slaves escaped, they succeeded in remaining at large an average of forty-nine days. Sixty-five percent were captured and the rest returned voluntarily. The distribution of compulsory and elective returns over the calendar year reveals that harsh weather was a significant factor in persuading slaves to give themselves up. Seventy-seven percent of those returning in the winter months did so voluntarily, while in the spring and summer eighty percent were brought back against their will. Weather and workload made summer the runaway season, and fifty-eight percent of all escape attempts occurred in June, July, and August.

While certain individuals—notably young males, particularly those without family ties—were most likely to become runaways, the slave community as a whole provided these individuals with assistance and support. Hammond himself recognized that runaways often went no farther than the nearby Savannah River swamps, where they survived on food provided by those remaining at home. The ties between the escapees and the community were sufficiently strong that Hammond endeavored to force runaways to return by disciplining the rest of the slave force. On at least one occasion Hammond determined to stop the meat allowance of the entire plantation until the runaways came in. In another instance, he severely flogged four slaves harboring two runaways, hoping thereby to break the personal and communal bonds that made prolonged absences possible. . . .

In the initial part of his tenure at the Bluff, Hammond recorded efforts to round up runaway slaves by means of extensive searches through the swamps on horseback or with packs of dogs. After the first decade, however, he made little mention of such vigorous measures and seems for the most part simply to have waited for his escapees to be captured by neighbors, turn up in nearby jails, or return home. In order to encourage voluntary surrender, Hammond announced a policy of punishment for runaways that allotted ten lashes for each day absent to those recaptured by force and three lashes per day to those returning of their own will. The establishment of this standardized rule integrated the problem of runaways into the system of rewards and punishments at Silver Bluff and rendered it an aspect of the understanding existing between master and slaves. Since no one escaped permanently, such a rule served to set forth the cost of unauthorized absence and encouraged those who had left in irrational rage to return as soon as their tempers had cooled. When the respected fifty-three-year-old driver John Shubrick was flogged for drunkenness, he fled in fury and mortification, but within a week was back exercising his customary responsibility in plantation affairs. . . .

While runaways disrupted routine and challenged Hammond's system of management, his greatest anxieties about loss of control arose from the fear that slave dissatisfaction would be exploited by external forces to threaten the fine balance of concession and oppression he had established. From the beginning of his tenure at the Bluff, he sought to isolate his bondsmen from outside influences, prohibiting their trading in local stores, selling produce to neighbors, marrying off the plantation or interacting too closely with hands on the steamboats that refuelled at the Bluff landing. Despite such efforts, however, Hammond perceived during the 1840s and 1850s an ever-growing threat to his power arising from challenges levelled at the peculiar institution as a whole. To Hammond's horror, it seemed impossible to keep information about growing abolition sentiment from the slaves. Such knowledge, Hammond feared, might provide the bondsmen with additional bases for ideological autonomy and greater motivation to resist his control. . . .

At the beginning of the war, Hammond was uncertain about the sympathies of his slaves. In 1861, he noted that they appeared "anxious," but remarked "Cant tell which side." As the fighting grew closer, with the firing of large guns near the coast audible at Silver Bluff, Hammond began to sense growing disloyalty among his slaves, and to confront intensifying problems of control. "Negroes demoralized greatly. Stealing right and left," he recorded in 1863. By the middle of that year, it seemed certain that the slaves expected "some great change." Despite his efforts, they seemed at all times "well apprised" of war news, sinking into "heavy gloom" at any Union reverse. Hammond observed the appearance of "a peculiar furtive glance with which they regard me & a hanging off from me that I do not like." They seemed to "shut up their faces & cease their cheerful greetings." Hammond felt the war had rendered his control tenuous, and he believed that even though his slaves sought to appear "passive . . . the roar of a single cannon of the Federal's would make them frantic—savage cutthroats and incendiaries."

Hammond never witnessed the Union conquest of the South or the emancipation of his slaves, for he died in November of 1864. Despite his dire prophecies, however, the people of Silver Bluff did not rise in revolution against those who had oppressed them for so long. Unlike many slaves elsewhere who fled during the war itself, the Hammond bondsmen did not depart even when freedom was proclaimed. "We have not lost many negroes," Hammond's widow complained in September 1865 as she worried about having too many mouths to feed. "I wish we could get clear of many of the useless ones."

Given the turbulent nature of the interaction between Hammond and his slaves in the antebellum years, it would be misguided to regard the blacks' decision to remain on the plantation as evidence either of docility or of indifference about freedom. Instead, it might better be understood as final testimony to the importance of that solidarity we have seen among bondsmen on the Hammond estate. These blacks were more concerned to continue together as a group than to flee Hammond's domination. In the preoccupation with the undeniable importance of the master-slave relationship, historians may have failed fully to recognize how for many bondsmen, the positive meaning of the web of slave interrelationships was a more central influence than were the oppressive intrusions of the power of the master. Silver Bluff had been home to many of these slaves before Hammond ever arrived; the community had preceded him, and now it had outlived him. Its maintenance and autonomy were of the highest priority to its members, keeping them at Silver Bluff even when any single freedman's desire for personal liberty might have best been realized in flight. The values central to this cultural group were more closely associated with the forces of tradition and community than with an individualistic revolutionary romanticism. . . .

. . . These freedmen saw themselves and their aspirations defined less by the oppressions of slavery than by the positive accomplishments of autonomous black community that they had achieved even under the domain of the peculiar institution.

PRIMARY SOURCES

Most of the sources in this chapter were produced by slaves or former slaves. Such documents are very helpful to historians who want to know what slavery was like. As you evaluate them, consider what evidence they provide for a separate slave culture and about slaves' opportunities to resist or escape the oppression of slavery.

2 Clark, a former slave, delivered this speech in 1842. It was recorded by abolitionist Lydia Maria Child and published in the *National Anti-Slavery Standard*. As you read it, consider whether Clark's sympathetic Brooklyn, New York, audience might have influenced what he said.

Leaves from a Slave's Journal of Life (1842)
LEWIS CLARK

"There was a widower in Kentucky, who took one of his women slaves into the house. She told her master one day that seven of the young girls had poked fun at her for the way she was living. This raised his *ambition*. 'I'll teach 'em to make fun!' said he. So he sent the woman away, and ordered the young girls to come to him, one by one." (An ill-mannered and gross laughter, among the boys of the audience, here seemed to embarrass him.) "Perhaps I had better not try to tell this story," he continued; "for I cannot tell it as it was; though surely it is more shameful to have such things *done,* than it is to tell of 'em. He got mad with the girls, because they complained to their mothers; but he didn't like to punish 'em for that, for fear it would make a talk. So he ordered 'em to go out into the field to do work that was too hard for 'em. Six of 'em said they couldn't do it; but the mother of the seventh, guessing what it was for, told her to go, and do the best she could. The other six was every one of 'em tied up naked, and flogged, for disobeying orders. Now, who would like to be a slave, even if there was nothing bad about it but such treatment of his sisters and daughters? But there's a worse thing yet about slavery; the worst thing in the whole lot; though it's all bad, from the butt end to the *pint*. I mean the *patter-rollers* (patrols.) . . . If a slave don't open his door to them at any time of night they break

Source: National Anti-Slavery Standard, October 20, 1842.

it down. They steal his money if they can find it, and act just as they please with his wives and daughters. If a husband dares to say a word, or even look as if he wasn't quite satisfied, they tie him up and give him thirty-nine lashes. If there's any likely young girls in a slave's hut, they're mighty apt to have business there, especially if they think any colored young man takes a fancy to any of 'em. Maybe he'll get a pass from his master, and go to see the young girl for a few hours. The patter-rollers break in and find him there. They'll abuse the girl as bad as they can, a purpose to provoke him. If he looks cross, they give him a flogging, tear up his pass, turn him out of doors, and then take him up and whip him for being out without a pass. If the slave says they tore it up, they swear he lies; and nine times out of ten the master won't come out agin 'em; for they say it won't *do* to let the niggers suppose they may complain of the patter-rollers; they must be taught that it's their business to obey 'em in everything; and the patter-roller knows that very well. Oh, how often I've seen the poor girls sob and cry, when there's been such goings on! Maybe you think, because they're slaves, they an't got no feeling and no shame? A woman's being a slave, don't stop her having genteel ideas; that is, according to their way, and as far as they can. They know they must submit to their masters; besides, their masters, maybe, dress 'em up, and make 'em little presents, and give 'em more privileges, while the whim lasts; but that an't like having a parcel of low, dirty, swearing, drunk patter-rollers let loose among 'em, like so many hogs. This breaks down their spirits dreadfully, and makes 'em wish they was dead.

"Now who among you would like to have your wives, and daughters, and sisters, in such a situation? This is what every slave in all these States is exposed to.—Yet folks go from these parts down to Kentucky, and come back, and say the slaves have enough to eat and drink, and they are very happy, and they wouldn't mind it much to be slaves themselves. I'd like to have 'em try it; it would teach 'em a little more than they know now."

Slave Interviews

Many former slaves were interviewed during and after the Civil War. Some of these interviews appeared in newspapers and magazines. In addition, the American Freedmen's Inquiry Commission, established in 1863, gathered testimony from numerous former slaves. Former bondsmen were also interviewed by scholars in the early twentieth century. In the 1930s, for instance, Works Progress Administration interviewers recorded the testimony of former slaves. As you read these interviews, note what they reveal about the treatment of slaves, the threat to families under slavery, and the female slave experience.

Also keep in mind that, as oral histories, they often attempted to capture the perceived slave dialect. Remember, too, that even though the interview subjects in this case had firsthand experience with slavery, their memories— like anyone's—may not always have been perfect. Finally, a word about a word. You will see "nigger" used repeatedly in some of these interviews. Remember that both the meaning and use of words, like language itself, change over time. Likewise, words can mean different things to different groups. In the early nineteenth century, "nigger" did not have the same offensive and racist character that it came to assume by the twentieth century. It or varied pronunciations have also been used by some, for instance, to denote any non-white or poor people and by others, as a term of solidarity. For slaves, or former slaves speaking to a white person in the early twentieth century for an oral history, it may well have been used in self-defense, signaling to listeners the perception that the speaker accepted white supremacy and his own inferior place in society.

3   Harry McMillan, Interviewed by the American Freedmen's Inquiry Commission (1863)

I am about 40 years of age, and was born in Georgia but came to Beaufort when a small boy. I was owned by General Eustis and lived upon his plantation.

Q. Tell me about the tasks colored men had to do?

A. In old secesh times each man had to do two tasks, which are 42 rows or half an acre, in "breaking" the land, and in "listing" each person had to do a task and a half. In planting every hand had to do an acre a day; in hoeing your first hoeing where you hoe flat was two tasks, and your second hoeing, which is done across the beds, was also two tasks. After going through those two operations you had a third which was two and a half tasks, when you had to go over the cotton to thin out the plants leaving two in each hill.

Q. How many hours a day did you work?

A. Under the old secesh times every morning till night—beginning at daylight and continuing till 5 or 6 at night.

Q. But you stopped for your meals?

A. You had to get your victuals standing at your hoe; you cooked it over night yourself or else an old woman was assigned to cook for all the hands, and she or your children brought the food to the field.

Q. You never sat down and took your food together as families?

A. No, sir; never had time for it.

Q. The women had the same day's work as the men; but suppose a woman was in the family way was her task less?

A. No, sir; most of times she had to do the same work. Sometimes the wife of the planter learned the condition of the woman and said to her husband you must cut down her day's work. Sometimes the women had their children in the field.

Source: John W. Blassingame, ed., *Slave Testimony: Two Centuries of Letters, Speeches, Interviews, and Autobiographies* (Baton Rouge: Louisiana State University Press, 1977), pp. 379–380. (Originally from American Freedmen's Inquiry Commission Interviews [1863].)

4   Charity Bowery (1847–1848)

Interviewed, 1847–1848. New York.
    by Lydia Maria Child

Age: sixty-five
b. 1782. North Carolina
Enslaved: North Carolina
House servant

The following story was told me by an aged colored woman in New York. I shall endeavor to relate it precisely in her own words, so oft repeated that they are tolerably impressed on my memory. Some confusion of names, dates, and incidents, I may very naturally make. I profess only to give "the pith and marrow" of Charity's story, deprived of the highly dramatic effect it received from her swelling emotions, earnest looks and changing tones.

"I am about sixty-five years old. I was born on an estate called Pembroke, about three miles from Edenton, North Carolina. My master was very kind to his slaves. If an overseer whipped them, he turned him away. . . .

"Sixteen children I've had, first and last, and twelve I've nursed for my mistress. From the time my first baby was born, I always set my heart upon buying freedom for some of my children. I thought it was of more consequence to them than to me; for I was old and used to being a slave. But mistress McKinley wouldn't let me have my children. One after another—one after another—she sold 'em away from me. Oh, how *many* times that woman broke my heart!"

Here her voice choked, and the tears began to flow. She wiped them quickly with the corner of her apron, and continued: "I tried every way I could to lay up a copper, to buy my children, but I found it pretty hard; for mistress kept me at work all the time. It was 'Charity! Charity, Charity!' from morning till night. Charity do this or that.

"I used to do the washings of the family; and large washings they were. The public road run right by my little hut, and I thought to myself, while I stood there at the wash-tub, I might just as well as not be earning something to buy my children. So I set up a little oyster-board, and when anybody came along that wanted a few oysters and a cracker, I left my wash-tub and waited upon them. When I got a little money laid up, I went to my mistress and tried to buy one of my children. She knew not how long my heart had been set upon it, and how hard I had worked for it. But she wouldn't let me have one! So I went to work again; and I set up late o'night, in hopes I could earn enough to tempt her. When I had two hundred dollars I went to her again; but she thought she could find a better market, and she wouldn't let me have one. At last, what do you think that woman did? She sold me and five of my children to the speculators! Oh, how I *did* feel when I heard my children was sold to the speculators!"

Source: Emancipation, April 5, 1848.

5   Uncle Ben (1910)

Interviewed, 1910. Alabama.   Enslaved: Alabama, Texas,
  by Mary White Ovington   N.C.

"Yes, we was worked hard in those days, we sure was. You think, maybe, people done have a rest on Sunday? I done never see it. Half-time work on Sunday pullin' fodder in the field for the mules an' cows. Then Sunday mornin' we'd build fences for the cattle, old fashion' bridge fences, we calls 'em. The women too was worked terrible. You see the railroad yonder? Women helped grade that railroad. Other times they'd plow in the field an' when night come they mus' spin two cuts o' cotton. Don't matter how tired they might be, they mus' spin their two cuts or in the morning they'd be whipt. That's what I's tellin' you.

"There were terrible persecution then. I's seen men with fly blows. You don't know what that mean, perhaps? Fly blows is what we calls the meat when it turns to maggots. They'd whip a man until he's so warm the blood creep thru his shirt, an' the flies 'ud come. Workin' out in the fiel' all the time, bendin' over the hoe, an' the flies suckin' the blood. Some men wouldn't stan' it. They'd take to the woods, an' then the dogs 'ud ketch 'em. After that they'd be chained, an' you'd hear rattling like they was chained logs. When night comes, there by deir bed there'd be a staple. The overseer'd come along an' lock the chain to the staple so they couldn't get away. In the mornin' the overseer let 'em out. They done put 'em, too, in screw boxes, what you call presses. When they put down the foller-block, then the nigger was tight. It was out-o-doors an' he was like to freeze. They chain him in the graveyard, too, keep him there all the night to skeer him. Oh, I knows what I's talking about, yes ma'am. Now an' den you can ketch some ole person who knows, who bear witness like hallelujah meeting, to what I say. . . ."

6   Sarah Fitzpatrick (1938)

Interviewed, 1938. Alabama.   Age: ninety
  by Thomas Campbell   b. 1847. Alabama
                               Enslaved: Alabama
                               House servant

In dem times "Niggers" had'ta hav'va pass to go to church too. White fo'ks axed you whut church ya' wan'na go to an' dey issue ya a pass, write on dere de name

Source: Independent 48 (May 26, 1910), pp. 1131–1136.

Source: Thomas Monroe Campbell Papers, Files of the Tuskegee Department of Records and Research, Hollis Burke Frissell Library, Tuskegee University.

ob de church an' de name ob de pu'son an' de time to git back home. Co'se when "Niggers" went to church wid deir white fo'ks dey didn't haf'ta have no pass. Ya'see, us "Niggers" had our meetin' in de white fo'ks Baptist Church in de town o' Tuskegee. Dere's a place up in de loft dere now dat dey built fer de "Nigger" slaves to 'tend church wid de white fo'ks. White preacher he preach to de white fo'ks an' when he git thu' wid dem he preach some to de "Niggers". Tell'em to mind deir Marster an' b'have deyself an' dey'll go to Hebben when dey die. Dey come 'round an' tell us to pray, git 'ligion, dat wuz on Sun'dy, but dey'ed beat de life out'cha de next day ef ya didn't walk de chalk line. Our white fo'ks made us go to church an' Sun'dy School too. Dey made us read de Catechism. G'ess de re'son fo' dat wuz, dey tho't it made us min' dem bedder. "Niggers" commence'ta wanna go to church by de'selves, even ef dey had'ta meet in de white church. So white fo'ks have deir service in de mornin' an' "Niggers" have deirs in de evenin', a'ter dey clean up, wash de dishes, an' look a'ter ever'thing. Den de white fo'ks come back at night an' have deir Church Service. Ya'see "Niggers" lack'ta shout a whole lot an' wid de white fo'ks al'round'em, dey couldn't shout jes' lack dey want to. . . .

Mos' all de "Niggers" use'ta steal in Slav'ry time, co'se 'bout all dey stole f'om dey Marster 'n Mistrus wuz sum'in t'eat, steal hogs 'n kill'um an' clean'um at night den dey dig a pit an' put'um 'way in de woods, den dey go back dere an' git some uv'it when dey want it, an' cook it. Som'times de white fo'ks ketch'em wid it an' beat'em. Didn't have no cook stove in dem times. Som' uv'em cook out doors, some uv'em in fi'place. Any "Nigger" would steal when he didn't get 'nuff t'eat. Ya'fam'ly didn't git but three an' haf' pounds uv meat, one an' er haf' pecks uv meal a week, dat wont e'nuff, so "Niggers" jes' had'ta steal. He didn't steal nothing' but sump'in t'eat dough. Co'se ma' white fo'ks wux high class, deir house gals didn't have no right to steal 'cause ma' mistrus tel' us anythin' we want, don't take it, but ax' fer it. Ef we wanna wear piece of her jewry we ax' her fer it an' she let us wear it, to church som'time. She leave money 'roun an' udder val'able things an' we didn't bodder it. Dey taught us not to take things. I knowed whar ma' marster kep' his money box: he kep'it right out in de sec'e'tary. He nuver did bodder 'bout lockin' it up fo'm us. We jes' didn't bodder his money. Durin' de war de white fo'ks sunt all de cot'on dey could get to de war. . . . "Niggers" didn't think dat stealin' wuz so bad in dem times. Fak' is dey didn't call it stealin', dey called it takin'. Dey say' "I ain't takin' fo'm nobody but ma' mistrus an' Marster, an' I'm doin' dat 'cause I'se hongry." "Niggers" use'ta steal cot'on an' anything dey could sell to 'nudder white man. Co'se dats whut de whites taught'em.

7   Henry Bibb, the author of this letter, escaped from slavery in 1840. He campaigned for the Liberty Party in 1844 and 1845 and, after the passage of the Fugitive Slave Law in 1850, moved to Canada. Note what this letter reveals about Bibb's treatment and his feelings toward his former master.

A Slave's Letter to His Former Master (1844)

Detroit, March 23d, 1844

William Gatewood

Dear Sir:—I am happy to inform you that you are not mistaken in the man whom you sold as property, and received pay for as such. But I thank God that I am not property now, but am regarded as a man like yourself, and although I live far north, I am enjoying a comfortable living by my own industry. If you should ever chance to be traveling this way, and will call on me, I will use you better than you did me while you held me as a slave. Think not that I have any malice against you, for the cruel treatment which you inflicted on me while I was in your power. As it was the custom of your country, to treat your fellow men as you did me and my little family, I can freely forgive you.

I wish to be remembered in love to my aged mother, and friends; please tell her that if we should never meet again in this life, my prayer shall be to God that we may meet in Heaven, where parting shall be no more.

You wish to be remembered to King and Jack. I am pleased, sir, to inform you that they are both here, well, and doing well. They are both living in Canada West. They are now the owners of better farms than the men who once owned them.

You may perhaps think hard of us for running away from slavery, but as to myself, I have but one apology to make for it, which is this: I have only to regret that I did not start at an earlier period. I might have been free long before I was. But you had it in your power to have kept me there much longer than you did. I think it is very probable that I should have been a toiling slave on your plantation today, if you had treated me differently.

To be compelled to stand by and see you whip and slash my wife without mercy, when I could afford her no protection, not even by offering myself to suffer the lash in her place, was more than I felt it to be the duty of a slave husband to endure, while the way was open to Canada. My infant child was also frequently flogged by Mrs. Gatewood, for *crying*, until its skin was bruised literally purple. This kind of treatment was what drove me from home and family, to seek a better home for them. But I am willing to forget the past. I should be pleased to hear from you again, on the reception of this, and should also be very happy to correspond with you often, if it should be agreeable to yourself. I subscribe myself a friend to the oppressed, and Liberty forever.

Henry Bibb
Windsor, Sept. 23, 1852

Source: Henry Bibb, *Narrative of the Life and Adventures of Henry Bibb, an American Slave* (New York, 1849).

8   Sometimes art captured scenes from slavery. At a dance in Virginia, one artist saw slaves playing musical instruments of both European origin (the fiddle) and African origin (the banjo and the bones). As you examine this picture, determine what it reveals about slave culture and plantation life.

Lynchburg Negro Dance, An Artist's View of Slavery (1853)

Abby Aldrich Rockefeller Folk Art Museum, The Colonial Williamsburg Foundation. Gift of Dr and Mrs. Richard M.Kain in memory of George Hay Kain

9   Although masters often used religion to teach obedience to their slaves, the slaves often derived other lessons from what they were taught. As you read this spiritual, ask yourself how religion helped sustain a slave culture. What lessons did slaves take from the Bible?

A Slave Spiritual (ca. 1863)

THE SHIP OF ZION.
Dis de good ole ship o' Zion,
Dis de good ole ship o' Zion,

Source: Atlantic Monthly, June 1867, pp. 685–694.

Dis de good ole ship o' Zion,
    And she's makin' for de Promise Land.
She hab angels for de sailors. (*Thrice.*)
    And she's, &c.
And how you know dey's angels? (*Thrice.*)
    And she's, &c.
Good Lord, shall I be de one? (*Thrice.*)
    And she's, &c.

Dat ship is out a-sailid, sailin', sailin',
    And she's, &c.
She's a-sailin' mighty steady, steady, steady,
    And she's, &c.
She'll neither reel nor totter, totter, totter,
    And she's, &c.
She's a-sailing' away cold Jordan, Jordan, Jordan,
    And she's, &c.
King Jesus is de captain, captain, captain,
    And she's makin' for de Promise Land.

---

10 Brer (Brother) Rabbit was a familiar figure to slaves. As in African folk
tales, slave stories assigned human qualities to animals. What traits
allow Brer Rabbit to survive against a much stronger Brer Fox? What
might these animal characters have stood for?

Brer Rabbit Outsmarts Brer Fox

De fox had a way goin' to de man hawg-pen an' eatin' up all his hawg. So de
people didn' know how to ketch de fox. An' so de rabbit was goin' along one
Sunday mornin'. Say was goin' to church. Ber Fox singin', "Good-mornin', Ber
Rabbit!" Ber Rabbit singin', "Good-mornin', Ber Fox!" Say, "Whey you goin'?"
Say, "I'm goin' to church." Ber Fox say, "Dis is my time. I'm hungry dis mornin'.
I'm goin' to ketch you."—"O Ber Fox! leave me off dis mornin'! I will sen' you to a
man house where he got a penful of pretty little pig, an' you will get yer brakefus'
fill. Ef you don' believe me, you can tie me here, an' you can go down to de house,
an' I'll stay here until you come back." So Ber Fox tie him. When he wen' down to
de house, de man had about fifty head of houn'-dawg. An' de man tu'n de houn'-
dawg loose on him. An' de fox made de long run right by Ber Rabbit. Ber Fox say,
"O Ber Rabbit! dose is no brakefus', dose is a pile of houn'-dawg."—"Yes, you

Source: Elsie Clews Parsons, *Foke-Lore of the Sea Islands of South Carolina, Memoirs of the
American Folk-Lore Society* (Cambridge, Mass.), XVI: pp. 26–27, 66–67.

was goin' to eat me, but dey will eat you for your brakefus' and supper to-night." An' so dey did. Dey cut [caught] de fox. An' Ber Rabbit give to de dawgs, "Gawd bless yer soul! dat what enemy get for meddlin' Gawd's people when dey goin' to church." Said, "I was goin' to school all my life an' learn every letter in de book but *d*, an' D was death, an' death was de en' of Ber Fox."

Artifacts from Slavery

Like other kinds of evidence, physical artifacts can tell historians much about what life was like for slaves. What does this evidence suggest about the opportunities for a separate existence in the slave quarters?

 This doll was found in the attic walls of a North Carolina plantation.

A Slave Child's Doll (ca. 1850)

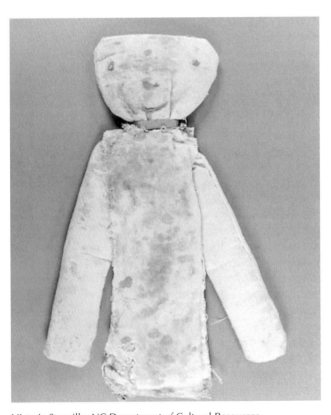

Historic Stagville, NC Department of Cultural Resources.

Bellegrove, a plantation built in 1857 in Louisiana, had twenty double cabins for slaves and a dormitory for 150 laborers.

A Plantation Plan (ca. 1857)

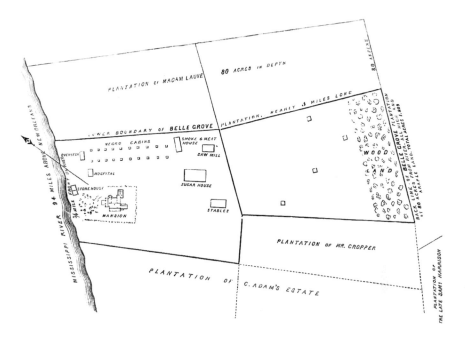

The Historic New Orleans Collection, acc# 1970.13.1.

CONCLUSION

The abolitionist Frederick Douglass, himself a runaway slave, made a point illustrated by this chapter. A free man, said Douglass, "cannot see things in the same light with the slave, because he does not, and cannot, look from the same point from which the slave does."[6] The study of slavery demonstrates the need to write history from several vantage points. Writing from the perspective of white masters and excluding the perceptions of slaves, as most historians did well into the last century, provides an incomplete and distorted view of slavery's nature and impact. Recently, historians have applied that insight about multiple vantage points in larger ways by comparing slave systems in the United States with those in other nations or by placing American slavery in a larger Atlantic or even global context. Looking at slavery from several vantage points provided by different locales or cultures also leads to insights that a narrow, unitary perspective misses.

The value of different vantage points—and comparative analyses—applies to many topics in history. In Chapter 11, you will have the opportunity to assess historians' conclusions about women in the North and South before the Civil War. Although most of these women had little in common with slaves, they also illustrate Douglass's argument. Northern women did not necessarily look at their roles in society "from the same point" as their Southern counterparts, and historians who ignore that fact will miss important differences between Northern and Southern society. Like conclusions about slavery, judgments about antebellum women depend heavily on which voices historians listen to from the past.

FURTHER READING

John W. Blassingame, *The Slave Community: Plantation Life in the Antebellum South,* rev. ed. (New York: Oxford University Press, 1979).

Edward D. C. Campbell, Jr., *Before Freedom Came: African-American Life in the Antebellum South* (Charlottesville: University Press of Virginia, 1991).

David B. Gaspar and Darlene Clark Hine, *More than Chattel: Black Women and Slavery in the Americas* (Bloomington: Indiana University Press, 1996).

Eugene Genovese, *Roll, Jordan, Roll: The World the Slaves Made* (New York: Pantheon Books, 1974).

Peter Kolchin, *American Slavery, 1619–1877* (New York: Hill and Wang, 1993).

Deborah Gray White, *Ar'n't I a Woman? Female Slaves in the Plantation South* (New York: W. W. Norton, 1985).

NOTES

1. Quoted in Robert V. Remini, *Andrew Jackson and the Course of American Empire, 1767–1821* (New York: Harper & Row, 1977), pp. 133–134.
2. Quoted in Kenneth M. Stampp, *The Peculiar Institution: Slavery in the Ante-Bellum South* (New York: Vintage Books, 1956), p. 188.
3. Gilbert Osofsky, ed., *Puttin' on Ole Massa: The Slave Narratives of Henry Bibb, William Wells Brown, and Solomon Northup* (New York: Harper & Row, 1969), p. 9.
4. Deborah Gray White, *Ar'n't I a Woman? Female Slaves in the Plantation South* (New York: W. W. Norton, 1985), p. 21.
5. Ibid., p. 22.
6. Quoted in John W. Blassingame, ed., *Slave Testimony: Two Centuries of Letters, Speeches, Interviews, and Autobiographies* (Baton Rouge: Louisiana State University Press, 1977), p. lxv.

Chapter

11

Ideology and Society: The Bounds of Womanhood in the North and South

This chapter presents two secondary sources and several primary sources related to an antebellum domestic ideology and the lives of Northern and Southern women. These documents will help you compare the ideals and circumstances regarding women in the North and South.

Secondary Sources

1. *The Bonds of Womanhood* (1997), NANCY F. COTT
2. Domestic Ideology in the South (1998), MARLI F. WEINER

Primary Sources

3. *Woman in America* (1841), MRS. A. J. GRAVES
4. *Treatise on Domestic Economy* (1841), CATHARINE BEECHER
5. *Lowell Offering* (1845)
6. The Evils of Factory Life (1845)
7. The Times That Try Men's Souls (1837), MARIA WESTON CHAPMAN
8. A'n't I a Woman (1851), SOJOURNER TRUTH
9. Address to the Daughters of Temperance Assembly (1852)
10. The Ideal Southern Woman (1835), THOMAS R. DEW
11. Memorial of the Ladies of Augusta to the General Assembly of Virginia (1832)
12. "Woman's Progress" (1853), LOUISA CHEVES MCCORD
13. "Memoir on Slavery" (1853), WILLIAM HARPER
14. "A Quilting Party in Western Virginia" (1854)

*T*he Southern "lady," beautiful and poised, has long occupied a secure place in American popular culture. For more than a century and a half, this mistress of the pre–Civil War plantation has symbolized life in the Old South. Although poorly educated, she was graceful, well mannered, and devoted to her husband and children. And like the younger "belle" who was submissive and concerned only with the private side of life (mostly numerous suitors), she never thought to question anything about her own society.

These images have a long history. They emerged first in popular novels, often written by Southerners in response to growing abolitionist attacks on slavery in the decades before the Civil War. By the late nineteenth century, when the issues of slavery and secession had been laid to rest, the plantation as depicted in popular literature often served as a place removed from the concerns of the world. It was a nostalgic sanctuary—in the words of one historian, "a kind of sunny Shangri-la."[1] This was the image that Hollywood movies broadcast starting in the early twentieth century, most notably with the hugely successful *Gone with the Wind* (1939). In the wake of the civil rights and women's movements in the 1960s and 1970s, that image was subjected to critical scrutiny and serious attack. Even at the beginning of the new century, however, television and romance novels have kept these idealized female inhabitants of the antebellum plantation alive in the popular consciousness.

Although the Southern belle or lady is still capable of evoking romantic images of the Old South, few people today realize that she had a "cousin" who was born and bred in the North about the same time. She, too, had a powerful impact on popular consciousness. She was the idealized housewife of the emerging urban middle class. Around her in the three decades or so before the Civil War Northern fiction writers, housekeeping advisers, ministers, and other opinion makers created a "cult of domesticity," a term modern historians use to describe the web of values and ideas—or ideology—pertaining to a unique feminine sphere. These commentators argued that women's proper place was the home or private "domestic sphere" as opposed to the masculine public sphere of commerce and politics. They also associated certain virtues with this feminine sphere and its idealized inhabitants, especially submissiveness, purity, and piety.

Today, historians understand that many women in the South and the North did not necessarily adhere to the domestic sphere or conform to the norms prescribed by an antebellum domestic ideology. Those women could be found on farms in the back country, in immigrant enclaves in the nation's growing cities, or elsewhere. If not involved in farmwork, they might be found working in textile mills or various sewing trades, as domestic servants, or even on the streets. Unlike their sisters higher up on the social scale, these women were not freed from the necessity of supplementing family incomes with meager wages. They often had little inclination or opportunity to absorb an emerging domestic ideology or reshape their lives to conform to it. Nonetheless, contemporary historians consider the images of the Southern lady and the virtuous Northern housewife essential for understanding the position of women in pre–Civil War American society. In fact, they ask the same questions of each: What impact did these culturally defined images have on free women in the North and South? To what extent did these images reflect the reality of women's lives in each section? What function did these images serve in each case and how were they related to social and economic changes in early nineteenth-century society? And to what extent do these images reflect actual differences between free women in the North and the South? In other words, were the Southern belle or lady and virtuous Northern housewife cousins or were they actually twins? This chapter considers these questions as we turn to the lives of free women in antebellum society.

SETTING

Historians who study women in the decades before the Civil War have focused much of their effort on distinguishing the realities of women's lives from ideal images. They have also sought to understand, in turn, how those images influenced women's lives. Indeed, few periods have proved more fertile ground for historians working in the field of gender relations than the three decades or so prior to the Civil War. Until the late 1960s, women rarely appeared in American history textbooks outside the usual appearances at the trial of Puritan Anne Hutchinson, the Salem Witch Trials, and the suffrage movement at the end of the nineteenth century. In fact, women's history as a distinct field of scholarly inquiry was nonexistent. This virtual exclusion of women from history began to change in the 1960s with the rise of the modern women's movement. Like many African Americans and Native Americans, women began to realize how they had been silenced on the pages of history and some of them set to work to recover their voices. Often, their work took the form of what one women's historian would later call "contribution history," that is, works primarily intended to demonstrate women's significant contributions to the American past. Perhaps more than anything, historians' explorations of antebellum society moved women's history beyond this approach. The starting point was the publication in 1966 of an essay titled "The Cult of True Womanhood." In it, historian Barbara Welter explored the relationship between the creation of a distinct ideal regarding women's domestic roles and the disruptive changes in early nineteenth-century American society related to industrialization and urbanization. By examining how a powerful ideology pertaining to women helped many men cope with social, economic, and social change, Welter's essay demonstrated that women were intimately related to important changes in the American past.

Historians quickly acknowledged the "cult of domesticity" as a key to under-standing early nineteenth-century society. At the same time, this concept also spurred scholars to take a closer look at the lives of antebellum women. Some began to explore the boundaries between the public and private sides of life, that is, between the male sphere of politics and business and the feminine sphere of the home. These historians discovered that the two spheres may not have been so separate after all. In an essay published in 1971, for instance, Barbara Smith-Rosenberg suggested that a "cult of domesticity" led many women out of the home and into the public sphere. By promoting the notion that women should be confined to their own feminine sphere, this ideology made it possible for many women to form close associations with other women. Moreover, by positing that women were uniquely qualified to instill morals, it gave rise to a widespread desire among antebellum Northern women to battle a host of social "evils," from alcohol to slavery. Indeed, the more historians explored the connection between a "cult of domesticity" and antebellum moral reforms, the less clear-cut the im-pact of this domestic ideology seemed to be. Did this ideology repress women by confining them to a subordinate, domestic role? Or did it actually help liber-ate them from traditional roles by providing an entree to the masculine, public sphere and even a basis to demand rights of their own? Or was it, in the words of one historian, a "double-edged sword" promoting both results?

By the 1980s, historians were raising numerous questions regarding ante-bellum women. Some, for instance, argued that the "cult of domesticity" was directed at a middle class, white audience and wondered whether it related in any way to the lives of working-class or free black women. Others pointed to a regional bias in the growing number of studies of antebellum women. Almost exclusively, this work had focused on women in the Northeast and some histo-rians wondered whether it applied at all to women in the South. As they turned to the South, these historians confronted the by-then long-standing myth of the Southern belle or lady. Beginning with Anne Firor Scott's *The Southern Lady* (1970), they began to explore how the lives of Southern women were affected by the gender expectations surrounding this ideal. Scott concluded that many women, unable to square the harsh realities of their own lives with the ideal of the lady, were critical of the patriarchal control exercised by their planter hus-bands. Later historians, however, continued to explore the impact of the ideal of the lady on women in the antebellum South. Like historians who focused on the hold of the "cult of domesticity," they wondered what role this feminine ideal played in a society based on slavery and the extent to which women actu-ally attempted to live up to it. And, like historians focused on the antebellum North, they did not always agree. Thus, Catherine Clinton's *The Plantation Mis-tress* (1982) argued that the ideal of the belle or lady was, in effect, a weapon used by plantation patriarchs to oppress their wives who, in Clinton's words, became "slave[s] of the slaves." Elizabeth Fox-Genovese's *Within the Plantation Household* (1988), however, concluded that most planters' wives attempted to live up to the ideal of the Southern lady and, in fact, realized its benefits to them as part of the elite in a class-bound society rooted in a race-based slavery.

In a way that also paralleled the studies of Northern antebellum women, historians wondered how widely the ideal of the lady could be applied in Southern society. In particular, they questioned the extent to which poorer Southern women, especially members of the yeoman-farmer class, were governed by the feminine ideal preached to their more affluent sisters. Meanwhile, others asked whether gender in some ways united white women in the South through a common culture that cut across class lines. Again, their conclusions differed. Suzanne Lebsock's *The Free Women of Petersburg* (1984), for instance, found evidence of a separate female culture in one part of the South that united women there much as "bonds of womenhood" united Northern women. On the other hand, Victoria Bynum's *Unruly Women* (1992), a study of poor and yeoman-class women, found no evidence of a female culture comparable to the one in the North that led to reform activism and, ultimately, a woman's rights movement. In addition, Christie Ann Farnham's *The Education of the Southern Belle* (1994) found that the daughters of the planter class were actually better educated than older accounts had assumed, calling into question one long-standing assumption regarding the differences between affluent women in the South and their supposedly better-educated Northern sisters.

More recently, historians have paid closer attention to the relationship between gender and other factors such as race and class. So rather than look at African American women only in terms of race, historians focus on relationships shaped as well by class and gender. Likewise, historians are now more sensitive to the ways white women were shaped not only by gender but also by race and class. Considering the interplay of these factors, while also taking into account regional variations, has yielded a far more complicated picture of women's lives and of history.

Since the publication of Barbara Welter's path-breaking essay, historians have clearly developed a much better understanding of early nineteenth-century assumptions about gender and the impact those assumptions and other factors had on women's lives. Still, many historians remain divided on two large questions that underlie all of their studies of women in this period. First, what does the interaction between women's circumstances and gender ideology in the South and North reveal about society in each region? Second, to what extent did the lives of free women of the North and South differ? Conflicting answers to these two questions are bound to inspire continuing interest among historians in the lives of antebellum women.

INVESTIGATION

In this chapter, we compare the ideal images of womanhood in the North and South and the impact of these images on women's lives in each section. To help you consider how and why the ideals and actual lives of free women in the North differed from their Southern counterparts, this chapter contains a small set of primary sources and two historians' arguments (Sources 1 and 2). The focus of each essay is different. One pertains to Northern women; the other concentrates on Southern white women. Because they deal with women in different regions and emphasize different responses to a domestic ideology, these two essays will provide a good basis for considering some of the ways in which the ideal images and real experience of women in the North and South differed. A good comparative analysis of the ideologies and experiences of Northern and Southern women will use the primary and secondary sources to address the following questions:

1. **According to the first essay, (Source 1) what was the impact of a domestic ideology on women in New England by the 1830s?** What was the relationship between this ideology and the emergence of women's rights as an issue?

2. **According to the second essay (Source 2), why did many Southerners embrace an ideology of domesticity even though the South did not undergo the social changes that historians assume led to its emergence in the first place?** How did expressions of the Southern domestic ideal differ from their Northern counterparts? What was its impact?

3. **Do the primary sources offer evidence that the domestic ideals in the North and South differed in significant ways?** What evidence do these sources offer regarding the influence of a domestic ideology in the North and South?

4. **What evidence do the primary sources offer regarding the limits of this ideology?** Do these sources reflect attitudes or behavior that contradicted the tenets of a Northern or Southern domestic ideology? Do they reveal factors that affected the hold of this ideology in the North and South?

The sections in your textbook on antebellum Southern society, the early nineteenth-century market revolution, and the rise of antebellum reform movements, including a woman's rights movement, will provide useful background for this assignment. As you read, note whether your textbook makes a connection between social or economic changes and the rise of a domestic ideology in the early nineteenth century. Note, too, how it compares the circumstances of Northern and Southern women in the early nineteenth century.

SECONDARY SOURCES

1
In this selection, historian Nancy Cott discusses an antebellum gender ideology based on the concept of separate male and female spheres. Focusing on women in New England, she confronts a paradox: a domestic ideology, which defined the role of women in domestic terms, emerged at the same time as feminism, which sought to broaden women's roles. What is her explanation for the simultaneous emergence of this domestic ideology and feminism?

The Bonds of Womanhood (1997)

NANCY F. COTT

It is fitting to begin with the decade of the 1830s in view . . . for it presents a paradox in the "progress" of women's history in the United States. There surfaced publicly then an argument between two seemingly contradictory visions of women's relation to society: the ideology of domesticity, which gave women a limited and sex-specific role to play, primarily in the home; and feminism, which attempted to remove sex-specific limits on women's opportunities and capacities. Why that coincidence? Objectively, New England women in 1835 endured subordination to men in marriage and society, profound disadvantage in education and in the economy, denial of access to official power in the churches that they populated, and virtual impotence in politics. A married woman had no legal existence apart from her husband's: she could not sue, contract, or even execute a will on her own; her person, estate, and wages became her husband's when she took his name. Divorce was possible—and, in the New England states, available to wives on the same terms as husbands—but rare. Women's public life generally was so minimal that if one addressed a mixed audience she was greeted with shock and hostility. No women voted, although all were subject to the laws. Those (unmarried or widowed) who held property had to submit to taxation without representation.

This was no harsher subordination than women knew in 1770, but by 1835 it had other grievous aspects. When white manhood suffrage, stripped of property qualifications, became the rule, women's political incapacity appeared more conspicuous than it had in the colonial period. As occupations in trade, crafts, and services diversified the agricultural base of New England's economy, and wage earning encroached on family farm production, women's second-class position in the economy was thrown into relief. There was only a limited number of paid occupations generally open to women, in housework, handicrafts and industry, and school-teaching. Their wages were one-fourth to one-half what men earned in comparable work. The legal handicaps imposed by the marriage contract prevented wives from engaging in business ventures on their own, and the professionalization of law and medicine by means of educational requirements, licensing, and professional societies severely excluded women from those avenues of distinction and earning power. Because colleges did not admit women, they could not enter any of the learned professions. For them, the Jacksonian rhetoric of opportunity had scant meaning.

Source: From Nancy F. Cott, *The Bonds of Womanhood:* "Woman's Sphere" *in New England,* 1780–1835, pp. 5–9, 199–201. Copyright © 1997. Reprinted by permission of the publisher, Yale University Press.

The 1830s nonetheless became a turning point in women's economic participation, public activities, and social visibility. New textile factories recruited a primarily female labor force, and substantial numbers of young women left home to live and work with peers. In the mid-1830s occurred the first industrial strikes in the United States led and peopled by women. "One of the leaders mounted a pump," the Boston *Evening Transcript* reported during the first "turn-out" in Lowell, Massachusetts, to protest wage reductions, "and made a flaming Mary Woolstonecraft [sic] speech on the rights of women." Middle-class women took up their one political tool, the petition, to demand legislation enabling wives to retain rights to their property and earnings. So many women pursued the one profession open to them, primary-school teaching, that their entry began to look like a takeover, although (or, to be accurate, because) they consistently commanded much lower salaries than men. Secondary schools and academies which could prepare young women to teach multiplied. Women's growing literacy, owed in part to the employment of some as teachers of girls, swelled the audience for female journalists and fiction writers. . . . Several ladies' magazines began publication during the decade, thereby increasing the editorial and publication possibilities for women authors and causing a female audience to coalesce.

Women also entered a variety of reform movements, to pursue objects in their own self-interest as well as to improve their society. Health reformers spotlighted women's physical condition. "Moral reformers" attacked the double standard of sexual morality and the victimization of prostitutes. Mothers formed societies to consult together on the rearing of children. Even larger numbers of women joined Christian benevolent associations, to reform the world by the propagation of the faith. An insistent minority of women became active in the antislavery movement, where they practiced tactics of recruitment, organization, fund raising, propagandizing, and petitioning—and initiated the women's rights movement in the United States, when some of them took to heart the principles of freedom and human rights. Although the Seneca Falls Convention of 1848 usually marks the beginning of organized feminism in this country, there were clearly feminist voices in the antislavery movement by the late 1830s.

At the same time, an emphatic sentence of domesticity was pronounced for women. Both male and female authors (the former mostly ministers) created a new popular literature, consisting of advice books, sermons, novels, essays, stories, and poems, advocating and reiterating women's certain, limited role. That was to be wives and mothers, to nurture and maintain their families, to provide religious example and inspiration, and to affect the world around by exercising private moral influence. The literature of domesticity promulgated a Janus-faced conception of women's roles: it looked back, explicitly conservative in its attachment to a traditional understanding of woman's place; while it proposed transforming, even millennial results. One might assume that this pervasive formulation was simply a re-action to—a conservative defense against—expansion of women's nondo-mestic pursuits. But women's educational, reform, labor force, and political activities were just beginning to enlarge in the 1830s when the concept of do-mesticity crystallized. Several decades' shift in the allotment of powers and functions inside and outside the household had created the constellation of ideas regarding women's roles that we call domesticity. . . . The particular-ization and professionalization taking place in the occupational structure between 1780 and 1835 affected women's domestic occupation as well as any other; and concomitant subtle changes in women's view of their domestic role established a substructure for their nondomestic pursuits and self-assertion. The ideology of domesticity may seem to be contradicted func-tionally and abstractly by feminism, but historically—as they emerged in the United States—the latter depended on the former. . . .

For several mutually reinforcing reasons, [the] domestic sphere became more conspicuous and more clearly articulated as woman's prerogative at the end of the eighteenth and beginning of the nineteenth centuries. The shift of production and exchange away from the household, and a gen-eral tightening of functional "spheres" (specialization) in the economy and society at large, made it seem "separate." But a cultural halo ringing the sig-nificance of home and family—doubly brilliant because both religious and secular energies gave rise to it—reconnected woman's "separate" sphere with the well-being of society. Statesmen of the Revolution had said that the republic of the United States would be great or weak as its citizens' char-acters were so; they believed as John Adams said in 1778, linking the Puritans to the Jacksonians in a chain of sentiment, that "the foundations of national Morality must be laid in private families." This ideology—colored by customary belief in women's domestic influence on men, strengthened by awareness of women's child-rearing obligations and by faith in the malle-ability of infant character—hinged the success of the national experiment on women's success in their sphere. The clergy, in addition, tended to focus the general concern for character formation specifically on *women's* performance as mothers. To accomplish their own social aims they solicited women, who comprised the majority of their congregations, to rear the next generation in piety. Religious and secular ideology thus made explicit what had been beneath the surface, for the most part: that women's domestic influence and maternal duties composed a positive social role. This was a social role that inherently justified certain greater opportunities for women—notably in education—without contradicting their family obligations. Its configuration took shape as early as 1780 and was well established by 1820.

The doctrine of woman's sphere opened to women (reserved for them) the avenues of domestic influence, religious morality, and child nurture. It articulated a social power based on their special female qualities rather than on general human rights. For women who previously held no particular avenue of power of their own—no unique defense of their integrity and dignity—this represented an advance. Earlier secular and religious norms had assumed male dominance in home, family, and religion as well as in the public world. (Husbands' legal authority over their wives and children, indeed, remained unchallenged until the 1830s.) The ideology of woman's sphere formed a necessary stage in the process of shattering the hierarchy of sex and, more directly, in softening the hierarchical relationship of marriage.

But woman's sphere had the defects of its virtues. In opening certain avenues to women because of their sex, it barricaded all others. It also contained within itself the preconditions for organized feminism, by allotting a "separate" sphere for women and engendering sisterhood within that sphere. It assigned women a "vocation" comparable to men's vocations, but also implying, in women's case, a unique sexual solidarity. When they took up their common vocation women asserted their common identity in "womanhood," which became their defining social role: gender ruled, in effect, their sentiments, capacities, purpose, and potential achievements. Without such consciousness of their definition according to sex, no minority of women would have created the issue of "women's rights."

---

2   In this selection, historian Marli F. Weiner discusses a Southern ideology of domesticity. Weiner relies heavily on the work of popular writers to reconstruct the ideal wife and mother of the antebellum South. Note her conclusion regarding the appeal of this ideal in women's lives. What did slavery have to do with the allure of a Southern domestic ideal? What did it have to do with the failure of women in the South to engage in organized reform movements that attracted many Northern women?

Domestic Ideology in the South (1998)

MARLI F. WEINER

Historians contend that the ideology of domesticity, with its strict division of public and private spheres for men and women, developed out of the social and economic changes of the late eighteenth century and the first twenty-five or so years of the nineteenth. As the consequences of independence and republican ideology unfolded, the lives of white middle-class Americans became increasingly complex. With greater economic diversification, men followed their work away from the home and farm and into the factories and

Source: Marli F. Weiner, *Mistresses and Slaves: Plantation Women in South Carolina, 1830–1880* (Urbana: University of Illinois Press, 1998), pp. 53–57, 61–62, 64–65, 68, 69, 70–71. Copyright 1998 by the Board of Trustees of the University of Illinois. Used with permission of the University of Illinois Press.

businesses of the growing cities of the Northeast. Yet the same forces that drew men out of the home simultaneously robbed the women who remained there of much of the work they had previously done. Women no longer needed to spin thread and weave cloth, make candles or soap, or produce any of a multitude of other things for which they had once been responsible because these items were increasingly manufactured in the marketplace. Although women's domestic responsibilities remained considerable, especially for those outside the orbit of the market economy, the focus gradually shifted from production to consumption. Women who had been active partners in the family economy became passive consumers of the goods men purchased with the money they earned outside the home. They were left to create an uplifting environment— a haven to which their men could return. Men, who needed a refuge from the competitiveness of the marketplace, and women, who resented the relative decline in their status, elaborated the ideology of domesticity both to justify keeping women at home and to enhance the status of what they did there.

A cardinal tenet of the ideology of domesticity—and what made it attractive to so many white middle-class women—held that women were morally superior to men. Finding themselves increasingly superfluous in the world of economic production and excluded from a public voice, middle-class women discovered in the notion of moral superiority not only a source of self-esteem but also a means of affecting the world at large, albeit from the sidelines. By setting women up as an example of Christian piety and virtuous conduct, the proponents of the ideology of domesticity offered the nineteenth-century woman the opportunity to believe herself capable of exerting influence over her husband and children. A beacon of morality in a world run amok, her very existence embodied the Christian ideal. And women could at least hope that their piety and purity would have an elevating effect on male callousness and brutality.

Even though masculine morality never attained the hoped-for standards, the ideology of domesticity did have other equally profound consequences for American middle-class culture. Not only did it justify the exclusion of women from the public world in terms acceptable to most women and men but, more importantly, it also cultivated common bonds among women. Relegated to a separate sphere, women found they had far more in common with one another than they had with men. They shared the biological experiences central to their definition as women and spoke the same language of virtue and piety. In short, the ideology of domesticity instilled an awareness among women of a set of common experiences and values specific to women and distinct from those of men. Key to this distinctly female culture were the extensive networks of female friends and relatives that women developed.

Since women were separate from and better than men, it was relatively easy to believe that women were obliged and privileged to work together to aid other women who were, for whatever reason, unable to put the ideology of domesticity into practice in their lives—"fallen" women, widows, poor women, orphan girls, abused women, and the wives of alcoholics. Many white middle-class women in the Northeast used the rhetoric of domesticity to explain their participation in a wide range of reform movements. By extending the sphere of their moral influence beyond the walls of their homes, they hoped to create a direct change in the world in which they lived. Not coincidentally, they also managed to create important work and a significant social role for themselves.

Historians who draw this picture of nineteenth-century womanhood almost invariably find the evidence for it in the northeastern part of the country; those who venture outside that region still focus on areas within its economic and cultural orbit. Industrialization, urbanization, and immigration had proceeded further in the Northeast than anywhere else, and the ideology of domesticity helped to assuage the anxieties these transformations produced in both men and women. The Northeast was the region most characterized by social dislocation and the corresponding need to try to establish or reestablish a sense of order. The majority of the most vocal proponents of the ideology of domesticity—women such as Sarah Josepha Hale of *Godey's Ladies Book* and Catharine Beecher as well as male ministers, doctors, publishers, and writers—lived and worked primarily in the Northeast. While they sought to bring their values to other regions of the country, they, like the historians who have written about them, assumed their most receptive audience was to be found in the Northeast.

Southern white women, however, were similarly acutely aware of the ideology of domesticity and tried to implement its teachings in their lives. Expectations of white womanhood were frequently articulated in the South; their content was quite similar to those in the North, even though few of the factors historians have identified as encouraging domesticity existed in the South. There was little industrialization, little urbanization, little immigration, and therefore little of the resulting social dislocation and sense of anxiety found in the North. With the important exception of slavery, southern anxieties were rooted in external threats—abolitionism and other challenges to the southern way of life—and not by changes within their society. Why, then, did white southern men and women advocate female moral superiority and the separation of spheres as central to definitions of appropriate behavior for women?

To some extent, southerners did so as a result of the cultural domination of northeasterners. The nation's largest and most influential publishers were located there, as were many of the popular writers who helped to shape public opinion for the nation. However, these ideas took root and flourished luxuriously in southern soil, suggesting that the ideology of domesticity resonated with social meaning there as well. For white southerners, increasingly on the defensive in the antebellum years, an articulated ideology of domesticity for white women helped to confirm both their regional superiority and the virtues of their racial beliefs and institutions. These ideas are illustrated by their pronouncements on the ideology of domesticity.

Southern proponents of domesticity drew on many of the same sources as those in other regions and came to many of the same conclusions. Of course, they defined domesticity in exclusively white terms; they considered the differences between blacks and whites as even more profound than those between white men and white women and certainly did not consider the possibility of any similarity among women. Southern writers had no doubts about the importance of what they considered fundamental differences between white men and women or about their meaning. Their primary concern, in numerous articles and books, was to elaborate the causes and implications of those differences. . . .

According to many of the southern proponents of the ideology of domesticity, differences between white men and women were best explained by references to the natural world and to women's biological role in childbearing. Thomas R. Dew, the author of "Dissertation on the Characteristic Differences between the Sexes, and on the Position and Influence of Woman in Society," defined his purpose as explaining "the constitutional differences between the sexes—to point out the effects which those differences have produced upon their moral, social and political characters—to show that the position of woman in society is not an accidental one, but results from the law of nature." . . .

The ideology of domesticity articulated in the South confirmed for white southerners their regional superiority and the virtues of their racial beliefs and institutions. This ideology also helped them to articulate the characteristics of the ideal woman. If southern society was beneficial for women, it also set high standards of behavior for them to follow. Once again, these standards echoed those articulated by northerners, but with a peculiarly southern perspective. Those shapers of southern public opinion who wrote about education, marriage, family life, women's rights, and individual behavior all defined expectations for white women distinctly. Together, their writings formed a guidebook of appropriate behavior and a powerful mechanism for reinforcing southern views about gender and race.

Proponents of the ideology of domesticity believed wholeheartedly in the importance of intellectual development for women, although none expected that education to have the same content as did men's or insisted that it be widely available. . . . Educating women offered a variety of advantages. Perhaps most important, it would create women who were suited for motherhood and able to raise virtuous and responsible children. . . .

Southern writers told women over and over again how to behave to guarantee a happy marriage. Women not only were expected to be good wives but they were also responsible for making men into good husbands. One author listed a series of maxims for women to follow, the first of which was "to be good yourselves. To avoid all thoughts of managing a husband. Never try to deceive or impose upon his understanding, nor give him uneasiness, but treat him with affection, sincerity, and respect. Remember that husbands, at best, are only men, subject, like yourselves, to error and frailty." Many writers warned women not to expect happiness from marriage: "Think not, that you are entering into a state of perpetual love, and joy, and peace. . . . It will produce new uneasiness, of various kinds, and will fill you with numberless fears, and disquiets, which, in a single state, might probably have been avoided." . . .

Like the ideal wife, the ideal mother was devoted and selfless. The best home was one in which "the pious, gentle mother, exercising her maternal rule in the fear and love of God, teaches obedience, virtue and self-restraint. The good mother needed "a patient temper, a cheerful spirit, and a good judgement" and should expect to find her work "laborious." Such a noble mother was one who "will tenderly chide and carefully correct; who will lift the ambition by gradual exercises; who will subdue the passions without outraging the nature; who will control the will without vexing the spirit; who will inform the moral, by daily habitual duties." . . .

Although southern men wanted to forbid women access to unacceptable ideas, they allowed, even encouraged under carefully controlled circumstances, women to extend the range of their interests beyond their homes and families. The southern ideology of domesticity, like its northern counterpart, offered women a model of behavior that could include extending charity and benevolence to those outside the family. In the North, women moved through benevolence to participation in a wide variety of reform movements. Such activity was not widely encouraged nor widely practiced in the rural South, but public benevolence was discussed in positive terms frequently enough to be considered an unquestioned part of the meaning of southern womanhood. . . .

Benevolence and charity were the responsibility of all women, but southern women were particularly urged to turn their benevolent impulses in the direction of their slaves. One father publicly advised his newly married daughter how to arrange domestic concerns effectively. "Unite liberality with a just frugality; always reserve something for the hand of charity; and never let your door be closed to the voice of suffering humanity. Your servants, in particular, will have the strongest claim upon your charity;—let them be well fed, well clothed, nursed in sickness, and never let them be unjustly treated." . . .

This message of benevolence was echoed by the lessons of paternalism taught by southern men. Southern rhetoric viewed slaves as dependents who needed the same protection and guidance white children did. Like children, slaves were considered unable to care for themselves, so it was the responsibility of slaveholders to provide for them physically, morally, and spiritually. This line of reasoning was developed by southern men partly to defend the institution of slavery from growing challenges by the northern antislavery movement. However, white men were rarely able to offer slaves the protection, care, and guidance required by paternalism; they were too busy with the demands of supervising their labor. They found it easier to delegate to white women the daily responsibility of caring for slaves, especially since women had already assumed concern for white dependents and moral issues.

Similarly, religious teachings in the white South offered plantation mistresses explicit instructions reinforcing the ideology of domesticity. According to Anne Firor Scott, "The image of the ideal Christian woman was very close to the image of the ideal southern lady so that religion strongly reinforced the patriarchal culture." Southern Christianity defined masters as morally obligated to care for their slaves and mistresses as the moral agents responsible for enacting that care. Together, these teachings ensured that mistresses would feel both a sense of responsibility toward slaves and empowered to act upon it.

White southern women were inundated from all directions with messages about what was considered appropriate behavior. The ideology of domesticity shaped the content of their educations, defined their roles as wives and mothers, and dictated a set of beliefs and practices regarding the society in which they lived. Like women in other regions of the country, plantation mistresses were expected to be benevolent and kind, moral and religious, and yielding to their husbands' authority. The reasons they were to behave in this fashion were familiar, but the institution of slavery gave a uniquely southern twist to the argument. The presence of slaves added a racial dimension to justifications for white women's proper place. The presence of slaves also made the threat of white women stepping out of their place quite alarming, because it was linked to the external threat of abolitionism. In addition, the presence of slaves forced a refinement of the ideology of domesticity that encouraged mistresses to see themselves as materially and morally responsible for those slaves. The ideology of domesticity in the South was a mechanism for defining and controlling race as well as gender differences.

The characteristics and expectations of southern white womanhood that emerged from the didactic literature suggest the importance the white South placed on beliefs about gender, race, and its own uniqueness. Influenced by these cultural messages and committed to the society that created them, slaveholding women were faced with the complex task of turning the expectations of the South's ideology of domesticity into a daily reality.

PRIMARY SOURCES

The sources in this section reflect early nineteenth-century gender ideology and offer clues regarding the relationship between that ideology and actual behavior. The first half of this set of sources relates to a Northern domestic ideal and its impact on women in the North. The second half relates to a Southern domestic ideal and its impact on Southern white women. Look for evidence demonstrating differences between the Northern and Southern ideals. Also note evidence that reveals a difference in behavior or attitudes about gender roles on the part of women in the North and South.

Mrs. A. J. Graves was one of many writers who wrote about "woman's sphere" in the early nineteenth century. On what grounds does she argue that women's duties are centered in the home? Why do you think she is so critical of organized reform efforts?

Woman in America (1841)

MRS. A. J. GRAVES

Next to the obligations which woman owes directly to her God, are those arising from her relation to the family institution. That *home* is her appropriate and appointed sphere of action there cannot be a shadow of doubt; for the dictates of nature are plain and imperative on this subject, and the injunctions given in Scripture no less explicit. Upon this point there is nothing equivocal or doubtful; no passage admitting of an interpretation varying with the judgments or inclinations of those who read. . . . "Let your women keep silence in the churches"—be "keepers at home"—taught "to guide the house." . . . And as no female of the present day can be so presumptuous as to suppose herself included in the miraculous *exceptions* mentioned in Scripture, these apostolic injunctions are doubtless to be considered as binding upon all: and if different views have been advocated, and a different practice has in many instances prevailed, the writer of these pages cannot but look upon such views and such practices as in direct violation of the apostle's commands, and as insidiously sapping the very foundations of the family institution. . . .

One of the most striking characteristics of the times is the universality of organized associations, and the high-wrought excitement so frequently produced by them. In these associations, where great numbers assemble together, whatever may be the object intended to be effected, there is a predominating influence which rules all minds, and communicates, as if by contagion, from one to another. When thus uniting in masses, men unconsciously give up their individual opinions, feelings, and judgments, and yield to the voice and the will of those around them. The power of sympathy, so potent in the human breast, makes the nerves of all thrill in unison, every heart throb with the same emotions, and every understanding submit to the same convictions, whether of truth or error, as though one spirit, and heart, and mind animated the whole. . . .

. . . The duty of charity is performed by societies instead of individuals, and thus it fails of its most beneficent effect, both as it regards the giver and

Source: Nancy F. Cott, ed., *Root of Bitterness: Documents of the Social History of American Women* (Boston: Northeastern University Press, 1986), pp. 141–145; originally from Mrs. A. J. Graves, *Woman in America: Being an Examination into the Moral and Intellectual Condition of American Female Society* (New York: Harper and Bros., 1841).

the receiver. Neither men nor women think, feel, or act for themselves, and from this it is that we see so few instances of individual greatness, either moral or intellectual. . . .

We would not undervalue the good, nor should we overlook the evils either necessarily or incidentally connected with this spirit of association; and we allude to it only for the purpose of showing its effects upon the character and usefulness of woman. Our chief aim throughout these pages is to prove that her domestic duties have a paramount claim over everything else upon her attention—that *home* is her appropriate sphere of action; and that whenever she neglects these duties, or goes out of this sphere of action to mingle in any of the great public movements of the day, she is deserting the station which God and nature have assigned to her. She can operate far more efficiently in promoting the great interests of humanity by supervising her own household than in any other way. Home, if we may so speak, is the cradle of the human race; and it is here the human character is fashioned either for good or for evil. It is the "nursery of the future man and of the undying spirit"; and woman is the nurse and the educator. Over infancy she has almost unlimited sway; and in maturer years she may powerfully counteract the evil influences of the world by the talisman of her strong, enduring love, by her devotedness to those intrusted to her charge, and by those lessons of virtue and of wisdom which are not of the world.

4   Catharine Beecher was perhaps the most influential of numerous Northern female writers who offered advice on housekeeping, child rearing, and family life in the early nineteenth century. In her *Treatise on Domestic Economy,* Beecher discussed in detail women's duties as housekeepers. In this excerpt, how does she relate that work to women's true mission? Do her remedies for problems facing housekeepers uphold the doctrine of separate spheres or potentially subvert it?

Treatise on Domestic Economy (1841)
CATHARINE BEECHER

The tendencies of democratic institutions, in reference to the rights and interests of the female sex, have been fully developed in the United States; and it is in this aspect, that the subject is one of peculiar interest to American

Source: Jeanne Boydston et al., eds., *The Limits of Sisterhood: The Beecher Sisters on Women's Rights and Woman's Sphere* (Chapel Hill: The University of North Carolina Press, 1988), pp. 131–134, 136; originally from Catharine E. Beecher, *Treatise on Domestic Economy for the Use of Young Ladies at Home and at School* (Boston: Marsh, Capen, Lyon, and Webb, 1841).

women. In this Country, it is established, both by opinion and by practice, that women have an equal interest in all social and civil concerns; and that no domestic, civil, or political, institution, is right, that sacrifices her interest to promote that of the other sex. But in order to secure her the more firmly in all these privileges, it is decided, that, in the domestic relation, she take a subordinate station, and that, in civil and political concerns, her interests be intrusted to the other sex, without her taking any part in voting, or in making and administering laws. . . .

In civil and political affairs, American women take no interest or concern, except so far as they sympathize with their family and personal friends; but in all cases, in which they do feel a concern, their opinions and feelings have a consideration, equal, or even superior, to that of the other sex.

In matters pertaining to the education of their children, in the selection and support of a clergyman, in all benevolent enterprises, and in all questions relating to morals or manners, they have a superior influence. In all such concerns, it would be impossible to carry a point, contrary to their judgement and feelings; while an enterprise, sustained by them, will seldom fail of success. . . .

The success of democratic institutions, as is conceded by all, depends upon the intellectual and moral character of the mass of the people. If they are intelligent and virtuous, democracy is a blessing; but if they are ignorant and wicked, it is only a curse, and as much more dreadful than any other form of civil government, as a thousand tyrants are more to be dreaded than one. It is equally conceded, that the formation of the moral and intellectual character of the young is committed mainly to the female hand. The mother writes the character of the future man; the sister bends the fibres that hereafter are the forest tree; the wife sways the heart, whose energies may turn for good or for evil the destinies of a nation. Let the women of a country be made virtuous and intelligent, and the men will certainly be the same. The proper education of a man decides the welfare of an individual; but educate a woman, and the interests of a whole family are secured.

If this be so, as none will deny, then to American women, more than to any others on earth, is committed the exalted privilege of extending over the world those blessed influences, that are to renovate degraded man, and "clothe all climes with beauty."

No American woman, then, has any occasion for feeling that hers is an humble or insignificant lot. The value of what an individual accomplishes, is to be estimated by the importance of the enterprise achieved, and not by the particular position of the laborer. The drops of heaven that freshen the earth are each of equal value. . . . The builders of a temple are of equal importance, whether they labor on the foundations, or toil upon the dome.

Thus, also, with those labors that are to be made effectual in the regeneration of the Earth. The woman who is rearing a family of children; the woman who labors in the schoolroom; the woman who, in her retired chamber, earns, with her needle, the mite to contribute for the intellectual and moral elevation of her country; even the humble domestic, whose example and influence may be moulding and forming young minds, while her faithful services sustain a prosperous domestic state;—each and all may be cheered by the consciousness, that they are agents in accomplishing the greatest work that ever was committed to human responsibility. It is the building of a glorious temple, whose base shall be coextensive with the bounds of the earth, whose summit shall pierce the skies, whose splendor shall beam on all lands, and those who hew the lowliest stone, as much as those who carve the highest capital, will be equally honored when its top-stone shall be laid, with new rejoicings of the morning stars, and shoutings of the sons of God.

Having pointed out the peculiar responsibilities of American women, and the peculiar embarrassments they are called to encounter, the following suggestions are offered, as the remedy for these difficulties.

In the first place, the physical and domestic education of daughters should occupy the principal attention of mothers. . . .

And it is to that class of mothers, who have the most means of securing hired service, and who are the most tempted to allow their daughters to grow up with inactive habits, that their country and the world must look for a reformation, in this respect. Whatever ladies in the wealthier classes decide shall be fashionable, will be followed by all the rest; while, if ladies of this class persist in the aristocratic habits, now so common, and bring up their daughters to feel as if labor was degrading and unbecoming, the evils pointed out will never find a remedy. . . .

A second method of promoting the same object, is, to raise the science and practice of domestic economy to its appropriate place, as a regular study in female seminaries. . . .

The third method for securing a remedy for the evils pointed out, is by means of endowed female institutions, under the care of suitable trustees, who shall secure a proper course of female education. . . .

The endowment of colleges, and of law, medical, and divinity, schools, for the other sex, is designed to secure a thorough and proper education, for those who have the most important duties of society to perform. . . . Liberal and wealthy men contribute funds, and the legislatures of the States also lend assistance, so that every State in this Nation has from one to twenty such endowed institutions . . . to carry forward a superior course of instruction . . . at an expense no greater than is required to send a boy to a common school and pay his board there. . . .

---

5   By the 1840s, Lowell, Massachusetts, was a major textile manufacturing center employing thousands of young, single women from all over rural New England. Given prevalent notions about women's domesticity, Lowell's managers realized that getting single young women to leave their homes to work for a wage in a distant city would not necessarily be easy. How

does this cover from the *Lowell Offering,* a management-sponsored literary magazine that published articles and poetry written by the factory operatives, attempt to reconcile the reality of female factory work with the ideal of domesticity? (The structure in the background on the right is a church; the one in the foreground on the left is a beehive.)

Lowell Offering (1845)

6   The following letter was published by a labor organization in Lowell
    after the *Lowell Offering* refused to publish it. How does its attack on
    "wage slavery" reflect the hold of traditional ideas regarding domes-
ticity even among factory operatives?

The Evils of Factory Life (1845)

Let us look forward into the future, and what does the picture present to our imagination! Methinks I behold the self same females occupying new and responsible stations in society. They are now wives and mothers! But oh! how deficient in everything pertaining to those holy, *sacred* names! Behold what disorder, confusion and disquietude reigns, where quiet, neatness and calm serenity should sanctify and render almost like heaven the home of domestic union and love! Instead of being qualified to rear a family,—to instruct them in the great duties of life—to cultivate and unfold the intellect—to imbue the soul in the true and living principles of right and justice—to teach them the most important of all lessons, the art of being *useful* members in the world, ornaments in society and blessings to all around them,—*they*, themselves, have need to be instructed in the *very first* principles of living well and thinking right. Incarcerated within the walls of a factory, while as yet mere children—drilled there from five till seven o'clock, year after year—thrown into company with all sorts and descriptions of minds, dispositions and intellects, without counsellor or friends to advise—far away from a watchful mother's tender care or father's kind instruction—surrounded on all sides with the vain ostentation of fashion, vanity and light frivolity—beset with temptations without, and the carnal propensities of nature within, what *must*, what *will* be the natural, rational result? What but ignorance, misery, and *premature decay* of both *body* and *intellect?* Our country will be but one great hospital filled with worn out operatives and colored slaves! Those who marry, even, become a curse instead of a help-meet to their husbands, because of having broken the laws of God and their own physical natures, in these modern prisons (alias palaces,) in the gardens of Eden! It has been remarked by some writer that the mother educates the man. Now, if this be a truth, as we believe it is, to a very great extent, what, we would ask, are we to expect, the same system of labor prevailing, will be the mental and intellectual character of the future generations of New England? What but a race weak, sickly, imbecile, both mental and physical? A race fit only for corporation tools and time-serving slaves?

Source: Rosalyn Baxandall et al., eds., *America's Working Women* (New York: Vintage Books, 1976), p. 67; originally from Julianna, "Factory Life as It Is, by an Operative" (Lowell, Mass.: Lowell Female Labor Reform Association, 1845).

7   Maria Weston Chapman was an upper-class founder of the Boston
Female Anti-Slavery Society. She wrote this poem in response to an
attack by church leaders on abolitionists Angelina and Sarah Grimke,
who spoke against slavery before a male audience. What is Weston's attitude
toward the doctrine of separate spheres?

The Times That Try Men's Souls (1837)

MARIA WESTON CHAPMAN

Confusion has seized us, and all things go wrong,
　　The women have leaped from "their spheres,"
And, instead of fixed stars, shoot as comets along,
　　And are setting the world by the ears!
In courses erratic they're wheeling through space,
In brainless confusion and meaningless chase.

In vain do our knowing ones try to compute
　　Their return to the orbit designed;
They're glanced at a moment, then onward they shoot,
　　And are neither "to hold nor to bind";
So freely they move in their chosen ellipse,
The "Lords of Creation" do fear an eclipse.

They've taken a notion to speak for themselves,
　　And are wielding the tongue and the pen;
They've mounted the rostrum; the termagant* elves,
　　And—oh horrid!—are talking to men!
With faces unblanched in our presence they come
To harangue us, they say, in behalf of the dumb.

They insist on their right to petition and pray,
　　That St. Paul, in Corinthians, has given them rules
For appearing in public; despite what those say
　　Whom we've trained to instruct them in schools;
But vain such instructions, if women may scan
And quote texts of Scripture to favor their plan.

Our grandmothers' learning consisted of yore
　　In spreading their generous boards;

*A boisterous scolding female.

Source: Elizabeth Cady Stanton, Susan B. Anthony, and Matilda Joslyn Gage, *History of Woman Suffrage* (New York: Fowler and Wells, 1881), I: pp. 82–83.

In twisting the distaff, or mopping the floor,
    And obeying *the will of their lords.*
Now, misses may reason, and think, and debate,
Till unquestioned submission is quite out of date.

---

8   Born a slave in New York, Sojourner Truth traveled throughout the
North speaking against slavery. She delivered this speech at a woman's
rights convention in Ohio. Suffragist Frances D. Gage recorded the
speech and the crowd's response to it. Does Sojourner Truth acknowledge a
separate female sphere?

A'n't I a Woman (1851)
SOJOURNER TRUTH

I rose and announced "Sojourner Truth," and begged the audience to keep
silence for a few moments. The tumult subsided at once, and every eye was
fixed on this almost Amazon form, which stood nearly six feet high, head
erect, and eye piercing the upper air, like one in a dream. At her first word,
there was a profound hush. She spoke in deep tones, which, though not
loud, reached every ear in the house, and away through the throng at the
doors and windows:—

"Well, chilem, whar dar is so much racket dar must be something out o'
kilter. I tink dat 'twixt de niggers of de Souf and de women at de Norf all a
talkin' 'bout rights, de white men will be in a fix pretty soon. But what's all
dis here talkin' 'bout? Dat man ober dar say dat women needs to be helped
into carriages, and lifted ober ditches, and to have de best place every whar.
Nobody eber help me into carriages, or ober mud puddles, or gives me any
best place [and raising herself to her full height and her voice to a pitch like
rolling thunder, she asked], and a'n't I a woman? Look at me! Look at my
arm! [And she bared her right arm to the shoulder, showing her tremendous
muscular power.] I have plowed, and planted, and gathered into barns, and
no man could head me—and a'n't I a woman? I could work as much and eat
as much as a man (when I could get it), and bear de lash as well—and a'n't
I a woman? I have borne thirteen chilern and seen 'em mos' all sold off into
slavery, and when I cried out with a mother's grief, none but Jesus heard—
and a'n't I a woman? Den dey talks 'bout dis ting in de head—what dis dey
call it?" "Intellect," whispered some one near. "Dat's it honey. What's dat
got to do with women's rights or niggers' rights? If my cup won't hold but

---

Source: Elizabeth Cady Stanton, Susan B. Anthony, and Matilda Joslyn Gage, *History of Woman Suffrage* (New York: Fowler and Wells, 1881), I: pp. 115–117.

a pint and yourn holds a quart, wouldn't ye be mean not to let me have my little half-measure full?" And she pointed her significant finger and sent a keen glance at the minister who had made the argument. The cheering was long and loud.

"Den dat little man in black dar, he say women can't have as much rights as man, cause Christ want a woman. Whar did your Christ come from?" Rolling thunder could not have stilled that crowd as did those deep, wonderful tones, as she stood there with outstretched arms and eye of fire. Raising her voice still louder, she repeated, "Whar did your Christ come from? From God and a woman. Man had nothing to do with him." Oh! what a rebuke she gave the little man.

Turning again to another objector, she took up the defense of mother Eve. I cannot follow her through it all. It was pointed, and witty, and solemn, eliciting at almost every sentence deafening applause; and she ended by asserting that "if de fust woman God ever made was strong enough to turn the world upside down, all 'lone, dese togedder [and she glanced her eye over us], ought to be able to turn it back and get it right side up again, and now dey is asking to do it, de men better let em." Long-continued cheering. "Bleeged to ye for hearin' on me, and now ole Sojourner ha'n't got nothing more to say."

9 Mary C. Vaughan was a Northern leader in the pre–Civil War temperance movement, one of the biggest reform causes of the era and the one involving the most women. Speaking at a temperance convention in 1852, Vaughan justified participation in such reform activity. How does she relate temperance to traditional female roles while also rejecting ideals associated with a "cult of domesticity"?

Address to Daughters of Temperance Assembly (1852)
MARY C. VAUGHAN

We have met to consider what we, as women, can do and may do, to forward the temperance reform. We have met, because, as members of the human family, we share in all the sufferings which error and crime bring upon the race, and because we are learning that our part in the drama of life is

Source: Mary C. Vaughan, "Address, Daughters of Temperance Assembly, Albany, New York, January 28, 1852" in Mari Jo Buhle and Paul Buhle, eds., *The Concise History of Woman Suffrage: Selections from* History of Woman Suffrage, *edited by Elizabeth Cady, Susan B. Anthony, Matilda Joslyn Gage, and The National American Woman Suffrage Association* (Urbana: University of Illinois Press, 2005), pp. 141–142.

something beside inactive suffering and passive endurance. We would act as well as endure; and we meet here to-day because many of us have been trying to act, and we would combine our individual experiences, and together devise plans for the future, out of which shall arise well-based hopes of good results to humanity. We are aware that this proceeding of ours, this calling together of a body of women to deliberate publicly upon plans to carry out a specified reform, will rub rather harshly upon the mould of prejudice, which has gathered thick upon the common mind.

. . . . There are plenty of women, as well as men, who can labor for reforms without neglecting business or duty. It is an error that clings most tenaciously to the public mind, that because a part of the sex are wives and mothers and have absorbing duties, that all the sex should be denied any other sphere of effort. To deprive every unmarried woman, spinster, or widow, or every childless wife, of the power of exercising her warm sympathies for the good of others, is to deprive her of the greatest happiness of which she is capable; to rob her highest faculties of their legitimate operation and reward; to belittle and narrow her mind; to dwarf her affections; to turn the harmonies of her nature to discord; and, as the human mind must be active, to compel her to employ hers with low and grovelling thoughts, which lead to contemptible actions.

There is no reform in which woman can act better or more appropriately than temperance. I know not how she can resist or turn aside from the duty of acting in this; its effects fall so crushingly upon her and those whose interests are identical with her own; she has so often seen its slow, insidious, but not the less surely fatal advances, gaining upon its victim; she has seen the intellect which was her dearest pride, debased; the affections which were her life-giving springs of action, estranged; the children once loved, abused, disgraced and impoverished; the home once an earthly paradise, rendered a fit abode for lost spirits; has felt in her own person all the misery, degradation, and woe of the drunkard's wife; has shrunk from revilings and cowered beneath blows; has labored and toiled to have her poor earnings transferred to the rum-seller's ill-gotten hoard; while her children, ragged, fireless, poor, starving, gathered shivering about her, and with hollow eyes, from which all smiles had fled, begged vainly for the bread she had not to bestow. Oh! the misery, the utter, hopeless misery of the drunkard's wife!

. . . . We account it no reason why we should desist, when conscience, an awakened sense of duty, and aroused heart-sympathies, would lead us to show ourselves something different than an impersonation of the vague ideal which has been named, Woman, and with which woman has long striven to identify herself. A creature all softness and sensibility, who must necessarily enjoy and suffer in the extreme, while sharing with man the pleasures and the ills of life; bearing happiness meekly, and sorrow with fortitude; gentle, mild, submissive, forbearing under all circumstances; a softened reflex of the opinions and ideas of the masculines who, by relation-ship, hold mastery over her; without individualism, a mere adjunct of man, the chief object of whose creation was to adorn and beautify his existence, or to minister to some form of his selfishness. This is nearly the masculine idea of womanhood, and poor womanhood strives to personify it. But not all women. This is an age of iconoclasms; and daring hands are raised to sweep from its pedestal, and dash to fragments, this false image of woman. We care not how soon, if the true woman but take its place. This is also, and most emphatically, an age of progress. One old idea, one mouldering form of prejudice after another, is rapidly swept away. Thought, written and spoken, acts upon the mass of mind in this day of railroads and telegraphs, with a thousandfold more celerity than in the days of pillions and slow coaches. Scarce have the lips that uttered great thoughts ceased to move, or the pen which wrote them dropped from the weary hand, ere they vibrate through the inmost recesses of a thousand hearts, and awaken deep and true responses in a thousand living, truthful souls. Thence they grow, expand, fructify, and the result is Progress.

10   Thomas R. Dew, the president of William and Mary College in Virginia, was one of the many Southern writers who created an image of the ideal Southern woman starting in the 1830s. Note the qualities that Dew assigns to this ideal. Does it differ from the feminine ideal advanced by Northern writers?

The Ideal Southern Woman (1835)
THOMAS R. DEW

The relative position of the sexes in the social and political world, may cer-tainly be looked upon as the result of organization. The greater physical strength of man, enables him to occupy the foreground in the picture. He leaves the domestic scenes; he plunges into the turmoil and bustle of an active, selfish world; in his journey through life, he has to encounter innu-merable difficulties, hardships and labors which constantly beset him. His mind must be nerved against them. Hence courage and boldness are his attributes. It is his province, undismayed, to stand against the rude shocks of the world; to meet with a lion's heart, the dangers which threaten him. He is the shield of woman, destined by nature to guard and protect her.

Source: Thomas Roderick Dew, "Dissertation on the Characteristic Differences Between the Sexes, and on the Position and Influence of Women in Society, No. III," *Southern Literary Messenger* (August 1835).

Her inferior strength and sedentary habits confine her within the domestic circle; she is kept aloof from the bustle and storm of active life; she is not familiarized to the out of door dangers and hardships of a cold and scuffling world: timidity and modesty are her attributes. In the great strife which is constantly going forward around her, there are powers engaged which her inferior physical strength prevents her from encountering. She must rely upon the strength of others; man must be engaged in her cause. How is he to be drawn over to her side? Not by menace—not by force; for weakness cannot, by such means, be expected to triumph over might. No! It must be by conformity to that character which circumstances demand for the sphere in which she moves; by the exhibition of those qualities which delight and fascinate—which are calculated to win over to her side the proud lord of creation, and to make him an humble suppliant at her shrine. Grace, modesty and loveliness are the charms which constitute her power. By these, she creates the magic spell that subdues to her will the more mighty physical powers by which she is surrounded. Her attributes are rather of a passive than active character. Her power is more emblematical of that of divinity: it subdues without an effort, and almost creates by mere volition;—whilst man must wind his way through the difficult and intricate mazes of philosophy; with pain and toil, tracing effects to their causes, and unravelling the deep mysteries of nature—storing his mind with useful knowledge, and exercising, training and perfecting his intellectual powers, whilst he cultivates his strength and hardens and matures his courage; all with a view of enabling him to assert his rights, and exercise a greater sway over those around him. Woman we behold dependant and weak; but out of that very weakness and dependance springs an irresistible power. She may pursue her studies too—not however with a view of triumphing in the senate chamber—not with a view to forensic display—not with a view of leading armies to combat, or of enabling her to bring into more formidable action the physical power which nature has conferred on her. No! It is but the better to perfect all those feminine graces, all those fascinating attributes, which render her the centre of attraction, and which delight and charm all those who breathe the atmosphere in which she moves. . . .

---

11 In the aftermath of the Nat Turner Rebellion, one of the largest slave uprisings in American history, some Southern women began to speak out against slavery. In Augusta County, Virginia, more than two hundred women did so publicly when they signed the petition that follows. Note how they acknowledge women's domestic roles in making this protest. How would you compare their approach to that of Mary C. Vaughan in Source 9?

Memorial of the Ladies of Augusta to the General Assembly of Virginia (1832)

Memorial of the Ladies of Augusta to the General Assembly of Virginia Praying the Adoption of Some Measure for the Speedy Extirpation of Slavery from the Commonwealth Signed by 215 Ladies

To the Hon, the General Assembly of the State of Virginia, memorial of the subscribing females of the county of Augusta humbly represents that although it be unexampled in our beloved State, that females should interfere in its political concerns, and although we feel all the timidity incident to our sex in taking this step, yet we hold our right to do so to be unquestionable, and feel ourselves irresistably impelled to the exercise of that right by the most potent considerations and the perilous circumstances which surround us. We pretend not to conceal from you, our fathers and brothers, our protectors by your investment with the political power of the land, the fears which agitate our bosoms, and the dangers which await us as revealed by recent tragical deeds. Our fears, we admit, are great, but we do not concede that they are the effects of blind & unreflecting cowardice; we do not concede that they spring from the superstitious timidity of our sex. Alas! we are indeed timid, but we appeal to your manly reason, to your more mature wisdom to attest the justice & propriety of our fears, when we call to your recollection the late slaughter of our sisters & their little ones, in certain parts of our land, & the strong probability that that slaughter was but a partial execution of a widely projected scheme of carnage. We know not, we cannot know the night, nor the unguarded moment, by day or by night, which is pregnant with our destruction, & that of our husbands, & brothers, & sisters, & children; but we do know that we are, at every moment, exposed to the means of our own excision, & of all that is dear to us in life. The bloody monster which threatens us is warmed & cherished in our own hearths. O hear our prayer, & remove it, yes protectors of our persons, ye guardians of our peace!

Tell us not of the labors & hardships which we shall endure when our bondservants shall be removed from us. They have no terrors for us. Those labors & hardships cannot be greater, or so great as those we now endure in providing for & ruling the faithless beings who are subjected to us. Or were they greater, still they are, in our esteem, less than the small dust in the balance, compared with the burden of our fears and our dangers. But what have we to fear, from these causes, more than females of other countries? Are they of the east, & of the West, of England, of France, more "cumbered with much serving" than we are? Are they less enlightened, or

Source: Lisa Grunwald and Stephen J. Adler eds., *Women's Letters: America from the Revolutionary War to the Present* (New York: The Dial Press, 2005), pp. 139–141.

less accomplished? However we may be flattered, we will not be argued out of our senses, & persuaded into a belief which is contradicted by experience, & the testimony of sober facts. Many, very many of our sisters & brothers have fled to other lands, from the evils which we experience: and they send us back the evidences of their contentment & prosperity. They lament not their labors & hardships, but exult in their deliverance from servitude to their quondam slaves: And we, too, fly—we, too, would exult in similar deliverance, were our destiny not otherwise ordered than it is. That destiny is in your hands, & we implore your high agency in ordering it for the best. We would enjoy such exultation on our native soil. Do not slight our importunities. Do not disregard our fears. Our destiny is identified with yours. If we perish, alas! what will become of you & your offspring?

We are not political economists, but our domestic employments, our engagements in rearing up the children of our husbands & brothers, our intimate concern with the interests & prosperity of society, we presume, cannot but inform us of the great & elementary principles of that important science. Indeed it is impossible that that science can have any other basis than the principles which are constantly developing themselves to us in our domestic relations. What is a nation but a family on a large scale? Our fears teach us to reflect & reason. And our reflections & reasonings have taught us that the peace of our homes, the welfare of society, the prosperity of future generations call aloud & imperiously for some decisive & efficient measure—and that measure cannot, we believe, be efficient, or of much benefit, if it have not for its ultimate object, the extinction of slavery, from amongst us. Without, therefore, entering upon a detail of facts & arguments, we implore you by the urgency of our fears, by the love we bear you as our fathers & brothers, by our anxieties for the little ones around us, by our estimate of domestic & public weal, by present danger, by the prospects of the future, by our female virtues, by the patriotism which flows in & animates our bosoms, by our prayers to Almighty GOD, not to let the power with which you are invested lie dormant, but that you exert it for the deliverance of yourselves, of us, of the children of the land, of future ages, from the direst curse which can befal a people. Signalize your legislation by this mighty deed. This we pray; and in duty will ever pray.

12 As in the North, feminine ideals were upheld in the South by women as well as men. In this poem, one of the region's most popular authors attacks (Northern) female reformers. What does this source reveal about the usefulness of a feminine ideal in the South in the face of growing—and often overlapping—abolitionist and woman's rights movements?

"Woman's Progress" (1853)

LOUISA CHEVES McCORD

And is this progress—Are these noisy tongues—
In fierce contention raised and angry war—
Fit boast for womanhood? Yon shrewish things,
In wordy boisterous debate,—are these
Perfected woman's exponents to show
Her model virtues to a later age?
And shall our daughters cast their woman robes,
A useless cumbrance aside, to seize
Some freer imitation of the man,
Whose lordly strut and dashing stride attract
Their envious love for notoriety?
Shall they, with flashing eye and clanging tongue,
Mount in the rostrum, lecture in the streets,
And, in the arena of election strife,
Claim with shrill voice, and rude dishevelled locks,
"Your votes! your votes!" ye loud-mouthed populace!
Nay;— should that peach-like cheek but feel the breath
Of yonder foul-mouthed crowd, methinks its bloom
Should wither in the contact. God hath made
A woman-nature holier than the man's—
Purer of impulse, and of gentler mould,—
Let her not stain it in the angry strife
Which these, our modern female Reverends,
Learned M. D's, and lecturing damsels, seek
To feed their hungry vanity, and bring
Unnoticed charms before the gaping crowd.
Tis surely not for this that God hath given
That soothing voice so sweetly taught to whisper.
. . . .

Then let our holy task be still to cleanse,
But not to change our natures. Let us strive
To be *more* woman,—never to be man.
These reverend Misses, doctors in mob caps,
And petticoated lecturers, are things
Which make us loathe, like strange unnatural births,
Nature's disordered works. You chirping thing
That with cracked voice, and mincing manners, prates
Of rights and duties, lecturing to the crowd,

Source: Southern Literary Messenger (November 1853).

And in strange nondescript of dress arrays
Unfettered limbs that modesty should hide;
Thus raising, as it were, rebellion's flag
Against her being's nature—call it not,
Sweet Sisters, call not that unsexed thing
By the pure name of Woman. Let us strive
With silent effort in the Woman's cause,
Perfecting in its destinies, our sex,
And cast aside this foul attempt which clings
To degradation as it were our pride.
Oh! let us be the woman of God's make;
No Mrs. Bloomer, Abby Kelly thing
Aping man's vices, while our weaker frame
Knows not his harsher virtues.

---

13 William Harper was one of numerous proslavery writers who took up the pen in response to the abolitionist assault on the "peculiar institution" starting in the 1830s. Harper's "Memoir on Slavery" was delivered to the South Carolina Society of the Advancement of Learning in 1837 and was published in 1853. In this excerpt, he discusses sexual relations between white masters and slaves and the alleged absence of prostitution and white female infidelity in the South. Was there a relationship between the sexual double standard discussed here and the Southern image of white womanhood? Do you think attitudes expressed here might have an impact on white women's attitudes regarding that image?

"Memoir on Slavery" (1853)
WILLIAM HARPER

It is true that . . . the morals of [the slave] class are very loose, (by no means so universally so as is often supposed,) and that the passions of men of the superior caste, tempt and find gratification in the easy chastity of the females. This is evil and to be remedied, if we can do so, without the introduction of greater evil. But evil is incident to every condition of society, and as I have said, we have only to consider in which institution it most predominates.

Source: William Harper, "Harper's Memoir on Slavery," in *The Pro-Slavery Argument; As Maintained by the Most Distinguished Writers of the Southern States* (Philadelphia: Lippincott, Grambo and Co., 1853), pp. 41–45.

Compare these prostitutes of our country, (if it is not injustice to call them so,) and their condition with those of other countries—the seventy thousand prostitutes of London, or of Paris, or the ten thousand of New-York, or our other Northern cities. . . .

Compare with this the female slave under similar circumstances. She is not a less useful member of society than before. If shame be attached to her conduct, it is such shame as would be elsewhere felt for a venial impropriety. She has not impaired her means of support, nor materially impaired her character, or lowered her station in society; she has done no great injury to herself, or any other human being. Her offspring is not a burden but an acquisition to her owner; his support is provided for, and he is brought up to usefulness; if the fruit of intercourse with a freeman, his condition is, perhaps, raised somewhat above that of his mother. . . .

It may be asked, if we have no prostitutes from the free class of society among ourselves. I answer, in no assignable proportion. With general truth it might be said that there are none. When such occurs, it is among the rare evils of society. And apart from other and better reasons, which we believe to exist, it is plain that it must be so, from the comparative absence of temptation. Our brothels, comparatively very few—and these should not be permitted to exist at all—are filled, for the most part, by importations from the cities of our confederate [Northern] States, where Slavery does not exist. . . . Never, but in a single instance, have I heard of an imputation on the general purity of manners, among the free females of the slaveholding States. Such an imputation, however, and made in coarse terms, we have never heard here—*here* where divorce was never known—where no Court was ever polluted by an action for criminal conversation with a wife—where it is related rather as matter of tradition, not unmingled with wonder, that a Carolinian woman of education and family, proved false to her conjugal faith. . . . And can it be doubted, that this purity is caused by, and is a compensation for the evils resulting from the existence of an enslaved class of more relaxed morals?

It is mostly the warm passions of youth, which give rise to licentious intercourse. But I do not hesitate to say, that the intercourse which takes place with enslaved females, is less depraving in its effects, than when it is carried on with females of their own caste. In the first place, as like attracts like, that which is unlike repels; and though the strength of passion be sufficient to overcome the repulsion, still the attraction is less. He feels that he is connecting himself with one of an inferior and servile caste, and that there is something of degradation in the act. The intercourse is generally casual; he does not make her habitually an associate, and is less likely to receive any taint from her habits and manners. He is less liable to those extraordinary fascinations, with which worthless women sometimes entangle their victims, to the utter destruction of all principle, worth and vigor of character. The female of his own race offers greater allurements. The haunts of vice often present a show of elegance, and various luxury tempts the senses. They are made an habitual resort, and their inmates associates, till the general character receives a taint from the corrupted atmosphere. Not only the practice is licentious, but the understanding is sophisticated; the moral feelings are bewildered, and the boundaries of virtue and vice are confused. Where such licentiousness very extensively prevails, society is rotten to the heart.

---

14 Keziah Miner was born in 1807 in western Virginia. Like other hill country areas in the rural South, this part of Virginia was home to poorer whites rather than large plantations. In 1854, Miner captured the lively scene at a quilting party, a common occurrence in such areas. What does this image suggest about opportunities for Southern women to overcome the isolation in an agricultural society? What does it also suggest about how pervasive the ideal of the "Southern belle" was in the pre–Civil War South?

Keziah Miner, "A quilting party in Western Virginia" (1854)

North Wind Picture Archives / Alamy

CONCLUSION

In 1910, the American Historical Association president Frederick Jackson Turner called on historians to "rework our history from the new points of view afforded by the present."[2] In heeding Turner's call, historians bring constant change to even thoroughly researched periods. Indeed, as this chapter demonstrates, they should never be too quick to close the books on any period or topic. In the case of the decades prior to the Civil War, the simple recognition that women played an important role in antebellum society in both the North and South sparked a significant reworking of history "from the new points of view afforded by the present." As a result, historians now have a much better understanding of the meaning of gender in the early nineteenth century and the importance of the ideas that Northerners and Southerners attached to it. Given the well-defined nature of antebellum gender ideals, few topics in the American past offer a better means to consider the function and impact of an ideology in society. Given the rapid social and economic changes in American society in the period and the growing sectional tensions between the North and South, the study of gender ideals has also given historians a much better understanding of the impact of historical change on ideas and values. Thus, by examining the images and circumstances of women in this period, they have an especially fruitful way to explore how and why the antebellum North and South differed. In Chapter 12, we will turn to another well-worked field that has lost none of its ability to produce an abundant crop of fresh historical insights—the war that resulted from those differences.

FURTHER READING

Victoria E. Bynum, *Unruly Women: The Politics of Social and Sexual Control in the Old South* (Chapel Hill: University of North Carolina Press, 1992).

Catherine Clinton, *The Plantation Mistress: Woman's World in the Old South* (New York: Pantheon Books, 1982).

Susanna Delfino and Michele Gillespie, eds., *Neither Lady Nor Slave: Working Women of the Old South* (Chapel Hill: University of North Carolina Press, 2002).

Lori D. Ginzberg, *Women and the Work of Benevolence: Morality, Politics, and Class in the Nineteenth-Century United States* (New Haven, Conn.: Yale University Press, 1990).

Suzanne Lebsock, *The Free Women of Petersburg: Status and Culture in a Southern Town, 1784–1860* (New York: W. W. Norton & Company, 1984).

Jean V. Matthews, *Women's Struggle for Equality: The First Phase, 1828–1876* (Chicago: Ivan R. Dee, 1997).

Christine Stansell, *City of Women: Sex and Class in New York, 1789–1860* (New York: Alfred A. Knopf, 1986).

NOTES

1. William R. Taylor, *Cavalier and Yankee: The Old South and the American National Character* (New York: Harper and Row, 1969), p. 128.
2. Quoted in Barton J. Bernstein, ed., *Towards a New Past: Dissenting Essays in American History* (New York: Vintage Books, 1969), p. v.

Chapter

12

Grand Theory, Great Battles, and Historical Causes: Why Secession Failed

The documents in this chapter address the question of why the North won the Civil War.

Secondary Sources

Primary Sources

*O*n July 3, 1863, Confederate general Robert E. Lee decided to attack the very center of the Union position at Gettysburg. The Confederates opened fire with 150 cannons from Seminary Ridge. The Union Army responded with eighty guns. One Union general said the Confederate barrage was "the heaviest artillery fire" he had ever known.[1] Yet it only pounded open ground behind the Union troops. When the fire finally died down and the smoke cleared, the Union soldiers looked over the fields and saw the enemy forming battle lines. "My brave boys were full of hope and confident of victory as I led them forth," said Confederate general George Pickett. Pickett's division would spearhead the attack of 10,500 men against the Federal position on Cemetery Ridge. The Union soldiers waited for the assault. "Every eye could see the enemy's legion, an overwhelming resistless tide of an ocean of armed men sweeping upon us!"[2]

At 700 yards, the Union artillery opened fire with devastating effect. Canisters (tin cans packed with slugs that created huge shotgunlike blasts) decimated the Confederate ranks. Witnesses saw body parts, rifles, and knapsacks hurled into the air. At least one soldier heard "a vast mournful roar" rise from the battlefield.[3] Undaunted, Pickett's men continued up Cemetery Ridge. Then the Union infantry opened fire. The Confederates stopped, returned fire, and resumed their advance. For a few moments the Confederate battle flag waved over Cemetery Ridge as the Confederates and Federals fired at nearly point-blank range. Then more Union troops swarmed in and the Confederates fell back. Within moments the battle was lost.

When the fighting was over, one Union general tried to ride over the field, but could not guide his horse through the dead and wounded soldiers. Pickett's charge had left 5,675 Confederate casualties and nearly 800 more captured. After three days of fighting at Gettysburg, 23,000 Union and nearly 20,500 Confederate soldiers were dead, wounded, captured, or missing. Lee took full responsibility. "All this has been my fault," he told his men after the futile charge.[4] Then he retreated back to Virginia, never to launch another assault so far into Union territory. In less than two years, Lee handed his sword to Ulysses S. Grant at Appomattox. The day after he surrendered, the Confederate general offered this explanation: "After four years of arduous service marked by unsurpassed courage and fortitude, the Army of Northern Virginia has been compelled to yield to overwhelming numbers and resources."[5]

More than 145 years later, historians continue to debate the reasons for the Confederacy's defeat. They have found them on Cemetery Ridge and other bloody battlefields. They have also found them in important developments on the home fronts of the North and South. Like Robert E. Lee after Pickett's charge, some historians argue that individual battles and military decisions were crucial to the outcome of the war. Like Lee after Appomattox, however, other historians have found the key to the Union's triumph in economic and other differences between the North and South. Which of Lee's explanations for defeat was more accurate? In this chapter we consider the role of factors both on and off the battlefield in explaining the Civil War's outcome.

SETTING

Each side had advantages at the outset of the Civil War. The Union had a much larger population, a growing factory system, and a superior transportation network. But Southerners needed only to defend their own territory to win. Historians who point to the superiority of Northern resources in explaining the triumph of the Union emphasize the "modern" nature of the Civil War. What counts in such wars is the ability to mobilize the entire society for a protracted struggle. Thus these historians maintain that the Union victory had more to do with home front morale than battlefield maneuvers. Other researchers see political leaders as the decisive factor. They point to Lincoln's political skills and his administration's ability to forestall foreign intervention in the conflict. They also emphasize Jefferson Davis's limitations as a political leader and his administration's inability to mobilize Southern resources. Other scholars cite additional factors far from the battlefield to explain the outcome of the Civil War, from the North's superior agricultural system to large numbers of slaves and other Union sympathizers in the South.

In these debates, it is easy to forget that the preservation of the Union was hardly a foregone conclusion at the beginning of the war. Indeed, the first two years of the war saw few Union victories on Eastern battlefields. Thus some scholars link the Union's early reverses and its eventual victory to men and events closer to the field of battle. They argue that military commanders, including the respective commanders-in-chief, were crucial to the outcome of the war. Many military historians argue that Confederate commanders were often better tacticians and generally more aggressive than their Union counterparts. Yet they also maintain that some Union generals demonstrated better strategic sense in adjusting to total war. These historians point to numerous reasons for the differences between Confederate and Union commanders. Some cite the impact on each group of the Swiss military strategist Antoine Henri Jomini, the most important writer on warfare in the early nineteenth century. Others have argued that the different way Union and Confederate generals fought was due to ethnic and cultural differences. One scholar has even suggested that each side's perceptions of the other's fighting abilities determined the way the generals fought.

Students of the Civil War can be forgiven if they conclude that there are as many explanations for the outcome of the war as there are Civil War historians. These competing conclusions clearly indicate that no single factor provides a satisfactory explanation for the outcome of the Civil War. In fact, historians today, recognizing the complicated nature of historical events and outcomes, embrace multifaceted explanation of the past, including this significant part of American history. As complicated as our understanding of this era is, however, it helps to think about the outcome of the Civil War with two basic questions in mind. Historians want to know if the North won the Civil War because of its inherent strengths or if the South lost the war because of its internal weaknesses. And they want to know whether it was military events or developments far from the battlefield that better explain the war's outcome. Historians' answers to the first question determine their conclusions about the Civil War. Their answers to the second question, as we shall see, reflect their assumptions about history itself.

INVESTIGATION

In this chapter, we compare two arguments about the outcome of the Civil War. One historian emphasizes the Union's tremendous advantages and attempts to relate them to a grand theory to account for the North's victory. The other points to military turning points as the crucial factor in the defeat of the South. As you read and think about the primary and secondary sources in this chapter, your main assignment is this: Explain why the Civil War turned out as it did. In your explanation, you should assess the two historians' arguments regarding the war's outcome and determine which one is more plausible. To do that, you need to determine whether factors far from the battlefield most influenced the outcome of the war or whether it can be better explained by focusing on commanders, campaigns, and battles. To complete this assignment, you should address the following questions:

1. **Do the historians argue that the South lost the Civil War or that the North won it?** Do they argue that the North's advantages or the South's weaknesses were more important? What is their most important evidence to answer that question?

2. **Was the outcome of the Civil War inevitable because it was determined by the balance of resources on each side?** What do the authors conclude? What do the primary sources reveal about that question?

3. **Cite the best examples of how developments on the home front, including those involving blacks and women, affected events on the battlefield and of the way events on the battlefield affected developments on the home front.** What problems do historians face in attempting to establish these connections?

Before you do this assignment, be sure to read the appropriate chapters in your textbook. They will give you valuable background and even suggest additional factors to consider. Pay attention to your textbook's reasons for the outcome of the war. When you are finished, you can compare its interpretation to those in this chapter's essays.

SECONDARY SOURCES

1   In this selection, historian George Fredrickson assesses a number of interpretations about the outcome of the Civil War that emphasize the North's advantages. He also builds his own case for the triumph of the Union, a kind of grand synthesis or theory. Note why Fredrickson thinks explanations that emphasize the North's advantages are flawed. Also consider his argument that Southern military leaders were rigid and conservative and how it relates to his overall theory about the reason for the Union's triumph. Does Fredrickson find the answer to the North's victory on the battlefield or on the home front? Does he make a connection between the way each side fought the war and the respective home fronts? Finally, what role does slavery play in his analysis?

Blue over Gray: Sources of Success and Failure in the Civil War (1975)

GEORGE M. FREDRICKSON

Historians have expended vast amounts of time, energy, and ingenuity searching for the causes and consequences of the Civil War. Much less effort has been devoted to explaining the outcome of the war itself. Yet the question is obviously important. One only has to imagine how radically different the future of North America would have been had the South won its permanent independence. It is also possible that a full comparison of how the two sides responded to the ultimate test of war will shed reflex light on both the background and legacy of the conflict. If northern success and southern failure can be traced to significant differences in the two societies as they existed on the eve of the war, then we may have further reason for locating the origins of the war in the clash of divergent social systems and ideologies. If the relative strengths of the North in wartime were rooted in the character of its society, then the sources of northern victory would foreshadow, to some extent at least, the postwar development of a nation reunited under northern hegemony.

A number of plausible explanations of "why the North won" have been advanced. The problem with most of them is not that they are wrong but that they are partial or incomplete. . . .

Perhaps the most widely accepted explanation of why the North won and the South lost derives from the time-honored proposition that God is on the side

Source: A Nation Divided: Problems and Issues of the Civil War and Reconstruction, ed by George M. Fredrickson. (1975 Burgess Publishing). Reprinted by permission of the Estate of George M. Fredrickson.

of the heaviest battalions. The North's advantages in manpower, resources, and industrial capacity were clearly overwhelming. According to the census of 1860, the Union, not counting the contested border states of Missouri and Kentucky, had a population of approximately 20,275,000. The Confederacy, on the other hand, had a white population of only about 5,500,000. If we include the 3,654,000 blacks, the total population of the eleven Confederate states adds up to slightly more than 9,000,000. Even if we consider the black population an asset to the Confederacy in carrying on a war for the preservation of slavery, the North still ends up with a more than two-to-one advantage in population. There was an even greater differential in readily available manpower of military age; the northern advantage in this respect was well in excess of three-to-one. In industrial capacity, the Union had an enormous edge. In 1860, the North had approximately 110,000 manufacturing establishments manned by about 1,300,000 workers, while the South had only 18,000 establishments with 110,000 workers. Thus for every southern industrial worker the North had a factory or workshop! Finally, in railroad mileage, so crucial to the logistics of the Civil War, the North possessed over seventy percent of the nation's total of 31,256 miles.

With such a decisive edge in manpower, industrial plant, and transportation facilities, how, it might well be asked, could the North possibly have lost? Yet history shows many examples of the physically weaker side winning, especially in wars of national independence. The achievement of Dutch independence from Spain in the seventeenth century, the colonists' success in the American Revolution, and many "wars of national liberation" in the twentieth century, including the Algerian revolution and the long struggle for Vietnamese self-determination, provide examples of how the physically weaker side can prevail. . . .

Recognizing the insufficiency of a crude economic or demographic explanation, some historians have sought psychological reasons for the Confederate defeat. It has been argued that the South "whipped itself" because it did not believe strongly enough in its cause. While the North could allegedly call on the full fervor of American nationalism and antislavery idealism, the South was saddled with the morally dubious enterprise of defending slavery and was engaged in breaking up a union of hallowed origin for which many southerners still had a lingering reverence. It has even been suggested that large numbers of loyal Confederates had a subconscious desire to lose the war. The northern victory is therefore ascribed to the fact that the North had a better cause and thus higher morale; the breakdown in the South's will to win is seen as the consequence of a deep ambivalence about the validity of the whole Confederate enterprise.

This thesis is highly speculative and not easily reconciled with the overall pattern of pro-Confederate sentiment and activity. It would seem to underestimate or even to belittle the willingness of large numbers of southerners to fight and die for the Confederacy. No northerner who fought the "Rebs" at places such as Shiloh, Antietam, and Gettysburg would have concluded that the South really wanted to lose. . . .

On the surface at least, it seems harder to explain what made the northern cause so compelling. Contrary to antislavery mythology, there is little evidence to sustain the view that a genuinely humanitarian opposition to black servitude ever animated a majority of the northern population. Most northerners defined their cause as the preservation of the Union, not the emancipation of the slaves. This was made explicit in a joint resolution of Congress, passed overwhelmingly in July 1861, denying any federal intention to interfere with the domestic institutions of the southern states. . . . But when considered simply as a formal ideology, Unionism seems too abstract and remote from the concrete interests of ordinary people to have sustained . . . the enthusiasm necessary for such a long and bloody conflict. In any case, the *a priori* proposition that the North had a more compelling cause, and therefore one that was bound to generate higher morale, seems questionable.

Morale in both sections fluctuated in direct response to the fortunes of war. . . . Throughout the conflict, morale seems to have been more a function of military victory and success than a cause of it. Furthermore, any comparison involving the will to win of the respective sides cannot ignore the different situations that they faced. Except for Lee's brief forays into Maryland and Pennsylvania, the northern people never had to suffer from invasion of their own territory. Whether the North's allegedly superior morale and determination would have stood up under pressures equivalent to those experienced by the South will never be known. But we do know that the resolve of the North came dangerously close to breaking in the summer of 1864, at a time when its territory was secure, its economy booming, and its ultimate victory all but assured. At exactly the same time, the South was girding for another nine months of desperate struggle despite economic collapse and the loss of much of its territory. Such a comparison hardly supports the thesis that the North excelled the South in its will to win. . . .

Some have attributed the North's success in outlasting the South to its superior leadership. One distinguished historian has even suggested that if the North and South had exchanged Presidents the outcome of the war would have been reversed. As a wartime President, Lincoln was unquestionably superior to Davis. A master politician, Lincoln was able through a combination of tact and forcefulness to hold together the bitterly antagonistic factions of the Republican party. . . . But perhaps Lincoln's greatest successes came in his role as commander in chief of the armed forces. Although lacking military training and experience, he had a good instinctive grasp of broad strategic considerations. Furthermore, he knew that he had neither the time nor the tactical ability to take direct charge of military operations and wisely refrained from interfering directly with his generals except when their excessive caution or incompetence gave him no choice. Lincoln's primary objective was to find a general who had a comprehensive view of strategic needs, a willingness to fight, and consequently the ability to take full charge of military activity. In late 1863, he found the right man and without hesitation turned the entire military effort over to General Grant, who proceeded to fight the war to a successful conclusion. In innumerable ways, Lincoln gave evidence of his common sense, flexibility, and willingness to learn from experience. Although not the popular demigod he would become after his assassination, he did provide inspiration to the North as a whole. Many who had been critical of Lincoln at the start of the war, seeing him merely as a rough, inexperienced, frontier politician, came to recognize the quality of his statesmanship. Furthermore, his eloquence at Gettysburg and in the Second Inaugural helped to give meaning and resonance to the northern cause.

The leadership of Davis was of a very different caliber. The Confederate President was a proud, remote, and quarrelsome man with a fatal passion for always being in the right and for standing by his friends, no matter how incompetent or unpopular they turned out to be. He fought constantly with his cabinet and sometimes replaced good men who had offended him with second-raters who would not question his decisions. . . . Most southern newspapers were virulently anti-Davis by the end of the war. Particularly harmful was Davis' military role. Because he had commanded forces in the Mexican war and served as Secretary of War of the United States, he thought of himself as qualified to direct all phases of operations. This belief in his own military genius, combined with a constitutional inability to delegate authority, led to excessive interference with his generals and to some very questionable strategic decisions. Unlike Lincoln, he lost touch with the political situation, and he failed to provide leadership in the critical area of economic policy. In the end, one has a picture of Davis tinkering ineffectually with the South's military machine while a whole society was crumbling around him.

It appears the North had a great war leader, and the South a weak one. Can we therefore explain the outcome of the Civil War as an historical accident, a matter of northern luck in finding someone who could do the job and southern misfortune in picking the wrong man? Before we come to this beguilingly simple conclusion, we need to take a broader look at northern and southern leadership and raise the question of whether the kind of leadership a society produces is purely accidental. If Lincoln was a great leader of men, it was at least partly because he had good material to work with. Seward was in some ways a brilliant Secretary of State; Stanton directed the War Department with great determination and efficiency; and even Chase, despite his awkward political maneuvering, was on the whole a competent Secretary of the Treasury. . . . The North, it can be argued, had not simply one great leader but was able during the war to develop competent and efficient leadership on almost all levels. Such a pattern could hardly have been accidental; more likely it reveals something about the capacity of northern society to produce men of talent and initiative who could deal with the unprecedented problems of a total war.

In the Confederacy, the situation was quite different. Among the South's generals there of course were some brilliant tactical commanders. Their successes on the battlefield were instrumental in keeping the Confederacy afloat for four years. But, in almost all other areas, the South revealed a sad lack of capable leadership. . . .

The contrast in leadership, therefore, would seem to reflect some deeper differences of a kind that would make one section more responsive than the other to the practical demands of fighting a large-scale war. Since both societies faced unprecedented challenges, success would depend to a great extent on which side had the greater ability to adjust to new situations. . . .

Lincoln himself set the pattern for precedent-breaking innovation. Whenever he felt obligated to assume extra-constitutional powers to deal with situations unforeseen by the Constitution, he did so with little hesitation. After the outbreak of the war and before Congress was in session to sanction his actions, he expanded the regular army, advanced public money to private individuals, and declared martial law on a line from Washington to Philadelphia. On September 24, 1862, again without Congressional authorization, he extended the jurisdiction of martial law and suspended the writ of habeas corpus in all cases of alleged disloyalty. The Emancipation Proclamation can also be seen as an example of extra-constitutional innovation. Acting under the amorphous concept of "the war powers" of the President, Lincoln struck at slavery primarily because "military necessity" dictated new measures to disrupt the economic and social system of the enemy. . . .

The spirit of innovation was manifested in other areas as well. In Grant and Sherman the North finally found generals who grasped the nature of modern war and were ready to jettison outworn rules of strategy and tactics. . . . In his march from Atlanta to the sea in the fall of 1864, Sherman introduced for the first time the modern strategy of striking directly at the enemy's domestic economy. The coordinated, multipronged offensive launched by Grant in 1864, of which Sherman's march was a critical component, was probably the biggest, boldest, and most complex military operation mounted anywhere before the twentieth century. Grant, like Lincoln, can be seen as embodying the North's capacity for organization and innovation. . . .

Businessmen also responded to the crisis and found that what was patriotic could also be highly profitable. There were the inevitable frauds perpetrated on the government by contractors, but more significant was the overall success of the industrial system in producing the goods required. . . . No small part of this success was due to the willingness of businessmen, farmers, and government procurement officials to "think and act anew" by organizing themselves into larger and more efficient units for the production, transportation, and allocation of goods.

It would be an understatement to say that the South demonstrated less capacity than the North for organization and innovation. In fact, the South's most glaring failures were precisely in the area of coordination and collective adaptation to new conditions. The Confederacy did of course manage to put an army in the field that was able to hold the North at bay for four years. . . . [But] Southern successes on the battlefield were in no real sense triumphs of organization or innovation. Before the rise of Grant and Sherman, most Civil War battles were fought according to the outdated tactical principles that generals on both sides had learned at West Point. In these very conventional battles, the South had the advantage because it had the most intelligent and experienced of the West Pointers. Since everyone played by the same rules, it was inevitable that those who could play the game best would win. When the rules were changed by Grant and Sherman, the essential conservatism and rigidity of southern military leadership became apparent.

Besides being conventional in their tactics, southern armies were notoriously undisciplined; insubordination was an everyday occurrence and desertion eventually became a crippling problem. There were so many men absent without leave by August 1, 1863, that a general amnesty for deserters had to be declared. For full effectiveness, southern soldiers had to be commanded by generals such as Robert E. Lee and Stonewall Jackson, charismatic leaders who could command the personal loyalty and respect of their men. The idea of obeying an officer simply because of his rank went against the southern grain.

Although the army suffered from the excessive individualism of its men and the narrow traditionalism of its officers, these defects were not fatal until very late in the war, mainly because it took the North such a long time to apply its characteristic talent for organization and innovation directly to military operations. But on the southern home front similar attitudes had disastrous consequences almost from the beginning. In its efforts to mobilize the men and resources of the South, the Confederate government was constantly hamstrung by particularistic resistance to central direction and by a general reluctance to give up traditional ideas and practices incompatible with the necessities of war.

Particularism was manifested most obviously in the refusal of state governments to respond to the needs of the Confederacy. The central government was rudely rebuffed when it sought in 1861 to get the states to give up control over the large quantity of arms in their possession. The states held back for their own defense most of the 350,000 small arms that they held. The Confederacy, initially able to muster only 190,000 weapons, was forced to turn down 200,000 volunteers in the first year of the war because it could not arm them. The states also held back men. . . .

. . . [T]he slaveholding planters, taken as a group, were no more able to rise above narrow and selfish concerns than other segments of southern society. Because of their influence, the Confederacy was unable to adopt a sound financial policy; land and slaves, the main resources of the South, remained immune from direct taxes. As a result, the government was only able to raise about one percent of its revenue from taxation; the rest came from loans and the printing of vast quantities of fiat paper money. The inevitable consequence was the catastrophic runaway inflation that made Confederate money almost worthless even before the government went out of existence. . . .

. . . What was there about the culture and social structure of the North that made possible the kinds of organizational initiatives and daring innovations that have been described? What was there about southern society and culture that explains the lack of cohesiveness and adaptability that doomed the Confederacy? Answers to such questions require some further understanding of the differences in northern and southern society on the eve of the war, especially as these differences related to war-making potential.

A fuller comprehension of what social strengths and weaknesses the two sides brought to the conflict can perhaps be gained by borrowing a well-known concept from the social sciences—the idea of modernization. Sociologists and political scientists often employ this term to describe the interrelated changes that occur when a whole society begins to move away from a traditional agrarian pattern toward an urban-industrial system. . . .

. . . [One] theorist has provided a simple rule of thumb to gauge the extent of modernization in various societies: the higher the proportion of energy derived from inanimate sources, as opposed to the direct application of human and animal strength, the more modernized the society. Modernization therefore has its intellectual foundations in a rationalistic or scientific world view and a commitment to technological development. . . .

By any definition of this process, the North was relatively more modernized than the South in 1861. To apply one of the most important indices of modernization, thirty-six percent of the Northern population was already urban as compared to the South's nine and six-tenths percent. As we have already seen, there was an even greater gap in the extent of industrialization. Furthermore, the foundations had been laid in the northern states for a rapid increase in the pace of modernization. The antebellum "transportation revolution" had set the stage for economic integration on a national scale, and the quickening pace of industrial development foreshadowed the massive and diversified growth of the future. Because of better and cheaper transportation, new markets, and a rise in efficiency and mechanization, midwestern agriculture was in a position to begin playing its modern role as the food-producing adjunct to an urban-industrial society. Literacy was widespread and means of mass communication, such as inexpensively produced newspapers, pamphlets, and books, were available for mobilizing public opinion. . . . In short, given the necessary stimulus and opportunity, the North was ready for a "great leap forward" in the modernization process.

The South, on the other hand, had little potentiality for rapid modernization. Overwhelmingly agricultural and tied to the slave plantation as its basic unit of production, it had many of the characteristics of what today would be called "an underdeveloped society." Like such societies, the Old

South had what amounted to a "dual economy": a small modern or capitalistic sector, profitably producing cotton and other commodities for export, coexisted with a vast "traditional" sector, composed of white subsistence farmers and black slaves. . . .

. . . The two main segments of the white South were united neither by a sense of common economic interests nor by a complete identity of social and political values. But the presence of millions of black slaves did make possible a perverse kind of solidarity. Fear of blacks, and more specifically of black emancipation, was the principal force holding the white South together. Without it, there could have been no broadly based struggle for independence.

The planter and the non-slaveholding farmer had one other characteristic in common besides racism; in their differing ways, they were both extreme individualists. The planter's individualism came mainly from a lifetime of commanding slaves on isolated plantations. Used to unquestioned authority in all things and prone to think of himself as an aristocrat, he commonly exhibited an indomitable sense of personal independence. The non-slaveholder, on the other hand, was basically a backwoodsman who combined the stiff-necked individualism of the frontier with the arrogance of race that provided him with an exaggerated sense of his personal worth. Southern whites in general therefore were conditioned by slavery, racism, and rural isolation to condone and even encourage quasi-anarchic patterns of behavior that could not have been tolerated in a more modernized society with a greater need for social cohesion and discipline. . . .

Such an attitude was obviously incompatible with the needs of a modernizing society for cooperation and collective innovation. Furthermore, the divorce of status from achievement made it less likely that competent leaders and organizers would emerge. Particularism, localism, and extreme individualism were the natural outgrowth of the South's economic and social system. So was resistance to any changes that posed a threat to slavery and racial domination. . . .

. . . [S]outhern politics, despite its high level of popular involvement, remained largely the disorganized competition of individual office seekers. Those who won elections usually did so either because they were already men of weight in their communities or because they came off better than their rivals in face-to-face contact with predominantly rural voters. In the North by 1861, politics was less a matter of personalities and more an impersonal struggle of well-organized parties. In urban areas, the rudiments of the modern political machine could already be perceived.

The fact that the South was economically, socially, and politically less "developed" or modernized than the North in 1861 may not by itself fully explain why war had to come, but it does provide a key to understanding why the war had to turn out the way it did. . . .

As it was, the only course open to southern leaders during the war was in effect a crash program of modernization in an attempt to neutralize the immense advantages of the North. When we consider the cultural heritage and economic resources they had to work with, their achievements went beyond what might have been expected. But the South had far too much ground to make up, and persisting rigidities, especially as manifested in the die-hard commitment to localism, racism, and plantation slavery, constituted fatal checks on the modernizing impulse.

The North, on the other hand, not only capitalized on its initial advantages during the war but was able to multiply them. In fact, the conflict itself served as a catalyst for rapid development in many areas. Modernizing trends that had begun in the prewar period came to unexpectedly rapid fruition in a way that both compounded the North's advantage in the conflict and helped set the pattern for postwar America.

---

2 The preceding essay examines differences between Northern and Southern society. In the following selection, historian James McPherson focuses on the military turning points. Note how he attempts to disprove other interpretations about the war's outcome. Also pay particular attention to how he tries to demonstrate that individual battles affected the will to fight. What would George Fredrickson, the author of the previous selection, have said about the reasons for the outcome of crucial Civil War turning points?

Why the North Won (1988)

JAMES M. McPHERSON

[A] persistent question has nagged historians and mythologists alike: if . . . Robert [E. Lee] was such a genius and his legions so invincible, why did they lose? The answers, though almost as legion as Lee's soldiers, tend to group themselves into a few main categories. One popular answer has been phrased, from the northern perspective, by quoting Napoleon's aphorism that God was on the side of the heaviest battalions. For southerners this explanation usually took some such form as these words of a Virginian: "They never whipped us, Sir, unless they were four to one. If we had had anything like a fair chance, or less disparity of numbers, we should have won our cause and established our independence." The North had a potential manpower superiority of more than three to one (counting only white men) and Union armed forces had an actual superiority of two to one during most of the war. In economic resources and logistical capacity the northern advantage was even greater. Thus, in this explanation, the Confederacy fought against overwhelming odds; its defeat was inevitable.

Source: "Why the North Won" from *Battle Cry of Freedom: The Era of the Civil War* by James M. McPherson. Copyright (c) 1988. By permission of Oxford University Press, Inc.

But this explanation has not satisfied a good many analysts. History is replete with examples of peoples who have won or defended their independence against greater odds: the Netherlands against the Spain of Philip II; Switzerland against the Hapsburg Empire; the American rebels of 1776 against mighty Britain; North Vietnam against the United States of 1970. Given the advantages of fighting on the defensive in its own territory with interior lines in which stalemate would be victory against a foe who must invade, conquer, occupy, and destroy the capacity to resist, the odds faced by the South were not formidable. Rather, as another category of interpretations has it, internal divisions fatally weakened the Confederacy: the state-rights conflict between certain governors and the Richmond government; the disaffection of non-slaveholders from a rich man's war and poor man's fight; libertarian opposition to necessary measures such as conscription and the suspension of habeas corpus; the lukewarm commitment to the Confederacy by quondam* Whigs and unionists; the disloyalty of slaves who defected to the enemy whenever they had a chance; growing doubts among slaveowners themselves about the justice of their peculiar institution and their cause. "So the Confederacy succumbed to internal rather than external causes," according to numerous historians. The South suffered from a "weakness in morale," a "loss of the will to fight." The Confederacy did not lack "the means to continue the struggle," but "the will to do so." . . .

In any case the "internal division" and "lack of will" explanations for Confederate defeat, while not implausible, are not very convincing either. The problem is that the North experienced similar internal divisions, and if the war had come out differently the Yankees' lack of unity and will to win could be cited with equal plausibility to explain that outcome. . . .

Nevertheless the existence of internal divisions on both sides seemed to neutralize this factor as an explanation for Union victory, so a number of historians have looked instead at the quality of leadership both military and civilian. There are several variants of an interpretation that emphasizes a gradual development of superior northern leadership. In Beauregard, Lee, the two Johnstons [Albert Sidney and Joseph Eggleston], and [Stonewall] Jackson the South enjoyed abler military commanders during the first year or two of the war, while Jefferson Davis was better qualified by training and experience than Lincoln to lead a nation at war. But Lee's strategic vision was limited to the Virginia theater, and the Confederate government neglected the West, where Union armies developed a strategic design and the generals to carry it out, while southern forces floundered under incompetent commanders who lost the war in the West. By 1863, Lincoln's remarkable abilities gave him a wide edge over Davis as a war leader, while in Grant and Sherman the North acquired commanders with a concept of total war and the necessary determination to make it succeed. At the same time, in [Secretary of War] Edwin M.

* Former.

Stanton and [Quartermaster General] Montgomery Meigs, aided by the entrepreneurial talent of northern businessmen, the Union developed superior managerial talent to mobilize and organize the North's greater resources for victory in the modern industrialized conflict that the Civil War became.

This interpretation comes closer than others to credibility. Yet it also commits the fallacy of reversibility—that is, if the outcome had been reversed some of the same factors could be cited to explain Confederate victory. . . .

Most attempts to explain southern defeat or northern victory lack the dimension of *contingency*—the recognition that at numerous critical points during the war things might have gone altogether differently. Four major turning points defined the eventual outcome. The first came in the summer of 1862, when the counter-offensives of Jackson and Lee in Virginia and Bragg and Kirby Smith in the West arrested the momentum of a seemingly imminent Union victory. This assured a prolongation and intensification of the conflict and created the potential for Confederate success, which appeared imminent before each of the next three turning points.

The first of these occurred in the fall of 1862, when battles at Antietam and Perryville threw back Confederate invasions, forestalled European mediation and recognition of the Confederacy, perhaps prevented a Democratic victory in the northern elections of 1862 that might have inhibited the government's ability to carry on the war, and set the stage for the Emancipation Proclamation which enlarged the scope and purpose of the conflict. The third critical point came in the summer and fall of 1863 when [Union victories at] Gettysburg, Vicksburg, and Chattanooga turned the tide toward ultimate northern victory.

One more reversal of that tide seemed possible in the summer of 1864 when appalling Union casualties and apparent lack of progress especially in Virginia brought the North to the brink of peace negotiations and the election of a Democratic president. But [Sherman's] capture of Atlanta and Sheridan's destruction of Early's [Rebel] army in the Shenandoah Valley clinched matters for the North. Only then did it become possible to speak of the inevitability of Union victory. Only then did the South experience an irretrievable "loss of the will to fight."

Of all the explanations for Confederate defeat, the loss of will thesis suffers most from its own particular fallacy of reversibility—that of putting the cart before the horse. Defeat causes demoralization and loss of will; victory pumps up morale and the will to win. Nothing illustrates this better than the radical transformation of *northern* will from defeatism in August 1864 to a "depth of determination . . . to fight to the last" that "astonished" a British journalist a month later. The southern loss of will was a mirror image of this northern determination. These changes of mood were caused mainly by events on the battlefield. Northern victory and southern defeat in the war cannot be understood apart from the contingency that hung over every campaign, every battle, every election, every decision during the war.

PRIMARY SOURCES

Northern and Southern Society

Even before the Civil War, many commentators saw differences between the North and South. Note the differences that these observers saw between the two regions. How could they have translated into advantages or disadvantages on the battlefield?

 Helper was a white, nonslaveholding Southerner who hoped the South would throw off the peculiar institution.

The Impending Crisis (1857)
HINTON ROWAN HELPER

And now to the point. In our opinion, an opinion which has been formed from data obtained by assiduous researches, and comparisons, from laborious investigation, logical reasoning, and earnest reflection, the causes which have impeded the progress and prosperity of the South, which have dwindled our commerce, and other similar pursuits, into the most contemptible insignificance; sunk a large majority of our people in galling poverty and ignorance, rendered a small minority conceited and tyrannical, and driven the rest away from their homes; entailed upon us a humiliating dependence on the Free States; disgraced us in the recesses of our own souls, and brought us under reproach in the eyes of all civilized and enlightened nations—may all be traced to one common source, and there find solution in the most hateful and horrible word, that was ever incorporated into the vocabulary of human economy—*Slavery!* . . .

. . . To undeceive the people of the South, to bring them to a knowledge of the inferior and disreputable position which they occupy as a component part of the Union, and to give prominence and popularity to those plans which, if adopted, will elevate us to an equality, socially, morally, intellectually, industrially, politically, and financially, with the most flourishing and refined nation in the world, and, if possible, to place us in the van of even that, is the object of this work. Slaveholders, either from ignorance or from a wilful disposition to propagate error, contend that the South has nothing to be ashamed of, that slavery has proved a blessing to her, and that her

Source: Hinton Rowan Helper, *The Impending Crisis of the South* (1857; repr., Cambridge, Mass.: The Belknap Press of Harvard University Press), pp. 25, 60–61.

superiority over the North in an agricultural point of view makes amends for all her shortcomings in other respects. On the other hand, we contend that many years of continual blushing and severe penance would not suffice to cancel or annul the shame and disgrace that justly attaches to the South in consequence of slavery—the direst evil that e'er befell the land—that the South bears nothing like even a respectable approximation to the North in navigation, commerce, or manufactures, and that, contrary to the opinion entertained by ninety-nine hundredths of her people, she is far behind the free States in the only thing of which she has ever dared to boast—agriculture. We submit the question to the arbitration of figures, which, it is said, do not lie. With regard to the bushel-measure products of the soil, of which we have already taken an inventory, we have seen that there is a balance against the South in favor of the North of *seventeen million four hundred and twenty-three thousand one hundred and fifty-two bushels,* and a difference in the value of the same, also in favor of the North, of *forty-four million seven hundred and eighty-two thousand six hundred and thirty-six dollars.* It is certainly a most novel kind of agricultural superiority that the South claims on that score!

 Olmsted, a Northern journalist and, later, urban landscape planner, traveled widely in the South in the 1850s.

The Cotton Kingdom (1861)
FREDERICK LAW OLMSTED

The whole number of slaveholders of this large class in all the Slave States is, according to De Bow's Compendium of the Census, 7,929, among which are all the great sugar, rice, and tobacco-planters. Less than seven thousand, certainly, are cotton-planters.

A large majority of these live, when they live on their plantations at all, in districts, almost the only white population of which consists of owners and overseers of the same class of plantations with their own. The nearest other whites will be some sand-hill vagabonds, generally miles away, between whom and these planters, intercourse is neither intimate nor friendly.

It is hardly worth while to build much of a bridge for the occasional use of two families, even if they are rich. It is less worth while to go to much pains in making six miles of good road for the use of these families. . . . It is not necessary to multiply illustrations like these. In short, then, if all the wealth

Source: Frederick Law Olmsted, *The Slave States* (New York: Capricorn Books, 1959), pp. 249–250.

produced in a certain district is concentrated in the hands of a few men living remote from each other, it may possibly bring to the district comfortable houses, good servants, fine wines, food, and furniture, tutors, and governesses, horses and carriages, for these few men, but it will not bring thither good roads and bridges, it will not bring thither such means of education and of civilized comfort as are to be drawn from libraries, churches, museums, gardens, theatres, and assembly rooms; it will not bring thither local newspapers, telegraphs, and so on. . . . There is, in fact, a vast range of advantages which our civilization has made so common to us that they are hardly thought of, of which the people of the South are destitute. They chiefly come from or connect with acts of co-operation, or exchanges of service; they are therefore possessed only in communities, and in communities where a large proportion of the people have profitable employment. They grow, in fact, out of employments in which the people of the community are associated, or which they constantly give to and receive from one another, with profit. The slaves of the South, though often living in communities upon plantations, fail to give or receive these advantages because the profits of their labour are not distributed to them; the whites, from not engaging in profitable employment. The whites are not engaged in profitable employment, because the want of the advantages of capital in the application of their labour, independently of the already rich, renders the prospective result of their labour so small that it is inoperative in most, as a motive for exerting themselves further than is necessary to procure the bare means of a rude subsistence; also because common labour is so poorly rewarded in the case of the slaves as to assume in their minds, as it must in the minds of the slaves themselves, a hateful aspect.

5   Numerous eyewitnesses, including journalists and those serving in the Union and Confederate forces, recorded the struggles on the battle-field of Gettysburg. Franklin Haskell, an officer in the Army of the Potomac, wrote one such account several weeks after the battle. What does this selection reveal about the factors determining the outcome of these battles? Could Gettysburg have easily turned out differently?

An Account of the Battle of Gettysburg (1863)
FRANKLIN A. HASKELL

Now came the dreadful battle picture, of which we for a time could be but spectators. Upon the front and right flank of [Union general] Sickles

Source: Harry A. Hagen and S. Lewis B. Speare, *A History of the Class of 1854 in Dartmouth College* (Boston: Alfred Mudge and Son, 1898).

came sweeping the infantry of [Confederate generals] Longstreet and Hill. Hitherto there had been skirmishing and artillery practice—now the battle begins; for amid the heavier smokes and longer tongues of flame of the batteries, now began to appear the countless flashes, and the long, fiery sheets of the muskets, and the rattle of the volleys mingled with the thunder of the guns. We see the long gray lines come sweeping down upon Sickles' front, and mix with the battle smoke; now the same colors emerge from the bushes and orchards upon his right, and envelop his flank in the confusion of the conflict. Oh, the din and the roar, and these thirty thousand rebel wolf-cries! What a hell is there down that valley!

These ten or twelve thousand men of the Third Corps fight well, but it soon becomes apparent that they must be swept from the field, or perish there where they are doing so well, so thick and overwhelming a storm of rebel fire involves them. But these men, such as ever escape, must come from that conflict as best they can. To move down and support them there with other troops is out of the question, for this would be to do as Sickles did, to relinquish a good position, and advance to a bad one. There is no other alternative,—the Third Corps must fight itself out of its position of destruction! Why was it ever put there?

In the meantime some other dispositions must be made to meet the enemy, in the event that Sickles is overpowered. With this corps out of the way, the enemy would be in a position to advance upon the line of the Second Corps, not in a line parallel with its front, but they would come obliquely from the left. To meet this contingency the left of the Second Division of the Second Corps is thrown back slightly, and two regiments . . . are advanced down to the Emmitsburg road, to a favorable position nearer us than the fight has yet come, and some new batteries from the artillery reserve are posted upon the crest near the left of the Second Corps. This was all General Gibbon could do. Other dispositions were made, or were now being made, upon the field, which I shall mention presently.

The enemy is still giving Sickles fierce battle,—or rather the Third Corps, for Sickles has been borne from the field minus one of his legs, and General Birney now commands,—and we of the Second Corps, a thousand yards away, with our guns and men, are, and must be, idle spectators of the fight. The rebel, as anticipated, tries to gain the left of the Third Corps, and for this purpose is now moving into the woods at the west of Round Top. We knew what he would find there. No sooner had the enemy got a considerable force into the woods . . . than the roar of the conflict was heard there also. The Fifth Corps and the First Division of the Second were there at the right time, and promptly engaged him; and then, too, the battle soon became general and obstinate.

Now the roar of battle has become twice the volume that it was before, and it's [*sic*] rage extends over more than twice the space. The Third Corps has been pressed back considerably, and the wounded are streaming to the rear by hundreds, but still the battle there goes on, with no considerable abatement on our part. . . .

. . . [F]resh bodies of the rebels continued to advance out of the woods to the front of the position of the Third Corps, and to swell the numbers of the assailants of this already hard pressed command. The men there begin to show signs of exhaustion,—their ammunition must be nearly expended,—they have now been fighting more than an hour, and against greatly superior numbers. . . .

. . . The Third Corps is being overpowered—here and there its lines begin to break,—the men begin to pour back to the rear in confusion,—the enemy are close upon them and among them,—organization is lost, to a great degree,—guns and caissons are abandoned and in the hands of the enemy,—the Third Corps, after a heroic, but unfortunate fight, is being literally swept from the field. That corps gone, what is there between the Second Corps and those yelling masses of the enemy? Do you not think that by this time we began to feel a personal interest in this fight? We did, indeed. . . .

. . . Five or six hundred yards away the Third Corps was making its last opposition; and the enemy was hotly pressing his advantage there, and throwing in fresh troops whose line extended still more along our front, when Generals Hancock and Gibbon rode along the lines of their troops; and at once cheer after cheer—not rebel mongrel cries, but genuine cheers—rang out along the line, above the roar of battle, for "Hancock" and "Gibbon," and our "Generals." These were good. Had you heard their voices, you would have known these men would fight.

Just at this time we saw another thing that made us glad: we looked to our rear, and there, and all up the hillside, which was the rear of the Third Corps before it went forward, were rapidly advancing large bodies of men from the extreme right of our line of battle, coming to the support of the part now so hotly pressed. There was the whole Twelfth Corps, with the exception of about one brigade . . . and some other brigades from the same corps; and some of them were moving at the double quick. They formed lines of battle at the foot of the hill by the Taneytown road, and when the broken fragments of the Third Corps were swarming by them towards the rear, without haltering or wavering they came swiftly up, and with glorious old cheers, under fire, took their places on the crest in line of battle to the left of the Second Corps. Now Sickles' blunder is repaired. Now, rebel chief, hurl forward your howling lines and columns! Yell out your loudest and your last, for many of your host will never yell, or wave the spurious flag again!

In this letter, Grant reported to the secretary of war the completion of his military assignment. What does Grant reveal about the reasons for the war's outcome?

General Ulysses S. Grant to Edwin M. Stanton (1865)

Washington D.C.
June 20th 1865

Hon. E. M. Stanton
Sec. of War,

Sir:

I have the honor, very respectfully, to submit the following report of operations of the Armies of the United States, from the 9th of March 1864, the date when the command was entrusted to me, to present date. Accompanying this will also be found all reports of commanders, subordinate to me, received at these Head Quarters. To these latter I refer you for all minor details of operations and battles.

From early in the War I had been impressed with the idea that active, and continuous operations of all the troops that could be brought into the field, regardless of season and weather, were necessary to a speedy termination of the gigantic rebellion raging in the land. The resources of the enemy, and his numerical strength, was far inferior to ours. But as an ofset [*sic*] to this we had a vast territory, with a population hostile to the government, to garrison, and long lines of river and rail-road communication, tr[thr]ough territory equally hostile, to protect to secure in order that the more active Armies might be supplied.—Whilst Eastern and Western Armies were fighting independent battles, working together like a balky team where no two ever pulled together, giving Summers and Winters to almost entire inactivity, thus enabling the enemy to use to great advantage his his interior lines of communication for transporting portion of his Armies from one theatre of War to an other, and to furlough large numbers of the Armyies during these seasons of inactivity to go to their home and do the work of producing for the suport of these Armies, it was a question whether our numerical strength was not more than balanced by these [dis]advantages.

My opinion was firmly fixed long before the honor of commanding all our Armies had been confered on me that no peace could be had that would be stable, or conducive to the happiness of North or South, until the Military power of the rebellion was entirely broken. Believing us to be one people,

Source: John Y. Simon, ed., *The Papers of Ulysses S. Grant* (Carbondale: Southern Illinois University Press, 1988), XV: pp. 164–166.

one blood and with identical interests, I do and have felt the same interest in the ~~welfa~~ ultimate welfare of the South as of the North. The guilty, no matter what their offence or to what section they belong, should be punished according to their guilt. The leaders in this rebellion against the Government have been guilty of the most heinous offence known to our laws. Let them reap the reward of their offence.

Here then is the basis of all plans formed at the onset. ~~1st~~ First to use the greatest number of troops practicable against the Armed force of the enemy. To prevent that enemy from using the same force, at different seasons, against first one Army and then another, and to prevent the possibility of repose for refitting and producing the necessary supplies for carrying on resistance. Second; to hammer continuously at the Armed force of the enemy, and his resources, until by mere attricion [*sic*], if in no other way, there should be nothing left to him but an equal submission with the loyal section of our common country to the universal law of the land. These views have been kept constantly before me and orders given and campaigns made to carry them out. How well it has been done it is for the public, who have to mourn the loss of friends ~~who have~~ fallen in the execution, and to pay the ~~expense~~ pecuniary cost of all this, to say. All I can say is the work has been done conscienciously and to the best of my ability. It has been done in what I concieved to be the interest of the whole country, South and North. . . .

Blacks and the Civil War

During the Civil War nearly 180,000 blacks served in the Union army and navy. An estimated 500,000 to 700,000 slaves found refuge with Union forces. As you read the following sources, note what they reveal about the role blacks played in the defeat of the Confederacy.

7   Affidavit of a Tennessee Freedman (1865)

My name is Makey Woods. I am 43 years old. I have lived with Mr. William Woods, of Hardaman County, Tennessee for about twenty years. I was his slave, about three years ago when the Union Army was in possession of Bolivar Tenn, and when nearly all the Black people were leaving their Masters and going to the Union Army Mr. Woods told me and such others as would stay with him that he would give us *one fourth* of the crop that we would raise while we stayed with him that he would clothe us and feed us and pay our doctor's bills. Since which time Mr. Wood has given *me* nothing

Source: Paul D. Escott and David R. Goldfield, eds., *Major Problems in the History of the American South* (Lexington, Mass.: D. C. Heath and Co., 1990), I: p. 525.

but my clothing: about that time and soon after he made this statement to us he ran off down South into the Rebel lines *fourteen of his slaves* among whom were three of my children, Mr. Woods is now living in Memphis and refus to perform his contract or fulfil his promises to me in any respect, and when I spoke to him a few days ago about carrying out his contract he told me that he was sorry he made such a bargain with us:

There has been raised on Mr. Woods' place this year 48 bales of Cotton most of which Mr. Wood has taken to Memphis last year there were 26 bales raised which Mr. Wood sold I do not know exactly how many black people on Mr. Woods' place at present. Mr. Woods told us that any little patches we might cultivate at odd hours he would not take into the count but would let us have it besides the ¼ of the regular crop.

 ### 8 Reverend Garrison Frazier on the Aspirations of His Fellow Blacks (1865)

Minutes of an interview between the colored ministers and church officers at Savannah with the Secretary of War and Major-General Sherman.

On the evening of Thursday, the 12th day of January, 1865, [twenty] persons of African descent met, by appointment, to hold an interview with Edwin M. Stanton, Secretary of War, and Major-General Sherman, to have a conference upon matters relating to the Freedmen of the State of Georgia. . . .

Garrison Frazier, being chosen by the persons present to express their common sentiments upon the matters of inquiry, makes answers to inquiries as follows:—

First. State what your understanding is in regard to the Acts of Congress, and President's [*sic*] Lincoln's Proclamation, touching the condition of the colored people in the rebel States.

Answer. So far as I understand President Lincoln's Proclamation to the rebellious States, it is, th[at] if they would lay down their arms and submit to the laws of the United States before the 1st of January, 1863, all should be well, but if they did not, then all the slaves in the rebel States should be free, henceforth and forever; that is what I understood.

Second. State what you understand by slavery, and the freedom that was to be given by the President's Proclamation.

Answer. Slavery is receiving by irresistible power the work of another man, and not by his consent. The freedom, as I understand it, promised by the Proclamation, is taking us from under the yoke of bondage, and placing

Source: Paul D. Escott and David R. Goldfield, eds., *Major Problems in the History of the American South* (Lexington, Mass.: D. C. Heath and Co., 1990), I: pp. 525–527.

us where we could reap the fruit of our own labor, and take care of ourselves, and assist the Government in maintaining our freedom.

Third. State in what manner you think you can take care of yourselves, and how you can best assist the Government in maintaining your freedom.

Answer. The way we can best take care of ourselves is to have land, and turn in and till it by our labor—that is, by the labor of the women, and children, and old men—and we can soon maintain ourselves, and have something to spare; and to assist the Government, the young men should enlist in the service of the Government, and serve in such manner as they may be wanted—(the rebels told us that they piled them up, and made batteries of them, and sold them to Cuba; but we don't believe that.) We want to be placed on land until we are able to buy it, and make it our own. . . .

Sixth. State what is the feeling of the black population of the South towards the Government of the United States; what is the understanding in respect to the present war, its causes and object, and their disposition to aid either side; state fully your views.

Answer. I think you will find there is thousands that are willing to make any sacrifice to assist the Government of the United States, while there is also many that are not willing to take up arms. I do not suppose there is a dozen men that is opposed to the Government. I understand, as to the war, that the South is the aggressor. President Lincoln was elected President by a majority of the United States, which guaranteed him the right of holding the office, and exercising that right over the whole United States. The South, without knowing what he would do, rebelled. The war was commenced by the rebels before he came into office. The object of the war was not, at first, to give the slaves their freedom, but the sole object of the war was, at first, to bring the rebellious States back into the Union, and their loyalty to the laws of the United States. Afterwards, knowing the value that was set on the slaves by the rebels, the President thought that his Proclamation would stimulate them to lay down their arms, reduce them to obedience, and help to bring back the rebel States; and their not doing so has now made the freedom of the slaves a part of the war. It is my opinion that there is not a man in this city that could be started to help the rebels one inch, for that would be suicide. There was two black men left with the rebels, because they had taken an active part for the rebels, and thought something might befall them if they staid behind, but there is not another man. If the prayers that have gone up for the Union army could be read out, you would not get through them these two weeks.

Seventh. State whether the sentiments you now express are those only of the colored people in the city, or do they extend to the colored population through the country, and what are your means of knowing the sentiments of those living in the country.

Answer. I think the sentiments are the same among the colored people of the State. My opinion is formed by personal communication in the course of my ministry, and also from the thousands that followed the Union army, leaving their homes and undergoing suffering. I did not think there would be so many; the number surpassed my expectation.

Eighth. If the rebel leaders were to arm the slaves, what would be its effect?

Answer. I think they would fight as long as they were before the bayonet, and just as soon as they could get away they would desert, in my opinion.

Ninth. What, in your opinion, is the feeling of the colored people about enlisting and serving as soldiers of the United States, and what kind of military service do they prefer?

Answer. A large number have gone as soldiers to Port Royal to be drilled and put in the service, and I think there is thousands of the young men that will enlist; there is something about them that, perhaps, is wrong; they have suffered so long from the rebels, that they want to meet and have a chance with them in the field.

Morale on the Home Front

Morale is a big factor in the ability of people to fight. What do these sources reveal about the problems on each side that may have affected morale?

9, 10   In July 1863, working-class Irish residents of New York City took to the streets to protest the draft. Over the course of five days, they destroyed draft offices, police stations, stores, homes, and the offices of Republican Horace Greeley's *Tribune* newspaper. Fueled by racial resentment and a long history of labor competition with poor blacks, the rioters also turned their wrath on the city's African-American population, beating and murdering scores of people and setting fire to an orphanage for black children. By the time the riots were over, 119 people lay dead and ten thousand federal troops occupied the city. The following sources reveal some of the riot's effects and the fate of some of its victims.

Destruction of the Coloured Orphan Asylum (1863)

THE RIOTS IN NEW YORK : DESTRUCTION OF THE COLOURED ORPHAN ASYLUM.

The New York Public Library/Art Resource, NY

Merchants Report on the Impact of the New York Riots (1863)
REPORT OF THE SECRETARY

Driven by the fear of death at the hands of the mob, who the week previous had, as you remember, brutally murdered, by hanging on trees and lamp posts several of their number, and cruelly beaten and robbed many others, burning and sacking their houses and driving nearly all from the streets, alleys and docks upon which they had previously obtained an honest though humble living—these people had been forced to take refuge on Blackwell's Island, at Police Stations, on the outskirts of the city, in the swamps and woods back of Bergen, New Jersey, at Weeksville and in the barns and out-houses of the farmers of Long Island and Morrissania. At these places were scattered some 5,000 homeless and helpless men, women, and children. . . .

Source: Report of the Committee of Merchants for the Relief of Colored People, Suffering from the Late Riots in the City of New York (New York, 1863), pp. 7, 14–15.

INCIDENTS OF THE RIOT

ABRAHAM FRANKLIN.

This young man who was murdered by the mob on the corner of Twenty-seventh St., and Seventh avenue, was a quiet, inoffensive man, 23 years of age, of unexceptionable character, and a member of Zion African Church in this city. Although a cripple, he earned a living for himself and his mother by serving a gentleman in the capacity of coachman. A short time previous to the assault upon his person, he called upon his mother to see if anything could be done by him for her safety. The old lady, who is noted for her piety and her Christian deportment, said she considered herself perfectly safe; but if her time to die had come, she was ready to die. Her son then knelt down by her side, and implored the protection of Heaven in behalf of his mother. The old lady was affected to tears, and said to our informant that it seemed to her that good angels were present in the room. Scarcely had the supplicant risen from his knees, when the mob broke down the door, seized him, beat him over the head and face with fists and clubs, and then hanged him in the presence of his mother.

While they were thus engaged, the military came and drove them away, cutting down the body of Franklin, who raised his arm once slightly and gave a few signs of life.

The military then moved on to quell other riots, when the mob returned and again suspended the now probably lifeless body of Franklin, cutting out pieces of flesh and otherwise mutilating it.

AUGUSTUS STUART.

Died at the Hospital, Blackwell's Island July 22d, from the effects of a blow received at the hands of the mob, within one block and a half of the State Arsenal, corner 7th Avenue and 35th street, on Wednesday evening, July 15th. He had been badly beaten previously by a band of rioters and was frightened and insane from the effects of the blows which he had received. He was running towards the Arsenal for safety when he was overtaken by the mob from whom he received his death blow.

Mrs. Stuart, his wife, says that some of the rioters declared that at the second attack upon him he had fired a pistol at his pursuers; but she says that if he did, he must have obtained the weapon from some friend after he had left home, a few minutes before, for he had no weapon then, nor was he ever known to have had one. He was a member of the church.

PETER HEUSTON.

Peter Heuston, sixty-three years of age, a Mohawk Indian, with dark complexion and straight black hair, who has for several years been a resident of this city, at the corner of Rosevelt and Oak streets, and who has obtained a livelihood as a laborer, proved a victim to the late riots.

His wife died about three weeks before the riots, leaving with her husband an only child, a little girl named Lavinia, aged eight years, whom the Merchants' Committee have undertaken to adopt with a view of affording her a guardianship and an education. Hueston served with the New York Volunteers in the Mexican War, and has always been loyal to our government. He was brutally attacked on the 13th of July by a gang of ruffians who evidently thought him to be of the African race because of his dark complexion. He died within four days at Bellevue Hospital from his injuries.

At the end of the Mexican War Heuston received a land warrant from the government, which enabled him to settle on a tract of land at the West, where be lived but a short time previous to his coming to this city.

JEREMIAH ROBINSON.

Mrs. Nancy Robinson, widow of the above, killed in Madison near Catherine street, says that her husband in order to escape dressed himself up in some of her clothes, and in company with herself and one other woman left their residence and went towards one of the Brooklyn Ferries.

Robinson wore a hood, which failed to hide his beard. Some boys seeing his beard, lifted up the skirts of his dress, which exposed his heavy boots. Immediately the mob set upon him and the atrocities they perpetrated upon him are so indecent, they are unfit for publication. They finally killed him and threw his body into the river.

His wife and her companion ran up Madison street and escaped across the Grand street Ferry to Brooklyn.

11 By 1863, women and children in the South had streamed into cities, swelling the Confederacy's urban population. At the same time, a Union naval blockade and hoarding had helped to create shortages of basic necessities. In the face of skyrocketing inflation, bread or food riots, often carried out by women, became a common occurrence in the South. The biggest such riot occurred in April 1863 in Richmond, Virginia.

Southern Women Feeling the Effects of Rebellion and Creating Bread Riots (1863)

Boston Athenaeum. Reprinted in Leslie's Illustrated Newspaper, May 23, 1863.

Excerpt from Diary of Margaret Junkin Preston (1862)

April 3d, 1862: . . .

Darkness seems gathering over the Southern land; disaster follows disaster; where is it all to end? My very soul is sick of carnage. I loathe the word—*War.* It is destroying and paralyzing all before it. Our schools are closed—all the able-bodied men gone—stores shut up, or only here and there one open; goods not to be bought, or so exorbitant that we are obliged to do without. I actually dressed my baby all winter in calico dresses made out of the lining of an old dressing-gown; and G. in clothes concocted out of old castaways. As to myself, I rigidly abstained from getting a single article of dress in the entire past year, except shoes and stockings. Calico is not to be had; a few pieces had been offered at 40 cents per yard. Coarse, unbleached cottons are very occasionally to be met with, and are caught up eagerly at 40 cents per yard. Such material as we used to give ninepence for (common blue twill) is a bargain now at 40 cents, and then of a very inferior quality. Soda, if to be had at all, is 75 cents per lb. Coffee is not to be bought. We have some on hand, and for eight months have drunk a poor mixture, half wheat, half coffee. Many persons have nothing but wheat or rye.

These are some of the *very trifling* effects of this horrid and senseless war. Just now I am bound down under the apprehension of having my husband again enter the service; and if he goes, he says he will not return until the war closes, if indeed he come back alive. May God's providence interpose to prevent his going! His presence is surely needed at home; his hands are taken away by the militia draught, and he has almost despaired of having his farms cultivated this year. His overseer is draughted, and will have to go, unless the plea of sickness will avail to release him, as he has been seriously unwell. The [Virginia Military] Institute is full, two hundred and fifty cadets being in it; but they may disperse at any time, so uncertain is the tenure of everything now. The College [Washington College] has five students; boys too young to enter the army.

Source: Elizabeth Preston Allan, *The Life and Letters of Margaret Junkin Preston,* (Boston: Houghton, Mifflin, 1903), pp. 134–135.

"Kate," whose first name only is known, wrote a letter to a friend in Baltimore after Robert E. Lee's army entered Frederick, Maryland.

"Kate," A Letter to a Friend (1862)

I wish, my dearest Minnie, you could have witnessed the transit of the Rebel army through our streets [of Frederick, Maryland] . . . Their coming was unheralded by any pomp and pageant whatever . . . Was this body of men, moving . . . along with no order . . . no two dresses alike, their officers hardly distinguishable from the privates—were these, I asked myself in amazement, were these dirty, lank, ugly specimens of humanity, with shocks of hair sticking through the holes in their hats, and the dust thick on their dirty faces, the men that had coped and encountered successfully and driven back again and again our splendid legions . . . ? I must confess, Minnie, that I felt humiliated at the thought that this horde of ragamuffins could set our grand army of the Union at defiance. . . .

Source: From *The Civil War and Reconstruction: An Eyewitness History*, edited by Joe Kirchberger.

CONCLUSION

The debate about the Civil War's outcome illustrates that historians are spectators in numerous arenas. In the Civil War, military leaders and events are in one amphitheater, political developments are in another, and economic and social developments are in still others. Of course, one venue is never entirely separate from another. Events on the battlefield affected in numerous ways politics and society in the North and South and vice versa. The challenge for historians is to demonstrate how they interacted.

The Civil War also illustrates the numerous ways in which historians explore the past. In searching for historical explanations, some historians look in several arenas. Others seek to understand everything about only one. Some historians conclude that leaders hold the key to understanding the past. Others insist that understanding the rank-and-file is more important. Some historians see large forces that give to events a certain inevitability. Others take a seat in the stands to witness all the unpredictable decisions and actions that took place.

Finally, the debate about the causes of the Civil War's outcome is also a reminder that the question of causation is at the heart of historical inquiry. If the Civil War's outcome was important in deciding the nation's future, then determining why the war turned out as it did is obviously crucial to our understanding of the nation's past. Yet to understand history, we must not only know the influence of past events on later generations, but appreciate how *interpretations* of those events may also influence those who come later. In Chapter 13, we shall turn to an especially powerful example of the power of historical interpretation.

FURTHER READING

Gabor S. Boritt, ed., *Why the Confederacy Lost* (New York: Oxford University Press, 1992).

David Donald, ed., *Why the North Won the Civil War* (Baton Rouge: Louisiana State University Press, 1960).

Doris Kearns Goodwin, *Team of Rivals: The Political Genius of Abraham Lincoln* (New York: Simon & Schuster, 2005).

Joseph T. Glatthaar, *Partners in Command: The Relationship Between Leaders in the Civil War* (New York: Free Press, 1994).

James M. McPherson, *The Negro's Civil War* (New York: Ballantine Books, 1991).

Harold E. Straubing, ed., *Civil War Eyewitness Reports* (Hamden, Conn.: Archon Books, 1985).

NOTES

1. James Ford Rhodes, *History of the Civil War 1861–1865* (New York: Frederick Ungar, 1961), p. 238.
2. Ibid., p. 240.
3. Bruce Catton, *Gettysburg: The Final Fury* (Garden City, N.Y.: Doubleday, 1974), p. 88.
4. Allan Nevins, *Ordeal of Union* (New York: Macmillan, 1971), IV: p. 111.
5. Lee's last general order, quoted in Joe H. Kirchberger, *The Civil War and Reconstruction: An Eyewitness History* (New York: Facts on File, 1991), p. 264.

Chapter
13

The Importance of Historical Interpretation: The Meaning of Reconstruction

This chapter provides two secondary sources and several primary sources on the highly controversial subject of Reconstruction.

Secondary Sources

1. "Seeds of Failure in Radical Race Policy" (1966), C. VANN WOODWARD
2. America's Reconstruction (1995), ERIC FONER

Primary Sources

3. Colored Rule in a Reconstructed (?) State (1874)
4. The Ignorant Vote—Honors Are Easy (1876)
5. Black Response to a South Carolina White Taxpayers' Convention Appeal to Congress (1874)
6. Statement of Colored People's Convention in Charleston, South Carolina (1865)
7. Testimony of Abram Colby (1872)
8. Testimony of Emanuel Fortune (1872)
9. Testimony of Henry M. Turner (1872)
10. A Former Slave Recalls Her Post-Emancipation Struggle (1937)

"I hope there will be . . . no bloody work after the war is over," declared Abraham Lincoln in April 1865, five days after Appomattox and hours before his assassination.[1] For the former Confederates whom Lincoln had in mind, there was no bloodshed; they were spared execution. However, there was much "bloody work" during Reconstruction, most of it visited upon the freedmen as Northerners and Southerners—black and white—struggled over the fate of the South and the place of African Americans in American society. And the "bloody work" did not end with the collapse of the last Reconstruction governments in 1877. The ground continued to be stained for a long time by those who challenged African Americans' inferior position in American society.

At the same time, the passions ignited by Reconstruction have produced another kind of "bloody work" in historians' interpretations of Reconstruction. Few areas of American history have engendered more controversy and conflict than this brief period after the Civil War. And few historical periods have given rise to such conflicting lessons. For some students, Reconstruction was a tragic period of carpetbag and black rule that justified the South's redemption at the hands of conservative, white Democrats. For others, it proves just the opposite: the need for radical government action to achieve social justice. For still others, it demonstrates the depth of racism in American society. The battles over Reconstruction's meaning have been so heated that one historian declared the entire field "devastated by passion and belief." Another went so far as to call Reconstruction history itself a "dark and bloody ground."[2]

If Reconstruction is an example of the past's power to shape the future, it also clearly shows the power of historical interpretation. For generations after Reconstruction, African Americans' second-class citizenship was maintained by law and the force of violence, and for much of that time, the historical justification for that position was found in the alleged horrors of Reconstruction. As historian Eric Foner put it, an image of these horrors "did much to freeze the mind of the white South in unalterable opposition to outside pressures for social change and to any thought of . . . eliminating segregation, or restoring the suffrage to disenfranchised blacks."[3] Thus, to this historian, the idea of Reconstruction was responsible for much of the South's later attitudes toward African Americans. Historians see other consequences in Reconstruction as well. In this chapter, therefore, we cross Reconstruction's "bloody ground" by examining its lessons and meaning today.

SETTING

It is an understatement to say that today's interpretations of Reconstruction differ from those eighty or one hundred years ago. Historians in the last two generations have effectively dismantled older views of this era and recon-structed a history shorn of the white supremacist assumptions that underlay older views. Thus students today have a very different understanding, com-pared to their counterparts even in the mid-twentieth century, of the often independent role of freedmen and freedwomen in this era, of the govern-ments established under Congressional Reconstruction, and of Reconstruc-tion's accomplishments and legacies. The long battle over Reconstruction history, like those fought over other parts of our past, is ongoing. Especially in the case of Reconstruction, however, this battle reveals much about the role that racism has played in the nation's past and its role for a long time in the re-telling of it.

For several generations after the turn of the century, most scholarly accounts of Reconstruction reflected a white Southern point of view. Led by William A. Dunning of Columbia University, most historians praised the Democratic governments established under Andrew Johnson's reconstruction plan and condemned the radicals in Congress and their "carpetbag" governments. Like the Democratic "Redeemers" who overthrew the Southern Republican govern-ments in the 1870s, Dunning historians pictured the "black Republican" gov-ernments as a disgraceful stew of corruption, ignorance, and mismanagement. The foundation of this view was the assumption of white racial superiority. In their accounts African Americans were helpless, ignorant, disrespectful, or menacing. Not only did they have a small role in influencing events, but they were unprepared for a competitive market economy and unfit for a republican political system. The fact that they participated at all in the Republican govern-ments was, in the words of one historian, to be "shuddered at."[4] The lesson of Reconstruction was clear. It had given too much freedom to the freedmen, and when it was over blacks had found their proper place in American society.

In the early twentieth century there were a few dissenters to the Dunning view, most notably the black historian W. E. B. Du Bois. His *Black Reconstruc-tion in America* (1935) portrayed Reconstruction as a laudable attempt to cre-ate a more democratic and just society. Du Bois lambasted historians whose accounts ignored the role of former slaves in Reconstruction. Historians' racial bias, he said, clouded their objectivity. "I stand . . . literally aghast at what American historians have done to this field," declared Du Bois, who went on to claim that "one fact and one fact alone explains the attitude of most recent writers toward Reconstruction; they cannot conceive Negroes as men."[5] Few historians paid much attention to Du Bois's work, and the Dunning School remained historical orthodoxy for decades.

By the 1940s, however, a handful of historians began to chip away at its edifice. In 1940, for instance, Howard K. Beale called upon his colleagues to discard the notion that "their race must bar Negroes from social and eco-nomic equality."[6] Meanwhile, black historian John Hope Franklin questioned the "facts" upon which Dunning historians had based their conclusions. Are these facts drawn, he asked, from "melodramatic" accounts of "wild-eyed conspirators" and "masses of barbarous freedmen"?[7] Still, the Dunning School did not come crashing down until the 1950s and 1960s. Then, as one historian put it, "Reconstruction history underwent its own reconstruction."[8]

The catalyst was changing racial attitudes and the growth of the civil rights movement. By the time such revisionist historians as Kenneth M. Stampp, Eric L. McKitrick, James McPherson, and Willie Lee Rose were finished, much of the Reconstruction story had been turned on its head. Later revisionists, in particular, demonstrated that the iniquity of "carpetbag rule" was a myth, especially when judged against political corruption elsewhere in the nation. They saw Radical Republicans as heroic champions of political and social change for the South. They contended that the great tragedy of Reconstruction was the Redeemers' assumption of power. The lesson was again clear. Reconstruction had been radical, but that had been a good thing. Those who were attempting to bring about a "second" Reconstruction with the civil rights movement could look to the first Reconstruction for inspiration.

When the demise of "Jim Crow" and the enfranchisement of blacks during the "second Reconstruction" of the 1960s failed to end the problems of racism and black poverty, some historians began again to revise their views about the first Reconstruction. By the 1970s, such postrevisionist historians as C. Vann Woodward, William Gillette, and Leon Litwack questioned just how radical Reconstruction had been. In the view of these postrevisionists, Reconstruction was limited by pervasive racism, by the conservativism of Republican leaders, and by the failure to distribute land to blacks. In other words, postrevisionists disagreed with both the Dunning and revisionist historians, who had at least agreed that Reconstruction had brought radical change. They questioned whether Reconstruction had wrought any lasting change at all. Rather than being too radical, it had actually been too conservative. Blacks had failed to achieve equality because the government had done too little and had failed to carry through on the promise of civil rights. Thus the postrevisionist interpretation taught an important lesson about the relationship between government action and social change.

In our own time, the historical reconstruction of Reconstruction is not finished. In the twenty-first century, such historians as Eric Foner and Michael Fitzgerald have placed the experience of former slaves rather than national political leaders and federal policy at the center of Reconstruction history. Others, such as Laura Edwards and Nina Silber, have done much the same for women during the period, placing issues relating to gender in the center of the Reconstruction story. These historians have shown that African Americans were not just passive objects manipulated by whites. They also demonstrated the roles that women families, churches, political organizations, and other black institutions played in the quest for independence and equal citizenship. At the same time the social, economic, and political experiences of African Americans have revealed dramatic changes in the period. Once again, historians have begun to see some revolutionary aspects to Reconstruction.

INVESTIGATION

Historians need to understand how interpretations of Reconstruction reflect changing circumstances. They also must judge the validity of these interpretations and the lessons they teach. Your primary challenge, therefore, is to offer an explanation for the way Reconstruction turned out and a conclusion about its lessons for us. To do that, you must carefully evaluate two secondary selections' explanations for the outcome of Reconstruction. Both essays focus on the Republican program, but their analyses may yield different lessons about the Reconstruction experience. Primary sources relating to political developments during the period will help you evaluate these essays and reach conclusions about Reconstruction's lessons. Before you begin, read your textbook's discussion of this period, carefully noting its interpretation regarding Reconstruction's accomplishments and failures. Your analysis should address the following questions:

1. **What explanations do Sources 1 and 2 offer for the outcome of Reconstruction?** In what ways were Republican policies flawed?

2. **What do the two historians see as the most important forces affecting Republican policy?** What role do they assign to racism, as opposed to class or ideological divisions, in explaining the outcome of Reconstruction?

3. **What do the sources reveal about the problems involved in reconstructing the South?** What most important changes needed to occur for Reconstruction to have turned out differently? Is the explanation for the fate of Reconstruction to be found in the South or in the North?

4. **What were the most important changes that came about as a result of Reconstruction?** In the end, was Reconstruction too radical or too conservative?

SECONDARY SOURCES

1   In this analysis of the Republican's Reconstruction policy at the national level, historian C. Vann Woodward offers an explanation for the failure of Reconstruction. Who or what does Woodward blame? Note his view about the Republicans' motives and his conclusions about Reconstruction's legacy.

Source: From *New Frontiers of the American Reconstruction* by Harold M. Human, ed., 1966, pp. 125–128, 130, 131–132, 133–134, 135, 136, 139–141, 143, 147. Copyright © 1966 by the Board of Trustees of the University of Illinois. Used with permission of the University of Illinois Press.

"Seeds of Failure in Radical Race Policy" (1966)
C. VANN WOODWARD

The Republican leaders were quite aware in 1865 that the issue of Negro status and rights was closely connected with the two other great issues of Reconstruction—who should reconstruct the South and who should govern the country. But while they were agreed on the two latter issues, they were not agreed on the first. They were increasingly conscious that in order to reconstruct the South along the lines they planned they would require the support and the votes of the freedmen. And it was apparent to some that once the reconstructed states were restored to the Union the Republicans would need the votes of the freedmen to retain control over the national government. While they could agree on this much, they were far from agreeing on the status, the rights, the equality, or the future of the Negro.

The fact was that the constituency on which the Republican congressmen relied in the North lived in a race-conscious, segregated society devoted to the doctrine of white supremacy and Negro inferiority. "In virtually every phase of existence," writes Leon Litwack with regard to the North in 1860, "Negroes found themselves systematically separated from whites. They were either excluded from railway cars, omnibuses, stagecoaches, and steamboats or assigned to special 'Jim Crow' sections; they sat, when permitted, in secluded and remote corners of theatres and lecture halls; they could not enter most hotels, restaurants, and resorts, except as servants; they prayed in 'Negro pews' in the white churches. . . . Moreover, they were often educated in segregated schools, punished in segregated prisons, nursed in segregated hospitals, and buried in segregated cemeteries." Ninety-three per cent of the 225,000 northern Negroes in 1860 lived in states that denied them the ballot, and 7 per cent lived in the five New England states that permitted them to vote. Ohio and New York had discriminatory qualifications that practically eliminated Negro voting. In many northern states discriminatory laws excluded Negroes from interracial marriage, from militia service, from the jury box, and from the witness stand when whites were involved. Ohio denied them poor relief, and most states of the old Northwest had laws carrying penalties against Negroes settling in those states. Everywhere in the free states the Negro met with barriers to job opportunities, and in most places he encountered severe limitations to the protection of his life, liberty, and property.

· One political consequence of these racial attitudes was that the major parties vied with each other in their professions of devotion to the dogma of white supremacy. Republicans were especially sensitive on the point because of their antislavery associations. Many of them, like Senator Lyman Trumbull of Illinois, the close friend of Lincoln, found no difficulty in reconciling antislavery with anti-Negro views. "We, the Republican party," said Senator Trumbull in 1858, "are the white man's party. We are for free white men, and for making white labor respectable and honorable, which it can never be when negro slave labor is brought into competition with it." Horace Greeley the following year regretted that it was "the controlling idea" of some of his fellow Republicans "to prove themselves 'the white man's party,' or else all the mean, low, ignorant, drunken, brutish whites will go against them from horror of 'negro equality.'" Greeley called such people "the one-horse politicians," but he could hardly apply that name to Lyman Trumbull, nor for that matter to William H. Seward, who in 1860 described the American Negro as "a foreign and feeble element like the Indians, incapable of assimilation"; nor to Senator Henry Wilson of Massachusetts, who firmly disavowed any belief "in the mental or the intellectual equality of the African race with this proud and domineering white race of ours." Trumbull, Seward, and Wilson were the front rank of Republican leadership and they spoke the mind of the Middle West, the Middle Atlantic states, and New England. There is much evidence to sustain the estimate of W. E. B. Du Bois that "At the beginning of the [Civil] war probably not one white American in a hundred believed that Negroes could become an integral part of American democracy."

As the war for union began to take on the character of a war for freedom, northern attitudes toward the Negro paradoxically began to harden rather than soften. This hardening process was especially prominent in the northwestern or middle western states where the old fear of Negro invasion was intensified by apprehensions that once the millions of slaves below the Ohio River were freed they would push northward—this time by the thousands and tens of thousands, perhaps in mass exodus, instead of in driblets of one or two who came furtively as fugitive slaves. The prospect of Negro immigration, Negro neighbors, and Negro competition filled the whites with alarm, and their spokesmen voiced their fears with great candor. "There is," Lyman Trumbull told the Senate, in April, 1862, "a very great aversion in the West—I know it to be so in my state—against having free negroes come among us. Our people want nothing to do with the negro." . . .

During the last two years of the war northern states began to modify or repeal some of their anti-Negro and discriminatory laws. But the party that emerged triumphant from the crusade to save the Union and free the slave was not in the best political and moral position to expand the rights and assure the equality of the freedman. There undoubtedly did emerge eventually an organization determined to overthrow Andrew Johnson's states' rights, white-supremacy policies and to take over the control of the South. But that was a different matter. On the issue of Negro equality the party remained divided, hesitant, and unsure of its purpose. The historic commitment to equality it eventually made was lacking in clarity, ambivalent in purpose, and capable of numerous interpretations. Needless to say, its meaning has been debated from that day to this.

The northern electorate the Republicans faced in seeking support for their program of Reconstruction had undergone no conversion in its wartime racial prejudices and dogmas. As George W. Julian, who deplored the fact himself, told his colleagues in the House in 1866, "the real trouble is that *we hate the negro*. It is not his ignorance that offends us, but his color."

In the years immediately following the war every northern state in which the electorate or the legislature was given the opportunity to express its views on issues involving the political rights of the Negro reaffirmed its earlier and conservative stand. This included the states that reconsidered—and reaffirmed—their laws excluding Negroes from the polls. Five states with laws barring Negro testimony in court against whites repealed them, and a few acted against school segregation. Throughout these years, however, the North remained fundamentally what it was before—a society organized upon assumptions of racial privilege and segregation. . . .

This is not to suggest that there was not widespread and sincere concern in the North for the terrible condition of the freedmen in the South. There can be no doubt that many northern people were deeply moved by the reports of atrocities, peonage, brutality, lynchings, riots, and injustices that filled the press. Indignation was especially strong over the Black Codes adopted by some of the Johnsonian state legislatures, for they blatantly advertised the intention of some southerners to substitute a degrading peonage for slavery and make a mockery of the moral fruits of northern victory. What is sometimes overlooked in analyzing northern response to the Negro's plight is the continued apprehension over the threat of a massive Negro invasion of the North. The panicky fear that this might be precipitated by emancipation had been allayed in 1862 by the promises of President Lincoln and other Republican spokesmen that once slavery were abolished the freedmen would cheerfully settle down to remain in the South, that northern Negroes would be drawn back to the South, and that deportation and colonization abroad would take care of any threat of northern invasion that remained. But not only had experiments with deportation come to grief, but southern white persecution and abuse combined with the ugly Black Codes had produced new and powerful incentives for a Negro exodus while removal of the shackles of slavery cleared the way for emigration.

The response of the Republican Congress to this situation was the Civil Rights Act of 1866, later incorporated into the Fourteenth Amendment. Undoubtedly part of the motivation for this legislation was a humanitarian concern for the protection of the Negro in the South, but another part of the motivation was concerned with the protection of the white man in the North. Senator Roscoe Conkling of New York, a member of the Joint Committee of Fifteen who helped draft the Civil Rights provisions, was quite explicit on this point. "Four years ago," he said in the campaign of 1866, "mobs were raised, passions were roused, votes were given, upon the idea that emancipated negroes were to burst in hordes upon the North. We then said, give them liberty and rights at the South, and they will stay there and never come into a cold climate to die. We say so still, and we want them let alone, and that is one thing that this part of the amendment is for." . . .

The author and sponsor of the Civil Rights Act of 1866 was Senator Lyman Trumbull, the same man who had in 1858 described the Republicans as "the white man's party," and in 1862 had declared that "our people want nothing to do with the negro." He had nevertheless fought for the Freedman's Bureau and civil rights in the South. Trumbull's bill was passed and after Johnson's veto was repassed by an overwhelming majority. Limited in application, the Civil Rights Act did not confer political rights or the franchise on the freedmen.

The Fourteenth Amendment, which followed, was also equivocal on racial questions and freedmen's rights. Rejecting Senator Sumner's plea for a guarantee of Negro suffrage, Congress left that decision up to the southern states. It also left northern states free to continue the disfranchisement of Negroes, but it exempted them from the penalties inflicted on the southern states for the same decision. The real concern of the franchise provisions of the Fourteenth Amendment was not with justice to the Negro but with justice to the North. The rebel states stood to gain some twelve seats in the House if all Negroes were counted as a basis of representation and to have about eighteen fewer seats if none were counted. The amendment fixed apportionment of representation according to enfranchisement. . . .

After two years of stalling, of endless committee work and compromise, the First Reconstruction Act was finally adopted in the eleventh hour of the expiring Thirty-ninth Congress. . . .

. . . It was not primarily devised for the protection of Negro rights and the provision of Negro equality. Its primary purpose, however awkwardly and poorly implemented, was to put the southern states under the control of men loyal to the Union or men the Republicans thought they could trust to control those states for their purposes. So far as the Negro's future was concerned, the votes of the Congress that adopted the Reconstruction Act speak for themselves. Those votes had turned down Thaddeus Stevens' proposal to assure an economic foundation for Negro equality and Sumner's resolutions to give the Negro equal opportunity in schools and in homesteads and full civil rights. As for the Negro franchise, its provisions, like those for civil rights, were limited. The Negro franchise was devised for the passage of the Fourteenth Amendment and setting up the new southern state constitutions. But disfranchisement by educational and property qualifications was left an option, and escape from the whole scheme was left open by permitting the choice of military rule. No guarantee of proportional representation for the Negro population was contemplated and no assurance was provided for Negro officeholding. . . .

The standard southern reply to northern demands was the endlessly reiterated charge of hypocrisy. Northern radicals, as a Memphis conservative put it, were "seeking to fasten what they themselves repudiate with loathing upon the unfortunate people of the South." And he pointed to the succession of northern states that had voted on and defeated Negro suffrage. . . .

There was little in the Republican presidential campaign of 1868 to con-
fute the southern charge of hypocrisy. The Chicago platform of May on which
General Grant was nominated contained as its second section this formulation
of the double standard of racial morality: "The guaranty by Congress of equal
suffrage to all loyal men at the South was demanded by every consideration
of public safety, of gratitude, and of justice, and must be maintained; while
the question of suffrage in all the loyal [i.e., northern] States properly belongs
to the people of those States." Thus Negro disfranchisement was assured in
the North along with enfranchisement in the South. No direct mention of the
Negro was made in the platform, nor was there mention of schools or homesteads for freedmen. Neither Grant nor his running mate Schuyler Colfax was
known for any personal commitment to Negro rights, and Republican campaign speeches in the North generally avoided the issue of Negro suffrage.

Congress acted to readmit seven of the reconstructed states to the
Union in time for them to vote in the presidential election and contribute
to the Republic majority. In attaching conditions to readmission, however,
Congress deliberately refrained from specifying state laws protecting
Negroes against discrimination in jury duty, officeholding, education,
intermarriage, and a wide range of political and civil rights. By a vote of
30 to 5 the Senate defeated a bill attaching to the admission of Arkansas the
condition that "no person on account of race or color shall be excluded from
the benefits of education, or be deprived of an equal share of the moneys or
other funds created or used by public authority to promote education. . . ."

Not until the election of 1868 was safely behind them did the Republicans
come forward with proposals of national action on Negro suffrage that
was to result in the Fifteenth Amendment. They were extremely sensitive
to northern opposition to enfranchisement. By 1869 only seven northern
states had voluntarily acted to permit the Negro to vote, and no state with
a substantial Negro population outside the South had done so. Except for
Minnesota and Iowa, which had only a handful of Negroes, Nebraska, which
entered the Union with Negro suffrage as a congressional requirement,
and Wisconsin by decision of her Supreme Court, every postwar effort to
enfranchise the Negro in northern states had gone down to defeat.

As a consequence moderates and conservatives among Republicans
took over and dominated the framing of the Fifteenth Amendment and
very strongly left their imprint on the measure. Even the incorrigibly radical Wendell Phillips yielded to their sway. Addressing other radicals he
pled, ". . . for the first time in our lives we beseech them to be a little more politicians and a little less reformers." The issue lay between the moderates and
the radicals. The former wanted a limited, negative amendment that would
not confer suffrage on the freedmen, would not guarantee the franchise and
take positive steps to protect it, but would merely prohibit its denial on the
grounds of race and previous condition. The radicals demanded positive and
firm guarantees, federal protection, and national control of suffrage. They

would take away state control, North as well as South. They fully anticipated and warned of all the elaborate devices that states might resort to—and eventually did resort to—in order to disfranchise the Negro without violating the proposed amendment. These included such methods—later made famous— as the literacy and property tests, the understanding clause, the poll tax, as well as elaborate and difficult registration tricks and handicaps. But safeguards against them were all rejected by the moderates. . . .

The Fifteenth Amendment has often been read as evidence of renewed notice to the South of the North's firmness of purpose, as proof of its determination not to be cheated of its idealistic war aims, as a solemn rededication to those aims. Read more carefully, however, the Fifteenth Amendment reveals more deviousness than clarity of purpose, more partisan needs than idealistic aims, more timidity than boldness.

Signals of faltering purpose in the North such as the Fifteenth Amendment and state elections in 1867 were not lost on the South. They were carefully weighed for their implications for the strategy of resistance. The movement of counter Reconstruction was already well under way by the time the amendment was ratified in March, 1870, and in that year it took on new life in several quarters. Fundamentally it was a terroristic campaign of underground organizations, the Ku Klux Klan and several similar ones, for the intimidation of Republican voters and officials, the overthrow of their power, and the destruction of their organization. Terrorists used violence of all kinds, including murder by mob, by drowning, by torch; they whipped, they tortured, they maimed, they mutilated. It became perfectly clear that federal intervention of a determined sort was the only means of suppressing the movement and protecting the freedmen in their civil and political rights. . . .

Finally, to take a longer view, it is only fair to allow that if ambiguous and partisan motives in the writing and enforcement of Reconstruction laws proved to be the seeds of failure in American race policy for earlier generations, those same laws and constitutional amendments eventually acquired a wholly different significance for the race policy of a later generation. The laws outlasted the ambiguities of their origins. It is, in fact, impossible to account for such limited successes as the Second Reconstruction can claim without acknowledging its profound indebtedness to the First.

---

2   This essay by leading Reconstruction scholar Eric Foner examines some of the accomplishments and the ultimate overturning of the Reconstruction governments in the South. What does Foner see as some of the major accomplishments of these regimes? What factors does he emphasize in discussing the failure of Reconstruction? How does his analysis

Source: Eric Foner and Olivia Mahoney, America's Reconstruction: People and Politics After the Civil War (Baton Rouge: Louisiana State University Press, 1995), pp. 93–95, 104, 106, 108–109, 112–115, 119–125, 126–127, 128, 134–136.

of events, especially regarding the role of blacks during Reconstruction, differ from that in Source 1?

America's Reconstruction (1995)
ERIC FONER

Among the former slaves, the passage of the Reconstruction Act of 1867, which brought black suffrage to the South, caused an outburst of political organization. Determined to exercise their new rights as citizens, thousands joined the Union League, an organization closely linked to the Republican party, and the vast majority of eligible African-Americans registered to vote. "You never saw a people more excited on the subject of politics than are the Negroes of the South," wrote a plantation manager.

By 1870, all the former Confederate states had met the requirements of Congress and been readmitted to the Union, and nearly all were under the control of the Republican party. Their new constitutions, drafted in 1868 and 1869 by the first public bodies in American history with substantial black representation (of about 1,000 delegates throughout the South, over one-quarter were black), represented a considerable improvement over those they replaced. They made the structure of Southern government more democratic, modernized the tax system, and guaranteed the civil and political rights of black citizens. A few states initially barred former Confederates from voting, but this policy was quickly abandoned by the new state governments.

Throughout Reconstruction, black voters provided the bulk of the Republican party's support. Although Democrats charged that "Negro rule" had come to the South, nowhere did blacks control the workings of state government, and nowhere did they hold office in numbers equal to their proportion of the total population (which ranged from about 60 percent in South Carolina to around one-third in Arkansas, North Carolina, Tennessee, and Texas). Nonetheless, the fact that well over 1,500 African-Americans occupied positions of political power in the Reconstruction South represented a stunning departure in American government.

During Reconstruction, blacks were represented at every level of government. Fourteen sat in the House of Representatives, and two, Hiram Revels and Blanche K. Bruce, represented Mississippi in the Senate. P. B. S. Pinchback of Louisiana served briefly as America's first black governor (a century and a quarter would pass until C. Douglas Wilder of Virginia, elected in 1989, became the second). Other blacks held major state executive positions, including lieutenant governor, treasurer, and superintendent of education. Nearly 700 sat in state legislatures during Reconstruction, and there were scores of black local officials, ranging from justice of the peace to sheriff, tax assessor, and policeman. The presence of black officeholders and their white allies made a real difference in Southern life, ensuring that those accused of crimes would be tried before juries of their peers, and enforcing fairness in such prosaic aspects of local government as road repair, tax assessment, and poor relief. . . .

The new Southern Republican party also brought to power whites who had enjoyed little authority before the Civil War. Many Reconstruction officials were Northerners who for one reason or another had migrated South during and after the war. Their opponents dubbed them "carpetbaggers," implying that they had packed all their belongings in a suitcase and left their homes, in order to reap the spoils of office in the South. Some carpetbaggers were undoubtedly corrupt adventurers. The large majority, however, were former Union soldiers who decided to remain in the South when the war ended, before there was any prospect of going into politics. Others were investors in land and railroads who saw in the postwar South an opportunity to combine personal economic advancement with a role in helping mold the "backward" South in the image of the modern, industrializing North, substituting, as one wrote, "the civilization of freedom for that of slavery." Still another large group of carpetbaggers were teachers, Freedmen's Bureau officers, and others who came to the region genuinely hoping to assist the former slaves.

The largest group of white Republicans had been born in the South. Former Confederates reserved their greatest scorn for these "scalawags," whom they considered traitors to their race and region. Some were men of stature and wealth, such as James L. Alcorn, a former Whig leader and Mississippi's first Republican governor. Others were business entrepreneurs who believed a "new era" had dawned in the South, and that the Republican party was more likely to promote economic development than the Democratic. The largest number of scalawags, however, were nonslaveholding white farmers from the Southern upcountry. Some had been wartime Unionists who cooperated with the Republicans in order to prevent Rebels from returning to power. Unionists, declared a North Carolina Republican newspaper, must choose "between salvation at the hand of the Negro or destruction at the hand of the rebel." Other scalawags hoped Reconstruction governments would help them recover from wartime economic losses by suspending the collection of debts and enacting laws protecting small property holders from losing their homes to creditors. Nowhere in the South during Reconstruction did the Republican party receive a majority of the white vote, but in states like North Carolina, Tennessee, and Arkansas, it initially commanded a significant minority.

Given the fact that many of the Reconstruction governors and legislators lacked previous experience in government, their record of accomplishment is remarkable. In many ways, Reconstruction at the state level greatly expanded the scope of public responsibility in the South. The new governments established the region's first state-supported public school systems, as well as numerous hospitals and asylums for orphans and the insane. These institutions were open to black and white Southerners, although generally, they were segregated by race. Only in New Orleans were the public schools integrated during Reconstruction, and only in South Carolina did the state university admit black students (elsewhere separate colleges were established for blacks). By the 1870s, in a region whose prewar leaders had made it illegal for blacks to learn and had done little to promote education among poorer whites, over half the children were attending public schools.

In assuming public responsibility for education, Reconstruction governments in a sense were following a path blazed by the North. Their efforts to guarantee African-Americans equal treatment in transportation and places of public accommodation, however, launched these governments into an area all but unknown in American law. Racial segregation, or the complete exclusion of blacks from both public and private facilities, was widespread throughout the country. Black demands for the outlawing of such discrimination produced deep divisions in the Republican party. But in the Deep South, where blacks made up the vast majority of the Republican voting population, laws were enacted making it illegal for railroads, hotels, and other institutions to discriminate on the basis of race. Enforcement of these laws varied considerably from locality to locality, but Reconstruction established for the first time at the state level a standard of equal citizenship and a recognition of blacks' right to a share of public services.

Republican governments also took steps to assist the poor of both races and to promote the South's economic recovery. The Black Codes were repealed, the property of small farmers protected against being seized for debt, and the tax system revised to shift the burden from propertyless blacks, who had paid a disproportionate share during Presidential Reconstruction, to planters and other landowners. The former slaves, however, were disappointed that little was done to assist them in acquiring land. Only South Carolina took effective action, establishing a commission to purchase land for resale on long-term credit to poor families.

Rather than land distribution, the Reconstruction governments pinned their hopes for Southern economic growth and opportunity for African-Americans on a program of regional economic development. Railroad construction was its centerpiece, the key, they believed, to linking the South with Northern markets, and transforming the region into a society of booming factories, bustling towns, and diversified agriculture. "A free and living Republic," declared a Tennessee Republican, would "spring up in the track of the railroad." The plantation would lose its dominant role in the economy, and new opportunities for employment and the acquisition of property would emerge for black and white alike. Every state during Reconstruction helped to finance railroad construction, and through tax reductions and other incentives, tried to attract Northern manufacturers to invest in the region. The program had mixed results. A few states—Georgia, Alabama, Arkansas, and Texas—witnessed significant new railroad construction between 1868 and 1872, but economic development in general remained weak. With abundant opportunities existing in the West, few Northern investors ventured to the Reconstruction South.

Thus, to their supporters, the governments of Radical Reconstruction presented a complex pattern of achievement and disappointment. The economic vision of a modernizing, revitalized Southern economy failed to materialize, and most African-Americans remained locked in poverty. On the other hand, biracial democratic government, a thing unknown in American history, for the first time functioned effectively in many parts of the South. Public facilities were rebuilt and expanded, school systems established, and legal codes purged of racism. The conservative oligarchy that had dominated Southern government from colonial times to 1867 found itself largely excluded from political power, while those who had previously been outsiders—poorer white Southerners, men from the North, and especially former slaves—cast ballots, sat on juries, and enacted and administered laws. The effect upon African-Americans was strikingly visible. "One hardly realizes the fact that the many Negroes one sees here ... ," a Northern correspondent reported in 1873, "have been slaves a few short years ago, at least as far as their demeanor goes as individuals newly invested with all the rights and privileges of an American citizen."

The South's traditional leaders—planters, merchants, and Democratic politicians—bitterly opposed the new Southern governments, denouncing them as corrupt, inefficient, and embodiments of wartime defeat and "black supremacy." There was corruption during Reconstruction, but it was confined to no race, region, or party. Frauds that existed in some Southern states, associated primarily with the new programs of railroad aid, were dwarfed by those practiced in these years by the Whiskey Rings, which involved high officials of the Grant administration, and by New York's Tweed Ring, controlled by the Democrats, whose depredations ran into the tens of millions of dollars.

The rising taxes needed to pay for schools and other new public facilities, and to assist railroad development, were another cause of opposition to Reconstruction. Planters resented the new tax systems, which forced them to bear a far higher share of the tax burden than in the past. Many poorer whites who had initially supported the Republican party turned against it when it became clear that their economic situation was not improving under the new governments.

The most basic reason for opposition to Reconstruction, however, was that most white Southerners could not accept the idea of former slaves voting, holding office, and enjoying equality before the law. They had always regarded blacks as an inferior race whose proper place was as dependent laborers. Reconstruction, they believed, had to be overthrown in order to restore white supremacy in Southern government, and to ensure planters a disciplined, reliable labor force. Even Southern Democrats like Benjamin H. Hill of Georgia, who believed the Civil War had demonstrated "the superiority of Yankee civilization," and who accepted the premise that the South must move from a plantation-oriented economy to one of small farms and developing industry, insisted that such policies could only be carried out by the region's traditional leaders, not blacks, carpetbaggers, and scalawags.

In 1869 and 1870, Democrats joined with dissident Republicans to win control of Tennessee and Virginia, effectively ending Reconstruction there. Elsewhere in the South, however, with Reconstruction governments securely entrenched, their opponents turned to a campaign of widespread violence in an effort to end Republican rule. Their actions soon posed a fundamental challenge both for Reconstruction governments in the South and for policy-makers in Washington. . . .

. . . In wide areas of the South, Reconstruction's opponents resorted to terror to secure their aim of restoring Democratic rule and white supremacy. Secret societies sprang up whose purpose was to prevent blacks from voting, and to destroy the infrastructure of the Republican party by assassinating local leaders and public officials.

The most notorious such organization was the Ku Klux Klan, which in effect served as a military arm of the Democratic party. Founded in 1866 as a Tennessee social club, the Klan was soon transformed into an organization of terrorist criminals, which spread into nearly every Southern state. Led by planters, merchants, and Democratic politicians, men who liked to style themselves the South's "respectable citizens" and "natural rulers," the Klan committed some of the most brutal acts of violence in American history. During the 1868 presidential election, Klansmen assassinated Arkansas congressman James M. Hinds, three members of the South Carolina legislature, and other Republican leaders. In Georgia and Louisiana, the Klan established a reign of terror so complete that blacks were unable to go to the polls to vote, and Democrats carried both states for Horatio Seymour.

Grant's election did not end the Klan's activities; indeed in some parts of the South, Klan violence accelerated in 1869 and 1870. The Klan singled out for assault Reconstruction's local leadership. White Republicans—local officeholders, teachers, and party organizers—were often victimized. In 1870 William Luke, an Irish-born teacher in a black school, was lynched in Alabama along with four black men. Female teachers were beaten as well as male.

African-Americans, however, especially local leaders, bore the brunt of Klan violence. In Georgia, Klansmen in 1869 forced black legislator Abram Colby into the woods "and there stripped and beat him in the most cruel manner for nearly three hours." One black leader in Monroe County, Mississippi, had his throat cut because he was "president of a republican club" and was known as a man who "would speak his mind." In York County, South Carolina, where nearly the entire white male population joined the Klan (and women participated by sewing the robes Klansmen wore as disguises), the organization committed eleven murders and hundreds of whippings. By early 1871, thousands of blacks hid out in the woods each night to avoid assault.

Occasionally, violence escalated from attacks on individuals to wholesale assaults on the local African-American community. Institutions like black churches and schools, symbols of black autonomy, frequently became targets. In Meridian, Mississippi, in 1871, some thirty blacks were murdered in cold blood, along with a white Republican judge. At Colfax, Louisiana, two years later, scores of black militiamen were killed after surrendering to armed whites intent on seizing control of the local government.

The Klan's purposes, however, extended far beyond party politics. Former slaves who had managed to obtain land were victimized, as well as those who had learned to read and write. The Klan, one white farmer commented, did "not like to see the Negro go ahead." Its aim was to restore white supremacy in all areas of Southern life—in government, race relations, and on the plantations.

The new Southern governments proved unable to restore order or suppress the Klan. Many sheriffs were too frightened to try to arrest those who committed acts of violence, and when they did, Klansmen—often the only witnesses—refused to testify against their compatriots. In a few states, including Arkansas and Texas, Republican governors used the state militia effectively against the Klan. Generally, however, the Reconstruction governments appealed to Washington for help.

Although some Northern Republicans opposed further intervention in the South, most agreed with Sen. John Sherman of Ohio, who affirmed that the "power of the nation" must "crush, as we once before have done, this organized civil war." In 1870 and 1871, Congress adopted three Enforcement Acts, outlawing terrorist societies and allowing the president to use the army against them. These laws continued the expansion of national authority during Reconstruction by defining certain crimes—those aimed at depriving citizens of their civil and political rights—as federal offenses rather than merely violations of state law. In 1871, President Grant authorized federal marshals, backed up by troops in some areas, to arrest hundreds of accused Klansmen. After a series of well-publicized trials, in which many of the organization's leaders were jailed, the Klan went out of existence. In 1872, for the first time since the Civil War, peace reigned in the former Confederacy.

Despite the Grant administration's effective response to Klan terrorism, the North's commitment to Reconstruction waned during the 1870s. Many Radical leaders, including Thaddeus Stevens, who died in 1868, had passed from the scene. Within the Republican party, their place was taken by politicians less committed to the ideal of equal rights for blacks. Many Northerners felt that the South should be able to solve its own problems without constant interference from Washington. The federal government had freed the slaves, made them citizens, given them the right to vote, and crushed the Ku Klux Klan. Now, blacks should rely on their own resources, not demand further assistance from the North.

In 1872, a group of Republicans, alienated by corruption within the Grant administration, bolted the party. Their ranks included some of the nation's most influential journalists, and a number of prominent Republican leaders, including Lyman Trumbull and other founders of the party. The Liberal Republicans, as they called themselves, claimed that the Civil War and Reconstruction had brought to power a new group of corrupt politicians, while men of talent and education like themselves had been pushed aside. They also believed that unrestrained democracy, in which "ignorant" voters such as the Irish immigrants of New York City could dominate politics in some locales, was responsible for such instances of corruption as the Tweed Ring. Governmental positions, they believed, should go to men who could pass demanding examinations, not to the political cronies of politicians, and that the propertyless and uneducated should have less of a say in government.

Democratic criticisms of Reconstruction found a receptive audience among the Liberals. As in the North, Liberals believed, the "best men" of the South had been excluded from power while "ignorant" voters controlled politics. The result was corruption and misgovernment. Government in the South should be returned to the region's "natural leaders.". . .

The Liberal attack on Reconstruction, which continued after Grant overwhelmingly won reelection, contributed to a resurgence of racism in the North. Journalist James S. Pike, . . . in 1874 published *The Prostrate State*, an influential account of a visit to South Carolina. In it, he depicted a state engulfed by political corruption and governmental extravagance, and under the control of "a mass of black barbarism." "Negro government," he insisted, was the cause of the South's problems; the solution was to see leading whites restored to political power. Pike's observations led even newspapers that had long supported Reconstruction to condemn black participation in Southern government. These same journals expressed their views visually as well. Increasingly, engravings depicting the former slaves sympathetically, as heroic Civil War veterans, upstanding citizens, or victims of violence, were replaced by caricatures presenting them as little more than unbridled animals. . . .

By the mid-1870s, Reconstruction was on the defensive. The depression dealt the South a severe economic blow, and further weakened the possibility that Republicans could create a revitalized Southern economy. Factionalism between blacks and whites and carpetbaggers and scalawags remained a serious problem among Southern Republicans. One by one, the South's Reconstruction governments were toppled. . . .

The collapse of Reconstruction deeply affected the future course of American development. In many parts of the South, the Republican party soon disappeared and the region long remained a bastion of one-party rule under the control of a reactionary elite who used the same violence and fraud that had helped defeat Reconstruction to stifle internal dissent. Despite its expanded authority over citizens' rights, the federal government stood by indifferently as the Southern states effectively nullified the Fourteenth and Fifteenth Amendments and, beginning in the 1890s, stripped African-Americans of the right to vote. Until then, blacks in some areas continued to hold public offices, but with Democrats firmly in command of state governments, black politicians found it extremely difficult to exercise authority on behalf of their constituents.

After the end of Reconstruction, Southern governments began to enact laws mandating racial segregation in schools, transportation, and public accommodations. In 1896, in *Plessy v. Ferguson*, the Supreme Court ruled that such segregation did not violate the Fourteenth Amendment's guarantee of equal protection before the law, so long as facilities for the two races were "separate but equal."

In practice, however, facilities for blacks, whether schools, hospitals, or railroad cars, were markedly inferior to those for whites. By the turn of the century, Southern blacks found themselves enmeshed in a complex system of oppression, each of whose components—segregation, economic inequality, political disempowerment—reinforced the others. Those accused of crimes, or who sought to challenge the South's new racial system, faced a rising threat of violence. Between 1880 and 1968, nearly 3,500 African-Americans were lynched in the United States, the vast majority in the South.

Although the black institutions created or strengthened after the Civil War—the family, church, and schools—survived the end of Reconstruction, governments in the New South fell far behind the rest of the nation in meeting their public responsibilities. White Southerners suffered as well as black, as expenditures on education, health, and public welfare remained well below those in other states. New laws strengthened the hands of landlords in disputes with tenants, and state governments resolutely opposed the introduction of labor unions. Long into the twentieth century, the South would remain the nation's foremost economic problem, a region of low wages, stunted economic development, and widespread poverty. Millions of poor Southerners, black and white alike, felt their only hope for economic opportunity and social justice was to migrate to other parts of the country.

Not until the 1950s and 1960s would the nation again attempt to come to terms with the political and social agenda of Reconstruction.

PRIMARY SOURCES

These sources offer additional insights into black political involvement during Reconstruction and the forces affecting Reconstruction's outcome. As you examine these sources, remember that they reflect attitudes as well as conditions.

Thomas Nast's Cartoons

Thomas Nast's cartoons appeared in *Harper's Weekly*. A Northern Republican, Nast reflected and shaped "respectable" opinion in the North. Note his view about black political activity during Reconstruction. In what ways did Northern white opinion shape the outcome of Reconstruction?

Colored Rule in a Reconstructed (?) State (1874)

NOTE: The female figure in the upper right corner is Columbia, the symbol of America. Boston Athenaeum. Reprinted in *Harper's Weekly*, March 14, 1874.

4   The Ignorant Vote—Honors Are Easy (1876)

NOTE: The figure on the right is a caricature of an Irishman.
Boston Athenaeum. Reprinted in *Harper's Weekly,* December 9, 1876.

5   The Associated Press wired a white Taxpayers' Convention's appeal to Congress and to newspapers across the country, but it refused to send this reply over the wires. The circulation of this response was therefore confined to the black press. What does this document reveal about obstacles blacks confronted as they asserted themselves politically during Reconstruction?

Black Response to a South Carolina White Taxpayers' Convention Appeal to Congress (1874)

Certain citizens of South Carolina, styling themselves "The Taxpayers' Convention," have memorialized your honorable bodies to grant them relief from unjust burdens and oppressions, alleged by them to have been imposed by the Republican State Government. We, the undersigned, members of the State Central Committee of the Union Republican party of South Carolina, beg leave to submit the following counter statement and reply:

The statement that "the annual expenses of the government have advanced from four hundred thousand dollars before the war to two millions and a half at the present time," is entirely incorrect, and the items of expenditures given to illustrate and prove this statement are wholly inaccurate and untrue, and skillfully selected to deceive.

We present a true statement of the appropriation of the fiscal year before the war, beginning October 1, 1859, and ending September 30, 1860, and the fiscal year beginning November 1, 1872, and ending October 31, 1873:

	1859–60	1872–73
Salaries	$81,100	$194,989
Contingents	73,000	47,600
Free schools	75,000	300,000
State Normal School	8,704	25,000
Deaf, dumb and blind	8,000	16,000
Military academies	30,000	. . . .
Military contingencies	100,000	20,000
Roper Hospital	3,000	. . . .
State Lunatic Asylum	. . . .	77,500
State Normal and High School	5,000	. . . .
Jurors and Constables	50,000	. . . .
State Orphan House (colored)	. . . .	20,000
State Penitentiary	. . . .	40,000
Sundries	184,427	444,787
	$618,231	$1,184,876

Source: The New National Era, April 16, 1874.

By the census of 1860, there were in South Carolina at that time 301,214 free population and 402,406 slaves. By the census of 1870 there were 705,606 free population. In 1860, the slave was no charge on the State Government, save when he was hung for some petty misdemeanor, and the State compelled to pay his loss.

It would be, therefore, but just and fair to divide the amount appropriated in 1859–60: $618,231 by the then free population, 301,214, and it will be found that the cost of governing each citizen was $2.05. Then divide the amount appropriated in 1872–73 by the free population now 705,606, and the cost of governing each citizen is $1.67–$2.05 during the boasted Democratic period and $1.67 under the so-called corrupt Radical rule—a difference of 38 cents *per capita* in favor of the latter. So that if the Democrats had the same number of free citizens to govern in 1859–60 that the Republicans had in 1972–73, it would have cost them $264,616 more than it has cost us.

The State organized upon a free basis necessarily created a larger number of officers, and, therefore, a larger amount of salaries. We are not ashamed of the fact that our appropriation for schools in 1872–73 is four times greater than in 1859–60. Ignorance was the corner-stone of slavery and essential to its perpetuity. Now in every hamlet and village in our state, the schoolmaster is abroad. In 1857 the number of scholars attending the free schools was only 19,356 while in 1873 the number of scholars attending the schools was 85,753.

There were no appropriations for the State Lunatic Asylum and Penitentiary in 1859–60. The Lunatic Asylum was then supported by the friends of its wealthy inmates, but in 1872–73 the State assumed its support and made liberal appropriation for its unfortunate patients. The erection of the Penitentiary was not begun until after the war and there was therefore no appropriation for it in 1859–60.

The appropriation in 1872–73 for military purposes was but $20,000. We had no occasion to appropriate $130,000 for military academies and contingencies in order to train the young to strike at the nation's life, and to purchase material for the war of secession.

There was no appropriation in 1859–60 for a colored State Orphan Home. The colored orphans that were then uncared for were free, but their parents, when living, were heavily taxed to support white orphans, while their own children, after their death, were neglected. . . .

The gentlemen who have assembled, constituting themselves representatives of the so-called taxpayers, are not what they would have the country believe. They are the prominent politicians of the old regime—the former ruling element of the State—who simply desire to regain the power they lost by their folly of secession.

The Republicans admit the existence of evils among them. They have committed errors which they deeply regret. But those errors are being daily corrected. There are enough able and good men among those who have the present charge of the government to right every existing wrong. They are determined to do so. The difficulties under which they have labored have been increased ten-fold by the hostility and the opposition of the Democratic party ever since Reconstruction. This is their third effort to regain power. First they expected it through the election of Seymour and Blair; second, through the midnight murders and assassinations of Ku Kluxism; and now, thirdly, by the distortion and misrepresentation of facts, in order to create a public sentiment in their favor and obtain relief from Congress.

Relying upon the justice of our cause we submit these facts to your impartial judgment.

> Samuel J. Lee, Chairman, pro *tem*, S. A. Swails,
> W. M. Thomas, Joseph Crews, H. H. Ellison,
> P. R. Rivers, John R. Cochran, Robert Smalls,
> E. W. M. Mackey, John Lee, H. L. Shrewsbury,
> George F. McIntyre, Wilson Cook, John H. McDevitt

Black Political Attitudes

As you read the following source, consider what it shows about black aspirations and divisions.

6 Statement of Colored People's Convention in Charleston, South Carolina (1865)

Heretofore we have had no firesides that we could call our own. The measures which have been adopted for the development of white men's children have been denied to ours. The laws which have made white men great, have degraded us, because we were colored. But now that we are freemen, now that we have been lifted up by the providence of God to manhood, we have resolved to come forward, and, like MEN, speak and *act* for ourselves.

We have not come together in battle array to assume a boastful attitude and to talk loudly of high-sounding principles or unmeaning platforms. Although we feel keenly our wrongs, still we come together in a spirit of meekness and of patriotic good will to all the people of the state. Thus we would address you, not as enemies, but as friends and fellow countrymen who desire to dwell among you in peace.

We ask for no special privileges or favors. We ask only for *even-handed* Justice. We simply ask that we shall be recognized as men.

Source: Proceedings of the Colored People's Convention of the State of South Carolina (Charleston, S.C., 1865).

White Violence

The following source is an account of violence against black Republicans during Reconstruction. What does this account reveal about the failure of Reconstruction policy?

 Colby was a black member of the Georgia legislature. His testimony was before a joint committee of Congress.

Testimony of Abram Colby (1872)

On the 29th of October 1869, they broke my door open, took me out of bed, took me to the woods and whipped me three hours or more and left me for dead. They said to me, "Do you think you will ever vote another damned radical ticket?" I said, "I will not tell you a lie." I supposed they would kill me anyhow. I said, "If there was an election tomorrow, I would vote the radical ticket." They set in and whipped me a thousand licks more, with sticks and straps that had buckles on the ends of them.

Q—What is the character of those men who were engaged in whipping you?

A—Some are first-class men in our town. One is a lawyer, one a doctor, and some are farmers. They had their pistols and they took me in my night-clothes and carried me from home. They hit me five thousand blows. I told President Grant the same that I tell you now. They told me to take off my shirt. I said, "I never do that for any man." My drawers fell down about my feet and they took hold of them and tripped me up. Then they pulled my shirt up over my head. They said I had voted for Grant and had carried the Negroes against them. About two days before they whipped me they offered me $5,000 to go with them and said they would pay me $2500 in cash if I would let another man go to the legislature in my place. I told them that I would not do it if they would give me all the county was worth.

The worst thing about the whole matter was this. My mother, wife and daughter were in the room when they came. My little daughter begged them not to carry me away. They drew up a gun and actually frightened her to death. She never got over it until she died. That was the part that grieves me the most.

Q—How long before you recovered from the effects of this treatment?

A—I have never got over it yet. They broke something inside of me. I cannot do any work now, though I always made my living before in the barbershop, hauling wood, &c.

Q—You spoke about being elected to the next legislature?

Source: Testimony Taken by the Joint Select Committee to Inquire into the Condition of Affairs in the Late Insurrectionary States (Washington, D.C., 1872).

A—Yes, sir, but they run me off during the election. They swore they would kill me if I staid. The Saturday night before the election I went to church. When I got home they just peppered the house with shot and bullets.

Q—Did you make a general canvas there last fall?

A—No, sir. I was not allowed to. No man can make a free speech in my county. I do not believe it can be done anywhere in Georgia.

Q—You say no man can do it?

A—I mean no Republican, either white or colored.

Black Landowning

The limited economic opportunities that most blacks had at the end of the Civil War were realized on the land. The following testimony before a congressional committee investigating conditions in the former Confederate states in 1872 reveals something about former slaves' chances to secure land. Consider why Republican political leaders did not attempt to create more opportunities for the freedmen.

8   Testimony of Emanuel Fortune (1872)

They will not sell our people any land. They have no disposition to do so. They will sell a lot now and then in a town, but nothing of any importance.

Q—What could you get a pretty good farm for—how much an acre?

A—Generally from $10 to $15 an acre. Very poor people cannot afford that.

Q—You can get it if you have the money?

A—They will not sell it in small quantities. I would have bought forty acres if the man would have sold me less than a whole tract. They hold it in that way so that colored people cannot buy it. The lands we cultivate generally are swamp or lowlands.

Q—Is there not plenty of other land to buy?

A—Not that is worth anything. I do not know of any Government land that will raise cotton.

Source: Testimony Taken by the Joint Select Committee to Inquire into the Condition of Affairs in the Late Insurrectionary States (Washington, D.C., 1872).

9   Testimony of Henry M. Turner (1872)

Q—You say that colored men employed in the country have not been able to get anything for their labor. Why is that?

A—During the year there is very little money paid to them and if they want to obtain provisions or clothing they are given an order on some store. At the end of the year these little bills are collected and however small a quantity of things have been taken, almost always the colored man is brought into debt. That is alleged as a reason why they should be bound to stay with their employers and work out what they say they owe them.

Q—A sort of practical peonage?

A—Yes, sir. Whenever there is fear that the laborer will go to work with someone else the following year, he is apt to come out $25 to $30 in debt and his employer calls upon him to work it out.

There was a bill introduced the other day to make it a penal offense for a laborer to break his contract. For instance, a white man writes out a contract. He reads the contract to the black man and, of course, reads just what he pleases. When the black man takes it to somebody else and gets him to read it, it reads quite differently. Among other things there is a provision in the contract that he must not go to any political gathering or meeting. If he does, he will lose $5 for every day that he is absent, and yet he is to receive only $50 or $75 a year. Every day that he is sick, a dollar or a dollar and a half is to be deducted. The man may want to quit and work for some person else who will pay him better wages.

Q—The effect of the legislation would be to render the laborer practically a slave during the period of his contract?

A—Or else he would be liable to punishment by imprisonment. There is no doubt that they will pass some kind of law to that effect.

Q—With a view to harmonize the relations of labor and capital?

A—Yes, sir, that is the phrase.

Source: Testimony Taken by the Joint Select Committee to Inquire into the Condition of Affairs in the Late Insurrectionary States (Washington, D.C., 1872).

Mattie Curtis was 98 years old and living in Raleigh, North Carolina, when the New Deal's Federal Writers Project conducted an interview with her as part of an oral history project involving former slaves. In discussing her life after emancipation, what does Curtis reveal about the challenges facing former slaves, in particular, women?

A Former Slave Recalls Her Post-Emancipation Struggle (1937)

When de Yankees come dey come an' freed us. De woods wus full of Rebs what had deserted, but de Yankees killed some of dem.

From: Slave Narratives: A Folk History of the United States from Interviews with Former Slaves, Vol. 13, North Carolina Narratives (St. Clair Shores, Mich.: Scholarly Press, 1976), pp. 220–221.

Some sort of corporation cut de land up, but de slaves ain't got none of it dat I ever heard about.

I got married before de war to Joshua Curtis. I loved him too, which is more dam most folks can truthfully say. I always had craved a home an' aplenty to eat, but freedom ain't give us notin' but pickled hoss meat an' dirty crackers, an' not half enough of dat.

Josh ain't really care 'bout no home but through dis land corporation I bought dese fifteen acres on time. I cut down de big trees dat wus all over dese fields an' I milled out de wood an' sold hit, den I plowed up de fields an' planted dem. Josh did help to build de house an' he worked out some.

All of dis time I had nineteen chilluns an' Josh died, but I kep' on an' de fifteen what is dead lived to be near 'bout grown, ever one of dem.

Right atter de war northern preachers come around wid a little book a-marrying slaves an' I seed one of dem marry my pappy an' mammy. Atter dis dey tried to find dere fourteen oldest chilluns what wus sold away, but dey never did find but three of dem.

But you wants ter find out how I got along. I'll never fergit my first bale of cotton an' how I got hit sold. I wus some proud of dat bale of cotton, an' atter I had hit ginned I set out wid hit on my steercart fer Raleigh. De white folks hated de nigger den, 'specially de nigger what wus makin' somethin' so I dasen't ax nobody whar de market wus.

I thought dat I could find de place by myself, but I rid all day an' had to take my cotton home wid me dat night 'case I can't find no place to sell hit at. But dat night I think hit over an' de nex' day I goes' back an' axes a policeman 'bout de market. Lo an' behold chile, I foun' hit on Blount Street, an' I had pass by hit seberal times de day before.

I done a heap of work at night too, all of my sewin' an' such an' de piece of lan' near de house over dar ain't never got no work 'cept at night. I finally paid fer de land. Some of my chilluns wus borned in de field too. When I wus to de house we had a granny an' I blowed in a bottle to make de labor quick an' easy.

Dis young generation ain't worth shucks. Fifteen years ago I hired a big buck nigger to help me shrub an' 'fore leben o'clock he passed out on me. You know 'bout leben o'clock in July hit gits in a bloom. De young generation wid dere schools an dere divorcing ain't gwine ter git nothin' out of life. Hit wus better when folks jist lived tergether. Dere loafin' gits dem inter trouble an' dere novels makes dem bad husban's an' wives too.

CONCLUSION

"In a certain sense," nineteenth-century writer Thomas Carlyle once said, "all men are historians."[9] As we saw at the beginning of this volume, all of us use history to make sense of the past. Whether trained as historians or not, we do so out of a shared assumption that the past has influenced the present. There are few clearer demonstrations of the validity of that assumption than the history of Reconstruction.

Reconstruction also shows that, as one historian put it, "To learn about the present in the light of the past is to learn about the past in the light of the present."[10] In other words, it demonstrates that all of us draw lessons from the past and that these lessons are influenced by our times and circumstances. Unlike most early twentieth-century historians, who argued that African Americans enjoyed too much freedom during Reconstruction, historians today debate how many political and economic opportunities freedmen really had. Thus, modern historians' views of Reconstruction no longer justify the need for a racial caste system. Instead, Reconstruction now yields lessons about racism's influence in American society, the power of government action to change people's circumstances, and the ability of people to control their lives under difficult conditions.

These lessons are relevant for us. Americans continue to confront the enduring problems of poverty and inequality and to debate the government's responsibility for the welfare of people. Reconstruction's "bloody ground," therefore, continues to teach lessons that may justify present-day policies. For that reason, it remains a powerful example of why all of us should care about interpretations of the past.

FURTHER READING

Richard H. Abbott, *The Republican Party and the South 1855–1877* (Chapel Hill: University of North Carolina Press, 1986).

W. E. B. Du Bois, *Black Reconstruction in America* (New York: Russell and Russell, 1935).

Laura F. Edwards, *Gendered Strife and Confusion: The Political Culture of Reconstruction* (Urbana: University of Illinois Press, 1997).

Michael W. Fitzgerald, *Splendid Failure: Postwar Reconstruction in the American South* (Chicago: Ivan R. Dee, 2007).

Eric Foner, *A Short History of Reconstruction, 1863–1877* (New York: Harper and Row, 1990).

Michael Perman, *Emancipation and Reconstruction 1862–1879* (Arlington Heights, Ill.: Harlan Davidson, 1987).

Dorothy Sterling, ed., *The Trouble They Seen: Black People Tell the Story of Reconstruction* (Garden City, N.Y.: Doubleday, 1976).

NOTES

1. Quoted in James Truslow Adams, *America's Tragedy* (New York: Scribner's, 1934), p. 371.
2. W. E. B. Du Bois, *Black Reconstruction in America* (New York: Russell and Russell, 1935), p. 725; Bernard Weisberger, "The Dark and Bloody Ground of Reconstruction Historiography," *Journal of Southern History* 25 (November 1959): pp. 427–447.
3. Eric Foner, *A Short History of Reconstruction, 1863–1877* (New York: Harper and Row, 1990), pp. 258–259.
4. Quoted in Eric Foner, *Reconstruction: America's Unfinished Revolution, 1863–1877* (New York: Harper and Row, 1988), p. xx.
5. Du Bois, *Black Reconstruction,* pp. 725–726.
6. Howard K. Beale, "On Rewriting Reconstruction History," *American Historical Review* 45 (July 1940): p. 819.
7. Quoted in Eric Anderson and Alfred A. Moss, Jr., eds., *The Facts of Reconstruction: Essays in Honor of John Hope Franklin* (Baton Rouge: Louisiana State University Press, 1991), p. 219.
8. Michael Les Benedict, "Preserving the Constitution: The Conservative Basis of Radical Reconstruction," *Journal of American History* 61 (June 1974): p. 65.
9. Thomas Carlyle, "On History," *The Complete Works of Thomas Carlyle* (New York: Kelmscott Society, 1869), V, Part II: p. 60.
10. E. H. Carr, *What Is History?* (New York: Alfred A. Knopf, 1962), p. 86.